ENGENDERINGS

Thinking Gender
Edited by Linda Nicholson

Also published in the series

Feminism/Postmodernism
Linda Nicholson

Gender Trouble
Judith Butler

Words of Power
Andrea Nye

Feminity and Domination
Sandra Bartky

Disciplining Foucault
Jana Sawicki

Beyond Accommodation
Drucilla Cornell

Embattled Eros
Steven Seidman

Erotic Welfare
Linda Singer

An Ethic of Care
Mary Jeanne Larrabee

Materialist Feminism and the Politics of Discourse
Rosemary Hennessy

Feminist Epistemologies
Linda Alcoff and Elizabeth Potter

Gender Politics and Post-Communism
Nanette Funk and Magda Mueller

ENGENDERINGS

Constructions of Knowledge, Authority, and Privilege

NAOMI SCHEMAN

Routledge New York London

Published in 1993 by

Routledge
29 West 35 Street
New York, NY 10001

Published in Great Britain by

Routledge
11 New Fetter Lane
London EC4P 4EE

Printed in the United States of America on acid free paper.

Library of Congress Cataloging-in-Publication Data

Scheman, Naomi.
Engenderings : constructions of knowledge, authority, and privilege / Naomi Scheman.
p. cm. — (Thinking gender)
Includes bibliographical references and index.
ISBN 0-415-90739-X.—ISBN 0-415-90740-3 (pbk.)
1. Feminist theory. I. Title. II. Series.
HQ1190.S34 1993
305.42′01—dc20 93-7337
CIP

British Library Cataloguing-in-Publication Data

Scheman, Naomi Beth
Engenderings : Constructions of Knowledge, Authority and Privilege. — (Thinking Gender Series)
I. Title II. Series
121

ISBN 0-415-90739-X (HB)
ISBN 0-415-90740-3 (PB)

To my mother, Blanche

my sisters, Carol and Judith

my nieces, Rebecca and Joanna Fiduccia and Ingrid Baumann
and my god-daughter, Lila Foldes

and to my father, Paul, of blessed memory

Contents

Preface: The Wizard of Oz, the Grand Canonical Synthesizer, and Me (1992) ix

Note on the Text xxi

1 Introduction: The Unavoidability of Gender (1990) 1

PART I. GENDER AND (INTER)SUBJECTIVITY

2 On Sympathy (1979) 11
3 Anger and the Politics of Naming (1980) 22
4 Individualism and the Objects of Psychology (1983) 36

PART II. CONSTRUCTIONS OF GENDER AND AUTHORITY

5 Othello's Doubt/Desdemona's Death: The Engendering of Scepticism (1987) 57
6 Though This Be Method, Yet There Is Madness in It: Paranoia and Liberal Epistemology (1992) 75
7 From Hamlet to Maggie Verver: The History and Politics of the Knowing Subject (1989) 106
8 Missing Mothers/Desiring Daughters: Framing the Sight of Women (1988) 126

PART III. CONVERSATIONS ON THE MARGINS

9 On Competition: Some Stray Thoughts on Baseball, Sex, and Art (1980) 155
10 Thinking about Quality in Women's Visual Art (1983) 158
11 Photography and the Politics of Vision (1985) 160

12 Art for Our Sake (1990) 167
13 Making It All Up (1987) 168
14 Coming to Know *Women's Ways of Knowing* (1990) 174
15 Changing the Subject (1992) 177

PART IV. THE BODY OF PRIVILEGE

16 The Body Politic/The Impolitic Body/Bodily Politics (1988) 185
17 Ground Is My Body: The Politics of Anti-Foundationalism (1991) 193
18 Who Wants to Know? The Epistemological Value of Values (1991) 205

PART V. (IN)CONCLUSION

19 Who Is That Masked Woman? Reflections on Power, Privilege, and Home-ophobia (1992) 229
20 Undoing Philosophy as a Feminist (1991) 239
21 Confessions of an Analytic Philosopher Semi-Manqué (1992) 245

Index 251

Preface: The Wizard of Oz, the Grand Canonical Synthesizer, and Me

"*This* is a philosopher?" my father used to ask as he produced me to colleagues and patients when we walked around the hospital where he worked. The incongruity between my appearance and what he took people to take philosophers to look like was a source of pride. He had no doubts about my being a philosopher, had, in fact, had none since I first fell in love with the field in my first year of college. His pride was tinged with the wonder he still felt about his own life, the distance between his Lower East Side childhood and his career as a surgeon, between the barrel-stave boat on Sheepshead Bay and the sailboat on Long Island Sound, and tinged as well with the radical iconoclasm that he and my mother had passed on to me, the refusal to accept the way the world happened to be, the passion to fight to change it.

In the intervening years I have come to look more like a philosopher. In part, that's simply because I don't look like a kid anymore, and in part it's because philosophers no longer look like they used to. This book charts those changes: along with many others in the largest and possibly most self-conscious cohort in history, I have been on uneasy terms with adulthood, with, in particular, the structures of power the more privileged among us were groomed to inherit. There seems to have been a race between our becoming, for example, professors, and our sufficiently changing the world for it to be morally acceptable for us to occupy such positions. This was not, of course, a race we could win: we were, that is, doomed to succeed (those of us who did succeed, and, of course, not all did) more quickly than we could change the world. We told ourselves, in part, that we were succeeding precisely in order to have the power to change the world, but the result is that we have become, structurally, "them." The moral questions we now face turn not on purity (hopelessly unavailable to us) but on acceptable, politically accountable, compromise: can we live the positions we occupy differently *enough*? In light of such questions papers such as those collected here are unavoidably ironic: as a body of work they enabled me to acquire the very forms of privilege and authority they challenge.

The earlier papers reflect the early days of my (and this wave's) feminism. As such, they are grounded in universalistic notions of gender as subordination, a politically and intellectually heady response of relatively privileged women to the discovery that we were members of an oppressed group. This was not all there was to the feminism of the 1970s: many of the early activists and theorists were poor and working class women and women of color; certainly many of them were lesbians, but within the academy the feminist theory that developed was shaped both by the resources and the limitations of the lives of the women privileged enough to be there and by the parameters of what was allowed a hearing by those who still held the reins of power.

As those of us who created the academic feminism of the seventies moved into faculty positions, we came up against the irony of our situation: though still subject to the sexism of the academy, not to mention what we encountered outside its walls, we were also acquiring positions of power and authority, on terms we had barely changed. We were, that is, less and less suited to the role of victim, a role that women of color in particular were quick to point out had never very well suited us in the first place and that we now looked simply foolish trying to play. (I need to mention here that I assume that very many feminist academics will not see themselves in my use of 'we': my choice to use it reflects my sense that there is a social phenomenon of some importance here: the relative ease with which some rebels have made it in the world against which we are rebelling, and, since we have made it, the disproportionate weight our voices have in what gets published and otherwise institutionally validated. I want to urge a collective responsibility for this social location: I mean to include in my use of 'we' those who share it with me. Such sharing is neither all-or-nothing nor uncontentious: you may share my social location in some ways, not in others; or you may disagree with me about whether, or to what extent, you do share it. Either of us may be, wholly or partly, wrong. But it is, I think, to evade both politics and responsibility to shirk these difficulties and claim instead to be speaking only for oneself.)

It is not, however, the case that, by and large, we just grabbed what we could get, simply advancing our own careers. To the extent that that has happened, it's reprehensible, but I don't think it's very *interesting*. What's interesting is that, while building our own careers, we have, through our choices about the research and teaching we have done, and through our commitments to building women's studies programs and departments and other institutionalized feminist presences on our campuses, changed the academy, including its receptivity to the contributions of people less privileged than we. But we have not done this nearly enough; that is, there is still cause for justifiable anger on the part of those who have been excluded and marginalized at those in positions of authority, including, now, us. It was, I think, inevitable that we would make the academy a more or less hospitable home for ourselves before we could make it anything like hospitable for those who lack our privilege. Having done the best we could (not that I think that we—or I—always or usually did, but even if we had . . .) clearly isn't good enough, and the fact that we ourselves are the immediate and principal beneficiaries of our efforts needs to give us pause, even if it could not have been otherwise.

The later papers here reflect this shift—from a focus on gender as a system of oppression in which I shared, to a focus on diverse systems of privilege, in some of which I was on the privileged side—a shift grounded partly in growing awareness about the forms of privilege that I have always had and partly in recognition of the privilege I was acquiring. It is very difficult to learn how to be responsible in the use of power one has defined oneself as lacking, hard to be a responsible occupant of a position of authority one has defined oneself against.

Like most academics I spend most of my time teaching. As an undergraduate at Barnard in the mid to late sixties I never thought of my teachers as those against whom I and my peers in SDS (Students for a Democratic Society) were rebelling. Our fury at the university was, rather, against those whom we perceived as selling its soul to the military industrial complex. We were intensely intellectual, passionate about connecting what we learned in the classroom with what we learned in the streets. We saw ourselves (correctly, I continue to believe) not as wrecking the university, but as fighting to save its soul. Becoming a teacher, acquiring that sort of authority, has, consequently, been relatively easy—it's not teachers *per se* who loom as "them" in my psyche. Only relatively recently have I begun to confront the need to reconfigure responsibility in the face of certain sorts of success, as, for example, feminist philosophy moves from a tiny fringe of my department to a center of gravity for, at least, the women graduate students. Learning how to live on the margins does not prepare one particularly well for dealing with the weightiness of influence. To the extent that we (I'm thinking here particularly of feminist philosophers, but of other feminist academics as well) have changed (our corners of) the world, we need to learn how to use the power we have gained responsibly, how, for example, to be good teachers to students who feel marginalized not because they share our intellectual and political commitments but because they are sceptical about them.[1]

This is another turn on the problem of responsibly exercising power and authority one has defined oneself as lacking. I am in many ways more comfortable when I can feel sure that students who share many of my views have had to fight to do so, when the pressures around them have pushed in some other way, when intellectual and social coercion are all on some other side. I need to relearn how to speak and write in spaces that have been significantly shaped by the efforts of those like me; I'm not yet used to the sound of my voice when it comes from

[1]For a very thoughtful discussion of these issues, including a sensitive account of student resistance, see Patti Lather, *Getting Smart: Feminist Research and Pedagogy with/in the Postmodern* (New York: Routledge, 1991).

somewhere other than way out in left field, and I don't yet know how to modulate it.

Learning this sort of responsibility is made more difficult by the instabilities of the current cultural and political scene. The backlash against feminism, gay liberation, and multiculturalism is real and frightening; politicians are unabashedly using the language of religious crusade against those, most notably gay men and lesbians, who threaten their vision of the patriarchal nuclear family, and white supremacists get away with portraying themselves as the victims of affirmative action and people of color as threats to the American way of life. The rhetoric of "political correctness" manages to make it appear that free speech includes the right not to be criticized or held accountable by those whose oppression is bolstered by the force of one's words. Groups like the National Association of Scholars work to maintain the centrality of privileged perspectives precisely by portraying themselves, with unrecognized irony, as the victims of those they continue to dominate. It is not, I think, an accidental side-effect of such tactics that progressive intellectuals are kept on the defensive, deprived of the space in which honest self-critique could flourish. It is, to say the least, disingenuous for those who are waging enormously well-funded battles to erase the gains of feminism and multiculturalism to accuse those who are fighting to save them of failing to be sufficiently open to criticism. But staying so open is, of course, imperative. It is one reason we need to fight to hold on to institutional spaces, such as autonomous women's studies and ethnic studies departments—not to serve as monolithic bastions, but precisely to be sites of constructive critique and diversity of opinion.

One aspect of the question of responsibility for social location that has especially come to concern me is the issue of voice. In philosophical discourse, especially since Descartes, it is not supposed to matter who is speaking: the philosophical subject, almost by definition, is generic. That the philosophical voice comes from nowhere in particular is the source of much of its authority: I think of it as the Wizard of Oz. Despite the bells and whistles, the important thing is that no one has ever seen the Wizard; he isn't one person among others, with a particular history and interests that might color and shape his pronouncements. When Toto discovers the little man behind the curtain, the Wizard urges us to ignore him, to go on attending to Oz, the Great and Powerful. It doesn't work, of course, and the balloonist from the Midwest who lost his way is exposed, and we see the fear and confusion that lay behind the stentorian pronouncements of the Wizard.

Many of us who became academic feminist theorists were schooled to be the Wizard of Oz. Part of what informed our feminist consciousness was the realization that there were incongruities between that schooling and what we had learned, and learned to be like, as women, and that not all the fault lay in the sexist nature of those latter lessons. We came, that is, to distrust the supposedly generic masculine, to reject the idea that it really did include us. But we had, it turned out, learned the lessons of wizardry well, so well that we were largely unaware of our surreptitious assumptions of authority, of the ease with which we universalized from our own perspectives.

My own response to having it pointed out, by women who felt as misrepresented, ignored, or marginalized by white academic feminist theorizing as we who created it had felt by white academic masculinist theorizing was not, I think, atypical. I vowed to incorporate more diverse women's experiences into my theorizing. Such a response, as María Lugones has argued,[2] shifts the problem away from the violence done to women of color by our racist failures of attention and onto the inadequacy of our theories. If the harm we perceive is to the theories we create, then solutions are aimed at changing those theories, typically in ways that perpetuate the inequalities of privilege we are supposed to be confronting. The Wizard of Oz becomes what I call the Grand Canonical Synthesizer. One "incorporates" others' experiences by "digesting" them, using them as raw material to be transformed into Theory. Meanwhile, as bell hooks has argued, white supremacy remains intact, as the division of labor is maintained between those who "have experiences," whose lives are nongeneric precisely because they lack one or another sort of privilege, and those who theorize, whose lives are, in their specifics, particularly in their privileged aspects, irrelevant to their theory.[3] Turning the tables, hooks puts words into the mouth of the Grand Canonical Synthesizer, speaking to those he or she has constructed as Other: "No need to hear your voice when I can talk about you better than you can speak about yourself. No need to hear your voice. Only tell me about your pain. I want to know your story. And then I will tell it back to you in a new way. Tell it back to you in such a way that it has become mine, my own. Re-writing you, I write myself anew. I am still author, authority. I am still the colonizer, the speaking subject, and you are now at the center of my talk."[4]

As Susan Bordo has argued,[5] we—those of us with the authority of academic positions—need to be responsible for the terms of that authority and for the power that goes with it: rather than worrying obsessively over whether we have

---

[2]María Lugones, "On the Logic of Pluralist Feminism," in Claudia Card, ed., *Feminist Ethics* (Lawrence: University Press of Kansas, 1991), pp. 40ff.

[3]See, especially, bell hooks, *Feminist Theory: From Margin to Center* (Boston: South End Press, 1984); *Talking Back: Thinking Feminist, Thinking Black* (Boston: South End Press, 1989); and *Yearning: Race, Gender, and Cultural Politics* (Boston: South End Press, 1990).

[4]bell hooks, "Choosing the Margin as a Space of Radical Openness," in *Yearning*, pp. 151ff.

[5]Susan Bordo, "The View from Nowhere and the Dream of Everywhere: Heterogeneity, Adequation, and Feminist Theory," *American Philosophical Association Newsletter on Feminism and Philosophy* 88, no. 2 (1989): 19–25; and "Feminism, Postmodernism, and Gender-Scepticism," in *Feminism/Postmodernism*, ed., Linda J. Nicholson (New York: Routledge, 1990).

adequately represented the voices of those who are excluded from the places where theory is made, we need to be actively engaged in opening those places up, in concrete programs of affirmative action and other forms of increasing access; we need to attend to the real politics that allows some people in and keeps some people out. We also need to learn to see as theory intellectual work that is done by people outside the academy; we need to accord it respect, not strip-mine it for what we can smelt out of it.[6] We need, that is, not just to understand the world, but to change it, and until and insofar as we have done that, no theoretical fancy dancing, no addition of more voices filtered through our word processors, will be an adequate response to those who charge us with abusing in fact the very privilege we deconstruct in theory.

A frequently noted feature of privilege is its invisibility, its passing for the generic, the unmarked. Part of what is needed, if we are to dismantle, not just deconstruct, privilege is a better, more honest, phenomenology. We need to hear from the little man behind the curtain. It sometimes gets said that we don't need men's studies as some sort of balance for women's studies, because the whole rest of the university is men's studies. But it isn't, quite. It's men-as-supposedly-generic studies—Wizard of Oz studies. We don't, similarly, know very much about the social constructions of whiteness,[7] or of heterosexuality.[8] Some of my most recent writing has followed from this recognition, and is an attempt to come out from behind the curtain, to write as one voice in a conversation, not as the last word, to say as honestly as I can how the world looks from here, the very particular place I occupy in it.

---

[6]See, for example, the essays in the section entitled "'Doing' Theory in Other Modes of Consciousness," in *Making Face, Making Soul/Haciendo Caras: Creative and Critical Perspectives by Women of Color*, ed., Gloria Anzaldúa (San Francisco: Aunt Lute, 1990).

[7]Some of what we do know, we know from the outside—from the observations of those whom white people have oppressed. See, for example, John Langston Gwaltney, ed., *Drylongso: A Self-Portrait of Black America* (New York: Random House, 1980). Bell hooks is theorizing various facets of Black women's perspectives on the world, including on white people: see "Representations of Whiteness," in *Black Looks: Race and Representation* (Boston: South End Press, 1992). Accounts from the inside are being crafted by, among others, Marilyn Frye, "On Being White," in *Politics of Reality* (Freedom, Calif.: Crossing Press, 1983), and "White Woman Feminist," in *Willful Virgin* (Freedom, Calif.: Crossing Press, 1992); Minnie Bruce Pratt, "Identity: Skin Blood Heart," in Elly Bulkin, Minnie Bruce Pratt, and Barbara Smith, *Yours in Struggle: Three Feminist Perspectives on Anti-Semitism and Racism* (Brooklyn, N.Y.: Long Haul Press, 1984); and Adrienne Rich, "Notes toward a Politics of Location," in *Blood, Bread, and Poetry: Selected Prose 1979–1985* (New York: Norton, 1986).

[8]Again, we have accounts from the outside, notably (in this case by a former insider writing from the chosen perspective of an outsider), Adrienne Rich, "Compulsory Heterosexuality and Lesbian Existence," *Signs* 5 (1980): 631–59.

None of these essays has the sort of history academic work is supposed to have: written simply because I chose to write it and then sent off to be judged by anonymous referees. Every one was requested by particular people for particular occasions, as part of particular conversations. Having discovered, as I was unsuccessfully trying to write a dissertation, that I was not very good at writing with no definite audience in mind, to answer no one's expressed need for what I had to say, I have been blessed by communities of feminist philosophers and theorists, including people with the energy and dedication to choreograph conferences, anthologies, and special issues of journals. Writing within such communities has been a delight, and my gratitude to them and to those who do the work of fostering them is immense.

The papers in the first section, "Gender and (Inter)subjectivity," were written at the time I should have been writing my dissertation. I was trying to puzzle out the differing ways in which we give accounts of different sorts of phenomena, in particular, accounts that are in some way constitutive of the phenomena they purport to describe, so that the usual notion of truth as adequate representation seems to trip over its own feet. As I focused on accounts of emotions as a central example, it became increasingly clear to me that among what structured and shaped those accounts were assumptions and attitudes about gender.

As I was puzzling over these issues, but unable to write, Mary Mothersill (who, with Sue Larson, had taught, guided, and believed in me so extraordinarily well that after two years of undergraduate study I was, and confidently knew myself to be, a philosopher) asked me to write a paper on sympathy for a special issue of the *Monist* on the ethical implications of concepts of the person. Shortly afterward, I unsuccessfully interviewed for a position in philosophy and women's studies at Cornell, and Sally McConnell-Ginet, Nelly Furman, and the late Ruth Borker asked me to write up the talk I had given on anger for an anthology they were putting together—my entry into the world of interdisciplinary feminist theory. Those two papers became two of the three parts of my dissertation; the third was an early version of the paper on individualism Sandra Harding requested for a collection she was editing with the late Merrill Hintikka. That collection of papers was the first to move feminist philosophy into, as its subtitle claims, "epistemology, metaphysics, methodology, and the philosophy of science"—realms where most of the profession believed (and much of it still believes) feminist perspectives are oxymoronic.

The essays in the next section, "Constructions of Gender and Authority," all reflect the influence of Stanley Cavell, my dissertation advisor. It is, I think, significant that his influence is most marked in the work I did after I left the country for four years, got my degree, and then moved to the Midwest. Harvard was, in many ways, a wonderful place to be, and Cavell was a wonderful teacher to have, as were, especially, Rogers Albritton and Burton Dreben, but the atmosphere of discipleship there made me uneasy. I appreciate in retrospect my position on the margins, a basically respected, thought-to-be-smart person in whom no one took a special interest, however ambivalent I may have been about it at the time.[9]

One mark of Cavell's influence in these essays is their starting with the placing of philosophical problems, notably scepticisms of various sorts, in the web of ordinary life, as expressions of anxieties of separation and estrangement, of finding and losing our way in the world. A talk I gave in a number of different forms in the years I was working on these essays was entitled "Who's This *We*, Paleface?"—Tonto's reply to the Lone Ranger, who has just informed him that "*we* are surrounded by an Indian war party." What I was trying to work out was my relationship as a woman philosopher to those problems, a relationship whose difficulties were emblematized in Cavell's discussion of Othello.[10] The lived experience out of which sceptical anxieties arise on Cavell's account is *gendered* experience. Reading him, and, subsequently, reading most philosophical texts, I had the experience Judith Fetterley describes in *The Resisting Reader*:[11] not only is the reader/philosopher constructed as male, but his maleness is set explicitly against the dark mystery of a corresponding femaleness. Desdemona does not have the problems of philosophy; she is the occasion for them, and because of them she dies. I found myself in a distressingly familiar position: invited to identify as a man, starting as my father's honorary son, I wondered about the women, starting with my mother, on whom I had turned my back. What, I came to wonder, can we make of the philosophical self—what can I, as a philosopher, make of myself—as a fully historical, gendered, raced, and classed being?

The papers on Othello and Descartes, Hamlet and Henry James, and mothers and daughters in films all respond to specific requests. Judith Genova organized a session of the International Association for Philosophy and Literature at which I presented a draft of "Othello's Doubt." (Roger Shiner's very insightful comments appear with my paper in the volume from the conference.) David Bleich called me up out of the blue (the first time to my knowledge that someone knew me only from what I had written) to invite me to a conference at the English Department of Indiana University on European empiricism and American hermeneuticism in the study of literature, assuring me, despite my incredulity, that I had something to say on the subject. The resulting paper on Hamlet, Henry James,

[9]Although I was not "his" student, Burton Dreben did take a special interest in me, at the crucial point at which I was struggling to write the noncommissioned portion of my dissertation. It is a pleasure to record publicly my appreciation for having been the object of his legendary critical intelligence, as well as my gratitude for his care, attention, and nagging.

[10]Stanley Cavell, *The Claim of Reason: Wittgenstein, Skepticism, Morality, and Tragedy* (New York: Oxford University Press, 1979), pp. 433–96.

[11]Judith Fetterley, *The Resisting Reader: A Feminist Approach to American Fiction* (Bloomington: Indiana University Press, 1978).

and Wittgenstein finally appeared, with some other papers from the conference, in *Poetics*.

The film paper was requested for a volume of *Psychiatry and the Humanities* on Cavell, psychoanalysis, and film, at his suggestion. It was, however, rejected (despite his pleas on its behalf) by the editors, one of whom engaged me in a lengthy correspondence concerning how wrong and wrong-headed I was about Freud and heterosexuality. The correspondence ended after he asked me to consider writing a book with him, in which the paper he had requested and was refusing to publish would appear first and we would alternate subsequent chapters. Having no idea how to answer that letter, I instead took up Cavell's suggestion to send the paper to *Critical Inquiry*.

The paper on method and madness has a longer history. I gave a number of versions of it as talks, initially as one of the Eunice Belgum Memorial Lectures I delivered at St. Olaf College in 1983; at a conference on Women and Reason at the University of Western Ontario in 1989; and finally at a conference on Gender, Rationality, and the Moderns at the University of Toronto in 1990. I wrote it in its present form when asked by Louise Antony and Charlotte Witt to contribute to *A Mind of Her Own*, a volume they have edited that constructs a conversation between feminists on different sides of the issue of the relevance of gender to epistemology. The conversation in and around this book and similar others seems to me to mark both a healthy maturity and a healthy openness in feminist philosophy, an openness that is fostered by the deep and responsible scepticism Antony and Witt have toward it, just as it is threatened by the fierce antagonism it arouses in others.

"Conversations on the Margins" are very brief, informal pieces written in dialogue with particular, mostly local, feminist audiences. I hope they give some sense of the connections between theory and practice that are needed to move beyond critique: my philosophical training equips me for the task of deconstructing the tradition, but not for the work of imagining alternatives to it. That work has drawn me into conversation, in particular, with feminist artists: the first two pieces were written for the journal of a women's art collective; the third, for an arts magazine; the fourth, for a writers' journal; the fifth, for an interdisciplinary humanities conference; the sixth, for a university publication on teaching; and the seventh, for an American Philosophical Association panel on teaching in ways that attract women and people of color to the profession. It is significant, I think, that conversations about concrete practice, including teaching, are more and more going on in philosophical circles: praxis is no longer something that happens only elsewhere.

The next section, "The Body of Privilege," moves the discussion about the relation between the social construction of privilege and the problems of philosophy onto the terrain of the body and of difference, in particular, of the body as the site of difference. It contains two papers that grew out of talks I gave at thematic, interdisciplinary symposia organized by Hans Ulrich Gumbrecht and

K. Ludwig Pfeiffer in Dubrovnik in 1987 and 1989. I often felt at sea there, understanding maybe half of what was going on (only partly because much of the time people were speaking French), but I was assured that what I was saying was, in fact, a contribution to the conversation, however little I was able to verify that for myself. Aptly, those papers have so far been published only in Pfeiffer's German translations, which, others assure me, are very well done. I am still bemused by existing in print, influencing people I have never laid eyes on; existing in translation is even odder: it's hard to feel responsible for words one cannot even competently read. The final paper in that section was requested by Ellen Messer-Davidow and Joan E. Hartman for *(En)gendering Knowledge*, as one of the synthesizing papers by philosophers at the end of each section of different disciplinary papers on issues in feminist research. Writing it required me explicitly to begin dealing with issues of race and with the particularities of my placement in the conversations in which I engage.

The concluding section continues this work. The essays in it reflect my increasing enmeshment in and debt to the community of feminist philosophers, notably the Midwest Society for Women in Philosophy (SWIP) and the APA Committee on the Status of Women, which has assisted Nancy Tuana in editing the *Newsletter on Feminism and Philosophy*. I have found there the ideal combination of support and critical challenge. More than perhaps anywhere else in the world, feminist philosophy has grown as a collective endeavor in Midwest SWIP; moving here in 1979 I joined a community that included, among many others, Sandra Bartky, Claudia Card, Marilyn Frye, Sarah Hoagland, Alison Jaggar, María Lugones, Peg Simons, Joyce Trebilcot, Iris Young, and Jacquelyn Zita. Alison Jaggar's work as chair of the APA committee and Nancy Tuana's as editor of the *Newsletter* have been exemplary, especially as they handled unprincipled attacks. I know I am not alone in benefiting from their efforts to deepen and widen the channels of responsible, honest, and searching critique. I have been pressed, writing for SWIP and the *Newsletter*, to examine my placement in the profession, the academy, and the world more generally, to learn who I am and how to be responsible as that person.

It is, I hope, clear, both in this preface and in the notes in the individual essays, that my intellectual debts are enormous. What may be less clear is how important it has been that all through the fifteen years during which these papers were written I have been a member of a number of groups, of varying degrees of formality and institutionalization. It is a pleasure to name them and to record my gratitude at the assurance they have afforded me that there are those to whom my words matter, who care enough to keep me honest, and whose voices make what I say not soliloquy but part of a vital, polyphonic conversation.

In Ottawa there was the Eiskreis, and now in Toronto there is the Gripe of Seven plus Two. I left Canada regretfully, but I am fortunate in the continuing friendship and intellectual companionship of Lynne Cohen, Naomi Goldenberg,

Debbie Gorham, Joy Kogawa, Andrew Lugg, Kathryn Morgan, Millie Morton, Ruth Roach Pierson, and Ronnie de Sousa. The Philosophy Department at the University of Minnesota has been, for the most part, a supportive and stimulating environment, notably in the Wittgenstein and the political economy discussion groups and in jointly led graduate seminars—in feminist theory and the philosophy of science with Ron Giere and in feminist ethics with Norman Dahl. My intellectual home at Minnesota has been in Women's Studies and the Center for Advanced Feminist Studies, an astonishing community of feminist scholars who have educated me and tolerated, even encouraged, my forays onto their various disciplinary turfs. The breakfast working group—Sara Evans, Amy Kaminsky, Elaine Tyler May, Riv-Ellen Prell, and Cheri Register—was wonderfully attentive, supportive, and critical when it came to figuring out how to put together a Book. The theater At the Foot of the Mountain was, for ten years before its demise in 1991, a touchstone for the relevance of theory outside the academy.

Courses I have taught have often blossomed into conversations and communities that wouldn't stop when the quarter ended. The students I teach, however much they may need the certification of a degree, are, rewardingly many of them, committed to an education—theirs and mine. Teaching at an urban public university is not something I knew enough to want when I was in graduate school, but I cannot now imagine classes without a wide range of adults, committed to lives outside the university, lives of work, relationship building, parenting, community involvement, political organizing, art making, and all the other things that people do when they are living what they take to be their real lives. And, finally, SOΦIA, the feminist philosophy discussion group, has grown over the past few years into a center both of gravity and of laughter. It's hard to remember the days when a handful of brave pioneers—especially Susan Bernick, Susan Heineman, and Ruth Ginzberg—planted the seeds of feminist work in the department, seeds that have taken root in SOΦIA and are flowering in profusion.

The final stages of preparing this manuscript have been handled, with skill, savvy, and unfailing good humor by Peg O'Connor, who also prepared the index, with the assistance of Veronica Weadock. I'm grateful as well to the other SOΦIA members who read the entire manuscript aloud to me for the final proofreading, thereby sacrificing—temporarily, I hope—their ability to read for content rather than for the minutiae of punctuation: Lisa Bergin, Jan Binder, Katy Brown, Carl Chung, Heidi Grasswick, Anne Phibbs, and Pauline Sargent. I appreciate Linda Nicholson's support and encouragement, as well as her responsibility for the company I get to keep in the "Thinking Gender" series. Maureen MacGrogan has been wonderful to work with: I will miss being in such extraordinarily capable and caring hands. As things moved along, I benefited as well from the expertise, patience, and friendliness of Katherine Lieber, editorial assistant, and Ray Walker, production editor. Over this past year, Ruth-Ellen Joeres in person and Amy Kaminsky on e-mail from Sweden have buoyed my spirits, while over the past decade Michael Root has done his best to keep my feet on the ground.

Note on the Text

"The Unavoidability of Gender" appeared in the *Journal of Social Philosophy,* Winter 1990, pp. 34–39, and is reprinted with permission.

"On Sympathy," originally published in *The Monist,* July 1979, pp. 320–330 (copyright © 1979, *The Monist,* La Salle, Illinois, 61301) is reprinted with permission.

"Anger and the Politics of Naming" appeared in *Women and Language in Literature and Society,* ed. Sally McConnell-Ginet, Ruth Borker, and Nelly Furman, (New York: Praeger, 1980), pp. 174–87, and is reprinted by permission of Praeger Publishers, an imprint of Greenwood Publishing Group, Inc., Westport, CT.

"Individualism and the Objects of Pyschology" appeared in *Discovering Reality: Feminist Perspectives on Epistemology, Metaphysics, Methodology, and the Philosophy of Science,* ed. Sandra Harding and Merrill B. Hintikka (Dordrecht: Reidel, 1983), pp. 225–44, and is reprinted by permission of Kluwer Academic Publishers.

"Othello's Doubt/Desdemona's Death: The Engendering of Scepticism" is reprinted from Judith Genova, ed., *Power, Gender, Values* (Edmonton, AB: Academic Printing and Publishing, 1987), pp. 113–33, by permission of Academic Printing and Publishing.

"Though This Be Method, Yet There Is Madness in It: Paranoia and Liberal Epistemology," is reprinted from *A Mind of One's Own: Feminist Essays on Reason and Objectivity,* ed. Louise Antony and Charlotte Witt, 1992, pp. 145–70, by permission of Westview Press, Boulder, CO.

"From Hamlet to Maggie Verver: The History and Politics of the Knowing Subject" appeared in *Poetics,* Vol. 18, 1989, pp. 449–69, and is reprinted with permission.

"Missing Mothers/Desiring Daughters: Framing the Sight of Women" was first published in *Critical Inquiry,* 1988, pp. 62–89, copyright © 1988 by the University of Chicago, all rights reserved, and is reprinted with permission. Excerpt from Adrienne Rich, "Sibling Mysteries" is reprinted from *Dream of a Common Language* by permission of W.W. Norton & Co. and Adrienne Rich.

"On Competition: Some Stray Thoughts on Baseball, Sex, and Art" is reprinted from the *Journal of the Women's Art Registry of Minnesota (WARM),* Fall 1980.

"Thinking about Quality in Women's Visual Art" is reprinted from the *WARM Journal,* Spring 1983.

"Photography and the Politics of Vision" appeared in *Artpaper,* April 1985.

"Art for Our Sake" appeared in *View from the Loft,* Fall 1990.

"Making It All Up" was originally published in *The Paradigm Exchange,* a publication of the University of Minnesota College of Liberal Arts, 1987.

"Coming to Know *Women's Ways of Knowing*" is reprinted from *Focus,* a publication of the University of Minnesota Office of Educational Development Programs, Winter 1990.

"Changing the Subject" will appear in the *American Philosophical Association (APA) Newsletter on Feminism and Philosophy,* Vol. 92, No. 2, Fall 1993, and is reprinted by permission of the APA.

"The Body Politic/The Impolitic Body/Bodily Politics" appeared as "Der Körper des Gemeinswesens/Der Unpolitische Körper/Körperpolitik," trans. K. Ludwig Pfeiffer, in *Materialität der Kommunikation,* ed. Hans Ulrich Gumbrecht and K. Ludwig Pfeiffer (Frankfurt: Suhrkamp, 1988), pp. 846–57.

"Your Ground is My Body: The Politics of Anti-Foundationalism" appeared as " 'Your Ground is My Body': Strategien des Antifundamentalismus," trans. K. Ludwig Pfeiffer, in *Paradoxien, Dissonanzen, Zummenbruche: Situationen offener Epistemologie* ed. Hans Ulrich Gumbrecht and K. Ludwig Pfeiffer (Frankfurt: Suhrkamp, 1991), pp. 639–54.

"Who Wants to Know?: The Epistemological Value of Values" is reprinted by permission of the University of Tennessee Press from *(En)Gendering Knowledge: Feminists in Academe,* ed. Joan E. Hartman and Ellen Messer-Davidow, (1991), pp. 179–200, copyright © 1991 by The University of Tennessee Press.

"Who is That Masked Woman?: Reflections on Power, Privilege, and Homeophobia" is reprinted from *Revisioning Philosophy,* ed. James Ogilvy, by permission of State University of New York Press. © 1992 SUNY Press. Excerpt from Rainer Maria Rilke's *Letters to a Young Poet,* trans. M.D. Herter Norton, is reprinted by permission of W.W. Norton & Co. and The Hogarth Press, Ltd.

"Undoing Philosophy as a Feminist" appeared in the *APA Newsletter on Feminism and Philosophy,* Vol. 91, No. 1, Spring 1992, and is reprinted by permission of the APA.

"Confessions of an Analytic Philosopher Semi-Manque" appeared in the *APA Newsletter on Feminism and Philosophy,* Vol. 91, No. 2, Fall 1992, and is reprinted by permission of the APA.

1

Introduction: The Unavoidability of Gender

Philosophers are distinguished from other people in part by the problems they have: how do we know whether the external world exists, or whether we have bodies or others have minds: and if we do have both minds and bodies, how are they connected? It isn't, of course, supposed to be only philosophers who have these problems. Rather, just as the problems of how to make sure bridges stay up are problems not solely for structural engineers, but for all of us who drive or walk across bridges, so we are all supposed to have philosophical problems, and philosophers are those who are equipped, by interest and training, to best answer them for the rest of us.

Feminist philosophers have queried the questions of philosophy, asking who is this "we" whose problems these are, out of whose experiences do they arise, and from whose perspective are they salient? The usual answer has, of course, been men (or some men: those who are white and otherwise privileged), that is, people like the people who have been philosophers.

I don't think this answer is quite right. As the feminist critics have argued,[1] the maleness of (most) philosophers, insofar as it has been reflected in their philosophy, has been a matter not of biology but of culture, not the possession of certain chromosomes, hormones, and bodily characteristics, but the learning of certain norms of thought, feeling, and behavior. But according to the usual way of understanding the feminist argument, call it the Standard Account, philosophers, having become men according to these norms, just do find some things rather than others interestingly problematic, and some methods rather than others useful for addressing those problems: philosophy is male in that its problems are born

[1]See, especially, Susan R. Bordo, *The Flight to Objectivity: Essays on Cartesianism and Culture* (Albany: SUNY Press, 1987); Evelyn Fox Keller, *Reflections on Gender and Science* (New Haven: Yale University Press, 1984); and Genevieve Lloyd, *The Man of Reason* (Minneapolis: University of Minnesota Press, 1984).

out of and its methods are recommended by distinctively masculine ways of being in the world.

Arguments about the maleness of philosophy, so understood, have been challenged, interestingly, by feminists, most notably by Jean Grimshaw,[2] who argues that being a man has historically been neither necessary nor sufficient for thinking like one. A recent project of recovery of women philosophers from antiquity onward would bear out the nonnecessity of maleness: many of the rediscovered women philosophized indistinguishably from their male contemporaries,[3] as certainly many women philosophers do today. And, conversely, Grimshaw gives examples of male philosophers whose views seem to diverge from masculinist orthodoxy, without there being any reason to believe that their sex role socialization did so. Such criticisms are, I believe, effective against the Standard Account, and to some extent against the actual arguments that get so construed. I want here to give a slightly different argument, leaving it open how closely this alternative account of the maleness of philosophy reflects the views of the various feminist critics: it is, at least, significantly different from the Standard Account, and it is, I think, true.

We can start by asking again who the philosophical "we" is. For those who use it unreflectively (and it is instructive—and dismaying—to note how readily and often even those of us who have learned to be suspicious of it do use it unreflectively)[4] it is assumed to be everyone. It is, we (philosophers) are taught, to mistake the philosophical tone of voice for the sociological or social psychological to reply to a question about the relation of the mind to the body by asking "whose mind to whose body?" But subtly or overtly many philosophers indicate that they don't entirely mean to include everyone in the "we," and it's frequently unclear where they mean to and where they don't. (One of the strongest arguments against the use of the supposedly generic 'he', 'man', etc., is that such terms are ambiguous, and the reader often can't tell which is meant.) Part of what is distressing to many women in reading philosophical texts is the experience of taking oneself to be included in the "we" and coming up short against the realization that one really wasn't.

One way to approach the question of the identity of the philosophical "we" is by looking at the problems that, as participants in philosophical conversation, we are supposed to have. One striking thing about the core epistemological problems defining modern philosophy is that the philosophers who discuss them acknowl-

---

[2]Jean Grimshaw, *Philosophy and Feminist Theory* (Minneapolis: University of Minnesota Press, 1986), pp. 36–75.

[3]See Mary Ellen Waithe, ed., *A History of Women Philosophers* (Dordrecht & Boston: M. Nijhoff, 1987).

[4]See Elizabeth V. Spelman's *Inessential Woman* (Boston: Beacon Press, 1988) for an account of how white feminist theorists have unreflectively used 'we' in writing about women, spuriously generalizing from their own positions of relative privilege.

edge that by and large people are not concerned with such questions, that even the philosophers themselves go about their daily lives untroubled by not being able to answer the questions they pose in their writing. Descartes, who, more than anyone else, got us started on these questions, explicitly regarded his insouciance in the face of unresolved doubt as merely provisional: he thought it was imperative for the development of a reliable science or ethics that fundamental metaphysical and epistemological questions be resolved and knowledge put on an unassailable footing. But, notoriously, his resolution, particularly as it relies on a Scholastic proof of the existence of God, has convinced far fewer readers than have his arguments for the doubt it was meant to lay to rest. Cartesian scepticism, for its inventor a powerful tool for the acquisition of certainty, has been, for those who have followed him, a slippery-sided abyss we cannot climb out of.

Humeans would have us simply steer clear of that abyss, noting that that way madness lies, and that without venturing to its edge we can give accounts of what the world is like and how we know about it that are good enough. Many contemporary philosophers would agree, eschewing the demands of foundationalism and absolute certainty in favor of one or another sort of naturalized epistemology.[5] That is, many philosophers have simply joined the rest of the world, which conducts its business on the other side of the abyss from where the philosophical subject as constructed by Descartes found himself. But there are unanswered questions about what that character (the one Hume failed to find on his introspective search) was doing over there, why he had the problems he had, and whether we can simply turn our backs on him.

The problems at the heart of modern epistemology concern the possibility of securely bridging one or another gulf: between the mind and the body, the self and others, the inner and the external world. The form of all those problems is the same: the philosophical subject finds himself on one side of the gulf and attempts to assess the possibilities of establishing reliable cognitive contact with what lies on the other side of it. What is striking is that the gulfs are not simply given: rather, the authoritative subject puts them in place with the very gestures by which he secures his authority. Again, the *Meditations* is the clearest expression of this activity of self-constitution, as the self of the cogito is discovered/created by successive gestures of estrangement from everything taken previously to constitute the self and to anchor it in the world.

Without the rigor of Cartesian doubt, authoritative modern subjectivity has deployed essentially the same gestures, of self-constitution through the achievement of independence from others and disidentification with and control over the body, the senses, and the emotions. Those who are taken to be in the best position to know are those who are believed to be objective, distanced, dispassionate,

[5]There are good reasons for considering such philosophy to be postmodern, even given the slipperiness of that term, in its rejection of foundational strategies of justification in favor of the *bricolage* that characterizes most contemporary analytic philosophy.

independent, and nonemotionally rational. That is, those who define themselves through the norms of epistemic authoritativeness acquire, as a residue of that act of self-constitution, the problems of philosophy. They don't, however, in New Age parlance, "own their problems." Instead, philosophical problems are mocked: they are for wimps, irrelevant eggheads who can't even match their own socks. The scorn masks the anxiety that is coded in those problems, anxiety about whether and how connections can actually be established and maintained with a potentially embarrassing body, with threateningly other people, and with an obdurately physical world. The anxiety is grounded in the norms that require that the body, other people, and the rest of the world be thought of in those ways, and consequently philosophical problems are originally problems for the fictive self that is constituted by those norms, and only derivatively for any real people, insofar as we identify ourselves with the project of living up to those norms.

It is evident in much, even contemporary, philosophical writing that the philosophical subject is not, in fact, any real person. Consider, for example, Kripke's Pierre.[6] Pierre, growing up in Paris, came to believe, from many descriptions and photographs, that, as he would have put it, "Londres est jolie." After moving to London, he came to believe that the city where he was residing was anything but pretty, a belief he expressed in English as "Whatever else you can say about it, it's certainly not true that London is pretty." He learned the name of the city he now resides in not by having 'Londres' translated, but ostensively, and, in fact, he never has learned that 'Londres' and 'London' refer to the same city. Invoking some apparently uncontroversial principles concerning translation and belief attribution, Kripke generates a puzzle about what Pierre believes about the prettiness of London. That the puzzle has in turn generated a small philosophical industry is an indication of how entrenched is the (typically unarticulated) assumption that the philosophical subject is not you or me, whatever gender we might be.

The puzzle is generated by noting that there seem to be adequate grounds for attributing to Pierre the belief that London is pretty, and also adequate grounds for attributing to him the negation of that belief, and there seem to be no grounds for calling him irrational. Worse, there seem equally to be adequate grounds for our both asserting and denying the statement that Pierre believes that London is pretty, and there's even less reason to think that we, as innocent observers of Pierre's confusion, are irrational.

Now, if Pierre were one of us (real people), what we (other real people) would say, as Wittgenstein is good at reminding us, is that there simply isn't any good answer to the question of what Pierre believes about the prettiness of London. It isn't that 'believes p' is vague, like 'is bald': if all we knew were the evidence in one of Pierre's linguistic homes, we would be justified in unequivocally

---

[6]Saul Kripke, "A Puzzle about Belief," in A. Margalit, ed., *Meaning and Use* (Dordrecht: Reidel, 1979).

affirming or denying of him that he believes that London is pretty. Rather, for us (real people) there are no necessary or sufficient conditions for belief attributions, nor any principles, about translation or anything else, that tell us what beliefs to attribute. We pay attention to what people say and do and, depending on an unspecifiable range of contextual circumstances, we interpret them (or, for that matter, ourselves) as having certain beliefs (or desires, attitudes, emotions, intentions . . .). And sometimes things aren't straightforward in the ways they usually are, and we don't know what to say, beyond telling the whole story: we can't sum up that story as "he believes p" or "he believes not-p."[7]

That's how it is with real people. But Pierre isn't a real person, nor are those who find his story genuinely puzzling. Pierre is a philosophical example, and those who puzzle over him are philosophers. Now, all the philosophers I know also happen to be real people, but it isn't *qua* real people that Pierre worries them. One worries about Pierre because one wants, and thinks it reasonable to expect to have, a theory about such things as belief, and one has certain ideas about what theories have to look like in order to be worth having. In order for it to be even remotely plausible that one will ever get such a theory, the phenomena, or at least the descriptions of them, have to be sufficiently orderly; the data have to be regimented. It has, for example, to be either true or false that Pierre believes that London is pretty. It won't do to say what real people say about other real people, that, if you look at it this way, he certainly seems to, and if you look at it that way, he certainly seems not to: why are you so intent on getting me to check one box or the other? (Think of how maddening survey research questions can be for us real people.)

One might reply that the philosophical subject—both the subject of the problems, like Pierre, and the subject who has the problems, the philosopher—are idealizations, like the gases that appear in the Ideal Gas Laws. But, I want to suggest, unlike airplane models in wind chambers or mathematical models of falling objects in perfect vacuums, philosophical subjects are normative. They aren't just how people will be assumed to be for the purpose of figuring something out about them. Rather, the regimentation of the data of experience and the assumption that, for example, such things as beliefs are definite states of individuals, reflect a view of persons as atomistically self-contained, which is how they ought to be if they are to acquire and exercise socially recognized authority.[8]

The modern philosophical "we" is akin to the "we" in such documents as the

[7]For a similar argument, see John Wallace and H. E. Mason, "On Some Thought Experiments about Mind and Meaning," in C. Anthony Anderson and Joseph Owens, eds., *Propositional Attitudes: The Role of Content in Logic, Language, and Mind* (Stanford: CSLI Press, 1990).

[8]For an elaboration of this connection, see my "Individualism and the Objects of Psychology."

U.S. Declaration of Independence and Constitution and the French Declaration of the Rights of Man. The kinship is, of course, nonaccidental. The modern philosophical subject was conceived, most explicitly by Descartes, as constituting himself[9] as epistemically authoritative, an authority that, as both its champions and its antagonists recognized, had far-reaching political, religious, and economic causes and effects. It is that subject—the bourgeois individual—who has held the center of the world-historical stage for the past two hundred years, and it is an open question whether or not he will—or should—continue to do so.

If one acknowledges the legitimacy of the claims of variously marginalized others to share center stage fully with the European and Euro-American men who have heretofore claimed it, that open question becomes one of the possibility of shedding the gender and race identifications that have characterized the fully authorized subject. Are those identifications merely contingent, in that only white men have been believed capable of approximating the norm or have had the opportunity, the encouragement, or the permission to do so? Or are those identifications intrinsic to the norms; can we meaningfully call the norms themselves white and male? That is, are the norms of authorized subjectivity the norms, not of personhood *per se,* but the norms of nonuniversalizable privilege?

Gender and, equally, race are, therefore, unavoidable epistemological issues, given the role of the norms of philosophical subjectivity in constituting epistemic authority. Furthermore, the connections between that authority and political, economic, and religious empowerment make it politically imperative that we answer the questions about the nature of the gender and race identifications of that normative subject. One may believe, as no doubt most philosophers currently do, that those identifications are merely contingent, as well as outdated and unjust.[10] Extending a line of argument going back at least as far as Descartes himself and made politically explicit by Mary Wollstonecraft, John Stuart Mill, and Harriet Taylor, they would argue that the norms of philosophical subjectivity have been wrongly offered for approximation only to European and Euro-American men and that such norms should be equally available to all, and we should expect all to be equally likely to approximate them and to be empowered by so doing. What is important to realize is that such a position is not well described as holding that epistemology has nothing to do with gender (or with race). Rather, it is to embrace, at least in part, the agenda of what is commonly known as liberal feminism (or civil rights, integrationist, or assimilationist race politics), which

---

[9]My use of the masculine pronoun here anticipates the argument that the normative philosophical subject is, in fact, normatively male.

[10]The only philosopher I know of to argue publicly that the preponderance of white males in philosophy is both natural and morally unproblematic (he takes the latter to follow from the former, which he takes to be nontendentiously specifiable) is Michael E. Levin, *Feminism and Freedom* (New Brunswick, N.J.: Transaction Books, 1987).

advocates the extension to women (or people of color) the privileges and forms of authority and empowerment currently available to white men.

Most self-identified feminist philosophers would disagree with this agenda, arguing that the norms of philosophical subjectivity are the norms of essentially inegalitarian gender privilege, and that such norms need to be challenged, not extended.[11] (Similar arguments are being made about the essentially inegalitarian race privilege encoded in those norms.)[12] On such views, the constitution of philosophical subjectivity is of a piece with the constitution of normative privileged masculinity, and, like it, gives a partial and distorted picture of what human beings can and should be like and which human capacities are epistemically fruitful and reliable.[13]

A frequently criticized feature of the projects of feminist philosophers such as Susan Bordo, Jane Flax, Evelyn Fox Keller, Jacquelyn Zita, and me are that we are, in differing ways, psychoanalytic. On the Standard Account we are taken to be psychoanalyzing particular philosophers or, perhaps, all men of their time, race, and class. I share the doubts of our critics about the plausibility of any such project, and would not describe what we are doing in those terms. (I am not sure here of the extent to which any of the others would agree with me.) Rather, I would take the analysand to be the normative philosophical subject: the persona of the *Meditations* as he discovers/constructs himself, the ideally rational scientist or citizen of the liberal state, or Pierre and those he puzzles. The problems they have need to be seen in the light of their distinctive project of self-constitution, as the epistemically authoritative modern subject. Such a project of self-constitution, like any developmental project, leaves a distinctive residue of unresolved problems, and psychoanalytic theory is defined by its undertaking to unearth and

---

[11]See, for example, Susan Bordo, *The Flight to Objectivity*, and Evelyn Fox Keller, *Reflections on Gender and Science*, and Jane Flax, "Political Philosophy and the Patriarchal Unconscious: A Psychoanalytical Perspective on Epistemology and Metaphysics," in Sandra Harding and Merrill B. Hintikka, *Discovering Reality: Feminist Perspectives on Epistemology, Metaphysics, Methodology, and Philosophy of Science* (Dordrecht: Reidel, 1983); Jacquelyn Zita, "Transsexualized Origins: Reflections on Descartes' *Meditations*," *Genders* 5 (Summer 1989): 86–105; and Naomi Scheman, "Othello's Doubt/Desdemona's Death: The Engendering of Scepticism."

[12]See, for example, *"Race," Writing, and Difference*, a special issue of *Critical Inquiry* 12, no. 1 (Autumn 1985); *The Nature of Minority Discourse*, a two-volume special issue of *Cultural Critique* 6 and 7 (Spring and Fall, 1987); and Cornel West, "The Politics of American Neo-Pragmatism," in John Rajchman and Cornel West, eds., *Post-Analytic Philosophy* (New York: Columbia University Press, 1985).

[13]See Alison M. Jaggar, "Love and Knowledge: Emotion in Feminist Epistemology" in Ann Garry and Marilyn Pearsall, eds., *Women, Knowledge, and Reality: Explorations in Feminist Philosophy* (Boston: Unwin Hyman, 1989), for an account of the ways in which emotions, especially the emotions of the marginalized, can be an epistemic resource.

examine those residues. (Freudian psychoanalytic theory, to take the best known example, is, I would argue, most helpfully understood as an account of certain culturally normative projects of self-constitution and of the neuroses that are the characteristic residues of unresolved aspects of those projects.)[14]

Thus, on such a view, philosophical problems become intellectualized sublimations of the neuroses of privilege, not to be solved, but, as Wittgenstein put it, dissolved by profound alterations in our forms of life: "The sickness of a time is cured by an alteration in the mode of life of human beings, and it was possible for the sickness of philosophical problems to get cured only though a changed mode of thought and of life, not through a medicine invented by an individual."[15]

Such a view of the problems of philosophy will, no doubt, appear implausible or even perverse to most philosophers. My concern here is not to argue for it, but to argue that whatever grounds one has for rejecting it, or for rejecting any other explicitly feminist account of the relation of gender to epistemology, are not grounds for claiming that gender is irrelevant to epistemology. Rather, those who think that the problems of philosophy we have inherited are everyone's, that the philosophical "we" as currently constituted is universal, are committed to the belief that the norms of self-constitution that give rise to those problems are appropriately thought of as human norms: they are, that is, committed to the extension of the ideals of liberalism to all women and to men of color.

One can deny the appropriate universality of these norms without claiming that various others reason in ways that are distinctively different from how white men reason: the claim is rather that we need to uncover and undo the implicit markings of gender and race privilege in the construction of subjectivity. The challenge of feminist philosophy is thus connected to the challenge of radical feminist and post-colonialist politics: do we need and can we formulate a radically different subjectivity, constituted by radically different norms, and authoritative on radically different grounds? Any answer needs to start with the question that began this paper: who is the "we" whose needs and capabilities frame these questions?

---

[14]Freud himself expresses at different times different views of his own project, and he is usually interpreted as theorizing ahistorically about human development. For a historically grounded picture of the neurosis-generating features of psychosexual development, see "'Civilized' Sexual Morality and Modern Nervous Illness" (1908) in vol. IX of the *Standard Edition*, ed. James Strachey (London: Hogarth Press, 1959).

[15]Ludwig Wittgenstein, *Remarks on the Foundations of Mathematics*, ed. G. H. von Wright, R. Rhees, and G. E. M. Anscombe (Cambridge, Mass: The M.I.T. Press, 1967), p. 57.

I

Gender and (Inter)subjectivity

2

On Sympathy

"I weep for you," the Walrus said: "I deeply sympathize."
With sobs and tears he sorted out
Those of the largest size,
Holding his pocket handkerchief
Before his streaming eyes.

—Lewis Carroll

I

What are we to make of the Walrus's sobs and tears and his claim to "deeply sympathize"? Alice, at least, makes *something* of them: when Tweedledee is done, she says, "I like the Walrus best . . . because he was a *little* sorry for the poor Oysters." She's indignant, however, when Tweedledee tells her, "He ate more than the Carpenter, though. . . . You see he held his handkerchief, so that the Carpenter couldn't count how many he took; contrariwise." The Oysters, understandably, take a thoroughly sceptical view of the sobs and tears: "O woeful, weeping Walrus, your tears are all a sham! You're greedier for Oysters than children are for jam."[1]

Clearly, the tears *were* a sham, especially since they served to explain the concealing handkerchief. But the Walrus wasn't *lying* when he said, "I weep for you," or not about the weeping anyway: the tears were real enough. Shedding sham tears is different from pretending to cry (harder, perhaps, but much more effective).

What about the proffered sympathy? It is natural to say that it, like the tears, was sham. Is this to say something other than that the claim to deeply sympathize was a lie? Was the Walrus expressing sham sympathy, shamming an expression of sympathy, or simply lying? Can we draw any genuine distinctions here? Was Alice naive to think the Walrus was "a *little* sorry for the poor Oysters"? What is the relevance of his feelings to questions about his sympathizing? The answer many people would give to these questions, based on what I will call "the inner-state view" is roughly this: There is no *essential* difference between expressing

[1]Sung by the ghost of the second Oyster, dancing a hornpipe on the sleeping Walrus's chest. Added by Carroll for Savile Clark's *Alice* operetta; see Martin Gardner, *The Annotated Alice* (Cleveland: Forum Books, 1963), p. 236.

sham sympathy or shamming an expression of sympathy, and lying. We are likely to use one of the first two descriptions rather than the third if we wish to stress a certain elaborateness of presentation, a degree of stage setting; lying is more a matter of simply stating as a fact what one believes to be false. The Walrus has both shammed sympathy and lied about his feelings. Genuine sympathy is a matter of genuine feeling. (Genuineness may admit of degrees; we can, for example, be moved by the poignancy of our own performance—so the line between genuine and real may not be a sharp one.) Alice was inferring from the Walrus's behavior, including his words, to his feelings; perhaps naively, but perhaps not—he may have had genuine sympathy for the poor Oysters, but eaten them anyway, his feelings not being strong enough to overcome his appetite. Or perhaps he acted akratically. In any event, on the inner-state view the question of whether or not he was sympathetic rests on what he did or did not *feel*.

When Alice is disillusioned by discovering that the handkerchief daubing the tears served to hide a larger consumption of Oysters, the inner-state view would have it that she has acquired new evidence that alters her inferred belief about the Walrus's feelings. These feelings are inferred to as the cause of his behavior, and when that behavior is seen differently, it is seen as likely to have different causes—in this case a desire to eat lots of oysters and the belief that he could better do so if the Carpenter didn't know. It's like discovering that someone apparently screaming in pain is rehearsing for a play.

There's a difference, on anyone's view, between sham or phony screams or tears, like the actor's or the Walrus's, and pretended crying or screaming (as one could pretend to scream in a photograph, a silent movie, or a very noisy place).[2] In the case of the shammed there's something there, something meant to be taken for the real thing, differing from the real thing primarily in what lies behind it, where it comes from. Pretense is like Monopoly money; sham, like counterfeit. As Austin makes us aware,[3] pretense is a much varied sort of thing: it needn't be true, given appropriate circumstances, that if one is pretending to ϕ, one is not actually ϕ-ing. Sham differs from pretense in the locus of its divergence from the genuine: words or behavior are sham when they are meant to be taken as, but are not in fact, the *expression* of something (an emotion, intention, character trait, belief). Austin's window washer who, in order to gain a view of an office, pretended to wash windows by actually doing so was not *shamming* washing windows, although had he gone on about how glad he was to do it for free, he

[2]That is to say, we all know how in some circumstances to draw this distinction, and we can have some idea of why we do. But the ordinary usage of 'sham' and 'pretend' and 'pretense' does not strictly speaking support the more thorough going distinction I mean to draw. It doesn't undermine it, either: the words overlap largely because we don't usually bother to draw the distinction.

[3]J. L. Austin, "Pretending," *Philosophical Papers* (Oxford: Oxford University Press, 1961), pp. 201–19.

would have been shamming generosity. The shammed, the ungenuine, and what makes it so, is what concerns us here.

Like counterfeit money, shammed sympathy can look very much, indistinguishably, like the real thing. In fact, unlike many central cases of pretense, it is in general important that shamming behavior appear to be the real thing. So we need to look at the connections that behavior has with other facts and features of the situation. On the inner-state view, we look for the presence of the appropriate sorts of feelings and causal connections between them and behavior. I want to suggest that we cannot, as the inner-state view would have us do, characterize feelings as sympathetic prior to situating them in a larger context, a pattern, including the agent's behavior, which pattern is one of meaning, of social significance. Sympathetic feelings are so because of how they fit with our actions and in our lives, not because of how they are in themselves, and although feelings we can so consider are certainly a typical part of genuine sympathy, they need not be present, and it is in any event not through an independent identification of them that we come to call the associated actions sympathetic.[4] I want to look first at cases where our concern is not with the agent's feelings and then at what such cases can lead us to suspect about the nature of our concern in those cases in which we do care about what someone is feeling.

II

Consider doctors, nurses, lawyers, teachers, judges, social workers, and so on. Much, though by no means all, of what we may expect of such people is that they respond to us sympathetically, that they be, not so much as a matter of personality or character, but in their professional roles, sympathetic. What we want from them in this regard is attentive listening (asking the right questions, taking the answers seriously), careful consideration of possible courses of action based on what we in particular need from them, willingness to spend time, etc. We don't expect them to have any particular feelings for us, and in certain crucial circumstances it would interfere with their being sympathetic if they did. If their thoughts and emotions are elsewhere, if they don't even like us especially well, if they forget about us as soon as their work is done—fine. It's not that the sorts of feelings we expect are different from those we expect of a sympathetic friend: feelings have essentially nothing to do with it.

This is not, of course, to say that their expressions of sympathy may not be sham. Rather, it is to suggest that the connections we need to find for them to be genuine are not with their feelings but with the larger course of action of which

[4]This talk of patterns, meanings, contexts, and social significance is, aside from its Wittgensteinian echoes, not particularly illuminating. I would in fact hope that the rest of the discussion could illuminate *it* somewhat, rather than the other way around. I hope eventually to explicate both phrases such as these and their Wittgensteinian echoes.

the expressions are a part. Do they follow up on what they say they will do, do they represent our needs, desires, fears, and so on fairly to others, are their actions genuinely in our interest? The expressions of sympathy are meant to indicate, not the presence of feelings about us and our plight, but certain settled and reliable patterns of behavior. We may talk about motivation here (the absence of ulterior motives), but we don't require of such people any nobility of motive: it may be just a job. Acting sympathetically as a way of earning their fee is fine; as a way of swindling our fortune, it's clearly not. The con artist may have no more hostile feelings toward us than the conscientious worker, but she or he is up to something different.

What concerns us in cases such as these is that the person's behavior and attitudes be appropriate—to the occasion and to us and our needs. Sympathy is essentially communicative, and as such it demands the cognitive skills necessary to know what sort of action or response is needed. Attempted expressions of sympathy can fail not just by being sham but by being ill-chosen, too blunt or too subtle, too obvious or clumsy. To be sympathetic in this way is in large part to be good at deciphering the ways in which needs are expressed and at suitably conveying one's own responses. In many cases no particular feelings at all are called for, and it is surely true that there is no one class of feelings, those of sympathy, that all such people are expected to have.

III

We may think the situation different, however, when we turn to sympathetic friends, or simply sympathetic people or behavior. And it is surely true that here we do characteristically care about how people feel; we want their responses to flow from their feelings for us, or at least for our plight. To this extent I agree with the inner-state view. But though phrases like 'sympathetic nurse' may be syncategorematic, I think that we can illuminate otherwise puzzling features of our concern in the more general case by keeping in mind how sympathy works when tied to a role.

Consider the Walrus again, not because Carroll is such a perceptive phenomenological psychologist or the Walrus so clearly Everyman, but because we do understand the story: silly as it is, the fact that we know how to read it is significant. One thing I want to suggest we know about it is that it is entirely possible that the Walrus has tender feelings toward the Oysters. We may think it unlikely that he does, but nothing in the story rules it out, and, importantly, Alice's and the Oysters' judgment of his proffered sympathy as sham would not fall if he did. Whatever the Walrus feels, his sympathy is sham, since the pattern into which those feelings fit is one of deception and betrayal. It is not an empirical generalization that deception and betrayal are incompatible with genuine sympathy; rather, not even the acutest pangs of identification and commiserative sorrow[5] will do if they serve to hide or disguise from the Walrus what his actions come to. What, as a matter of introspection, we *feel* is not always a reliable guide to what our actions express, or to what those feelings themselves mean.

One way of putting this point is to say that if the Walrus has any feelings (other than hunger) for the Oysters, these feelings are sham. This could easily happen: it is a common form self-deception takes. We are engaged in a project we feel somewhat uneasy about, and we find ourselves with feelings that run counter to what we are doing. The feelings may be behind the uneasiness or the other way around, but we are often deceiving ourselves if, as we are tempted to do, we identify with the feelings, and think of them as being somehow truer of us than our actions. It is as though our actions couldn't be quite what they seem because the feelings, the inner self they flow from, is not nasty or mean or possessive or greedy. We have a picture of what people who characteristically act as we are acting are like, and comfort ourselves with the thought that because of the feelings we have we are surely not like them.

But we do have those feelings, and sometimes they do count a very great deal—what makes the difference? We feel sympathetic toward a student and are pained to have to give him or her a low or failing grade. We may even feel critical of the system of grading to which we (have to, we say) adhere. What makes our feelings here genuine, our expressions of sympathy sincere? We need to do for ourselves what others would do were they asking the question about us—assemble what on the inner-state view would be *evidence* for our true feelings: did we try to help the student to do better in the course; have we made any attempt to alter the system of grading; do we manifest attitudes of, for example, elitism or academic isolation in other contexts; etc.? But we *know* our feelings; we can't be gathering evidence for them, so what are we doing? (And what does it mean to talk of "true feelings"?)

Freud, and much of the Western world after him, would say we were looking for evidence not for our conscious feelings, the ones we know about, but the deeply hidden, unconscious ones that are really behind it all. But even in cases where we do something like this the same problem arises: we can ask again what makes those feelings, intentions, beliefs, etc., the unconscious ones, genuine? The usual answer, the one Freud wants to give (though not, I would argue, the one one gets from looking at the practice of psychoanalysis), is that it is these feelings that cause the behavior.

Whatever truth there may be to this claim, I think we have reason to worry over its ability to account for the explanatory power that both commonsense and

---

[5]It should be clear that I do not mean to be defining feelings of sympathy as "pangs of identification and commiserative sorrow": if you have a favored definition, substitute it. Part of my point is that there is no such definition: it's not wholly something about feelings as feelings that makes them sympathetic.

psychoanalytic explanations have for us. These explanations do explain, not always and not universally, but often convincingly and insightfully, clearly—we want to say—correctly, and importantly, therapeutically. And all this is quite undisturbed by the aura of controversy, not to mention the radical incompleteness, of the causal theory meant to underlie them and account for their force. If the causal theory were the explanation of the power and the efficacy of particular explanations, the least we would expect would be that the latter would inherit some of the shakiness of the former. But our sense of having hit upon a way of seeing the situation that makes sense of it, and, often, the therapeutic efficacy of such insight, seem independent of the scientific claims made for the causal theories on which they would seem to be based. We do, though not always, know where to stop, when we've reached the motivations that explain the behavior and the feelings, though we may have little confidence in, and we surely have little knowledge of, the causal mechanisms meant to provide the justification for our confidence.[6]

The Walrus's expressions of sympathy are surely sham not because we have reason to be convinced of the empirical claim that genuinely sympathetic feelings could not coexist with the gluttonous devouring of the objects of those feelings. Rather, the meaning of whatever feelings he may have in part has to do with their situation within a social context. In other words, we have to assess the Walrus's feelings, along with his actions, in basically the same sort of way that we assess the behavior of sympathetic professionals. The particular standards of appropriateness will be different, importantly in concern with feelings. But equally in this sort of case, there is nothing to appeal to, the presence or absence of which will settle the question. No matter what we learn about the state of the Walrus's feelings or inner states or whatever, we can go on to ask what, in this particular context, it means, how it should be taken, what it comes to.

Although the genuineness of our feelings is connected with our actions and we often deem feelings ungenuine because the appropriate actions are not done or radically inappropriate ones are done, the connection is not nearly as simple as this. We have all known people, and most of us have been people, who have been unable, or even perhaps unwilling, to act on feelings they nonetheless genuinely have, and not just once or on isolated occasions but often or always. That they are so may be the reason for anger or pity or scorn or, depending on the feelings and the reasons, admiration or respect. Sometimes we regard such unacted-on feelings as less than genuine, not deeply felt, perhaps self-deceptive. But not always. What is it to regard them as deep and real? And what can our reasons be for so regarding them?

---

[6]None of this, of course, argues against the possibility that the underlying causal theory is right and will eventually account for the efficacy of particular explanations. Although I do not believe this is possible (see below and note 7), the question I am concerned with here is a different one, namely, why do these explanations work for us now?

We care, as in the most straightforward cases, about what the feelings mean, how to read them, how they fit in, not just with particular actions, but with all the other things we know about the person, who may be ourselves, and about people in general. (And patterns, of course, can be ignored or mis-seen or simply missed, and nonetheless present: significance is relative to a particular social setting; that doesn't make it in the eye of the beholder.) We understand, accept as genuine, love that remains hidden because of honor or fear or shame, but not because of greed or embarrassment. It's not that we believe those couldn't in fact be strong enough, but rather that we have standards about such things, about what sorts of feelings, in what sorts of contexts, get to count as genuine love. And feelings that are swamped by greed don't. Nor do feelings capable of being swamped by greed get to count as sympathy either: witness the Walrus.

The case will not always be clear, nor will the unclarity always be attributable to ignorance. Often there just is no answer, beyond the telling of how it is and how it is not like the wholly real thing. This is one reason why trust, of ourselves as well as of others, can be extremely important: it can make all the difference to how we go on that our feelings be taken seriously in cases where we cannot or are not ready to act on them. And it is perhaps why love is seen as both blind and uncannily perceptive: it can lead us to be both less and more willing and able to put things together, add them up, see the patterns.

Whether or not such questions of significance will ultimately be answered in terms of causal connections between inner states and actions, it is important to note that that could not be how we now answer them. And we do now answer them.[7] Rather than considering what *must* be the case to satisfy certain conceptions of a scientific or realist theory of mind, we will do better to consider the sorts of constraints we are actually inclined to put on acceptable explanations. What I want to suggest is that these are irreducibly social and irreducibly involve notions of appropriateness.

Consider various sorts of failures in expressions of sympathy. It is a commonplace that such expressions do not travel well, especially not across the Atlantic. The touching that is common in North America is, among people who are not intimate, simply not done in England, and it carries a sexual charge that, far from being comforting, is often disturbing. Our ability to characterize a gesture as nonetheless sympathetic, albeit a failure, comes from our ability to place it in a milieu more familiar to the person who made it: we know what it was meant to express because we know what it does express elsewhere. Similarly, I mean water

---

[7]A response, such as Hilary Putnam's, that we are all along referring to what we discover to be constraining our use of words, in ways that we may be unaware of, could not, in the case of sympathy at any rate, lead us to inner states, if I am right that many of the constraints are social and nonindividual. My argument here is essentially the same as the one Putnam uses to similar ends in the case of meaning; see "The Meaning of 'Meaning'," *Mind, Language, and Reality* (Cambridge: Cambridge University Press, 1975), pp. 215–71.

when I say 'water' to the uncomprehending waiter in Sicily because that's what the word means in the language I share with a lot of other, albeit absent, people. It doesn't follow that, to use Wittgenstein's example, I can simply say 'bububu' and mean 'If it doesn't rain I shall go for a walk'[8]—no matter what may be in my head as I say it.

If someone is a failure on her or his home ground, we become less certain what to say. It is certainly part of what we expect of people when we expect that they be sympathetic or act sympathetically that they be reasonably good at ascertaining what sorts of response will be genuinely helpful and be perceived as such. A number of different things can go wrong: they can have no idea, or a very wrong one, of how to respond, or the genuinely helpful and the perceived-as-helpful responses can be different, leaving one uncertain as to what the sympathetic thing to do would be.

Cases like this are rather like those Wittgenstein asks us to consider concerning what dogs can and cannot do: simulate pain, be hopeful or remorseful, or fear being beaten tomorrow.[9] Such notions have their natural homes in the characterization of people, where they get applied in response to a multifarious range of behavior, importantly including verbal behavior, feelings, and thoughts in certain sorts of situations. If we treat these as evidence for some state or event or process which just *is* the hope, the fear, the remorse, we are tempted to ask whether that state can be found in animals—a straightforwardly empirical question. Wittgenstein is not, of course, a priori giving a negative answer to that question, but rather urging that we see such notions as applying not to something hidden, behind and responsible for all the "evidence," but to those phenomena themselves or, better, to certain socially significant patterns of phenomena. What we then say about the beasts is how they are like us, how unlike. Such are the facts of the matter, and one applies the term in question if the similarities are especially striking and the differences seem less crucial, influenced often by moral and emotional attitudes toward the animals in question.

So it is with the various sorts of failure in the expression of sympathy: there is no special something, the presence or absence of which is definitive. Rather, we have certain generally accepted but varying notions of what sorts of behavior, feeling, attitude will count as sympathetic in particular circumstances, and failures are often failures to fit closely enough the pattern of our expectations. Sometimes we will care most about the feelings someone has, their ability to "feel with," and we will call them and their actions sympathetic although the latter may be sadly and ineptly off the mark. But we may not: in a different sort of relationship, caring about different sorts of things, such actions, such people are not really

---

[8]Ludwig Wittgenstein, *Philosophical Investigations* (New York: Macmillan, 1953), p.18n. (Hereafter, *P.I.*)

[9]Wittgenstein, *P.I.* 250; *P.I.*, p. 174; *Zettel* (Oxford: Blackwell, 1967), 518; *P.I.*, p. 650.

sympathetic, though they may point or yearn in that direction and we judge them utterly differently than we judge failure from indifference or meanness.

It is true neither that a sympathetic response is always genuinely helpful, nor that it is always perceived to be, but both genuine helpfulness and perceived helpfulness exert tugs, differing in their strength in different circumstances, on our use of 'sympathetic': they are part of what concerns us when sympathy does, but how large or important a part is a question of appropriateness, of circumstances, of the precise focus of our concern. And that focus will not be the same for all those in a position to have an opinion: to point out to someone who feels harshly dealt with that the action was a sympathetic one because motivated by a belief in good faith about her true interests, is not to confront her false belief with a true one but to reinterpret the situation, show it from another point of view, alter the focus and the stresses, urge on her a more sympathetic reading of the other person's actions and motivations. And there may be no fact about the other person to appeal to if she resists your reinterpretation because she finds the behavior patronizing rather than sympathetic. Not that we can't settle such questions in at least some cases, not that everything is the way it appears to anyone to be, but that there are no facts about that person, i.e., about his or her inner events, states, or processes, that by themselves just are the answers. The difference between patronizing and sympathetic behavior lies in the social world in which actions and feelings have meaning, not in the inner world of their causes.

Consider another sort of example. Some people characteristically or at particular times find it very difficult to accept sympathy. There is nothing one can do that can help or that will even be acknowledged as an expression of feeling. Or relationships can be such that within them nothing could be recognized as an expression of sympathy: this can happen between parents and children, with the actions of the parents perceived as either indifferent or infantilizing; they can lack the vocabulary of word and gesture with which to express concern while respecting separateness (often a cultural problem rather than just a personal one). In such circumstances we characteristically feel pulled between saying, "There was no way he would allow me to be sympathetic, nothing I could do would count," and, "No matter how sympathetic I was, no matter how sympathetically I acted, he was unwilling or unable to acknowledge it."

When we feel relatively secure in saying something of the second sort, it is usually because we think of him as being, always or for a while, on the other side of an emotional Atlantic. We judge the appropriateness of our responses—and of our feelings—by imagining them in other circumstances in which they would have been and have been perceived as being helpful or in some other way sympathetic. What underlies this perception is our confidence in our own reactions and in the imagined reality of those other circumstances. And our confidence may be well or ill-placed. If we are generalizing merely from how *we* would like to be treated or to have others feel about us, our responses are probably not genuinely sympathetic because they are too self-centered, too unimaginative. And even if we are relying on how we know him normally to want us to be, there may be room for argument: "If you really cared you'd have seen that he just wanted to be left alone today."

I want to suggest that we can helpfully see that sentence not as a (causal) counterfactual conditional but as (part of) an urged stipulative (though by no means arbitrarily so) definition of what—here and now and for him—it would be to care, to have one's feelings count, to have them mean what one wants them to. We can argue against this urging, argue that we do care really and as much as anyone could or could be expected to, perhaps even that we saw he wanted to be alone, and we cared too much to let him be. And I am not claiming that we can never settle such disputes, that there are no rights and wrongs. But I do want to relocate what it is that must be appealed to from where the inner-state view would have it be: what matters is what our actions and our feelings mean, and that is not settled by anything inside our heads or our breasts.

Not only do our social surroundings predispose us to feel the ways we do, help make us the people we are, but they form the framework within which what we do and feel is meaningful and significant; they set the limits of what gets to count as sympathy—in feeling or in deed. And they can, in the extremest cases, make it impossible that anything *could* count, leave us so boxed and hedged that even our feelings are not what we would have them be and our actions are all failed gestures. More happily, sympathy can be the natural language of a group, the reading that is placed on the unchecked immediacy of feeling and expression: the sharing of *any*thing can be taken as strengthening the bonds of caring and support. Between these poles, where most of us live, small details of circumstance will determine the focus of concern, the standards of appropriateness, the range of what will count, the meaning of what we feel and do.

IV

One important consequence of all of this is the suggestion that at least a certain part of our moral discourse—that concerned with sympathy—cannot be applied simply to individuals. Not only, as is obviously true, are certain circumstances more likely to elicit sympathetic responses and nurture sympathetic people, but it is in part social circumstances that determine the meaning of our actions and feelings, determine what will count as sympathetic.

Some recent moral philosophy shows an extremely salutary thrust (connected with the revival of attention to Aristotle) beyond the action to the actor, to a concern with character. I am suggesting that, perhaps for similar reasons, our concern has to extend beyond the individual to the social setting, that at least part of our moral language cannot straightforwardly be applied to individuals abstracted from their social worlds.

We are inclined to find this thought disturbing: moral judgments seem to demand an attachment to the individual. This demand may be connected with the lingering, though by no means weak, influence of religious conceptions of salvation and damnation and with the more contemporary influence of legal and quasi-legal conceptions of responsibility, praise, and blame. What I am urging is that certain less well-charted areas of the moral landscape may not be helpfully mapped in these individualistic ways, that persons may be units too small to capture much of what needs remarking about this part of the world.[10]

[10]For stimulating suggestions and constructive disagreements I would like to thank the members of the Society for Women in Philosophy in Toronto in March 1977, and at Lehigh in April 1978, the Committee on Women's Studies and the department of philosophy at Cornell, the junior faculty seminar in the philosophy department at Harvard, and Burton Dreben, whose philosophical help and moral support have been invaluable. Andrew Lugg and Adam Morton were of considerable help with the penultimate draft. Peter Shea assisted with the final editing.

3

Anger and the Politics of Naming

> As interworked systems of construable signs . . . , culture is not a power, something to which social events, behaviors, institutions, or processes can be causally attributed; it is a context, something within which they can be intelligibly described.
>
> —Clifford Geertz, *The Interpretation of Cultures*

To discover what we are feeling (our emotions) is not necessarily or usually to discover some new feelings (pang, *frisson*, wave, or whatever); rather, it is to discover what all of that means, how it fits in with who we are and what we are up to. It is to put a name to a mass of rather disparate stuff, to situate the otherwise inchoate "inner" in a social world, to join (introspectible) feeling and behavior in a significant way, to note a meaningful pattern.

The ways we have for doing this, our vocabulary of the emotions, are given socially: the patterns to be found are various but not infinite and not wholly in our individual power to change. Societies categorize at least some of the emotions in at least slightly different ways. They find different conjunctions of feeling and behavior significant, and the significance can change over time.[1]

On an individual level poetry and novels can change the ways we read ourselves —not just tell us we have been in love, but enable us to be by showing us what

---

The long history of this paper has implicated, beyond my ability to disentangle their contributions, many members of the Canadian and American Societies for Women in Philosophy and the Canadian Research Institute for the Advancement of Women. I am grateful for the criticism, the ideas, the support, and the entanglement. Burton Dreben and David Hills were particularly helpful with the penultimate version, which appeared in my doctoral dissertation "Depsychologizing Psychology: Essays against Individualism in the Philosophy of Mind" (Harvard, 1978). Sally McConnell-Ginet was an encouraging and insightful editor, particularly when it came to recasting the essay in a more intelligible form. The preparation for the final version was managed, with the most tactful bullying, by Eta Schneiderman, to whose stylistic sensibilities and clearheadedness this paper owes whatever clarity it may have.

[1]See Denis DeRougemont, *Love in the Western World* (New York, N.Y.: Pantheon, 1956). Also Virginia Woolf, *Night and Day* (New York, N.Y.: Harcourt Brace Jovanovitch, 1948), for a discussion of whether intense and obsessive feelings are to count as love for two sensible, "modern" people.

it would mean for *that* to be love (perhaps homosexual love, or nonspectacular, quiet attachment).[2] This enabling is not just freeing us to feel in the future but, equally important, showing us how to read the past. In addition, changes can be seen as political and ideological. As we change our beliefs and opinions about, for instance, the existence and nature of sexual oppression, we can come to change the ways in which we interpret our own feelings and behavior.

In this paper I will examine three different sorts of changes that can occur in the case of anger. One is *becoming angry*, the second is *discovering that one has been angry*, and the third is *changing what counts as being angry*. While the first is (philosophically) uncontroversial, the second and (especially) the third pose difficulties for the traditional picture of mind and language, a picture that stands opposed to the view I have just outlined. After sketching the traditional picture, I will elaborate the alternative model as a way of giving a better account of what we are learning through the practices of the women's movement, in particular, through the experiences of the creation and the discovery of anger in consciousness-raising groups.

The Traditional Picture

The traditional picture of mind comes from Descartes: on the surface of the stream of consciousness float leaves that are our sensations, thoughts, and feelings, each unmistakably labeled.[3]

Freud has modified this picture: not all the leaves float on the surface. Some leaves, by the force of the directional flow of the stream (the ego), have been thrust to the bottom and covered with silt (repression). Because they are there, they disturb in gross or subtle ways the flow of water over them and thus the behavior of the leaves still on the surface (neuroses, parapraxes, dreams, and so on). In order to free the leaves and hence free ourselves from the disturbances they cause while hidden, we need to uncover them. We can do this by interpreting the clues we gather from the eddies and whirlpools they create (psychoanalysis).

The heart of the traditional picture is this: when we talk about the emotions, conscious or unconscious, we are talking about some particular mental or physical state that is "in" us (or that we are in) that makes what we are saying true. The anger, the joy, the love, the grief are supposed to have been there all along, awaiting discovery and naming. It is this picture I want to argue against through

---

[2]In his portrayal of Oscar Wilde, Vincent Price tells of an early friendship with a younger boy and the awesome sweet pain of discovering, after a blithely obtuse parting, left in a railway car with the other boy's tears on his face and his kiss on his lips, that *that* had been love. Not a new feeling, caused by the parting, but the old one, revealed and interpreted by it.

[3]Descartes (and Freud, see below) are of course more subtle than my impressionistic account, but I do not think the subtlety affects my argument.

a consideration of the three ways in which our emotions and our knowledge of them can change.

Becoming Angry

The first sort of change is this: as women come to believe that it is neither natural nor inevitable that they stay at home and experience most of the world at one remove, that their sacrifices of goals and dreams and freedom were not in their real interest, they often become angry. Their lives could be a whole lot better than they are, and someone or something is to blame. The object of their blame and anger varies from the closeness and specificity of a husband to the political generality of society and social institutions.

We can question whether the anger these women feel is justifiable, and if so what its appropriate objects are. We can even question whether emotions are the sorts of things that can be justifiable or appropriate at all. However, the claim that people do become angry in this way appears uncontroversial.

The traditional picture of mind can account for becoming angry by explaining how changes in leaves in or beneath the stream engender new ones. To give such an account strains only my metaphor, but the account itself is strained when we turn to the second and third sorts of changes.

Discovering That One Has Been Angry

To begin with, we need a clear and detailed account of what is meant to have happened when someone is said to have discovered that she was angry. Alice belongs to a consciousness-raising group. When she first joined she was generally satisfied with her life. But she became gradually more aware of those times when she felt depressed, or pressured and harried, as though her time were not her own. However, she didn't believe her time ought to be her own, so in addition, she felt guilty. She would sometimes snap at her husband or children, or cry without quite knowing why, and then put her "moodiness" down to various *causes*, such as her neuroses or her menstrual cycle. She didn't think she had any *reason* to feel this way; she never took the bad feelings as justified or reasonable; she didn't identify with them; they came over her and needed to be overcome.

Within the group Alice's feelings are responded to differently. She is encouraged to acknowledge and to express them in a safe environment, in which she has little fear that her feelings will disappoint, disillusion, hurt, or anger those around her. Furthermore, there is a growing shared sense, not only of the reality, but of the legitimacy and, finally, the justifiability of Alice's feelings.

We must distinguish here among the reality, the legitimacy, and the justifiability of feelings. One can acknowledge the reality of an emotion while believing that it is in some way illegitimate. And to acknowledge that one's feelings are legitimate—sincere, not self-deceptive—is not necessarily to take those feelings to be justifiable. They may, no matter how deeply or fully felt, be irrational, unfounded, needlessly self- or other-destructive.

It is likely that the other women in the group will urge Alice to acknowledge the reality of her depression and guilt, but to deny the legitimacy of those feelings. This denial amounts to the claim that she is in some way feeling something that she is unable to face. The guilt and the depression are a response to and a cover for those other feelings, notably feelings of anger. Alice is urged to recognize her anger as legitimate and justifiable in this situation.

If Alice comes to this recognition, we may describe her as having discovered that she had been angry, though she hadn't previously recognized it. She would, in fact, have denied it if she were asked: "Why *should* I be angry?" It is significant that a denial that one is angry often takes the form of a denial that one would be justified in being angry. Thus one's discovery of anger can often occur not from focusing on one's feelings but from a political redescription of one's situation.

If we accept the plausibility of the notion that Alice can discover that without knowing it she had been angry, we may initially be tempted by the analogy of the submerged leaves. We may think that the anger must have been there all along, to make Alice's anger not just a politically helpful fiction. But we cannot, of course, actually produce her past anger to satisfy the critic who says we manipulated Alice into a suspiciously revisionist rewriting of history. Even if she is now clearly and straightforwardly angry, couldn't it be that she just *became* so? It's *yesterday's* anger we need here, and there seems no way of laying our hands on that.

Not only would no newly discovered leaf provide conclusive evidence of past anger, but it may be that there is no particular item in our mental life left to be discovered. What is primarily keeping us as women from acknowledging our anger is an inability to interpret our feelings and behavior in the proper political perspective. At least three different aspects of sexist ideology help prevent our synthesizing the pieces and naming the puzzle of our feelings.

One is the myth about the emotions, women's emotions in particular, that tells us that they are irrational or nonrational storms. They sweep over us and are wholly personal, quite possibly hormonal. The emotions that fit with this picture tend to be diffuse, like moods, or episodic and undirected. They don't, in any event, *mean* anything. Thus we have outbursts of anger aimed at children, the weather, or a piece of balky machinery. We often feel there's something not quite right about the anger; it's out of proportion, and, especially if aimed at children, feels unfair and wrong. Instead of encouraging us to interpret these outbursts, the myth makes us feel guilty for having succumbed.

A second feature of our lives that keeps us from putting the pieces together is our own insecurity. The central cases of anger are judgmental, a way of feeling that someone (or some group) has acted badly. In order to be straightforwardly angry, one standardly has to trust one's own reactions and take oneself to be in a position to judge.[4] That can be very hard to do from a position of dependency, where one's welfare and happiness depend on pleasing others. Even outside of marriage women are expected to be uncritical and unchallenging, and it can be very threatening to step back from this network of expectations.

A third thing keeping us from seeing ourselves as angry is the picture we are likely to have of what the good life for a woman consists in. Anger is "object-hungry": if there is no one and nothing to be angry at, it will be harder to see oneself as really angry. If the life one has is just what one has expected would be most satisfying and fulfilling, and if one's sacrifices are seen merely as the transcending of childish dreams, then it will be hard to find anyone or anything to be properly angry at. It is similarly hard to be properly angry if one thinks one's life as a woman is "natural," ordained by biology. The limitations that flow socially from one's being a woman are seen as on a par with those that flow from physical or biological factors.[5]

It is, of course, possible to be irrationally angry at a situation that is as one thinks it should be or that no one is to blame for. We may find ourselves angry and wonder why; it seems so uncalled for and childish. But the difference between someone who is irrationally angry and someone who is not may not be a difference in what they *feel* so much as a difference in what sorts of feelings, under what sorts of circumstances, they are ready to take as anger. When we judge that people are right to deny the name of anger to their irrational reactions, we are often judging that their situation, unlike Alice's, does not really call for anger.

But those who do take those reactions as anger may not be mistaken. Having noted this point, we are faced with the complex relationship between being angry and taking ourselves to be. If we take ourselves to be angry, whether justifiably or not, our anger changes. We begin to see things differently, as it were *through* the anger; it colors our world, both inner and outer. We find, because we are looking for them, more reasons for our anger and more feelings

---

[4]Not, of course, that all anger is so explicitly judgmental or sees itself so clearly in the right. But although people can be angry while knowing they have no good reason to be, those who find it difficult to acknowledge anger are often helped by coming to see that it would be justifiable for them to feel it.

[5]Freud is often mistakenly seen as holding this view ("anatomy is destiny"), but his actual view, although more subtle, serves the same ends. He is well aware both of the social origin of the norms of femininity and of their mutilating effects, but it is perhaps the clearest evidence of the deep pessimism of his later life that he saw the alternative to such socialization (and to the corresponding socialization of men) as barbarism: the situation may be awful, but there is nothing to blame but civilization itself, a barely more appropriate object of anger than biology.

we can take as anger, which we may before have labeled differently or not have noticed. Our feelings, judgments, and behavior become organized around the fact of our anger.[6]

Or we can resist this. We can either let our feelings and our behavior remain uninterpreted or search for some other meaning. We can be mistaken in doing this. Thus, to discover that we have been angry is to correct an earlier interpretation. But we are never simply mistaken, the way others can be about us. We can be confused, but we cannot be "merely or wholly wrong."[7] If we are confused about our emotions, those emotions themselves are confused.

We can recognize this difference between how I see my emotions and how others see them and go on to ask why this difference exists. One point is clear. If I fail to interpret my feelings and behavior as anger, they are likely to be both odd and erratic, and therefore less coherent and predictable than you would expect of someone who was angry straightforwardly. The patterns we pick out when we name the emotions have to do with the needs of social life: seeing people as angry is connected with a complex set of expectations of them, and their not seeing themselves in the same way affects the validity of those expectations.

In light of these observations, the theory of privileged access (the philosophical view that we are each the ultimate authority about our own emotions) can be seen less as a fact of epistemology than as a piece of social theory—a clue to what we care about in our interpretations of people. That we are inclined not to notice this, in part because of the emotions-as-inner-states picture of mind, is typical of the workings of an ideology: matters of political choice come to seem to be matters of unchangeable fact. We think that emotions just *are* particular states of individuals, specifiable independently of social context.

The individualism that characterizes this view of the mind and the emotions is historically nonaccidental. It fits with the essentially atomistic view of persons underlying liberal economic and political structures, of agents entering the marketplace freely with already formed motivations and desires. We treat each other as psychologically detachable units and regard ourselves as the owners of ourselves. We are both the legal and epistemic authorities. Since the view about psychological predicates (such as 'is angry') that I am urging is that they pick out socially significant patterns, ways of organizing feeling and behavior in accordance with particular social needs, it would be expected that in a society like ours primacy

---

[6]For a similar view in the context of a different sort of theory, see Ronald deSousa, "The Rationality of Emotions," *Dialogue: Canadian Philosophical Review*, and in *Explaining Emotions*, ed. Amelie Ockensberg Rorty (Berkeley and Los Angeles: University of California Press, 1980).

[7]Stuart Hampshire, "Sincerity and Singlemindedness," *Freedom of Mind and Other Essays* (Princeton, N.J.: Princeton University Press, 1971), p. 237. My discussion here owes much to his, although his does not extend beyond the limits of the individual.

would be given to first-person perception. We care most about our own view of ourselves since we are the ones who are allowed to determine how we are to be taken as feeling: privileged access functions as a sort of property right.

I may think, and you may disagree, that you are angry with me, or in love with me, but are afraid to admit it even to yourself. That may seem to me to be the clearest sense to be made of the confusing ways you feel and the strange ways you act. And I may, insofar as I can, treat you as someone who is angry at (or in love with) me, thus making our relationship to a certain extent what it would be if you acknowledged these things. But are you *really* angry or in love? There may be no answer to this. What you are is confused and conflicted; you haven't settled yet on a clear way to be. There is no reason to think that under the muddle is a clear fact, a leaf beneath the silt.

Now why do you get to do the settling? What is wrong with my taking you to be some way you don't take yourself? What I want to suggest is not that I am any less likely than you to be right, but that I haven't got the right: I am an intruder, failing to respect your privileged access to yourself.[8] It is certainly true that we take people to have these sorts of rights to their own(ed) feelings; we may think they are wrong, but we do not normally have the right to treat them according to our conception of them rather than their own. People can confer on others the right to interpret their feelings, or can lose their right to do it themselves, by being declared insane, which means, among other things, that one's own view of oneself is not the one the rest of us have to respect.

Less extremely, this right is unequally distributed. Adults, for example, often tell children what they are and are not feeling, and what those feelings mean ("You're just overtired"). And the interpretation of women's feelings and behavior is often appropriated by others, by husbands or lovers, or by various psychological "experts." Autonomy in this regard is less an individual achievement than a socially recognized right, and, as such, people with social power tend to have more of it.

But, as with other sorts of property rights, we can recognize and seek to change an inequality of distribution while working ultimately for more fundamental changes. We can, that is, explore the possibility of allowing our emotions to be fully and openly social constructions, rather than needing, as we do now, to acquire and keep to ourselves the final authority about them.

Consider, for example, the interactions of feeling and perception in a consciousness-raising group. A frequently remarked feature of such groups is that each woman's ability to recognize and change her situation depends on the others' doing the same. Part of why this is important lies in how it is that one is being seen and responded to. Although it is true that women are taught to be overly

---

[8]For an interesting discussion of the nature and importance of our consideration of other people's self-conceptions, see Elizabeth V. Spelman, "Treating Persons as Persons," *Ethics* 88 (1978): 150–61.

dependent on our reflections in the eyes of others, it is a serious mistake to conclude from this that we ought not to care about or attend to how others see us. We need to be selective about whose views we care about and why and about how people's views are distorted and manipulative. But to attempt to cease to care is to adopt an asocial, individualistic picture of people that it has been one of the important goals of feminism to deny. The serious question posed by the experience of such groups is how to characterize the connections between how we really are and how we are seen. This question is at once normative and descriptive.

There are many such connections apparent in the workings of a consciousness-raising group: that between being listened to and taken seriously and the development of self-respect, or between being genuinely sympathetic and having one's expressions of sympathy acknowledged.[9] Here I want to focus on the relevance of these considerations to the discovery of anger.

For example, when Alice finds herself snapping at the children or complaining to her husband, she is apt to feel like some sort of monster for not being made happy by her life. The crystallization of her feelings will be impeded in part by her unwillingness to face the sort of person she thinks she would be were she really angry. But in the group, women she has grown to know and to like confess to similar feelings. As the other women realize that they are angry, Alice's certainty that they are not monsters will make it easier for her to accept that she is angry too. Shifting notions of normality function like this: as it becomes more expected that children will be angry at their parents, it becomes easier for people to interpret a lot of darkly baffling feeling and seemingly perverse behavior.

Conversely, R. D. Laing draws our attention to the ways in which family members can invalidate each other's experiences.[10] A powerful family mythology about what someone ought to be feeling can override otherwise much more plausible readings, warping her interpretations, leading her to focus on or to ignore certain aspects of her feeling and behavior. One reason this can happen is that feelings don't bear their meanings on their faces: we need to learn socially what they add up to. We interpret our reactions and our behavior in the light of this family mythology, so when, as happens in a consciousness-raising group, it is challenged and undermined, we are apt to see our lives and our emotions differently.

The bestowing or the withholding of a name can be personally and politically explosive. To see that some state of affairs counts as oppression or exploitation, or that one's own feelings count as dissatisfaction or anger is already to change the nature of that situation or those feelings.

---

[9]For a discussion of this and related issues, see my "On Sympathy."

[10]R. D. Laing and Aron Esterson, *Sanity, Madness and the Family* (New York: Basic Books, 1965).

Changing What Counts as Being Angry

We inherited from Freud, whether he intended it or not, a way of accounting for the discovery of anger. There is supposed to be a particular state people are in when they are angry, a state that can be either conscious or unconscious. Unconscious anger is the same sort of thing as conscious anger, just as a submerged leaf is the same sort of thing as an unsubmerged leaf: it is supposed to be obvious that whatever is repressed is *anger*. What Freud is supposed to have discovered is that emotions, intentions, beliefs are not necessarily conscious; precisely those things can be hidden from us.

To put the matter this way is to represent Freud as holding a sophisticated version of the view of emotions as inner states. Most of the time this is how he represents himself. By demonstrating that the processes that characterize our conscious lives also appear in unconscious forms, Freud claims to be taking the sort of insight into feeling and behavior we receive from poets, novelists, playwrights, and both extending it and making it scientific (ultimately neurophysiological).

Freud defines "psychical acts" as those that "have a sense." In showing that, for example, parapraxes, dreams, and neuroses have a sense, that is, "meaning, intention, purpose and position in a continuous psychical context," rather than arising "immediately from somatic, organic and material influences," he takes himself to be making "a quite considerable extension to the world of psychical phenomena and [to] have won for psychology phenomena which were not reckoned earlier as belonging to it."[11]

This description of Freud's achievement is, I think, apt, but it admits of two divergent interpretations, one that fits with the emotions-as-inner-states view and one that fits with my alternative. Under the first interpretation there is a mechanism of the mind, a set of basic processes, that produce all the contents of consciousness and all intentional behavior. On this view Freud takes himself to have discovered convincing evidence for the claim that many pieces of behavior we had been taking as caused by a distinct sort of physical mechanism are in fact caused by an underlying and hidden extension of the mechanism of the mind and by underlying states essentially like their conscious counterparts (which cause pieces of straightforwardly intentional behavior). It is in terms of this (as yet only programmatically specified) mechanism of the mind that unconscious intentions, motivations, and beliefs are identified. Psychoanalysis uncovers evidence for the causal structure of this mechanism, and thus for the unconscious states and processes that can be recognized by their roles in it. This is a natural way of

---

[11]Sigmund Freud, *Introductory Lectures on Psychoanalysis,* eds. James Strachey and Angela Richards, Pelican Freud Library, vol. I (Harmondsworth, Middlesex: Penguin Books, 1976), pp. 87–88.

taking what Freud means when he says that to have sense is to have a "place in a continuous psychical context."

But there is another, I think more plausible, interpretation, which neither relies on nor supports the view of emotions as inner states. We could take what Freud marshals as *evidence* (parapraxes and dreams and what people spontaneously say about them, the behavior of children, neurotic symptoms) as itself significant, as constituting a meaningful pattern of mental occurrences and behavior, without the postulation of ghostly entities and a ghostly mechanism holding it all together.

Consider the following picture: we have some pieces of intentional behavior, say, my shouting at and then walking out on someone I take to have wronged me. We also have a number of relevant beliefs (in particular, that he has wronged me and that he could have avoided it) and some conscious feelings.

The traditional picture tells us that these fit together causally. The focal point is the feeling (one of the feelings?), which is the anger, caused by (my beliefs about) his behavior, and in turn causing mine.[12] When we turn from the conscious case to a case of parapraxis or a piece of neurotic behavior or a dream, we are supposed to see the causal chain clearly enough for us to infer the existence of the central, apparently missing piece: the emotion itself. So, for example, we infer the existence of my repressed anger as caused by my belief (perhaps itself repressed, a complication) that I have been somehow avoidably wronged and as causing my otherwise inexplicable behavior or symptoms.

The problem here is not with the convincingness of the analogy between the conscious and the unconscious cases but with the initial picture of how the feelings, beliefs, and behavior fit together when the whole affair is conscious. Simply, there is no justification for identifying the anger with the feeling, because most of the time there is no one feeling (sometimes there are none; sometimes there are many, possibly conflicting), and there is most certainly no *sort* of feeling characteristic of anger (it can feel like almost anything, from exhilarating to crushing to nothing at all). Nor is there any real reason to infer that behind it all is some identifiable, peculiar state that is the anger and causes the behavior *and* the feelings.

What makes the whole affair a case of someone's being angry is how it is as a whole similar, in ways we particularly care about, to other cases. The similarity is not inferred similarity of mechanism but conferred similarity of meaning. There is no particular state, conscious or unconscious, mental or physical, that will by itself settle the question of whether someone is angry. In order to settle this question, we need to learn more about the person's behavior, feelings, circumstances, and we need to know how to interpret what we learn.

I have argued that by extending the range of phenomena we can see as

---

[12]For a criticism of this point similar to mine but from a slightly different angle, see J. L. Austin, "Other Minds," *Philosophical Papers*, eds. J. O. Urmson and G. J. Warnock (Oxford: Oxford University Press, 1961), esp. p. 77.

meaningful Freud has given us an alternative way of thinking about our psychic lives. We can speak of unconscious motivations, emotions, and so on, just as we speak of conscious ones: as ways of interpreting feelings and behavior that are complex and otherwise inchoate (despite whatever causal links science may uncover). Thus Freud has led us to expand the range of cases that count as cases of anger, not just in the sense that we can now point to some we couldn't have pointed to before (as biologists increased our repertoire of organisms by discovering the existence of many invisible to the naked eye), but by changing our notions of what it is to be angry. Although unconscious anger is anger in just the same sense as conscious anger is, to see that this is so is not so much to uncover some new datum as to learn to see the old data differently. Freud's insight leads us away from focusing on the nature of the emotion itself as some identifiable thing, toward looking at the meaning of feelings and behavior seen in historical and interpersonal context.

Speculations on the Emotions, Politics, and the Power of Naming

I have suggested that to account for the phenomenon of discovering that someone has been angry it is necessary to change the sorts of patterned situations that are seen as significant. Even people not otherwise sympathetic to psychoanalysis are now inclined to identify emotions by their place in an individual's history, not just by how they feel. What I want to consider now is the possibility that we can come to name and classify emotions differently for reasons that are not just individually historical—a sort of "political psychoanalysis."

One thing that led us to see unconscious anger as genuine anger was that we saw someone's feelings and behavior hanging together coherently and pointing in a certain direction. And we came to see this by seeing a stretch of her life as a whole: the judgment that she was angry embodied not just a claim about her present state but facts about the past and expectations about the future. We can come to a similar realization about a group—that it has a history, an organized present, a probable future. And coming to see this can lead us to think differently about the feelings and behavior of individuals of that group.

Consider women and anger. Part of what makes it true that a woman is angry today is that her vague and unfocused feelings are apt to crystallize in the future as she becomes clearer about the nature of sexism and its role in her life. We identify her feelings and behavior today as straightforwardly angry partly with reference to this possible future, their natural one. Calling this future course "natural" means here that the political beliefs she comes to have are *true*, and her not having had them previously can be explained as part of the distorting effect of a false ideology. The requirement that the future course be in this sense natural supports one of the central points of this essay—that substantive political considerations are prior to the correct identification, even to the identity, of the emotions.[13]

But this future course has become at all likely only quite recently. Although, of course, having feminism in the air has a great deal to do with how people (introspectively) feel, there is another, subtler difference. I want to suggest that someone who felt like a woman who is unstraightforwardly angry today would not previously have been considered to be, and *would not have been*, angry. There was then neither the likelihood of future crystallization nor any way of thinking that would have made it appropriate to gather together some odd jumble of feelings and behavior and call it "anger." The meaning that the jumble has for us today is the product of social change; it has acquired a way to organize itself and grow.

We can look back and say of someone that she was angry because it enables us to explain more of what was going on. But it doesn't follow that it would have been correct to say it of her then: what counts as anger has changed. We have given a meaning to what previously had none; it had none because there was no future for it within the social, political, and economic reality of earlier times. We can see confused and obscure anger today as anger by seeing it as embryonic, as a state that would become straightforward anger were certain social pressures, false beliefs, and internalized fears removed. But the corresponding feelings and behavior of women in the past were not leading anywhere, not for most women in their lifetime anyway, and so there was no reason to see them as meaning anything; they didn't count as anger because they lacked even the potential social significance such feelings and behavior have today.

In the light of this claim I think we can make sense of the defensiveness and belligerence of the critics of consciousness-raising groups. If there is the connection that I have been suggesting between politics and the discovery—and even the nature—of anger, then emotions become much more threatening than they would be were they simply inner states. Anger could on that view lead people to act in ways we might reasonably fear, but it wouldn't be intimately bound up with collective political action.

We can thus make sense of the current craze for psychological individualism: "you just feel what you feel; get in touch with what's really there inside you." It is no accident that such a view is flourishing. It functions as a reaction to and a damper on the sorts of personal and political changes central to feminism, making the sort of discovery of anger I have been discussing impossible. As long as only you can really know what's going on in your own head, the odds are fairly high you never will.

Another, more intellectually serious way in which consciousness-raising groups are criticized is that they are seen as manipulative of the feelings of the women

---

[13]This point about naturalness needs both clarification and defense. Both are beyond the scope of the paper and, at the moment, of its author.

in them, that people come to feel (or to think they feel) what the group deems proper. If I am right and there actually is something like this going on, it is important to acknowledge, define, and ultimately defend it, rather than simply accept the terms in which the criticism is couched and try to refute it. Some groups undoubtedly are manipulative in a way any disinterested person would recognize and deplore—I'm not concerned with them here. But the idea that there is a context in which you can simply "get in touch with your feelings," free from the influence of other people or of political concerns, is a dangerous myth.

The idea that I am the way I am no matter what anyone else thinks is not politically neutral. To take this position is to stifle the possibility of particular sorts of political change. But it's also to blind ourselves to the truth that we are in many deep and important ways what others take or at least allow us to be. Whether or not we are really angry, beneath the confusion and the pain, depends in part on the particular social processes, which will give or fail to give our feelings the possibility of definition.

The structure that consciousness-raising groups provide for the interpretation of feelings and behavior is overtly political; it should be immediately obvious that one is presented with a particular way of making sense of one's experience, a way intimately linked with certian controversial political views. Consciousness-raising groups are not, however, unique in this respect. What they are is unusually honest: the political framework is explicit (though often vague) and openly argued for. The alternative is not "a clear space in which to get your head together" but a hidden political framework that pretends not to be one and hence is spared the bother (and the risk) of argument.

Apologia

In this paper I have attempted to identify a source of discomfort, a project that makes complete sense only to those whose discomfort it is. I have gone on to suggest how we might construct an alternative framework, a project that is likely to seem simply perverse to someone committed to the old one.

We experience this discomfort as feminists when we realize that our experiences are leading us to think differently about people and human relationships, while the only concepts available to think with are suited to forms of social organization shown to be outmoded by those very experiences. Forms of practice such as consciousness-raising groups can lead us to a fundamental revision of the conceptual structures in terms of which we name our experiences. We can, in particular, question the underlying individualism of the traditional picture of mind.

It would be satisfying to think I could marshal arguments sufficiently cogent to convince any (rational) reader: philosophers are supposed to aim at that, not just preach to the converted. But there's another kind of philosophical task: to bring to light, clarify, and explain the nature and sources of dimly perceived contradictions in or between our concepts and our social practice. Such contradictions may have been there all along, but their presence causes particular trouble when social practice is changing. One doesn't choose here between explaining the world and changing it; rather one explains (and perhaps facilitates) the changes by changing the explanations.

4

Individualism and the Objects of Psychology

> . . . it was men mostly who did the talking and what they were talking about was themselves although they used such generic terms as people or mankind these terms were really a euphemism for men but we didn't know that since the men didn't think it was necessary to say so and the women permitted the men to do most all the talking it was easy to conclude that we were all humans and when one human spoke that human spoke for all of us all of which means that until recently very few of us realized we were women.
>
> —Jill Johnson, *Lesbian Nation*

Much philosophical discussion has been devoted to the questions about what sort of existence to attribute to the objects[1] of psychology. Recent focus on scientific realism as a way of answering ontological questions[2] has subtly shifted the center of these questions. Thus, Descartes claimed to have demonstrated that psychological states were of (or in) a mind, a substance wholly different from the body. The question of causal interaction between the two arose, but he took his ultimate inability to answer it to indicate not the inadequacy of his dualism but the limits of metaphysical investigation. In contrast, for modern scientific realists what exists is whatever has to exist for our best theories to be true, and causality plays a central role in these accounts. Psychological states are whatever they have to be to have the (physical or psychological) causes and effects that they do.[3]

This focus has generally led to some sort of physicalism, construed very broadly: types of psychological states (like being angry or in pain) actually are types of physical states (like certain patterns of neurons firing), or, more weakly,

---

[1]I'm using the term 'objects' very broadly, in the sense of objects of attention or study. Often it will serve as short for 'events, states, and processes'. I am not attending particularly to the distinctions among these, in part because I'm not convinced that they are genuine or genuinely helpful and in part because, be that as it may, my discussion will, I think, apply equally to all three. I will most often speak of states, as they have figured most prominently in recent discussions.

[2]See especially Hilary Putnam, *Mind, Language and Reality: Philosophical Papers*, Vol. 2 (Cambridge: Cambridge University Press, 1975).

[3]In addition to Putnam, this has been argued (in different ways and to rather different ends) by David K. Lewis, "An Argument for the Identity Theory," in *Materialism and the Mind-Body Problem*, ed. David M. Rosenthal (Englewood Cliffs, N.J.: Prentice Hall, 1971), pp. 162–71; and Donald Davidson, "Mental Events," in *Experience and Theory*, ed. L. Swanson and J. W. Foster (Amherst: University of Massachusetts Press, 1970), pp. 79–101.

each particular psychological state (an occasion of anger or pain) is a particular (though perhaps each time a different type of) physical state. There are a plethora of arguments for positions that are variations of one or the other of these two, and some arguments for why one or the other must be true, given the causal roles of psychological states.[4]

What there are no arguments for, to the best of my knowledge, is the underlying assumption that, whatever they may be, psychological states can be assigned and theorized about on an individualistic basis.[5] Here, as in discussions in political theory and social science methodology, it is difficult to make clear what is meant by 'individualism' or 'individualistic'. What I have in mind is the assumption that my pain, anger, beliefs, intentions, and so on are particular, (in theory) identifiable states that I am in, which enter as particulars into causal relationships. Some examples of individualistic states are being five feet tall, having pneumonia, missing three teeth, and having some immediate subjective experience (though how to describe the last is by no means clear). Being the most popular girl in the class or a major general or divorced are not individualistic states: nor, I want to argue, are being in love or angry or generous, believing that all eels hail from the Sargasso Sea, knowing how to read, intending to be more honest, or expecting an explosion any minute now.

This largely unquestioned assumption, that the objects of psychology—emotions, beliefs, intentions, virtues, and vices—attach to us singly (no matter how socially we may acquire them) is, I want to argue, a piece of ideology. It is not a natural fact, and the ways in which it permeates our social institutions, our lives, and our senses of ourselves are not unalterable. It is deeply useful in the maintenance of capitalist and patriarchal society and deeply embedded in our notions of liberation, freedom, and equality. It is connected with particular features of the psychosexual development of males mothered by women in patriarchal society, with the development of the ego and of ego-boundaries. It is fundamentally undercut by an examination of female experience, if that experience is seen in its own terms and not as truncated male experience.

My aim in this paper is to make the claims of the last paragraph reasonably clear and at least somewhat plausible. I want to argue that (1) what I will call the individualist assumption does underlie contemporary philosophical accounts of the nature of the objects of psychology, as much as these differ from each other; (2) this assumption is substantive, not merely formal, and the underlying reasons that might be advanced for it are inadequate; (3) we can illuminate the grip the

---

[4]Lewis and Davidson in particular argue for the claim that some sort of identity theory must be true. These various positions are well represented in Rosenthal's collection and laid out in the introduction.

[5]For arguments very different from mine against this claim, see Putnam, "The Meaning of Meaning," in *Mind, Language and Reality*, and Tyler Burge, "Individualism and the Mental," in *Midwest Studies in Philosophy* 4 (1979), pp. 73–121.

assumption has on us by seeing it as forming part of the ideology of liberal individualism; and (4) part of the functioning of that ideology is the structure of the bourgeois family, producing men who see themselves as conforming to the assumption and men and women who see such conforming as natural.

I

Why is this assumption so nearly universal? I want to suggest four different sorts of answers to this question, not as alternatives, but as complementary attempts to grasp the depth and power this assumption has for us. The first two are reasons that might be offered for thinking the assumption true, one a straightforwardly theoretical demand and the other an appeal to (philosophically colored) common sense.

Nearest to the argumentative surface, the assumption that psychological objects are particular states of individuals is required by the claim that they are physiological objects, since, presumably, physiology needs to ascribe states to us singly. This claim is in turn connected with the demands of physicalism, that the world be one causally closed system, containing one kind of stuff, governed at bottom by one coherent system of laws, and that those laws be the ones of the physical sciences. Reduction on the level of explanation has fared ill enough that it has, even as a possibility, been widely rejected in favor of the autonomy of levels of explanation, along with the irreducibility of the natural kinds of one explanatory level to those of a lower. But there is hope for another sort of reduction that is much more tenacious—the view that the objects of one theory are complex objects of a more basic, lower-level theory, and that as such each particular one will be explicable in terms of that lower-level theory.

This view is plausible whenever we have some idea of how to individuate the objects in question in terms of the lower-level theory whose elements are their parts. We need to be able to do this in a way that shows the objects as appropriate objects of explanation, that is, as particulars rather than as motley conglomerations. Typically (always?) this will be done in terms of causal connections among the parts and ways in which the complex objects enter as wholes into causal relationships. Thus, for example, even if chemistry is as a theory nonreducible to physics, it could still be that all the objects of chemistry—molecules, chemical bonds, and such—are each particular physical objects or states, subject as coherent wholes to physical law. I suspect that this sort of reduction will always be possible except when the higher-level theory is ontologically holistic, except, that is, when in order to individuate a particular object of the theory one needs to refer to structural features of the theory as a whole. Thus, chemistry is not generally thought to be ontologically holistic: it is assumed that its objects can be specified singly as complex objects of physics. Economics and sociology are—debatably

—holistic; that is to say, e.g., classes cannot be picked out independently of the framework of those theories, not, say, as the collection of all the people in them.[6]

In general, the objects of the social sciences, including psychology, are, I want to suggest, objects only with respect to socially embodied norms, and thus any reduction would have to proceed via the whole social system, explaining a particular object as an object-with-respect-to-that-system. Since such a project is, to say the least, unrealistic, we must acknowledge that our explanations in such fields are of objects whose existence as particulars is relative to a social framework.

This claim is likely to seem obviously false; in fact, the projects of philosophers of psychology in the empiricist tradition can often be seen as attempts to explain how we can best theorize about such things as emotions, beliefs, occasions of understanding, thoughts, and pains in a way that is simultaneously responsible to the social complexity of our ordinary attributions and explanations and to what they take to be the obvious, particular existence of such things in each of us. And typically our ordinary talk is seen as more likely to be wrong or misleading or theoretically unhelpful than is the clear conviction that we are in particular states of belief or emotion, that we do experience particular episodes of coming to understand, of having a thought, or of feeling a pain.

Similarly, in attempting to understand Quine's thesis about the indeterminacy in the actual reference of words many people are most disturbed by his claim that "there is no fact of the matter" about what our own words refer to. This also, for much the same reason, seems obviously false: surely there is some real difference to be marked in me corresponding to my referring to rabbits or to their undetached parts or temporal stages. Many people relatively comfortable with indeterminacy as an epistemological thesis about the limits of our knowledge of others balk at it as an ontological thesis denying the real, particular existence in us of determinate states of belief.

Worries of this sort are connected with the second reason for the individualist assumption, namely, that it seems so obviously, and so importantly, true. Arguments against Quinean philosophy or behavioral psychology often center on the conviction that there is something important we are not being enabled to account for or allowed to take adequately seriously: our inner lives, subjective experiences, the richness of what seems to each of us to mediate between stimulus and response. There is a great deal that is going on in us that is expressed in our behavior only inadequately, if at all, states that we seem clearly and definitely to know ourselves to be in, as well as some we may be ignorant of or wrong or confused about. It

---

[6]It is this sort of holism that Quine has in mind when he marks, with the thesis of the indeterminacy of translation, a sharp break between all the natural sciences and psychology, linguistics, and related fields. His theory of analytical hypotheses is meant to make the relativization precise for the case of translation. See *Word and Object* (Cambridge: M.I.T. Press, 1960), esp. chap. 2.

seems clear to us that there is much about our inner lives to *discover*, much that is true of us though no one may be able to observe it.

Wittgenstein is also usually taken to be denying that we can make any sense of these claims, talk coherently about inner lives or private experiences. Although he is deeply critical of what, particularly as philosophers, we are inclined to say about such things, including our calling them "inner" or "private," I think it is a mistake to take him this way. (He was aware that people would; he asks throughout the *Investigations*, "what gives the impression we mean to deny anything?" It is not a rhetorical question.) I want to offer in response to these worries what I believe to be a reading of Wittgenstein, although I cannot here defend it as such.[7]

There are things—sensations, for example—that are definite particulars, events, states, or processes that may be introspectively accessible, immediate objects of awareness, whose identity or relation to physical events, states, or processes is (perhaps) an open philosophical or even scientific question. But *most* of what we care about—emotions, beliefs, understanding, motives, desires—are not such particulars. We make one sort of mistake (that it is the task of Wittgenstein's private language argument to address)[8] when we are tempted to think that objects of introspective awareness, like sensations or color patches in our visual fields, are the objects our words most directly hook on to, independently of interpersonal criteria. But we make quite another (the one I am here concerned to address) when we assimilate all psychological objects to objects of introspection or to introspectible bodily states.

The problem with this assimilation is that it ignores the nature of the complexity of our identification of our own (let alone others') complex psychological objects. What we take to be our emotion, our belief, our desire is a bundle of introspectible states and behavior, unless we are simply assuming that some one thing underlies them all. What it is that we know, what it is that is so definitely and particularly there in us, is not the thing itself (our *feeling* of anger is not the anger itself, surely not all of it) but, we usually think, some sign of it. We can, I think, maintain that our twinges, pangs, and so on are particular events no matter what our social situation, but it does not follow that the same is true for more complex psychological objects, such as emotions, beliefs, motives, and capacities. What we need to know in order to identify them is how to group together introspectible states and behavior and how to interpret it all. The question is one of meaning, not just at the level of what to call it, but at the level of there being an "it" at all. And

---

[7]For various reasons I would not expect this response to be taken as support by a Quinean or behavioral psychologist, but it is no part of my intent to offer such support: I want to argue that the realm of the psychological is essentially social, not that it is in any way unreal or unworthy of serious investigation.

[8]Ludwig Wittgenstein, *Philosophical Investigations*, trans. G. E. M. Anscombe (Oxford: Basil Blackwell, 1967), esp. secs. 269–315.

questions of meaning and interpretation cannot be answered in abstraction from social setting.[9]

For all I've said so far, it might of course be that what connects introspectible states and behavior to make them manifestations of a psychological object could be an underlying causal mechanism, or even some one underlying state. I don't think that that could be the case, but I don't intend to argue here that it couldn't. Rather, I want to suggest that the nearly universal failure even to see the need to argue that emotions, beliefs, and so on *are* particular states, that is, the tendency to make the individualist assumption, is in need of explanation.

Our attachment to the reality of the contents of our own minds and to our often unshared (and in an important way always unshareable) experience of them is, I think, part of such an explanation. But it is not enough: we can acknowledge the existence, even the importance, of such things, without its following that emotions and so on are themselves among them—as, in fact, they do not obviously seem to be. It may well be misleading in many or most cases (surely not in all) to say that I infer on the basis of evidence that I am angry or jealous or that I understand calculus or believe that primates can learn language, but nothing I immediately encounter just *is* my emotion, my understanding, or my belief, the way something I encounter *is* my itch or my sudden awareness of music in the room.

What I want to suggest in the remainder of this essay is that there is an underlying ideology of individualism and a set of child-rearing practices connected to it that can help us to understand the seeming obviousness of the individualist assumption and to account for the difficulty we feel about relinquishing it.

II

My first two answers to the question of the universality of the individualist assumption took the form of reasons for believing the assumption to be true: its apparently being demanded by a commitment to physicalism and its seeming to follow from our access to and our commitment to the reality of the constituents of our inner lives. The other two answers I would like to suggest are of another sort: rather than purported justifications of the assumption, they are attempts at explaining how it has come to have the hold on us that it does. Thus the third answer articulates the connections between the individualist assumption in the

[9]Hilary Putnam's work on the division of linguistic labor, the irreducibly social dimension of meaning, has similar consequences for individualist functionalist accounts. In Putnam's writing, as in Davidson's, an acute perception of this social dimension undercuts his programmatic work in philosophical psychology. (Putnam himself has acknowledged this effect, though perhaps not as extremely as I argue.) See esp. "The Meaning of Meaning."

philosophy of mind and the notion of the self embodied in the ideology of liberal individualism, and the fourth answer ties that notion of the self to the psychosexual development of males in a patriarchal culture where childcare is primarily in the hands of women.

To see the individualist assumption as stemming from the ideology of liberal individualism is to see that what purports to be a statement about how things naturally are is instead an expression of a historically specific way of structuring some set of social interactions. The supposed naturalness and the various theories that support it are essential components of that ideology. Thus, it is supposed to be a natural fact about human beings, and hence a constraint on any possible social theory, that, no matter how social our development may be, we exist essentially as separate individuals—with wants, preferences, needs, abilities, pleasures, and pains—and any social order has to begin by respecting these as attaching to us determinately and singly, as a way of respecting *us*.

Classical liberal social theory gets off the ground with the observation that individuals so defined are in need of being enticed—or threatened—into enduring and stable associations with one another. The societies thus envisioned aim at maximally respecting the separateness of their members by providing mechanisms for adjudicating the claims that one member may make against another, while leaving as intact as possible the rights of each to be self-defining.

Central to this liberal vision, as Ronald Dworkin persuasively argues,[10] is the conviction that the state ought not to discriminate among conceptions of the good life. The state ought not to embody or even favor any among the alternative pictures of human nature or human flourishing that may be favored by individuals or groups within the society. This evenhandedness is seen as constitutive of the equal respect that all citizens can expect from the liberal state: no vision of how human beings ought to live is to be favored over any other. Such visions, and the people who hold them, cannot always, of course, be *treated* equally: I may respect your desire to eat the whole cake as much as the desires of the rest of us to share it, without giving it all to you, and I can continue to respect your desire for the cake even if I decide that the children should get it all.

Making these distinctions is no easy matter, but they are central to liberal political theory because, among other reasons, liberals need to affirm an individualism of *method*, a counting of each of us as one and only one, a respect for separateness, without being committed to an individualism of *substance*, an anti-communitarian view of how society ought to work. This is for two reasons: we may be required by facts about developmental psychology to see human beings as springing from, perhaps even necessarily continuing to see themselves as members of, particular social groups, and communitarian ideals may well be among the possible visions the state is committed to respecting equally.

---

[10]Ronald Dworkin, "Liberalism," in *Public and Private Morality*, ed. Stuart Hampshire (Cambridge: Cambridge University Press, 1978), pp. 113–43.

The feasibility of this project (as, for example, John Rawls pursues it in *A Theory of Justice*) has been called into question: whether, that is, methodological individualism in political and social theory does not discriminate against communitarian ideals.[11] An alternative way of framing this concern is to ask whether in claiming neutrality among views of human nature and human flourishing the state is in fact expressing some particular set of views to the exclusion of others. A view of human beings as socially constituted, as having emotions, beliefs, abilities, and so on only insofar as they are embedded in a social web of interpretation that serves to give meaning to the bare data of inner experience and behavior, would in fact seem to be incompatible with a social and political theory that sees social groups as built on the independently existing characteristics of individuals.

If this incompatibility is real (as I think it is) the liberal has good reason to resist the view of the social construction of the objects of psychology: only if psychological states can be seen as attaching to individuals in abstraction from their social setting can we expect to appeal to them to justify forms of social organization; otherwise, we are in the position of attempting to evaluate a system that is constructing the data on which the evaluation is based. I would argue that we are in fact in this position, and the attendant circularity is unavoidable, but one of the hopes of liberalism is precisely to avoid this situation. As Larry Scidentop argues,[12] English liberalism (the sort we have come to think of as liberalism) is based on empiricist epistemology, using the individual as a foundation on which to justify both scientific and political theories.

Even if liberals give up this project of constructing social theory on an asocial foundation, the individual as self-defining and the state as neutral among these definitions remain important: the problem becomes one of characterizing these self-definitions in individualistic terms. Although psychological individualism as a realist thesis (emotions, beliefs, and so on are really there as particular states) is a natural way of doing this, one could attempt to salvage liberal individualism without it. I suspect, however, that the difficulties inherent in such an attempt contribute to the attraction of the realist thesis.

Nonrealist individualism would acknowledge that the psychological objects are constructions, ways of making sense of the observed regularities of individual and social life (and even that social considerations, such as the meanings of words we use, must enter in), but reserve to the individual the ultimate authority over these constructions: my psychological life may not be simply as I *find* it, but respect for me entails that it is as I construct it. On such a view privileged access (the epistemological thesis that I and only I have direct knowledge of my psychological states) becomes a social thesis affirming a sort of property right.

---

[11]This point was argued by Mary Gibson in a session of the Radical Caucus of the American Philosophical Association on "Rawls and the Left," New York, December 1979.

[12]Larry Scidentop, "Two Liberal Traditions," in *The Idea of Freedom: Essays in Honor of Isaiah Berlin*, ed. Alan Ryan (London: Oxford University Press, 1979), pp. 153–75.

But consider what this entails. The realist will see psychological states as definite particulars analogously to the way the liberal theorist sees individuals, with identities and entitlements attached to them. Internal respect, like political respect, would demand that evenhanded consideration be given to all these states. But (as Charles Taylor argues)[13] this position is untenable: we don't value all our feelings, inclinations, and so on equally, or even equally identify with them, and we would be abandoning an important aspect of our intelligence and humanity were we to do this. We need morally to evaluate our psychological states even if we are realist about them, and this need for moral evaluation is of course increased if the states themselves are not simply facts about us. We cannot treat our own feelings, inclinations, and so forth as though we were liberal states and they the citizens.

How are we to make these evaluations? For the liberal they must be made in terms of one's own true nature, deepest desires, or self-definition. But it is difficult to give these notions sufficient content to do the work we need them for. We may start by thinking of our true nature as an objective fact about us: we can be wrong in how we evaluate our feelings; we can be self-deceived, victims of false-consciousness, or simply muddled. But if we can appeal neither to psychological realism nor to social constraints, it is hard to see how to make sense of these claims; there seems to be nothing in terms of which to settle their truth.

Alternatively, we can focus on the idea of self-definition, on the freedom to constitute ourselves in any way we choose. But this sort of voluntarism (exemplified most starkly by Sartre) makes this ultimate choice irrational and inaccessible to criticism. What we choose today as central to our self-definition we may repudiate tomorrow. And we are unable to account for our deep, shared conviction that some activities of self-constitution are misguided, silly, futile, or immoral. The liberal doesn't want us (certainly not in the name of the state) to make these judgments about each other, but without psychological realism to fall back on, it's unclear how we can give any content to such judgments about *ourselves*, or why it should matter to us, as it clearly does, that we make them.

The problem is this: if individuals, their identities and life-plans are to be identifiable independently of forms of social organization (as the liberal needs them to be),[14] then we are hard pressed to come up with anything that could make

---

[13]Charles Taylor, "What's Wrong with Negative Liberty," in *The Idea of Freedom*, pp. 175–95.

[14]Strictly speaking, the liberal wants individuals to be prior to forms of *political* organization. This split allows free reign to forces of social and economic coercion. The liberal needs to argue that these forces are less powerful or less reprehensible than political forces, or, quite implausibly as soon as one considers the socialization of children, extend liberalism to social forces as well. Problems of this sort are raised by Marx in "On the Jewish Question" and discussed in relation to pluralism by Robert Paul Wolff in "Beyond Tolerance," in *Critique of Pure Tolerance*, with Herbert Marcuse and Barrington Moore, Jr. (Boston: Beacon Press, 1965), and by Lorenne Clark in "Sexual Equality and the Problem of an Adequate Moral Theory: The Poverty of Liberalism," in *Contemporary Moral Issues,* 3rd ed., ed. Wesley Cragg (Toronto: McGraw Hill, Ryerson, 1992): 157–65.

this identification nonarbitrary—unless we accept psychological realism. The idea that psychological states are definite particulars is the natural mirror to the liberal conception of individuals, since on this conception we are deprived of anything to guide the choosing and the weighing that would need to be involved were these states to be seen as constructions.

This situation is reflected in disputes in psychological theory. Freudian metapsychology needs to postulate real forces within each individual in terms of which the organization of the self occurs. In contrast, object-relations theory (which I will discuss below), sees the self as developing essentially in relation to particular others—and the principles of self-organization as arising out of those relationships. The more individualist the theory the greater the need for psychological realism, particularly since the competing notion of free choice makes even less sense for infants than it does for adults. I want to suggest that these connections account for some of the strength of psychological individualism: our liberal view of persons as separable individuals would seem to require, or at least to fit most naturally with, a view of psychological objects as existing brutely in us.

III

My fourth reason for the widespread acceptance of the individualist assumption ties this view of the self to patriarchal child-rearing practices. I want to suggest that if certain recent accounts of gender differences in psychosexual development are correct, they would lead us to expect that precisely such an individualistic view of the self would come to be both exemplified by men and taken by men and women alike as essentially human. Although most of the work I know in this area follows Freud in giving what the authors take to be causal accounts, I think there are grave difficulties with this approach. In what follows I mean the account to function as a sort of narrative framework, in terms of which we can make sense of the functioning of institutions such as the bourgeois family. We can think of the family as serving, *inter alia*, to produce heterosexual adults who will go on to form families like the ones they grew up in: in any particular case the causal story, whether or not it has this outcome, is very much more complicated.

Two recent books—Dorothy Dinnerstein's *The Mermaid and the Minotaur* and Nancy Chodorow's *The Reproduction of Mothering*[15] —explore the consequences of early, intimate child rearing's being nearly exclusively in the hands of women. My discussion will rely heavily on both books, in particular Chodorow's discus-

---

[15]Dorothy Dinnerstein, *The Mermaid and the Minotaur: Sexual Arrangements and Human Malaise* (New York: Harper and Row, 1976); Nancy Chodorow, *The Reproduction of Mothering: Psychoanalysis and the Sociology of Gender* (Berkeley: University of California Press, 1978).

sion there and elsewhere[16] on gender differences in the development of the self. (Chodorow in turn draws heavily from object-relations theorists.)[17] I will argue that the view of a separate, autonomous, sharply individuated self embedded in liberal political and economic ideology and in individualist philosophies of mind can be seen as a defensive reification of the process of ego development in males raised by women in a patriarchal society. Patriarchal family structure tends to produce men of whom these political and philosophical views seem factually descriptive and who are, moreover, deeply motivated to accept the truth of those views as the truth about themselves. In turn, the acceptance by all of us of those views as views about *persons* sustains these child-rearing practices by leading us to devalue, to see as truncated, as less than fully, healthily adult, the very different psychical structures of *women* raised by women. Since men (tend to) exemplify the psychical structures declared by political and philosophical theories to be universal (or if they don't, to see that as a personal failing), we are kept from criticizing those structures and from considering alternatives based on female experience. This interrelationship is characteristic of an ideology: a set of views purports to tell us the facts, what is "naturally" true, in the nature of things, and through doing this helps to structure social institutions in such a way as to produce people who tend to exemplify those views, thereby providing evidence for their own truth.

Chodorow and Dinnerstein offer theories of psychosexual development based on those of Freud, but differing sharply from his in emphasizing particular historically and socially contingent features of the family and its relationship to male-dominated society. The principal feature is the nearly exclusive role of women in early, intimate child rearing. It is obvious that this fact plays an important role in Freud's account, but since he doesn't treat it as an alterable social arrangement, it remains insufficiently examined, and its effects remain undifferentiated: we seem to be presented with an account of what it's like to grow up, period. And although this account is different for girls and for boys, Freud never considers the development of girls sufficiently in its own terms, but rather in relation to, or as a truncated and altered version of, the development of boys.

The usual reason given for this failure on Freud's part (one he recognized) is

---

[16]See especially "Being and Doing: A Cross-Cultural Examination of the Socialization of Males and Females," in *Woman in Sexist Society: Studies in Power and Powerlessness*, ed. Vivian Gornick and Barbara K. Moran (New York: Basic Books, 1971); "Family Structure and Feminine Personality," in *Women, Culture and Society*, ed. Michelle Z. Rosaldo and Louise Lamphere (Stanford: Stanford University Press, 1974); and "Mothering, Male Dominance, and Capitalism," in *Capitalist Patriarchy and the Case for Socialist Feminism*, ed. Zillah R. Eisenstein (New York: Monthly Review Press, 1979).

[17]Chodorow cites principally Alice Balint, Michael Balint, W. R. D. Fairbairn, Harry Guntrip, Hans Loewald, Margaret Mahler, Roy Shafer, and D. W. Winnicott.

that, although a large proportion of his patients were women, they remained for him, as for most men, a mystery. A deeper reason, I want to suggest, is that he was concerned to chart the path from infancy to civilized adulthood, and his model of civilized adulthood was that of bourgeois patriarchy, a model applicable only to men.

Related to this concern with this particular path is Freud's emphasis on the Oedipal period, on the vicissitudes of desire and sexual orientation, at the expense of the pre-Oedipal period and questions of individuation and core gender identity (that is, a sense of oneself as fitting in one of two utterly distinct social categories—the masculine or the feminine). One casualty of this relative lack of attention has been the question of gender differences in the infant's achievement of a sense of self and the connections between that achievement and the achievement of core gender identity. What we learn from the recent work that addresses these questions supports my hypothesis that philosophical and political individualism are connected with the psychosexual development of males raised by women. The lack of attention by psychologists, philosophers, and social theorists to the specific effects of this social practice and to gender differences in the pre-Oedipal period have led us to see individualism as somehow natural, as reflecting brute facts about the nature of persons.

When we focus on the pre-Oedipal period, two striking achievements in the way of psychosexual development stand out: before (possibly well before) the age of three, children become aware of themselves as social persons who are distinct from all others, in particular from their mothers, and they become aware of themselves as feminine or masculine, an identity it is next to impossible to change, even when it contradicts biological sex (difficult as that is to provide clear criteria for). Chodorow argues that these two feats are connected and are accomplished differently for girls and for boys.

Given our child-rearing arrangements, all infants start out intimately connected with a woman, and their development of a sense of self flows from their relationship with her. For a boy that relationship is colored by the mother's sense of difference from her son: since in our society the genders are utterly and profoundly distinct, a son is experienced and treated as other, as different. Achieving masculinity thus becomes a central part of what the male infant must do to establish his independence. In becoming himself he defines himself as both separate and different from his mother, and his achievement of masculinity is emblematic of this separation and difference.

As Freud argues that the girl has a harder time in establishing a heterosexual orientation because of the need to switch the gender of her object choice, so the boy has a harder time establishing core gender identity, since this identity is different from that of the person with whom he has identified. His initial experience of gender is an experience of difference. Thus a boy's sense of self is and remains reactive and defensive, something to be protected by an emphasis on his differences from others, his separateness and distinctness from them. It is through this emphasis that he comes to fit the picture underlying individualism in the philosophy of mind and in political theory: he is defined as a person by those properties that he senses as uniquely his and that seem somehow internal to him.

This process is profoundly affected by the relative absence of fathers in early childcare. Boys are urged to identify with their only distantly experienced fathers, and later, in the Oedipal stage, the power promised by this identification becomes a bribe to the boy to give up his desire for his mother. But this identification remains relatively abstract: in industrial society the father seems to have the independence the boy craves; he moves out of the family into the wider world, in ways that the boy knows little about. Being a man is exciting and attractive, but extremely vague and scary. About the only clear thing he knows about it is that it is *not* being a woman, and the importance of this fact is underscored by the social devaluation of women.

A boy's father serves, of course, not only as an attractive figure to identify with, but also as the embodiment of punishment and threat: during the Oedipal phase he is seen as the agent of social authority, and it is his voice that becomes internalized as the boy's superego. The intense fear generated by the power of this threat, which Freud sees as the threat of castration, accounts, on his view, for the strength of the male superego necessary for the maintenance of morality and civilization. And the relative abstractness of the father gives the superego an air of impersonality that I believe is connected with the centrality of objectivity and universalizability in moral theory. Thus, unsurprisingly, our moral notions reflect the socially dominant view of the nature of persons: if individuals are distinct and not necessarily connected with one another, then morality can be expected to concern itself not with the particularity of relationships among people, but with the abstractly characterizable features of interactions among individuals whose natures are taken as given.

The emphasis on externally conceived, rule-governed morality and the development of liberal individualist politics are connected with the increasing absence of fathers from the home with the development of industrial capitalism. Before this development, what it was to be a man was more closely connected with becoming like one's father, in relatively concrete and easily understood ways. (The speculative nature of these remarks can be summed up by saying that this view commits one to holding that serfs had weaker ego boundaries than workers in modern industrial society.) It may be significant in this regard that moral worth was often, in European societies, defined in religious ways, to be punished or rewarded not in this world, but in the next, and to be determined by how well one's life conformed to the model of the life of Christ, an absent, distant, relatively abstract "role model." Only when the demands of industrialization moved fathers far enough away to play this role did individual merit become attached to earthly achievement.

In turn, as Chodorow argues, sons growing up with absent fathers were better suited for industrial life—more responsive to abstract and impersonal demands, more likely to internalize a need to conform to authority.[18] Putting the matter this way emphasizes the extent to which, for the vast majority of men, the ideal of autonomous self-creation has been a myth. Very few men have a significant amount of control over their lives, but the myth encourages the illusion, generated by the promise held out by identification with their fathers, that the obedience to authority required by industrial capitalism is their free choice and will be rewarded.

Turning to the psychosexual development of girls, we can discover the psychological meaning of the claim made by Marxists in economic terms that women's position in capitalist society is essentially feudal. A girl achieves a sense of herself much less sharply differentiated from her mother. In part she is responding to the fact that in a society in which gender categories structure all social relations, her mother is likely to identify with her. There is furthermore no particular sharp difference she can seize upon to break the primitive identification all infants must develop with their primary caretaker. Nor does her father typically provide this for her as he does for her brother: he urges her not to identify with him, but to relate to him, and to do so as a woman, that is, as someone like her mother. And the person she is to grow up to be like is someone she knows intimately, concretely, and who is defined for her not as a separate, mysteriously self-actualizing individual, but only through family relations.

Thus, for a girl neither a sense of herself nor her gender identity consists, as it does for a boy, in a free leap in the dimly perceived direction of self-definition, defined mainly by difference from the mother. Her gender identity is characteristically less tenuous (compare the relative scarcity of female to male transsexuals) and less connected with heterosexual orientation, which, if it occurs, is a later, more difficult achievement. (Consider here the fact that, whereas the "macho" element in gay male life is connected with an understandable need to assert to a sexist world that they are "real men," the butch and femme roles lesbians have adopted at certain times in certain societies have more to do with survival than with a need to be seen as "real women.") But although core gender identity tends to be easier to achieve, a girl's sense of self is typically weaker than a boy's; her ego-boundaries are less strong. Who she is is much more closely bound up with intimate relationships and with how she is perceived by others; it is less natural for her to separate how others react to and treat her from how she perceives herself to be.

Given that the masculine model of a sharply distinguished self is our cultural norm (since men have had both the need and the power to define as fully human this sort of self, to turn their experience of infancy on its head and define 'feminine' as 'not masculine'), women have been perceived as less than fully

---

[18]For the discussion on the need for men's personality structures to change to accommodate the demands of industrial capitalism, see Heidi Hartmann, "Capitalism, Patriarchy, and Job Segregation by Sex," in *Capitalist Patriarchy*.

human, or at least as less than fully adult. We are less likely to consider ourselves, or to be considered by others, as having an identity, a character, talents, and virtues independently of our particular intimate relationships and of how we are perceived by others.

Thus, if we accept the picture of a person embedded in political and philosophical individualism, the picture of healthy autonomous adulthood embedded in psychological theory, and the picture of conscience and morality embedded in moral philosophy, we come to the conclusion that there is something deficient in the natural character of girls or in their upbringing. Traditionally, of course, this deficiency has been seen as natural: women have quite consistently been excluded from the centrally important metaphysical, epistemological, moral, and political conceptions of personhood.[19] Freud is often read as being in this tradition, but he is at least from time to time explicit about the unnaturalness and painful deformation involved in the making of women and men from female and male children, and even to some extent of how this process is more destructive of females than of males.[20]

Liberal feminism, in line with liberal social theory in general, sees most women's failure to exemplify fully the culture's ideals of personhood as due not to our nature but to constraints imposed upon us by that culture. As a rule, the more radical the thinking, the further back in our lives these constraints are located and the deeper and more difficult eradicating their effects is taken to be. Thus, the use made by Dinnerstein and Chodorow of the Freudian stress on the family, infancy, and early childhood. As Juliet Mitchell has argued,[21] we can read Freud as providing a theory of how children develop under patriarchy, a theory we have reason to learn both to explain ourselves better, including how we came to be the way we are, and to help discover the constraints on changes we might want to make in the mechanisms of enculturation in order to allow women better to conform to the norms of adult personhood. (For Freud the constraints were absolute: he writes as though our only alternatives were the Hobbesian state of nature or the turn-of-the-century bourgeois patriarachal family.)

Chodorow and Dinnerstein are far more revisionist than Mitchell in their neo-Freudianism, and, in particular, Chodorow's use of object-relations theory can lead us to question not only the mechanisms of enculturation and their crippling

---

[19]This point is argued and historically illustrated by Susan Moller Okin, *Women in Western Political Thought* (Princeton: Princeton University Press, 1979).

[20]See especially Sigmund Freud, "'Civilized' Sexual Morality and Modern Nervous Illness," 1908 *Standard Edition*, vol. 9, ed. James Strachey (London: Hogarth Press, 1959), esp. pp. 194–95.

[21]Juliet Mitchell, *Psychoanalysis and Feminism* (New York: Pantheon Books, 1974).

effects on females, but the norms of adult personhood those mechanisms are designed to enable some men to achieve (and others to strive for).

In the final section I would like briefly to question those norms. There are, of course, many changes necessary in the upbringing of girls, but we ought not to accept the masculinist pictures of persons, of healthy adulthood, or of morality as the goals of those changes.

IV

These norms have been at least tacitly questioned, in the forms of women's lives, work, and conversations, for as long as they have existed. The recent flourishing of feminism is having two effects: this questioning is more and more going on in (a deliberate subversion of) the "father tongue," the allegedly universal but socially masculine language of philosophy and science.[22] Women who have been allowed and trained to "think like men" are using that training to think more clearly—which means more radically—like women, that is, like people who are living real, embodied lives, shared in deep and important respects with others of our culturally devalued gender, at a particular time in history involving, crucially, a re-evaluation of gender.

The other effect is a backlash of fear that liberals are ill-equipped to deal with. The fear arises from a recognition of the fact that men have been free to imagine themsleves as self-defining only because women have held the intimate social world together, in part by seeing ourselves as inseparable from it. The norms of personhood, which liberals would strive to make as genuinely universal as they now only pretend to be, depend in fact on their not being so—just what we would expect from an ideology. Thus, the fear aroused by liberal feminism's ideal of opening to women the sort of autonomy previously reserved for men is, I think, a real one.

There is every reason to react with alarm to the prospect of a world filled with self-actualizing persons pulling their own strings, capable of guiltlessly saying "no" to anyone about anything, and freely choosing when to begin and end all their relationships. It is hard to see how, in such a world, children could be raised, the sick or disturbed could be cared for, or people could know each other through their lives and grow old together.

Liberal feminism does have much in common with this sort of "human potential" individualistic talk, but it is my suspicion that it was in reaction to the deeper, and more deeply threatening, insights and demands of feminism that the current vogue for self-actualization developed—urging us all back inside the apolitical

---

[22]The notion of a father tongue and its difference from a mother tongue is Thoreau's. See Stanley Cavell, *The Senses of Walden* (New York: The Viking Press, 1972), pp.15ff.

confines of our own heads and hearts and guts. What I hope I have begun to suggest here is that the psychological individualists might be wrong and we are responsible for the meaning of each other's inner lives, that our emotions, beliefs, motives, and so on are what they are because of how they—and we—are related to others in our world—not only those we share a language with, but those we more intimately share our lives with.

We cannot and do not want to see this because men, who have traditionally had the power to define what it is to be human, to be adult, to be moral, have done so in response to their own experience of and need for separateness and distinctness. And, as women, we have accepted this view of the self as truly, fully human—despite our own inevitable sense of failure in the face of it—because (as Dinnerstein powerfully argues) we share with men deep ambivalence about birth, death, dependence, and the body, its needs and demands. We too have our earliest and deepest associations of these things with a woman and we too evade the difficult resolution of this ambivalence by splitting off these aspects of experience. We allow—and require—men to express a vision, which even at the cost of self-denigration we need as they do, of pure, clean, free, uncontaminated humanness.

Chodorow's and Dinnerstein's books are not particularly optimistic. Unlike Freud, they allow for the possibility of changes in the deepest structures of enculturation, but the path to these changes is not well marked, and all that is clear about it is that it is difficult both to find and to keep to. Part, though by no means all, of finding this path is saying what we can about its destination. We may not be able to say very much about it since, as Marx has argued, the very ideas of new forms of human existence are created out of forms of practice. But we can learn something about where we are or ought to be going by looking at the practices that form our lives as women, by taking them seriously, listening to what we do, and finding the voices with which to speak what we hear.

My contention in this paper has been that one of the things we will learn is a radically different conception of the nature of persons and a deep suspicion of some of the underpinnings of philosophical psychology, metaphysics, epistemology, ethics, and political theory: the essential distinctness of persons and their psychological states, the importance of autonomy, the value of universal principles in morality, and the demand that a social theory be founded on an independent theory of persons, their natures, needs, and desires.

These issues have been traditionally discussed in Western culture by upper or middle class white males who have taken themselves to be speaking in a universal human voice. Our very varied experiences as women have been crucially different from theirs, in part because of the often limited and limiting social roles we have been constrained to fill (defined by our bodies' sexual appeal and reproductive capacity and by our immersion in the intimate social world) as well as by what we have chosen to do with our lives (for example, in art and in the interconnectedness of experience and perception in consciousness-raising groups). We are less likely to speak naturally in voices at once abstractly disembodied and autonomously self-defining.

Rather than claim our right to speak in such voices, to transcend our experience as women, I would urge us to speak out of that experience, in part as a way of changing it, but also out of a recognition of what there is to learn from the perspectives on human life that have been distinctly ours.[23]

---

[23]It has been pointed out to me (by Jane Gallop) that this paper seems to have been written by at least two different people. I have made no attempt to change that: it reflects something important about feminist scholarship today—the complexities of our relationships to traditional disciplines, their problems and methodologies, and to politics, to our histories and to our audiences. I am grateful to my colleagues at the University of Minnesota for their criticism and suggestions and, especially, for their making it possible for me comfortably to be all the authors of this paper. I read earlier versions at the University of Wisconsin at Milwaukee and the University of Minnesota and profited from those discussions, as well as from extensive ones with Peter Shea, Burton Dreben, and Sandra Harding, and from Kathryn Morgan's work on autonomy. Adam Morton brought to my attention various flaws in the penultimate draft.

II

Constructions of Gender and Authority

5

Othello's Doubt/Desdemona's Death: The Engendering of Scepticism

I

Toward the end of *The Claim of Reason* Stanley Cavell gives a reading of *Othello* that is at the same time a reading of philosophical scepticism.[1] Upon first encountering these readings, I was struck by their aptness and by their mutual illumination. Doubting, for Othello or for the sceptic, responds to an unease at the heart of the experiences of immersion in the world and connectedness to others. The immersion and the connection are at the same time terrifying and tenuous and then terrifying in their tenuousness. Embodied human experiences, notably of sexuality, are central to Cavell's account;[2] gender is not: it figures only briefly and then as a symmetrical difference.[3]

In this essay I want to suggest a rereading of some of the texts that engage these questions, a rereading that places the asymmetries of gender at the crux of sixteenth-century Europe, a time and place that was profoundly and disturbingly disordered.[4] Shakespeare explored the disorder, attendant in part on the loss of centering authority, most notably in *King Lear*. Many of his other works continue this exploration, playing out a range of responses to the disorder of the world.

---

[1]Stanley Cavell, *The Claim of Reason*: *Wittgenstein, Skepticism, Morality, and Tragedy* (New York: Oxford University Press, 1979), pp. 433–96.

[2]See Cavell's "Knowing and Acknowledging," and "The Avoidance of Love: A Reading of *King Lear*," in *Must We Mean What We Say?* (New York: Scribner's, 1969).

[3]See Luce Irigary, "The Blind Spot of an Old Dream of Symmetry," Part 1 of *Speculum of the Other Woman*, trans. Gillian C. Gill (Ithaca: Cornell University Press, 1985), for a critical exploration of the (male) view of gender difference as symmetrical.

[4]Questions about a possible "gender inflection" to scepticism are ones Cavell has addressed since the publication of *The Claim of Reason*. See, in particular, his essay, "Psychoanalysis and Cinema," in *Psychiatry and the Humanities* 10 (1986).

One such response is the "problem comedic."[5] It is, I think, best represented by *All's Well That Ends Well.* The philosophical analogue is the "mitigated scepticism" of Montaigne. Another response is tragically played out in *Othello.* I want to argue that the impulse Shakespeare is exploring in that play, which leads Othello to embrace Iago's view of the world, is the impulse that informs Descartes's *Meditations*[6] and the subsequent course of Western science and epistemology. It is a consequence of my argument that this impulse is as necessarily murderous and tragic in "real life" as it is in Shakespeare's play.

II

As narrated by Richard Popkin,[7] sixteenth-century Europe underwent a threefold sceptical crisis: theological, sparked by the Reformation and fueled by fideistic defenses of Catholicism; humanistic, as a relativistic response to learning about the different ways of life in the recently discovered new world and recently rediscovered ancient world; and scientific, with the undermining of the bases of Aristotelian science and the debates about what, if anything, could replace them. Popkin situates Montaigne, especially *The Apology for Raymond Sebond*, in this context:

> By extending the implicit sceptical tendencies of the Reformation crisis, the humanistic crisis, and the scientific crisis, into a total *crise pyrrhonienne*, Montaigne's genial *Apologie* became the *coup de grâce* to an entire intellectual world. It was also to be the womb of modern thought, in that it led to the attempt either to refute the new Pyrrhonism, or to find a way of living with it.[8]

Montaigne himself chose to live with it, and his *Essays* are largely a record of the sort of life thereby chosen: forgiving of oneself and others, discursive, amused, literate, and nondogmatically conservative, a place from which the world is

---

[5]The term and its history are discussed by Carol Thomas Neely, *Broken Nuptials in Shakespeare's Plays* (New Haven: Yale University Press, 1985), pp. 58–65. I don't take it to be precise; my use of it should become clear and is strongly influenced by her discussion.

[6]My reading of Descartes takes as its starting point an interpretation that is already controversial in its viewing scepticism for Descartes as a genuine threat, not just a philosophical tool. It is presented, with some variations, in Richard H. Popkin, *The History of Scepticism from Erasmus to Descartes* (New York: Harper and Row, 1964), and E. M. Curley, *Descartes against the Skeptics* (Cambridge: Harvard University Press, 1978). I don't want to argue the merits of this interpretation, although I do find it convincing. Rather, I would hope that the use to which I put it will lend it additional support.

[7]Popkin, *The History of Scepticism*, esp. chaps. 1–3.

[8]Ibid., p. 55.

attentively observed, but never definitively known. Such a life and the world within which it is lived can be seen as the subjects of Shakespeare's problem comedies, at least one of which—*All's Well That Ends Well*—has been argued to be drawn in part directly from Montaigne.[9]

The accommodation to scepticism is historically uneasy, poised between nostalgia for a (mis)remembered world of unquestioned certainty and stability and the hope that scientific rationality will bring the world under our practical and epistemic control. This uneasiness has tinged many critical readings of the problem plays (so that the plays themselves *are* the problems—like problem children). E. K. Chambers, for example, writes of *All's Well*, *Troilus and Cressida*, and *Measure for Measure*: "They are all unpleasant plays, the utterances of a puzzled and disturbed spirit, full of questionings, sceptical of its own ideas, looking with new misgivings into the ambiguous shadows of a world over which a cloud has passed and made a goblin of the sun."[10]

Arthur Kirsch offers a more redemptive reading of *All's Well*.[11] He sees Bertram the way he suggests Montaigne would see him, as an adolescent boy, prey to "the nakedness of sexuality,"[12] in need of acceptance and, Kirsch argues, redemption into Pauline marriage through the agency of a virtuous heroine.[13] Kirsch, whose interpretive framework is Freudian and Christian, finds "the fabric of Montaigne's essay" ("On Some Verses of Virgil") in "the elegiac cast of *All's Well*, its pervasive opposition of age and youth, the association of that opposition with marriage and lust and with virtue and nobility, the depiction of Bertram as a 'princock boy . . . in season . . . in the age next unto infancy.' " The play and the essay have as "their common denominator, an unremitting focus upon erotic love and a consciousness of sexuality itself as a supreme instance of the mixed nature of our being."[14]

As a woman and a feminist I am ambivalent about the attitudes Kirsch finds in the play, as I am ambivalent about Montaigne. I am attracted by the epistemic modesty, the air of humane acceptance of embodied, sexual humanness, and the room in such a world, with such men, for women of strength, intelligence, and maturity. I am, however, at the same time, and prompted by many of the same

---

[9]In particular, from "On Some Verses of Virgil." See Arthur Kirsch, *Shakespeare and the Experience of Love* (Cambridge: Cambridge University Press, 1981), p. 38; and A. P. Rossiter, *Angel with Horns and Other Shakespeare Lectures*, ed. Graham Storey (London: Longmans, Green & Co. Ltd., 1961), p. 98.

[10]E. K. Chambers, *Shakespeare*: *A Survey* (London: Sidgewick & Jackson, 1925), p. 210, quoted in Neely, p. 225 n.4.

[11]Kirsch, *Shakespeare and the Experience of Love*, pp. 37ff, 111–36.

[12]Ibid., p. 118.

[13]Ibid., p. 186 n.8.

[14]Ibid., p. 127. Kirsch is quoting from Montaigne, "On Some Verses of Virgil," and the elisions are his.

words and images, disturbed by the central and structuring role of marriage as redemptive—for men—and the view of women as the natural agents of that redemption.[15]

Consider, for example, Helena's remarks to Diana and her mother after the bed-trick: "But, O, strange men, / That can such sweet use make of what they hate, / When saucy trusting of the cozen'd thoughts / Defiles the pitchy night; so lust doth play / With what it loathes for that which is away."[16] The thought here is a perceptive, critical insight into a profoundly disturbing feature of male sexuality—the easy compatibility of desire and contempt. Such an insight might well ground feminist unease about that sexuality and about one's prescribed place as a woman in relation to it. But the lines are introduced by Helena's reassurance that all will turn out as it should: "Doubt not but heaven / Hath brought me up to be your daughter's dower, / As it hath fated her to be my motive / And helper to a husband."[17]

Thus, Helena embodies the humane acceptance of (male) human sexuality, even in one of its most distressing forms, with a sigh of "boys will be boys" and the confidence, or at least the hope, that marriage—"real" marriage, consummated and fecund—will make everything all right.[18] Men seem by this state of affairs to be spared the hard labor of maturity, having it done for them by virtuous and more than faintly maternal young women.

Connected, I think, to the historically uneasy accommodation to scepticism is

---

[15]For an alternative, feminist view of marriage and institutionalized heterosexuality in women's lives, see Adrienne Rich, "Compulsory Heterosexuality and Lesbian Existence," *Signs* 5 (1980): 631–60.

[16]*All's Well* IV. iv. 21–5. All references to plays of Shakespeare are from *The Riverside Shakespeare*, ed. G. Blakemore Evans (Boston: Houghton Mifflin, 1974).

[17]Neely (*Broken Nuptials*, pp. 75ff) discusses the friendships between Shakespearean women as intimate, mutually sympathetic and helpful, and supportive and furthering of heterosexual, marital bonds. Although she goes on to argue that "comic action characteristically weakens or breaks old bonds to make way for new ones" (ibid., p. 77), she explicitly excludes bonds of female friendship from this fate. The argument that such bonds *do* succumb to the comedic ending has been made by Shirley Nelson Garner, "*A Midsummer Night's Dream*: 'Jack shall have Jill; / Nought shall go ill,'" *Women's Studies* 9 (1981): 47–63.

The disagreement may reflect, in part, the choice of plays: the more the classic world of romantic comedy is intact, the more heterosexual romantic love may sweep away all other attachments and sentiments. But there is an additional issue of perspective: an explicitly nonheterosexist perspective, such as Garner's—one which does not accept heterosexuality as normative—is more likely to reveal the limitations, losses, and betrayals of female relationships exacted by the comedic marriage ending.

[18]Kirsch (*Shakespeare and the Experience of Love*, p. 137) finds in Helena's words a "sense of paradoxical wonder," an attitude he takes to pervade the play as a whole. He argues that Rossiter is wrong to find "horror or revulsion" in Helena's words.

male ambivalence about this picture. The cost of having one's sexual appetites indulged and then indulgently forgiven has typically been seen as exorbitant. Maternal female power is experienced as castrating, and the redemption of marriage is seen, like the redemption of socially proper religion, as a trap. As attractive as being forever a little boy may appear, the attendant (sense of) powerlessness usually evokes at least ambivalence.

Kirsch both captures and expresses this ambivalence when he writes of *All's Well* that "... throughout the play Bertram is confronted by a conspiracy of women whose nurturing affections threaten to control and therefore deprive him of the energy of his aggressive sexual instincts, to bring him to what he calls 'the dark house and the detested wife'" (II. iii. 285).[19] Kirsch finds the resolution to the ambivalence in the bed-trick: Bertram is drawn into marriage through acting (so he believes) "freely"—i.e., out of aggressive and unlawful sexual instinct. As Kirsch puts it, "Bertram's freedom enables him to conquer Helena and discover her as a woman, a conquest that provides the basis for a marriage in which there can be desire as well as affection. . . ."[20]

Another locus of male ambivalence is the awareness that the voracious sexuality being humanely accepted is not one's own exclusive possession: one is in danger of being cuckolded by *other* naughty boys. Acknowledgment of *female* (hetero)-sexual desire (as in *All's Well*), and of male desire for that desire, also raises the fear of cuckoldry. Genuine, autonomous desire—the only sort worth desiring—is uncontrollable by its object: "O curse of marriage! / That we can call these delicate creatures ours, / And not their appetites!"[21] As Coppelia Kahn notes, Touchstone and Lavatch, the clowns in *As You Like It* and *All's Well*, turn "shame to witty advantage by spurious logic": each "shows himself a wise fool by recognizing and accepting the folly that is inevitably his as a married man."[22] Needless to say, wise or not, such attitudes are not stable: (imagined) cuckoldry becomes in later plays, notably *Othello* and *The Winter's Tale*, the locus of real or narrowly and magically averted tragedy.[23]

---

[19]Ibid., p. 141.

[20]Ibid., p. 142.

[21]*Othello* III. iii. 268–70.

[22]Coppelia Kahn, *Man's Estate: Masculine Identity in Shakespeare* (Berkeley: University of California Press, 1981), chap. 5, "'The Savage Yoke': Cuckoldry and Marriage," pp. 124ff.

[23]Similar paths through Shakespeare are being traced by a number of feminist critics, such as Madelon Sprengnether, who reads "the development from the comedies through the problem plays and the major tragedies in terms of an explosion of the sexual tensions that threaten without rupturing the surface of the earlier plays." Published under Madelon Gohlke, "'I wooed thee with my sword': Shakespeare's Tragic Paradigms," in Carolyn Swift Lenz, Gayle Greene, and Carol Thomas Neely, eds., *The Woman's Part: Feminist Criticism of Shakespeare* (Urbana: University of Illinois Press, 1980), pp. 150–70; quotation, p. 154.

III

For the remainder of this essay I want to look at the other response to the pyrrhonian crisis, the one that Shakespeare explores in *Othello* and that finds its major philosophical expression in Descartes. It can arise either out of the ambivalence engendered by the problem comedic resolution or more directly out of the fears and threats to the ego presented by an apparently stabler (mis)remembered earlier world. The historical breaking apart of that world became the ground on which a new conception of the self emerged, a self whose definition rested on a violent repudiation of the presumed power of the earlier world to engulf and submerge the individual. The remembered experience of maternal power became in this process an intrapsychic trope for what had in historical fact been the nearly exclusively male power of feudalism.

Alongside the figure of the phallically powerful mother is a fantasy of exclusively possessing her from a position of omnipotence. The fantasy is, of course, itself unstable: the mother is desired *as* powerful, as the source of nurturance and life itself, but as such she is perceived as a threat not only to infantile omnipotence but to the self as independently existing. This fantasy, along with the ambivalence it engenders, rather than becoming integrated into a sexual economy that recognizes the otherness of the object of desire, remains intact as the basis of culturally normative male desire.

Ambivalence, and the violent warding off of ambivalence, are thus inevitable in a world in which men are expected to dominate, in part by the expression and evocation of sexual desire, women—whose bodily presence reawakens infantile experiences of dependency and symbiotic intimacy.[24] The playing out of these anxieties is evident in "Shakespeare's recurrent preoccupation with betrayal and with feminine powers to create and destroy *suddenly*, and in the repeated desire of his male characters both to be that all-powerful woman and to control the means of nurturance themselves, to the exclusion of the otherness of others."[25]

Othello and Descartes's *Meditations* are permeated by this anxiety. Descartes's world, as Popkin argues,[26] is in the throes of scepticism. Although we may read Descartes as self-confidently working toward the overthrow of Scholasticism and the institutionalization of the epistemology of modern science, he saw his project equally as one of warding off the threat of epistemic nihilism, a threat he perceived the Montaignean sceptic as posing. Similarly, although a number of critics have noted the resemblance of the plot and setting of *Othello* to comedy,[27] Othello, in

---

[24]See Dorothy Dinnerstein, *The Mermaid and the Minotaur: Sexual Arrangements and Human Malaise* (New York: Harper & Row, 1976).

[25]Murray Schwartz, "Shakespeare through Contemporary Psychoanalysis," *Hebrew University Studies in Literature* 5 (1977): 182–98, quoted in Kahn, p. 153, n.4.

[26]Popkin, *The History of Scepticism*, esp. chaps. 9, 10.

[27]See Neely (*Broken Nuptials*, pp. 109ff), especially on the roles of sexuality and gender in comedic structure.

his sense of himself and his love for Desdemona, is shown to be as antithetical to the comedic spirit as Descartes's epistemic desires are to Montaigne's humane scepticism.

One important reason why *Othello* seems like a comedy gone horribly wrong is that at the start Desdemona is a perfect comedic heroine: apparently and unremarkedly motherless and strongly attached to a powerful father,[28] perceptively and bawdily witty, strong-willed, passionate and unconventionally adventurous, realistic and mocking of Othello's extravagant romanticism, with an intimate female confidante and friend who is not her social peer (a relationship that counterpoints but never hinders the thematically central heterosexual one).

Othello loves her for her (their) conversation:[29] he is drawn by it into the comedic world, described by Susan Snyder as one of "multiple possibilities held in harmonious balance . . . anarchic dislocations of order and identity . . . the world where lovers always win, death always loses, and nothing is irrevocable. . . . "[30] In this world, Othello's military life becomes an adventure story to tell to Desdemona: "She lov'd me for the dangers I had pass'd, / And I loved her that she did pity them. / This only is the witchcraft I have us'd."[31]

The "witchcraft" is, rather, Desdemona's: through her perception of Othello ("I saw Othello's visage in his mind")[32] she weaves from his own words, actions, and feelings a world of magical delight. And he comes to feel that his continued

---

[28]Cavell addresses this feature of the lives of the heroines of the '30s and '40s film comedies he discusses in *Pursuits of Happiness*: *The Hollywood Comedy of Remarriage* (Cambridge: Harvard University Press, 1981). For further discussion, see his essay in *Psychiatry and the Humanities* 10 (1986); also my "Missing Mothers/Desiring Daughters: Framing the Sight of Women."

My account of Desdemona and of the comedic elements in *Othello* owes much to Neely's (*Broken Nuptials*, pp. 109–17). For an illuminating account of why such a spirited Desdemona should respond so helplessly to Othello's jealous rages, see S. N. Garner, "Shakespeare's Desdemona," *Shakespeare Studies* 9 (1976): 233–52.

[29]Conversation as a marital (and democratic) ideal is a topic throughout *Pursuits of Happiness* (a connection that leads me to suggest that the interpretation of *Othello* I'm urging is one we'd have seen had Katharine Hepburn played Desdemona). The degeneration of Desdemona's language, its "increasing obliqueness" and opacity, and her becoming "the victim of her ambiguities" are explored in Madelon Gohlke, "'All that is spoke is marred': Language and Consciousness in *Othello*," *Women's Studies* 9 (1982): 157–76; quotations, 167.

[30]Susan Snyder, *The Comic Matrix of Shakespeare's Tragedies* (Princeton: Princeton University Press, 1979). Although I find Snyder's readings perceptive and I draw on them extensively, I differ with her in attempting to locate the tragedy not—as she does—in "the tragic implications in any love relationship" (p. 84), but in a historically specific, and gendered, set of attitudes.

[31]*Othello* I. iii. 167–69.

[32]*Othello* I. iii. 252.

existence rests on the continued reality of this magical world—that is, on Desdemona's continued, faithful weaving of it. In railing about his horror that he can no longer believe in her, Othello speaks of Desdemona's love and fidelity as a *place* ". . . where I have garner'd up my heart, / Where either I must live, or bear no life; / The fountain from the which my current runs / Or else dries up. . . . "[33]

The dependency and vulnerability of living in a world magically constructed from lovers' conversation and of having one's sense of self mirrored in a woman's eyes pose a threat—to which Iago and his alternative metaphysics and epistemology are an answer. Iago offers Othello a place to stand, off to the side, hidden, eavesdropping, from which he can put Desdemona, their love, and the world they wove to the test. Stepping back, outside that world, he interrogates her and it, assembling evidence, demanding proofs, imagining, as he moves further into madness, that the movement is toward the greater clarity of dispassionate objectivity.

Proximity to Desdemona is epistemically dangerous: "I'll not expostulate with her, lest her body and beauty unprovide my mind again. . . . "[34] It is because Othello comes to see his relationship to Desdemona as one of intolerable vulnerability and epistemic dependency (what, in better times, one would call trust or faith) that he manages *not* to see how vulnerable to and dependent upon Iago he eventually becomes. Male bonding, in this play as elsewhere, is not experienced as the threat to autonomy that connection to women is.[35]

Iago's perspective, the one he offers to Othello, has been described as scientific[36] or, with a slight shift of emphasis, as judicial.[37] Terence Hawkes describes Iago's method of reasoning as Baconian, based on what in scholastic terminology was called *ratio inferior*, to be distinguished from *ratio superior*, the faculty of wisdom—intuitive, inspired, and theological—represented in the play by the transcendence of Desdemona's love. Hawkes situates the play in the Elizabethan struggle between "lower" and "higher" reason, between those who would "observe, analyze, explain, define, and . . . interpret . . . with . . . validity, logical

---

[33]*Othello* IV. ii. 58–61.

[34]*Othello* IV. i. 200–202.

[35]Toni McNaron has drawn my attention to Othello's picking up Iago's speech patterns as he picks up his epistemic stance, and to the homoeroticism in the relationship between the two men, including a mock marriage in which they swear undying loyalty (III. iii. 460–80). Othello fails to perceive Iago's increasing possession of his soul in part because he thinks of eroticism and its attendant threats of dependency wholly in relation to women, and he regards the world of men and soldiering as a refuge from those threats.

[36]See W. H. Auden, "The Joker in the Pack," in *The Dyer's Hand and Other Essays* (New York: Random House, 1948), pp. 246–72; and Terence Hawkes, "Iago's Use of Reason," *Studies in Philology* 58 (1961): 160–69.

[37]See Winifred M. T. Nowottny, "Justice and Love in *Othello*," *University of Toronto Quarterly* 21 (1952): 330–44.

necessity, and rational certitude,"[38] and those like Montaigne who would chasten the ambitions of scientific reason.

Hawkes's point is that Iago's skillful manipulation of the appearances (he doesn't exactly *lie*) is not a perversion of scientific reason, but, in its power to seduce Othello, a demonstration both of the incapacity of such reason to comprehend aspects of the world that lie beyond it and of the defenseless inability of that world to provide a logical, rational proof of its own reality. It needs—demands—no proof, but pressed to give one, it will inevitably fail. Montaigne might be warning Othello: "take heed lest any man deceive you by Philosophie and vain seducement, according to the rudiments of the world."[39]

W. H. Auden sees Iago similarly as "a parabolic figure for the autonomous pursuit of scientific knowledge through experiment which we all [i.e., modern Westerners], whether we are scientists or not, take for granted as natural and right." He goes on to distinguish such knowledge by the ascetic disinterest of the investigator, the necessary absence of reciprocity (unlike the knowing of a friend, which requires reciprocity), and the having of power over the object of knowledge.[40]

Both Auden's and Hawkes's characterizations of scientific epistemology are as applicable to Cartesian rationalism as to Baconian empiricism. Although Bacon was more likely to have been in the air Shakespeare was breathing, the fundamental objectifying stance was common to both perspectives. If, as we shall see, nature is unlikely to survive the distancing tactics to which the empiricist subjects her, she fares no better with the rationalist, for whom she is an even less active epistemic partner.[41]

Auden argues that "Iago treats Othello as an analyst treats a patient. . . . Everything he says is designed to bring to Othello's consciousness what he has already guessed is there. Accordingly, he has no need to tell lies."[42] But Auden attributes the *motivation* for this process solely to Iago: " . . . the fall of Othello is the work of another human being; nothing he says or does originates with himself. In consequence, we feel pity for him but no respect; our aesthetic respect

---

[38]Hawkes, "Iago's Use of Reason," p. 165.

[39]Quoted in ibid., p. 169.

[40]Auden, "The Joker in the Pack," p. 270.

[41]Kant's criticism of the sceptical consequences of both empiricism and rationalism makes a similar link: once the self imagines the "external world" as in need of proof, a proof that it is in a position to demand, search for, and recognize, it has placed that world on the other side of a gulf nothing can span. See *Critique of Pure Reason*, trans. Norman Kemp Smith (New York: St. Martin's Press, 1965), esp. "The Refutation of Idealism," B274–79, and "The Fourth Paralogism: Of Ideality," A366–80. Kant argues that the self cannot in fact coherently so imagine the world, since it can have no sense of itself apart from the world in which it finds itself.

[42]Auden, "The Joker in the Pack," p. 266.

is reserved for Iago."[43] This final claim, and its consequence that *Othello* is not a proper tragedy, have been hotly debated. I want to argue against it by suggesting that we see Iago not just as exploiting what he finds in Othello, but as answering a need: if Iago hadn't been there, Othello would have had to invent him.[44]

Which is, of course, what Descartes did, with the evil genius of his first Meditation. The evil genius is invoked to steel Descartes's resolve not to be seduced into belief in a world that has presented itself to him through his sometimes deceptive senses, the "charm" of fables, the "power and beauty" of eloquence, the "ravishing delicacy and sweetness" of poetry, and the soberer delights of mathematics, philosophy, theology, morals, jurisprudence, and medicine.[45] He withdraws from the world—even, ultimately, from his own body—in order to put his relationship with it on a different footing: he aims to find and maintain himself in a position of epistemic control, knowing himself (i.e., his mind) while agnostic of all else, and admitting knowledge of the world only after it has been subjected to tests and proofs.

Descartes's doubt in the *Meditations* is clearly self-induced, and he confidently expects to regain the world he has willed away.[46] But, as Popkin argues, we need to take seriously the threat scepticism posed to Descartes. Epistemic dependency was both intolerable and increasingly unreliable, and his central interest in the growth of science demanded foundations more secure than the scepticism of Montaigne would allow. His response to doubt was very much Othello's: "Think'st thou I'ld make a life of jealousy? / To follow still the changes of the moon / With fresh suspicions? No, to be once in doubt / Is once to be resolv'd."[47]

Othello goes on to express the (increasingly desperate) hope that Desdemona will survive the tests he is putting her to, as though he could reconstruct the world of their love from a position outside of it, secure in the knowledge that it was

---

[43]Ibid., p. 247. Hawkes also sees Iago as the active incarnation of scientific reason, with Othello torn between him and Desdemona.

[44]For a related discussion of Othello's need to believe in Desdemona's infidelity, see Shirley Nelson Garner, "Male Bonding and the Myth of Women's Deception in Shakespeare's Plays," in Norman N. Holland and Sidney Homan, eds., *Shakespeare's Personality* (Berkeley: California University Press, 1989). Garner draws attention to the role such a belief plays in the maintenance of connections between men. Her argument has interesting implications about the nature and role of the (male) scientific community in the acquisition and validation of knowledge.

[45]René Descartes, *Discourse on the Method*, in Elizabeth S. Haldane and G. R. T. Ross, eds., *The Philosophical Works of Descartes*, vol. I (Cambridge: Cambridge University Press, 1977); quotations, p. 84.

[46]The psychological process of decathecting the world and "recreating" it under the control of the narcissistically aggrandized ego is at the heart of Freud's account of paranoia. See "Psycho-Analytic Notes upon an Autobiographical Account of a Case of Paranoia," *Standard Edition* 12 (London: Hogarth Press, 1958): 9–82.

[47]*Othello* III. iii. 178–81.

really, "objectively," all that, while wrapped up in it, he had taken it to be. Descartes displays greater confidence, and the apparently comedic resolution to the *Meditations* presents the solemnized Baconian "chaste marriage" of the knowing mind with nature already pregnant with scientific possibility.[48]

Descartes's confident relation to the world is grounded in his confidence about God as his true and nondeceiving parent. Othello is, by contrast, radically unparented, a foreigner who is accepted and admired as a soldier but who is barred by racism from real connection to the world he moves in—except for the miracle of Desdemona's love. Descartes establishes the relationships the other way around: his untouchably certain existence as God's creature (his letters patent of noble lineage) licenses his establishing a relationship with nature in which his own identity and status are not at risk.

The shift that Descartes effects is a radical revisioning of what it is to be parented, one that replaces maternity with paternity as the relationship from which the self derives its identity. To be mothered is to find oneself helplessly in a situation over which one can initially exercise no conscious, rational control; one's mother and one's relationship to her are *given*, and the relationship grows and changes as one's self does. One's ability to affect consciously the nature of the bond grows along with one's emerging sense of self, rather than proceeding from that self.

Paternity, on the other hand, is notoriously uncertain. 'Being fathered' refers most usually not to the sort of ongoing, evolving, interactive process that being mothered is, but to a discrete causal event whose particulars are shrouded in mystery and are the subject of speculation and attempts at scientific proof. To place oneself in the world as one's father's son is to claim a lineage, a heritage, a name. As Freud put it, the "turning from the mother to the father [the triumph of patriarchy over matriarchy] points . . . to a victory of intellectuality over sensuality—that is, an advance in civilization, since maternity is proved by the evidence of the senses while paternity is an hypothesis, based on an inference and a promise. Taking sides in this way with a thought-process in preference to a sense perception has proved to be a momentous step."[49]

Connected with the transformed meaning of parentage is the transformed meaning of nature and the natural. Descartes rejects nature as a seductive and misleading teacher, whose lessons can be genuinely profited from only when they are brought under the epistemic quality control of the individual knower. Strictly

---

[48]For a discussion of the complicated sexual imagery in Bacon, see Evelyn Fox Keller, *Reflections on Gender and Science* (New Haven, Conn.: Yale University Press, 1985), esp. "Baconian Science: The Arts of Mastery and Obedience," pp. 33–42.

[49]Sigmund Freud, *Moses and Monotheism* (London: Hogarth Press, 1949), pp. 23, 114. Quoted in Peggy Kamuf, "Writing like a Woman," Sally McConnell-Ginet, Ruth Borker, and Nelly Furman, eds., *Women and Language in Literature and Society* (New York: Praeger, 1980), p. 289. The insertion and elision are Kamuf's.

regulated laboratory science must replace common sense as the route to nature's secrets: we cannot trust what she chooses to show us but must force her to reveal herself to us. "Natural light," on the other hand, illuminates that which cannot be doubted: "I possess no other faculty whereby to distinguish truth from falsehood, which can teach me that what this light shows me to be true is not really true. . . . But as far as natural impulses are concerned . . . when I had to make active choice between virtue and vice . . . they have often enough led me to the part that was worse. . . . "[50]

The activity of self-induced doubt is used to split the self and its impulses into parts that are and that are not to be trusted, to be identified with. The self as mothered—desiring, sensual, embodied, interactive, continuously influenced, and dependent—must yield to the self as fathered—autonomous, related statically to the law, in a position to judge, armed, and vigilant.

Nature in *Othello* undergoes a similar transformation: it "appears to have changed sides. Love's ally is now love's enemy, partly because the angle of vision has changed: nature as instinctual rightness [at odds with reason, as in the comedies] gives way to nature as abstract concept, susceptible like all concepts to distortion and misapplication." Snyder's discussion focuses on the shift from the "particular" to the "general" sense of nature, from an appeal to "particular and personal . . . individual essence" to "common experience and prejudice" and "observed law(s) of nature."[51]

I want to draw the distinction slightly differently: between aspects of nature that emerge out of experience, whether they be someone's true desire, motivation, or character or the comedic force of nature that runs counter to all rational, judicious attempts to dam it up, and nature as the object of scientific—or pseudo-scientific—generalization. In this latter sense, the concept of nature needn't be "distorted" or "misapplied" (by its *own* lights, anyway) radically to disorder a world of interdependency, trust, vulnerability, and epistemic reciprocity. Disordering that world is exactly what it's been invented to do, by being that from which the knowing self must be alienated and over which that self must learn to exercise control.

Othello and the *Meditations*, in passages that have posed enduring exegetical and critical difficulties, record the attempts of each of their protagonists to exercise this control over a representative "natural" object: Desdemona's handkerchief and Descartes's ball of wax. The natural world Othello is fleeing is the comedic one; hence, the associations of female, sexual magic with the handkerchief and its origins.[52] The handkerchief becomes a "free-floating

[50]Meditation III, in Haldane and Ross, vol. 1, pp. 160ff.

[51]Snyder, *The Comic Matrix*; all quotations in this paragraph are from p. 77.

[52]*Othello* III. iv. 53–73. I am most persuaded by the account of the handkerchief in Neely, *Broken Nuptials*, pp. 128–31. See also her critical discussion of alternative readings, pp. 237f, n.33.

signifier":[53] various characters attempt to fix and control its meaning—as love token, talisman, or hard evidence of adultery.

Initially the handkerchief symbolizes for Othello Desdemona's power over him, passed on to her by his mother, who got it from a sibyl. Losing it, he says, she would lose that power and face ". . . such perdition / As nothing else could match."[54] She does, of course, lose it, in part because for her its sentimental value is overshadowed by what she hopes will be its usefulness in soothing Othello's headache: when he brusquely rejects it, and her attempts to comfort him, she lets it fall.

The juxtaposition here of Othello's romantic attitude with Desdemona's more quotidian view of love mirrors the interchange between them when, upon landing in Cyprus, Othello tells her, "If it were now to die, / 'Twere now to be most happy; for I fear / My soul hath her content so absolute / That not another comfort like to this / Succeeds in unknown fate," and she replies, "The heavens forbid / But that our loves and comforts should increase / Even as our days do grow."[55]

Appropriately, at the end of the play, when the handkerchief has fallen entirely into the world of ocular proofs and pieces of evidence, its origin also shifts: Othello describes it as " . . . an antique token / My father gave my mother."[56] Part of the attempt to pin the handkerchief down, to make it hold fast with sufficient evidential weight to justify a murder, is recasting its lineage as patriarchal: it came from the father.

Descartes's ball of wax is a similarly free-floating signifier. He encounters it first through his senses: "that sweetness of honey, . . . that particular whiteness, . . . that figure, . . . that sound."[57] It is pleasantly, seductively, sensual, and it is particular: it is *that* ball of wax. But, he goes on to argue, it is as such unknowable; all those qualities are subject to change: "While I speak and approach the fire what remained of the taste is exhaled, the smell evaporates, the color alters, the figure is destroyed, the size increases, it becomes liquid, it heats, scarcely can

---

[53]The term is Timothy Murray's, from an unpublished paper entitled "*Othello*, An Index and Obscure Prologue to Foul Generic Thoughts," cited in Neely, *Broken Nuptials*, p. 234, n.21, and p. 238, n.33. Neely argues against Murray that, although characters do struggle over the symbolism of the handkerchief, it "like Desdemona, has an essence which is independent of the fantasies surrounding it" (p. 238, n.33). The argument comes down to a tension at the heart of feminist theory: are *women* "free-floating signifiers" or do we "have an essence which is independent of the fantasies surrounding us"? It's not a tension I think we can—or should try to—resolve: we need both to explore the terrifying extent to which we have been reduced to men's dreams and theories of us *and* to hold on to our deeply felt, though perhaps unaccountable, untheorizable conviction that we are something other than those dreams and theories.

[54]*Othello* III. iv. 67–68.

[55]*Othello* II. i. 189–95. See Neely, *Broken Nuptials*, p. 116.

[56]*Othello* V. ii. 217–18.

[57]Meditation II, p. 154. Subsequent quotations from pp. 154–56.

one handle it, and when one strikes it, no sound is emitted . . . yet the same wax remains." Seduced immersion in the sensuous particularities of the wax is epistemically dangerous.

Descartes needs to step back, "abstracting from all that does not belong to the wax . . . [to] see what remains." The first step is from sensory engagement with the piece of wax to the imagination of its possible changes of state. Imagination, however, encompasses only finitely many such changes, while the wax can maintain its identity through a literal infinity of changes. "We must then grant that I could not even understand through the imagination what this piece of wax is, and that it is my mind alone which perceives it. . . . Its perception is neither an act of vision, nor of imagination, and has never been such although it may have appeared formerly to be so."

Othello's "knowledge" of Desdemona went through a similar process: from immediate, engaged perception of her particularity, through Iago-prompted pornographic imagining of her possible changes, to subsuming her under supposed general laws of female sexual behavior. Epistemically, the loss was a double one: of Othello's concrete engagement with her as a ground of his knowledge and of Desdemona's particularity. In practice, of course, the principal loss was of Desdemona's life.

Descartes claims to have achieved "a more evident and perfect conception of what the wax was." He claims for his new conception greater "distinctness," though not, of course, of *this* piece of wax as compared to all others: "nothing remains excepting a certain extended thing which is flexible and movable." But that is precisely to say that it has no particular size or shape nor, he argues, any particular smell, taste, color, or sound. There remains nothing in his final, trustworthy conception of the ball of wax to distinguish it from any other piece of wax or, for that matter, from any other relatively plastic physical object. Its identity consists essentially in its being subject to the laws of geometry and physics. Descartes describes how he has reached this point with the wax: "I distinguish the wax from its external forms, and . . . just as if I had taken from it its vestment, I consider it quite naked. . . . "

Although vision is for Descartes as fundamentally unreliable as any other sense, the *metaphor* of vision is central to the epistemology of modern science. As Evelyn Fox Keller and Christine Grontkowski argue,[58] vision played a central role in Greek epistemology as well, but with a difference. For the Greeks vision was an activity, analogous to illumination; it partook of the divine and was for Plato quite literally the philosopher's mode of apprehension of the Forms. For

[58]Evelyn Fox Keller and Christine R. Grontkowski, "The Mind's Eye," in Sandra Harding and Merrill B. Hintikka, eds., *Discovering Reality: Feminist Perspectives on Epistemology, Metaphysics, Methodology, and Philosophy of Science* (Dordrecht: Reidel, 1983), pp. 207–24.

Descartes and his contemporaries, as for us, vision has been taken to be a relatively passive affair, involving the action of light on receptors in the eye. As such it is an unreliable ground for knowledge for an agent whose epistemic authority rests on his [*sic*] autonomous agency and his control over what he knows.

Vision does, however, as Keller and Grontkowski go on to show, provide an excellent *metaphor* for knowledge so conceived.[59] One sees best at some distance from the object, one can see without being seen and without affecting or being (otherwise) affected by the object, and seeing is spatial rather than temporal: one can take in "all at once" an array of objects, some changing and some static. Furthermore, one can, if one chooses, fix the object in one's gaze; as one cannot, for example, dominate someone by one's intensely focused *listening*.[60]

On Keller and Grontkowski's account, Descartes "enabled us to retain *both* the conception of knowledge as active and the use of the visual metaphor by severing the connection between the 'seeing' of the intellect and physical seeing—by severing, finally, the mind from the body."[61] Thus, the "natural light of reason" and the "inborn light" reveal truths to us wholly independently of our senses, and by them we see with otherwise unattainable clarity—in our mind's (incorporeal) eye.[62]

Robert B. Heilman explores in detail the role of a "vocabulary of seeing" in

---

[59]Keller and Grontkowski's account of the phenomenology of vision as a ground for its epistemological pre-eminence is drawn from Hans Jonas, "The Nobility of Sight," *Philosophy and Phenomenological Research* 14 (1954), esp. pp. 507, 513–18.

[60]Note the centrality of the gaze to Sartre's characterization of the fundamental impulse toward the other as sadistically objectifying. *Being and Nothingness,* trans. Hazel E. Barnes (New York: Washington Square Press, 1966), pp. 441–504.

[61]Keller and Grontowski, "The Mind's Eye," p. 215.

[62]Vision itself reappears in Descartes's epistemology. Once knowledge is secured on a footing independent of the senses, properly controlled observation, vigilantly policed, is admitted as a necessary source of knowledge about the world, and vision is pre-eminently the observing sense. Descartes's extensive work in visual optics testifies to his concern to establish the conditions under which visual evidence is admissible testimony, ranking just below—and, of course, answerable to—sensorily unaided reason as a guide to the truth. Object-relations psychoanalytic theorists (such as Winnicott and Mahler) and Lacan, followed by feminist theorists influenced by them, have begun the development of an alternative epistemology that, as Keller and Grontkowski recommend, eroticizes vision (while perhaps also sharing the central metaphorical role with other senses). See, for example, Caroline Whitbeck, "A Different Reality: Feminist Ontology," in Carol Gould, ed., *Beyond Domination: New Perspectives on Women and Philosophy* (Totowa, N.J.: Rowman and Allanheld, 1983), and "Love, Knowledge and Transformation," *Hypatia* 2 (1984): 393–405. For a different but related approach to an erotics of vision, see Marilyn Frye, *The Politics of Reality: Essays in Feminist Theory* (Trumansburg, N.Y.: The Crossing Press, 1983), esp. "In and Out of Harm's Way: Arrogance and Love," and "To Be and Be Seen: The Politics of Reality."

Iago's manipulation of Othello's relation to Desdemona.[63] What Othello comes to believe he needs is the distanced, unaffected, objective view of Desdemona achieved by covert observation and conclusive pieces of evidence. Heilman contrasts with this stance Desdemona's practice of "a doctrine of sight more profound and veracious than Othello's system of ocular proof . . . [which] rests firmly on the imaginative perception of quality that may deny or transcend the visual evidence."[64]

A similar contrast is drawn by Keller and Grontkowski. They argue that neither literal nor metaphorical vision need carry implications of disembodiment and domination. Going back to Plato, they find another aspect of sight, namely that of communion, found in Plato's ideal relation to the Forms as well as in the common experience of "locking eyes." Fundamental to both is the eroticism of vision—the aspect most notably exorcized from its rational and scientific employment.[65]

The contrast between Iagoan and Desdemonean visual epistemology thus does not mirror that between natural (sensory) vision and the natural light of reason in Descartes, as a purely empiricist reading of Iago and his reliance on visual evidence might lead one to believe. Iago's stance is one essentially shared by empiricists and rationalists alike. Descartes distrusts the senses, and Iago gets Othello to (mis)place his faith in what they (can be made to) show, but what the two have in common is the adoption of a fundamentally paranoid alienation from a form of belief experienced as dangerously seductive in favor of a detached and controlling objectivity.

I want to argue, finally, that nature in the *Meditations* (and in the theory and practice of modern science) is, like Desdemona, murdered on the altar of this paranoid epistemology. Winifred Nowottny's account of Desdemona's murder as an execution, the final triumph of justice over love,[66] is helpfully supplemented by Madelon Sprengnether's argument that Othello fears Desdemona's power (which consists in his vulnerability to her) and feels humiliated by what he takes to be her betrayal of him: " . . . it is the fear or pain of victimization on the part of the man that leads to his victimization of women. It is those who perceive themselves to be powerless who may be incited to the acts of greatest violence."[67]

That is, Othello embraces Iago's view of Desdemona for refuge against the fear induced by his vulnerability to her, by his need for her to be an autonomous,

---

[63]Robert B. Heilman, *Magic in the Web: Action and Language in Othello* (Lexington: University of Kentucky Press, 1956), pp. 58–64.

[64]Ibid., p. 62.

[65]Another closely connected aspect of vision is the much-discussed mirroring phase of infant development, in which the reciprocal gaze of mother and child becomes the field in which the infant's sense of self initially takes root.

[66]Nowottny, "Justice and Love," esp. p. 343.

[67]Gohlke, " 'I wooed thee with my sword'," p. 156.

desiring other (loving him, showing him pure in her eyes) and his terror at his identity's being thus "garner'd up" in another. Embracing Iago's view has the result of bringing him to believe what he (thought) he most feared—that Desdemona was unfaithful to him; but, as awful as that belief was for him, it warded off one more awful yet: that Desdemona was not a "whore," that the world she wove by loving him was *real*, far more real than the one Iago offered, though (because) not in his control.

IV

Francis Barker writes about the "metaphysics of death" at the heart of the discourse of modernity: his primary texts are Pepys's diary, *Hamlet*, Rembrandt's *Anatomy Lesson*, Marvell's "To His Coy Mistress," and Descartes's *Meditations* and *Discourse on Method*.[68] He remarks on the startling return of the body in Descartes's texts, but notes that it is a different body from the one banished in the First Meditation. The one that returns is the object of knowledge, to be anatomized, dissected, studied, scrutinized, and controlled—by the knowing subject, who knows himself quite apart from it. There are, however, two problems with this body: it is dead (or machine-like; anyway, its soul has fled), and it's on the other side of an epistemic divide—to which it has been banished in the name of epistemological hygiene, and where it is kept by a continuing paranoia. Consequently, knowledge of it is always uncertain. Discourse

> departs from itself in order to have something corporeal to represent—for in a positivist universe, without an object of knowledge there is strictly nothing to say—but in so far as it is constrained to operate this structure of separation it must set at a permanent distance the signs which are to be interpreted if meaning is to inhere. It founds itself on a gulf which is to a degree unbridgeable, and necessarily so for this discourse to function meaningfully at all.[69]

One of the distinctive marks of modernity is the importance of the individual, including individual sentiment in relation to marriage and individual certainty in relation to knowledge. We needn't be wishing our way back to an earlier time to note the costs of individualism, particularly those associated with gender: until quite recently—and in many, conceptual and practical ways, still—individuals are male, and maleness has had at its definitional heart a paranoid flight from femininity and a need for administrative structures to control and contain it, and, of course, us. The failure of those structures, or the fear, however ill-founded,

---

[68]Francis Barker, *The Tremulous Private Body* (London: Methuen, 1984), esp. pp. 95–112.

[69]Ibid., p. 105.

that they might fail, has characteristically precipitated violence against women and against those aspects of men and of the world—most notably nature (herself) —that are associated with us.

Shakespearean problem comedy and Montaignean scepticism represent one response to the failure of the magically or religiously guaranteed conjunction of sexuality with marriage and certainty with knowledge. It's a response in which one's individual (male) agency is limited—in exchange for an acceptance of one's nature, which is precisely to be thus limited. Nothing will ever again be quite as it was, but high-spirited, intelligent virgin mother/wives will make it—almost—all right.

This response did not prevail. Rather, there has been an attempt—*per impossibile*—to *force* the comedic ending, to bring about Bacon's "chaste and lawful marriage" of the knower with the known through the adoption of a distanced and controlling posture toward the world. The hope is for a sadistic encounter (chaste and lawful though it may be) in which nature is stripped bare and forced to reveal herself. Sadism's border with necrophilia is not, however, well marked: particularly when nature—or women—are desired *as* maternally powerful, they are likely to arouse murderous feelings of infantile impotence in those who in fact dominate them. Consequently, the prospects for this union are not good: though we are meant not to notice, the heroine was killed in the first act.[70]

---

[70]I am enormously indebted to the several feminist communities in which I have thought about the issues in this essay—notably, the Women's Studies Program and the Center for Advanced Feminist Studies at the University of Minnesota and the Midwestern and Eastern chapters of the Society for Women in Philosophy. Conversations with Michael Root have improved both my ideas and my writing style, though he would still quarrel with both.

6

Though This Be Method, Yet There Is Madness in It: Paranoia and Liberal Epistemology

> When you do not see plurality in the very structure of a theory, what do you see?
>
> —María Lugones, "On the Logic of Pluralist Feminism"

> Somewhere every culture has an imaginary zone for what it excludes, and it is that zone we must try to remember today.
>
> —Catherine Clément, *The Newly Born Woman*

In an article entitled "The Politics of Epistemology," Morton White argues that it is not in general possible to ascribe a unique political character to a theory of knowledge.[1] In particular, he explores what he takes to be the irony that the epistemologies developed by John Locke and John Stuart Mill for explicitly progressive and democratic ends have loopholes that allow for undemocratic interpretation and application. The loopholes White identifies concern in each case the methods by which authority is granted or recognized.

Neither Locke nor Mill acknowledges any higher epistemic authority than human reason, which they take (however differently they define it) as generic to the human species and not the possession of some favored few. But for both of them, as for most other democratically minded philosophers (White discusses also John Dewey and Charles Sanders Peirce), there needs to be some way of distinguishing between the exercise of reason and the workings of something else, variously characterized as degeneracy, madness, immaturity, backwardness, ignorance, passion, prejudice, or some other state of mind that permanently or temporarily impairs the development or proper use of reason. That is, democracy is seen as needing to be defended against "the excesses of unbridled relativism and subjectivism" (White, "Politics," p. 90).

The success of such a defense depends on the assumption that if we eliminate the voices of those lacking in the proper use of reason, we will be eliminating (or at least substantially "bridling") relativism. This, I take it, can only mean that those whose voices are listened to will (substantially) agree, at least about those things that are thought to be matters of knowledge, whether they be scientific or commonsense statements of fact, fundamental moral and political principles, or specific judgments of right or wrong. To some extent this assumption is tautological: it is frequently by "disagreeing" about things the

[1]Morton White, "The Politics of Epistemology," *Ethics* 100 (October 1989): 77–92.

rest of us take for granted that one is counted as mad, ignorant, or otherwise not possessed of reason. But precisely that tautologousness is at the root of what White identifies as the loophole through which the anti-democratic can pass. Moral, political, and epistemological elitism is most attractive (to the elite) and most objectionable (to others) when the non-elite would say something different from what gets said on their behalf, allegedly in the name of their own more enlightened selves.

White argues that the democratic nature of an epistemology cannot be read off its face but is in part a matter of its historically specific application: "Whether such a philosophy will be democratic in its effect depends on the ease with which the ordinary man may attain the privileged status described in the epistemology of the democratically oriented thinker. Where, because of social conditions, large numbers of persons in the community are not thought by such a philosopher to be able to see what their moral duties and rights are because they lack the attributes of a fully equipped moral judge, then the democratic intentions stand a good chance of being subverted" (White, "Politics," pp. 91–92). It's unclear to me why White thinks that the anti-democratic subversion of an intentionally democratic epistemology depends specifically on the philosophers' beliefs about who can exemplify their theories. Surely, such subversion depends at least as much on the ways in which that theory is understood and applied by others and on the beliefs of those others about who does and does not satisfy the philosopher's criteria of enfranchisement. Such beliefs may even, as I will argue is the case with René Descartes, contradict the philosopher's own explicit statements. Authorial intent is not determinative of how democratic an epistemology is: having constructed a loophole, theorists do not retain the authority to determine what can pass through it.

White's own unselfconscious use of 'man' in what I assume he intends to be a generic sense is, ironically, a case in point. As has been argued by many feminist theorists[2] masculine nouns and pronouns do not, in fact, have genuinely generic senses. Rather, in designating the masculine *as* generic, they designate the feminine as different, thereby requiring an act of self-estrangement on the part of female readers who would take themselves to be included in their scope. And all too often (frequently despite the stated beliefs of philosophers themselves), women have *not* been included among the rational, the mature, the unprejudiced. Historically, more often than not, in the real worlds in which philosophers' theories have been interpreted, the vast majority of women—along with many men—have been barred from or thought incapable of attaining "the privileged status described in the epistemology (or the moral philosophy) of the democratically oriented thinker[s]."

---

[2]For one of the earliest and most thorough of such arguments, see Janice Moulton, "The Myth of the Neutral 'Man'," in *Feminism and Philosophy*, ed. Mary Vetterling-Braggin, Frederick Elliston, and Jane English (Totowa, N.J.: Littlefield, Adams & Co., 1977).

A striking feature of the advance of liberal political and epistemological theory and practice over the past three hundred years has been the increase in the ranks of the politically and epistemically enfranchised. It would seem that the loopholes have been successively narrowed, that fewer and fewer are being relegated to the hinterlands of incompetence or unreliability. In one sense, of course, this is true: race, sex, and property ownership are no longer explicit requirements for voting, office holding, or access to education in most countries. But just as exclusionary gestures can operate to separate off groups of people, so similar gestures can operate intrapsychically to separate those aspects of people that, if acknowledged, would disqualify them from full enfranchisement. We can understand the advance of liberalism as the progressive internalization—through regimes of socialization and pedagogy—of norms of self-constitution that (oxymoronically) "democratize privilege."

Thus various civil rights agendas in the United States have proceeded by promulgating the idea that underneath the superficial differences of skin color, genitalia, or behavior in the bedroom, Blacks, women, and gays and lesbians are really just like straight white men. Not, of course, the other way around: difference and similarity are only apparently symmetrical terms. In the logic of political identity, to be among the privileged is to be among the same, and for the different to join those ranks has demanded the willingness to separate the difference-bearing aspects of their identity, to demonstrate what increasingly liberal regimes were increasingly willing to acknowledge: that one didn't need, for example, to be a man to embrace the deep structure of misogyny. It is one of my aims to argue that the norms that have structured modern epistemic authority have required the internalization of such exclusionary gestures, the splitting off and denial of (or control over) aspects of the self that have been associated with the lives of the disenfranchised, and that those gestures exhibit the logic of paranoia.

This process of "democratizing privilege" is inherently unstable. Materially, it runs up against the requirement of capitalism for significant numbers of people who are outside the reasonably affluent, paid labor force: the vast majority of people in the Third World, as well as those in affluent countries who are unemployed or marginally employed or who work only in the home—that is, those whose bodies literally are the foundation on which privileged subjectivity rests. As more and more of those others lay claim to stand on the ground their bodies have constituted, that ground gets predictably unstable.[3] Ideologically, expanding the ranks of the same runs up against the rise of the wide varieties of nationalisms and identity politics that have followed on the recognition by large numbers of people that they have all been attempting to impersonate a small minority of the

---

[3]I have argued for this dependence in "Your Ground Is My Body: Stratagien des Anti-Fundamentalismus."

world's population, and that it might instead be both desirable and possible to claim enfranchisement as the particular peoples they happen to be. Recent work in epistemology and philosophy of science, much of it explicitly influenced by Ludwig Wittgenstein or W. V. Quine (neither of whom would embrace either the explanations or the political agenda at issue here), can be seen as responsive to the need, given these challenges, for an epistemology that breaks with the structures of modernity by eschewing the homogenization of foundationalism and allowing for the democratic enfranchisement of explicitly and irreducibly diverse subjects. Knowledge rests not on universally recognizable and unassailable premises but on the social labor of historically embodied communities of knowers.

Part of my aim is to provide an account of what I think underlies this shift in mainstream Anglo-American epistemology and philosophy of science, to place that shift in social and historical context. But I am also concerned with the extent to which much current work is still captive to older pictures, notably in the continuing dominance of individualism in the philosophy of psychology. A fully social conception of knowledge that embraces diversity among knowers requires a corresponding conception of persons as irreducibly diverse and essentially interconnected. The individualism of modern personhood entails a denial both of connection and of individuality: modern subjects are distinct but not distinctive. Philosophers have taken this subject as theirs: it is his (*sic*) problems that have defined the field, the problems of anyone who takes on the tasks of internalizing the norms of privilege. As these norms change, so must the corresponding conceptions of personhood.

It is in this light that I want to examine the influence of Descartes's writings, works of intentionally democratic epistemology that explicitly include women in the scope of those they enfranchise. I have argued elsewhere, as have many others,[4] for the undemocratic nature of the influence of Cartesian epistemology, an influence that extends even to those epistemologies standardly treated as most antithetical to it (notably, empiricism). In particular, I want to argue that the structures of characteristically modern epistemic authority (with science as the central paradigm) normalized strategies of self-constitution drawn from Cartesian method. The discipline that is meant to ensure that proper use of the method will not lead to "unbridled relativism and subjectivism," although intended by Descartes to be both liberatory and democratic, has come to mirror the repressions that mark the achievement of privilege. Those strategies find, I believe, a peculiarly revelatory echo in the autobiographical writings of Daniel Paul Schreber

[4]See Genevieve Lloyd, *The Man of Reason* (Minneapolis: University of Minnesota Press, 1984); Susan Bordo, *The Flight to Objectivity: Essays on Cartesianism and Culture* (Albany: SUNY Press, 1987); my "Othello's Doubt/Desdemona's Death: The Engendering of Scepticism"; and Jacquelyn Zita, "Transsexualized Origins: Reflections on Descartes's *Meditations*," *Genders* 5 (Summer 1989): 86–105.

and in their use in Freud's theory of paranoia.[5] Ironically, by the very moves that were meant to ensure universal enfranchisement, the epistemology that has grounded modern science and liberal politics not only has provided the means for excluding, for most of its history, most of the human race but has constructed, for those it authorizes, a normative paranoia.

I. Schreber

> The pedagogical conviction that one must bring a child into line . . . has its origin in the need to split off the disquieting parts of the inner self and project them onto an available object. . . . The enemy within can at last be hunted down on the outside.[6]

> [Anti-Semites] are people who are afraid. Not of the Jews, to be sure, but of themselves, of their own consciousness, of their instincts, of their responsibilities, of solitariness, of change, of society, and of the world —of everything except the Jews. . . . Anti-Semitism, in short, is fear of the human condition. The Anti-Semite is a person who wishes to be a pitiless stone, a furious torrent, a devastating thunderbolt—anything except a human being.[7]

Daniel Paul Schreber, a German judge, was thrice hospitalized for mental illness. After a brief confinement in a Leipzig clinic in 1884–1885, he recovered sufficiently to serve as *Senatspräsident* (head of a panel of judges) in Dresden. He was re-hospitalized from 1893 until 1903, when he left the asylum after succeeding in a legal suit for his release from "tutelage" (that is, involuntary state guardianship). He returned to the asylum in 1907 and remained there until his death in 1911, the same year Freud published the case history based on the *Memoirs of My Nervous Illness*, which Schreber published in 1903 to draw attention to what he took to be happening to him.

Subsequent discussions of Schreber's case and of the *Memoirs* have taken issue with Freud's account. Sam Weber, in his introduction to recent re-publications (in German and English) of the *Memoirs*, gives a Lacanian reading of the text, and

---

[5]Daniel Paul Schreber, *Memoirs of My Nervous Illness*, tr. and ed. Ida Macalpine and Richard A. Hunter (Cambridge: Harvard University Press, 1988); Sigmund Freud, "Psycho-Analytic Notes upon an Autobiographical Account of a Case of Paranoia (Dementia Paranoides)," *Standard Edition* (hereafter *SE*) 12 (London: Hogarth Press, 1958): 9–82.

[6]Alice Miller, *For Your Own Good: Hidden Cruelty in Child-Rearing and the Roots of Violence*, tr. Hildegarde Hannum and Hunter Hannum (New York: Farrar, Straus, and Giroux, 1984), p. 91.

[7]Jean-Paul Sartre, *Anti-Semite and Jew*, quoted in Erica Sherover-Marcuse, *Emancipation and Consciousness: Dogmatic and Dialectical Perspectives in the Early Marx* (Oxford: Basil Blackwell, 1986), p. 158.

Morton Schatzman, in *Soul Murder: Persecution in the Family*,[8] takes Schreber's account as a transformed but intelligible description of what was done to him as a child by his father, Daniel Gottlieb Moritz Schreber. The elder Schreber was a renowned doctor whose theories of child rearing were exceedingly influential in the development of some of the more extreme forms of what Alice Miller describes as "poisonous pedagogy,"[9] by which she means the accepted, even normative, use of coercion and violence against children supposedly "for their own good." I find helpful correctives to Freud both in Weber's Lacanian remarks and, especially, in Schatzman's anti-psychoanalytic analysis,[10] (to which I will return); but I want to start with Freud's account, in part because its logical structure mirrors that of the *Meditations* and the *Discourse on Method.*

Freud suggests that central to symptom formation in paranoia is the process of projection, but that this process can't be definitive of paranoia, in part because it appears elsewhere—for example, "when we refer the causes of certain sensations to the external world, instead of looking for them (as we do in the case of others) inside ourselves" (Freud, *SE*, 12, p. 66). He expresses the intention of returning to a general theory of (nonpathological as well as pathological) projection, but he never does. I want to suggest that the account he does give—of projection as a mechanism of paranoia—is closer to such a general theory than he thought it to be, because the relationship to the external world that was epistemically normative in his time and in ours is, by that account, paranoid.

Paranoia, for Freud, starts with the repression of a homosexual wishful fantasy —that is, for a man, sexual desire for another man.[11] In paranoia, as in all cases of repression more generally, there is a detachment of libido: what is previously cathected becomes "indifferent and irrelevant" (Freud, *SE*, 12, p. 70). In paranoia this decathexis spreads from its original object to the external world as a whole, and the detached libido attaches itself to the ego, resulting in megalomania.[12] It is the

[8]Morton Schatzman, *Soul Murder: Persecution in the Family* (New York: Random House, 1973).

[9]Miller, *For Your Own Good.*

[10]It is anti-psychoanalytic in the manner of Jeffrey Moussaieff Masson's later but better known work, *The Assault on Truth: Freud's Suppression of the Seduction Theory* (New York: Farrar, Straus and Giroux, 1984), i.e., in reading patients' reports and symptoms as expressions not of fantasies but of what was actually done to them as children.

[11]Freud's account is almost entirely in masculine terms, but here, as elsewhere, he took his analysis to apply also to women, *mutatis mutandis*. As I will go on to argue, the phenomena he describes are, in fact, wholly gender inflected and are grounded in distinctively masculine experiences.

[12]Freud gives two reasons for the attachment of the libido to the ego: that, detached from the entire external world, it has nowhere else to go (*SE*, 12, p. 65), and that narcissism is the stage at which paranoids are characteristically fixated, hence the stage to which they regress (*SE*, 12, p. 72). This latter view is connected to Freud's notorious association of homosexuality with narcissism, a stage intermediate between auto-eroticism and object-love (*SE*, 12, pp. 60–61).

subsequently megalomaniacally re-created world that is permanently hostile to the paranoid: "The human subject has recaptured a relation, and often a very intense one, to the people and things in the world, even though the relation is a hostile one now, where formerly it was hopefully affectionate" (Freud, *SE*, 12, p. 71).

The hostility of the re-created world is a function of the mechanism of projection. The repression of the fantasy of loving a man takes the form of its contradiction: "I *hate* him," which is transformed by projection into "*he* hates—and persecutes—*me,* which justifies my hating him." Freud says only that the "mechanism of symptom-formation in paranoia requires that internal perceptions—feelings—shall be replaced by external perceptions" (Freud, *SE*, 12, p. 63). Presumably an account of just why such replacement should be required was to await the never-delivered general account of projection, but the mechanism isn't very mysterious. Placing all the initiating feeling out there, on what had been its object, is a far more effective way of shielding the ego from the acknowledgement of its own forbidden desires than would be a simple transformation of love into (inexplicable) hate.

The hostile forces in Schreber's world—God and his "rays"—are unequivocally male, and he believes that part of their plan is to transform him into a woman. The meaning of the transformation is twofold. Men, according to Schreber, have "nerves of voluptuousness" only in and immediately around their penises, whereas women's entire bodies are suffused with such nerves (Schreber, *Memoirs*, p. 204). God is directing toward Schreber, who has captured all of God's attention, rays that stimulate these nerves, requiring Schreber to "strive to give divine rays the impression of a woman in the height of sexual delight," by imagining himself "as man and woman in one person having intercourse with myself," an activity that Schreber insists, obviously protesting too much, "has nothing whatever to do with any idea of masturbation or anything like it" (Schreber, *Memoirs*, p. 208). The rays also impose demands, in the form of compulsive thinking, on Schreber's "nerves of intellect," and he is forced to strike a balance between intellectual thought and sensual ecstasy. But, most important, he must attempt always to be engaged in one or the other:

> As soon as I allow a pause in my thinking without devoting myself to the cultivation of voluptuousness—which is unavoidable as nobody can either think all the time or always cultivate voluptuousness—the following unpleasant consequences . . . occur: attacks of bellowing and bodily pain; vulgar noises from the madmen around me, and cries of "help" from God. Mere common sense therefore commands that as far as humanly possible I fill every pause in my thinking—in other words the periods of rest from intellectual activity—with the cultivation of voluptuousness" (Schreber, *Memoirs*, pp. 210–11).

In addition to being provided with soul-voluptuousness, God's other aim in "unmanning" him was eventual "fertilization with divine rays for the purpose of creating new human beings." Schreber was cognizant of the humiliating aspects of his position. The rays themselves taunted him, saying such things as, "Fancy a person who was a *Senatspräsident* allowing himself to be f . . . d [*sic*]." He initially entered into complicity with his transformation into a woman at a time when he believed that he was the only real person existing: "all the human shapes I saw were only 'fleeting and improvised,' so that there could be no question of any ignominy being attached to unmanning" (Schreber, *Memoirs*, p. 148). He subsequently defends the essential honor of his position as an accommodation with necessity and with God's will: "Since then I have wholeheartedly inscribed the cultivation of femininity on my banner. . . . I would like to meet the man who, faced with the choice of either becoming a demented human being in male habitus or a spirited woman, would not prefer the latter" (Schreber, *Memoirs*, p. 149).

The logic of Schreber's madness seems to me not that of homosexuality, repressed or otherwise. His delusions mirrored his treatment as a boy at the hands of his father, and his madness indicts that treatment even while preserving the idealization of the powerful father who administered it. What that combination of terror and enthralled submission in the face of remembered or imagined male power does reflect is the logic of male homophobia. 'Homophobia' is often used as though it meant the same thing for women as for men, but, given the very different social constructions of female and male sexuality, there is no reason to think this should be so. In particular, male homophobia attaches with greatest force not to the general idea of sexual desire for another man, but to the specific idea of being in the receptive position sexually. Given a culturally normative definition of sexuality in terms of male domination and female subordination, there is an understandable anxiety attached to a man's imagining another man's doing to him what men are expected to do to women: real men, *Senatspräsidenten* or not, are not supposed to allow themselves to be fucked. (Thus in men's prisons, the stigma attaches not to rapists, but to their victims.)

Male homophobia combines this anxiety with its corresponding desire, that of being, as we might say, ravished,[13] or swept away. It's notoriously difficult to speak—or think—clearly about such desires or pleasures, a difficulty made apparent by the intertwinings of rape and rapture (which themselves share a common Latin root) in the *Oxford English Dictionary*'s definition of 'ravish'. The story seems to be the bad old one of the woman falling in love with the man who rapes her, a staple of pornography and Gothic romance, and barely veiled in Freudian accounts of normative femininity and in fairy tales. (Did Sleeping Beauty consent to the Prince's kiss?) Part of what is so insidious about these stories is that they link violence and domination to the pleasures of release—for example, the pleasure that sneezing can be, the sudden unwilled flood of sensation.

[13]The term 'ravished' comes from a conversation with Gary Thomas about music and sexuality: 'ravishing' seems the best word for the effect on us of certain, especially Romantic, music.

Not, that is, *against* our will, inflicted upon us and a threat to our integrity, but *un*willed, a respite from will, a momentary reprieve from the exigencies of bodily discipline, an affront not to our humanity but to our solemnity, not to our self-respect but to our self-conceit. (The unlinking of such pleasure from the sadomasochistic structure of normative sexuality—the uncoupling of rape from rapture—is a fairy tale worth believing in, even if we can't quite tell it clearly.)

Schreber enacts both the anxiety and the desire. His body and mind are wracked by the struggle to resist what he ultimately succumbs to—being "unmanned" in the name of perpetual feminine "voluptuousness." His compensation for being subjected to such humiliating pleasure is the knowledge both that God has singled him out to receive it and that from his feminized loins will issue a new race of humans to re-create the world. Homophobia thus gets joined to another venerable fantasy structure: the usurpation by men of women's reproductive power. At least as far back as Socrates, men have taken the imagery of childbirth to describe their allegedly nobler, sublimated creative activities. Schreber's fantasies expose the homophobic anxieties that underlie the use of this imagery: you can't give birth without being fucked.

II. Descartes

> They are, in essence, captives of a peculiar arrogance, the arrogance of not knowing that they do not know what it is that they do not know, yet they speak as if they know what all of us need to know.[14]

Cartesian philosophy is a paradigmatic example of White's thesis about the subversion of the democratic intent of an epistemology, although not because of Descartes's own views about whom it authorized. Descartes's explicit intent was the epistemic authorization of individuals as such—not as occupiers of particular social locations, including the social location of gender.[15] Most important, Descartes wanted to secure epistemic authority for individual knowers who would depend on their own resources and not on the imprimatur of those in high places, and, he argues, those resources could only be those of mathematized reason, not those of the senses. Only such a use of reason could ensure the sort of stability that distinguishes knowledge from mere opinion. Descartes's method was designed to allow anyone who used it to place him- or herself beyond the influence of anything that could induce error. Human beings, he argued, were not created as naturally and inevitably subject to error: God wouldn't have done that. What we are is

[14]Molefi Kete Asante, *The Afrocentric Idea* (Philadelphia: Temple University Press, 1987), p. 4.

[15]Cartesian philosophy was, in fact, influential on and in some ways empowering for contemporary feminists. See Ruth Perry, "Radical Doubt and the Liberation of Women," *Eighteenth Century Studies* 18 (1985): 472–93.

finite, hence neither omniscient nor infallible. But if we recognize our limits and shield ourselves from the influence of what we cannot control, we can be assured that what we take ourselves to know is, in fact, true.

The method is a form of discipline requiring acts of will to patrol a perimeter around our minds, allowing in only what can be determined to be trustworthy and controlling the influence of the vicissitudes of our bodies and of other people. Purged of bad influences, we will be struck by the "clarity and distinctness" of truths like the cogito.[16] We will have no real choice but to acknowledge their truth, but we ought not to find in such lack of choice any diminution of our freedom. Because the perception of truth comes from within us, not "determined by any external force," we are free in assenting to it, just as we are free when we choose what we fully and unambivalently want, even though it makes no sense to imagine that, given our desire, we might just as well have chosen otherwise.[17]

Freedom from determination by any external force requires, for Descartes, freedom from determination by the body, which is, with respect to the mind, an external force. Thus when Descartes invokes the malicious demon at the end of the First Meditation to help steel him against lazily slipping back into credulity,[18] his efforts are of a piece with his presentation at the end of *The Passions of the Soul* of "a general remedy against the passions."[19] Passions are no more to be dispensed with entirely than are perceptions (or, strictly speaking, *other* perceptions, given that passions are for Descartes a species of perception). But no more than other perceptions are passions to be taken at face value: they can be deceptive and misleading. Still less are they to be taken uncritically as motives to act, whether the action in question be running in fear from the dagger I perceive before me, or assenting to its real existence. In both cases, I (my mind) need to exercise control over my perceptions or, at least, over what I choose to do in the face of them. Seeing ought *not* to be believing in the case of literal, embodied vision, but when ideas are seen by the light of reason in the mind's eye, assent does and should follow freely.[20]

---

[16]It is a frequently remarked problem that the original argumentative role of the cogito depends on the absolute uniqueness of its claim to our credulity, yet it is then supposed to stand as a paradigm for other successful claimants.

[17]Descartes, Meditation 4, in *The Philosophical Writings of Descartes,* 2 vols., tr. John Cottingham, Robert Stoothoff, and Dugald Murdoch (Cambridge: Cambridge University Press, 1985), p. 40 (hereafter CS&M).

[18]Descartes, Meditation 1, CS&M, 2, p. 15.

[19]Descartes, *Passions of the Soul*, part 3, sec. 211, CS&M, 1, p. 123. I owe the suggestion to look again at *The Passions of the Soul* to Adam Morton, who may, however, have had something else entirely in mind.

[20]Evelyn Fox Keller and Christine R. Grontkowski provide an excellent account of the role and fate of vision in Cartesian dualism in "The Mind's Eye," in *Discovering Reality: Feminist Perspectives on Epistemology, Metaphysics, Methodology, and Philosophy of Science*, ed. Sandra Harding and Merrill B. Hintikka (Dordrecht: Reidel, 1983).

The individualism of Cartesian epistemology is yoked to its universalism. Though we are each to pursue knowledge on our own, freed from the influence of any other people, what we come up with is not supposed to be our own view of the world—it is supposed to be the truth, unique and invariable. When Descartes extols, in the *Discourse*,[21] the greater perfection of buildings or whole towns that are the work of a single planner over those that sprang up in an uncoordinated way, he may seem to be extolling the virtues of individuality. But what he finds pleasing are not the signs of individual style; it is the determining influence of reason as opposed to chance. Individualism is the route not to the idiosyncrasies of individuality but to the universality of reason.

This consequence is hardly accidental. Scepticism, which was a tool for Descartes, was for some of his contemporaries the ultimate, inevitable consequence of ceding epistemic authority to individual reason. If epistemic democratization was not to lead to the nihilism of the Pyrrhonists or the modesty of Montaigne, Descartes needed to demonstrate that what his method produced was knowledge, not a cacophony of opinion.[22] It could not turn out to be the case that the world appeared quite different when viewed by people differently placed in it. More precisely, everyone had to be persuaded that if it *did* appear different from where they stood, the remedy was to move to the Archimedean point defined by the discipline of Cartesian method. Those who could not so move were, in the manner of White's discussion, relegated to the ranks of the epistemically disenfranchised.

Descartes himself does not, so far as I know, consider the possibility that not everyone of sufficient maturity could actually use his method. The only disqualifying attribute I know that he explicitly discusses is youth.[23] He does, of course, briefly consider in the First Meditation the possibility that he is mad, or asleep and dreaming, but his aim there is to argue that it makes no difference: the cogito would still be true and knowable. Later, when he needs to go beyond those confines to areas in which sanity and a certain degree of consciousness can be presumed to make a difference, he needs, for the sake of his argument, to rely on first person accessible signs that his mind is in working order: there's no way in which the judgment of others could be allowed to undercut the agent's own sense of being epistemically trustworthy.

It is central to Descartes's project, as it is to the social and political significance of that project, that no one and nothing other than agents themselves can confer or confirm epistemic authority (despite God's being its ultimate guarantor, His guarantee consists precisely in our each individually possessing such authority). Epistemic authority resides in the exercise of will that disciplines one's acts of assent—principally to refrain from assenting to whatever is not perceived clearly

[21]Descartes, *Discourse on the Method*, part 2, CS&M, 1, pp. 116–17.

[22]On Pyrrhonist and Montaignean scepticism, see Richard Popkin, *The History of Scepticism from Erasmus to Descartes* (New York: Humanities Press, 1960).

[23]See, for example, part 2 of the *Discourse on the Method*, CS&M, 1, p. 123.

and distinctly.[24] And the will, for Descartes, is not only equally distributed among all people, but is also, in each of us, literally infinite. What is required is not the acquisition of some capacity the exercise of which might be thought to be unequally available to all; rather it is the curbing of a too-ready willingness to believe.

Of course, such restraint will lead only to the avoidance of error; in order actually to acquire knowledge, one has also clearly and distinctly to perceive ideas to which one will, freely and inevitably, assent. But even such acquisition is, for Descartes, not reserved for the few, and even it is more a matter of disciplining the interference of distracting and misleading influences from the body, and from the external world through the body, than it is a positive matter of access to recondite truths. We need to train ourselves to quiet the ceaseless chatter of inner and outer perception, to curb, for example, the wonder we feel at the appearance of what seems to us unusual and extraordinary. A certain degree of wonder is useful for retaining in memory what we might otherwise fail to register sufficiently, but wonder, if unchecked, draws our attention hither and yon, when we should be intentionally directing it along the lines of thoughtful investigation. In his discussion of wonder Descartes does distinguish among people who are "dull and stupid," or "ignorant" because "not naturally inclined to wonder," or inclined to excessive, distracting wonder because "though equipped with excellent common sense, [they] have no high opinion of their abilities."[25] But none of these differences are differences in *intellect*: in our active capacities as knowers we are all, for Descartes, absolutely equal, and by disciplining our overactive wills, we can all bring our problematic (and unequal) bodies into line.

But, as I argued above, there is no reason why philosophers' own views about who can and cannot fully exemplify their requirements of epistemic enfranchisement should carry any special weight when the question concerns the democratic or anti-democratic effect of their theories, especially as those theories have been influential far beyond those philosophers' lifetimes. Descartes is a paradigmatic case in point.

The Cartesian subject was revolutionary. The individual bearer of modern epistemic authority became, through variations on the originating theme of self-constitution, the bourgeois bearer of rights, the self-made capitalist, the citizen of the nation state, and the Protestant bound by conscience and a personal relationship to God. In Descartes's writings we find the lineaments of the construction of that new subject, and we see the centrality of discipline to its constitution. Such discipline is supposed in theory to be available to all, not only to those whose birth gave them a privileged place in the world. If one was placed where one could not see the truth, or obtain riches, or exercise political or religious

[24]See Margaret Dauler Wilson, *Descartes* (London: Routledge & Kegan Paul, 1978), pp. 17–31.

[25]Descartes, *The Passions of the Soul*, part 2, secs. 75–79, CS&M, 1, pp. 354–56.

freedom, the solution was to move to some more privileged and privileging place. The "New World" was precisely constituted by the self-defining gestures of those who moved there from Europe and who subsequently got to determine who among those who followed would be allowed to take a stand on the common ground. (That constitution of the "New World" is one reason why the people who already lived there merited so little consideration in the eyes of those who invaded their home. The relationship the Indians took—and take—themselves to have to the land, a relationship grounded in their unchosen, unquestionable ties to it , was precisely the wrong relationship from the perspective of those who came to that land in order to define themselves anew by willfully claiming it, unfettered by history.)

With the success of the revolutions prefigured in the Cartesian texts, it became clear that the theoretical universalism that was their underpinning existed in problematic tension with actual oppression. Those who succeeded in embodying the ideals of subjecthood oppressed those whose places in the world (from which, for various reasons, they could not move)[26] were (often) to perform the labor on which the existence and well-being of the enfranchised depended and (always) to represent the aspects of embodied humanness that the more privileged denied in themselves.

The 'often' and 'always' in the preceding sentence reflect differences in the form taken by the oppression of various groups and the concomitant applicability of various methods for explaining that oppression. With respect to certain groups, most clearly the working class but also many women and people of color, oppression has been in large measure a matter of exploitation. Members of privileged groups benefit directly from the labor done by the exploited, whose oppression is a function both of the theft of their labor and of the ideological representation of that labor as disenfranchising. Such labor is disenfranchising either positively, in that its nature (for example, the bearing and rearing of children) is taken to be incompatible with intellection, or negatively, in that it doesn't allow for the leisure to cultivate the "higher" capacities that authorize the enfranchised.

For other oppressed groups, notably gay men, lesbians, and the disabled, the element of exploitation is either missing or at least far less evident, and an economic analysis of why they are oppressed is less evidently promising. It is striking, however, that such groups share with the others the representation of their supposed natures as incompatible with full social, political, and epistemic

[26]The most heinous case of such oppression is slavery, and the U.S. slave trade, of course, *required* the movement of slaves from their homes. But such movement was the denial, rather than the expression, of those people's will, and it served to confirm what, in the nonliteral sense, was their place in the world, as defined by Europeans and Euro-Americans, part of which was that they had no say over where, literally, their place in the world was to be.

authority. For various reasons they are portrayed in hegemonic discourses as incapable of full participation in public life: they are put into one or more of the categories of disenfranchisement that White discusses. All the oppressed—the obviously exploited and the others—share in the minds of the privileged a defining connection to the body, whether it is seen primarily as the laboring body, the sexual body, the body insufficiently under the control of the rational will, or some combination of these. The privileged are precisely those who are defined not by the meanings and uses of their bodies for others but by their ability either to control their bodies for their own ends or to seem to exist virtually bodilessly. They are those who have conquered the sexual, dependent, mortal, and messy parts of themselves—in part by projecting all those qualities onto others, whom they thereby earn the right to dominate and, if the occasion arises, to exploit.

Exploitation and oppression are, of course, enormous and enormously complicated phenomena, and there is no reason to believe that one theory will account for all their aspects and ramifications, all their causes and effects.[27] There are also reasons for being generally suspicious of the felt need for, what are called by their critics, grand or totalizing theories or master narratives.[28] It is certainly not my intent either to give or to invoke any such theory. Rather, as Sandra Harding argues,[29] we (those who would seek to understand these phenomena with the aim of ending them) need to embrace not only methodological pluralism but even the "instabilities and incoherencies" (Harding, *Science Question*, p. 244) that come with theorizing during times of large-scale intellectual, social, and political change. In that spirit, I see this essay as part of what we might call the social psychology of privilege, an examination not of the apparently economically rational grounds for exploitation-based oppression, but of the deep springs that feed such oppression as well as the oppressions that seem on their face less rational.

Privilege, as it has historically belonged to propertied, heterosexual, able-bodied, white men, and as it has been claimed in liberal terms by those who are variously different, has rested on the successful disciplining of one's mind and its relation to one's body and to the bodies and minds of others. The discourses

---

[27]For a helpful discussion of the intertwinings of oppression and exploitation, see Marilyn Frye, "In and Out of Harm's Way: Arrogance and Love," in *Politics of Reality: Essays in Feminist Theory* (Freedom, Calif.: The Crossing Press, 1983).

[28]The literature on these disputes is vast and growing. For an introduction and overview, see Sandra Harding, *The Science Question in Feminism* (Ithaca, N.Y.: Cornell University Press, 1986), pp. 163–96; and Linda Nicholson, ed., *Feminism/Postmodernism* (New York: Routledge, 1989). For some of us, myself included, the later Wittgenstein is an independent source of a deep scepticism toward theories, though not necessarily toward the activity of theorizing. For a discussion of that distinction, see Barbara Christian, "The Race for Theory," *Cultural Critique* 6 (Spring 1987): 51–63.

[29]Harding, *The Science Question in Feminism*, and "The Method Question," *Hypatia* 2, no. 3 (Fall 1987): 19–35.

of gender, race, class, and physical and cognitive ability have set up dichotomies that, in each case, have normalized one side as the essentially human and stigmatized the other, usually in terms that stress the need for control and the inability of the stigmatized to control themselves. Acts of violence directed against oppressed groups typically are presented by their oppressors as preemptive strikes, justified by the dangers posed by the supposedly less-civilized, less-disciplined natures of those being suppressed. Workplace surveillance through lie detectors and drug testing (procedures in which subjects' bodies are made to testify to the inadequacies of their minds and wills), programs of social control to police the sexual behavior of homosexuals, the paternalistic disempowerment of the disabled, increasing levels of verbal and physical attacks on students of color by other students, and the pervasive terrorism of random violence against women all bespeak the need on the part of the privileged to control the bodies and behavior of those who are "different," a need that both in its targets and in its gratuitous fierceness goes beyond securing the advantages of exploitation.

Cartesian strategies of epistemic authorization, viewed through the lens of Schreber's paranoia, are illuminating here. As the authorized subject constitutes himself by contrast with the disenfranchised others, so he constitutes himself by contrast with the world that is the object of his knowledge. He also, by the same gestures, reciprocally constitutes that world. Freud, in his discussion of Schreber, quotes Goethe's *Faust*:

> Woe! Woe!
> Thou hast it destroyed,
> The beautiful world,
> With powerful fist!
> In ruins 'tis hurled,
> By the blow of a demigod shattered!
>
> Mightier
> For the children of men,
> More splendid
> Build it again,
> In thine own bosom build it anew![30]

The gesture is not only Schreber's; it is, of course, Descartes's. Like Schreber, Descartes imaginatively destroys the world through the withdrawal of his attachment to it (he becomes agnostic about its very existence), and like Schreber, his ego is thereby aggrandized and goes about the task of reconstituting the world,

---

[30]Freud, "Notes on a Case of Paranoia," *SE*, 12, p. 70. The quotation is from part I, scene 4 of *Faust*.

or a semblance of it, under the problematic aegis of an all-powerful father. This reconstituted world is perceived as hostile—made up as it is of everything the ego has split off—and as permanently in need of vigilant control. It is also perceived, and needs to be perceived, as independent of the self as the self needs to be perceived as independent of it. There can be no acknowledgement of the self's complicity in the constitution of the world as an object of knowledge. "Indeed," as Paul Smith puts it, "it is the desired fate of both paranoia and classical realism to be construed as interpretations of an already existing world, even though the world they both create is their own."[31]

Smith notes the need of the paranoiac (or of the humanist intellectual—he has in mind, in particular, hermeneutically inclined anthropologists such as Clifford Geertz) "to objectify or *realize* a reality and yet to proclaim the 'subject's' innocence of its formation" (Smith, *Discerning the Subject*, p. 87; emphasis in the original). Not only as hostile—or exotic—but as *real*, the world has to be regarded as wholly independent of the self. And the very activity of securing that independence has to be repressed; the subject and the world have to be innocent of each other, unimplicated in each other's identity.[32]

Despite Descartes's genuinely democratic intentions, as his epistemology was taken up by those who followed him, it authorized those—and only those—whose subject positions were constituted equally by their relationship to a purportedly objective world and by their relationship to the disenfranchised others, defined by their inescapable, undisciplined bodies.

III. Paranoia, Discipline, and Modernity

> Whatever we seek in philosophy, or whatever leads us to ask philosophical questions at all, must be something pretty deep in human nature, and what leads us to ask just the questions we do in the particular ways we now ask them must be something pretty deep in our tradition.[33]

---

[31]Paul Smith, *Discerning the Subject* (Minneapolis: University of Minnesota Press, 1988), p. 98. Smith's parallels between paranoia and what he calls "humanist epistemology," which I came across in the very final stages of writing this paper, are very similar to mine, as is his aim to articulate a conception of human subjectivity and agency that is politically and socially usable.

[32]See my "From Hamlet to Maggie Verver: The History and Politics of the Knowing Subject"; and "Missing Mothers/Desiring Daughters: Framing the Sight of Women."

[33]Barry Stroud, *The Significance of Philosophical Scepticism* (New York: Oxford University Press, 1984), p. x.

The most influential theorist of surveillance, discipline, and control is Michel Foucault. His *Discipline and Punish: The Birth of the Prison* traces the development and deployment of characteristically modern systems of power as pervasively applied to the bodies of the subjugated; his *The History of Sexuality*, volume 1, looks at those systems largely as they shape subjectivity, desire, and knowledge.[34] In both cases power is not the simple possession of certain individuals or groups; rather, it is omnipresent, constitutive as much as constraining, expressed through the tissue of our personal and institutional lives.[35] But whereas the forms of administrative power discussed in *Discipline and Punish* construct individuals as objects, the discursive constructions of sex construct us rather *as subjects* in what we take to be our freedom, the expression of our desire. As we struggle against what we have learned to call repression, we speak our desire in terms that construct it—and us—according to a distinctively modern regime, even as we take ourselves to be striving toward the liberation of timelessly human wants and needs.[36]

I want to use Foucault to bring together Descartes and Schreber. With the success of the economic, social, cultural, and political revolutions that empowered the Cartesian subject,[37] the discipline Descartes called for moved from being the self-conscious work of self-constituting radicals to finding expression in the

---

[34]I owe this juxtaposition of the two books to a suggestion by Michael Root. See Hubert L. Dreyfus and Paul Rabinow, *Michel Foucault: Beyond Structuralism and Hermeneutics*, 2nd ed. (Chicago: University of Chicago Press, 1983), pp. 143–83.

[35]Feminists and others have expressed concerns that despite the attractiveness of Foucauldian theory we need to be wary that by following him we risk losing politically indispensable notions like oppression and power (as something some people have unjustly more of). It is similarly unclear how in Foucauldian terms to formulate effectively coordinated strategies of resistance. See, for example, *Feminism and Foucault: Reflections on Resistance*, ed. Irene Diamond and Lee Quinby (Boston: Northeastern University Press, 1988); and Cornel West, *The American Evasion of Philosophy: A Geneaology of Pragmatism* (Madison: University of Wisconsin Press, 1989), pp. 223–26. I share these concerns but find some of Foucault's analyses helpfully illuminating. I want to "go a piece of the way with him," a notion I owe to an unpublished paper by Angelita Reyes, "Derridada . . . Don't Leave Home without Him, or, Going a Piece of the Way with Them."

[36]The unspecified 'we' in these sentences is a reflection of one thing many feminists and other liberationist theorists find problematic in Foucault—the homogenization of subject positions. It is striking to me how difficult it is not to do this, to be always conscious of the diversity of different people's experiences. Philosophy as a discipline makes such consciousness especially difficult, because the philosophical subject is defined precisely by its (alleged) universality.

[37]See, for example, Francis Barker, *The Tremulous Private Body: Essays on Subjection* (London: Methuen, 1984), for an account of the emergence of the distinctively modern subject.

pedagogy of the privileged.[38] The soul-shaping regimes of the elder Schreber are a particularly stark version of that pedagogy, which finds coded expression in the *Memoirs* of Freud's Schreber and a chilling critique in the works of Alice Miller.

Morton Schatzman's *Soul Murder* is a detailed argument for the thesis that Schreber's *Memoirs* recount in coded form what his father did to him when he was a child. Daniel Gottlieb Moritz Schreber wrote prolifically about child-rearing regimes aimed at suppressing a child's will and replacing it with automatic obedience to the will of the parent while simultaneously inculcating in the child enormous powers of self-control, which the child was to exercise over his or her own body and desires. That is, the goal was not an attitude of subservient obedience, such that children would have no idea of what they were to do until commanded by their parents. Rather, the child's will was to be replaced by the will of the parent in such a way that the child would not notice (or, at least, would not remember)[39] that this was done and would henceforth act "autonomously," as though the now-internalized commands came from her or his own true self. And that commanding self needs precisely not to be weak and unassertive, charged as it is with keeping under control the child's unruly body, emotions, and desires.

Not surprisingly, prominent among the desires and unruly impulses that need to be kept under control are those connected with masturbation and sexual curiosity. Foucault's characterization of modern Europe as hardly silent about sexuality is borne out by Miller's examples of instructional techniques for extracting from children confessions of masturbation (Miller, *For Your Own Good*, pp. 18–21) and of arguments that sexual curiosity needs to be (albeit perhaps fraudulently) satisfied, lest it grow obsessive. One recommended means is to have children view naked corpses, because "the sight of a corpse evokes solemnity and reflection, and this is the most appropriate mood for a child under such circumstances" (Miller, *For Your Own Good*, p. 46). J. Oest, whose advice this was in 1787, also advised

> that children be cleansed from head to foot every two to four weeks by an old, dirty, and ugly woman, without anyone else being present; still, parents should make sure that even this old woman doesn't linger unnecessarily over any part of the body. This task should be depicted to the children as disgusting, and they should be told that the old woman

---

[38]The echo of Paulo Freire's *Pedagogy of the Oppressed* is intentional. Freire's aim is to develop an explicit pedagogy that will be empowering to those who are currently oppressed; I want to examine the implicit pedagogy that actually empowers the currently privileged.

[39]Alice Miller stresses the importance for the success of "poisonous pedagogy" that its victims not have any memory of what was done to them, that they never see their parents as anything other than good and loving. My discussion draws heavily on her *For Your Own Good.*

> must be paid to undertake a task that, although necessary for purposes of health and cleanliness, is yet so disgusting that no other person can bring himself to do it (Miller, *For Your Own Good*, pp. 46–47).

Miller quotes extensively from the elder Schreber as well as from these and other, similar eighteenth- and nineteenth-century pedagogues who counseled parents on how, for example, "exercises can aid in the complete suppression of affect" (Miller, *For Your Own Good*, p. 25; the counsel comes from J. Sulzer, whose *Essay on the Education and Instruction of Children* was published in German in 1748). The same theorist made it clear that such suppression of autonomy was not intended only or even primarily for those whose place in society was subordinate:

> Obedience is so important that all education is actually nothing other than learning how to obey. It is a generally recognized principle that persons of high estate who are destined to rule whole nations must learn the art of governance by way of first learning obedience. . . . [T]he reason for this is that obedience teaches a person to be zealous in observing the law, which is the first quality of the ruler (Miller, *For Your Own Good*, pp. 12–13).

The choreography of will breaking and will strengthening has one additional turn: the shaping fiction of the enterprise is that the unruliness of children, however omnipresent, is nonetheless unnatural. In Schreber's words, "[t]he noble seeds of human nature sprout upwards in their purity almost of their own accord if the ignoble ones, the weeds, are sought out and destroyed in time."[40] Thus the parental will that replaces the child's is in fact more truly expressive of the child's true nature than was the "bad" will the child took to be her or his own; it is not only that children should come to think so.

All this is, of course, much more reminiscent of Kant than of Descartes. It is Kant who argued that our passions are not expressive of our true, autonomous selves and, hence, that acting on them is neither morally right nor autonomous, and that those categories—the lawbound and the free—are actually identical. It is Kant who most clearly taught us to control our passions[41] and to identify with a self that we experience not as idiosyncratic but as speaking in the voice of

---

[40]Quoted in Miller, *For Your Own Good*, p. 90; from Schatzman, *Soul Murder*, p. 19, quoting Schreber.

[41]But we should not obliterate them. Kant suggests, for example, that we should visit places that house the poor and the ill to reinvigorate in ourselves sympathetic feelings that can be enlisted on the side of motivating us to do what duty commands. Immanuel Kant, *The Doctrine of Virtue: Part II of the Metaphysics of Morals*, trans. Mary J. Gregor (Philadelphia: University of Pennsylvania Press, 1964), sec. 35, p. 126.

impartial reason. Descartes, on the other hand, seems far more human, more playful, more respectful of the body and the emotions, more intrigued by the diversity in the world around him, more—and this is the crucial difference—anti-authoritarian than Kant.

As, of course, he was. He was in the midst of making the revolution that the pedagogues and Kant inherited, and it was a revolution precisely against entrenched authority, a revolution waged in the name of the individual. There is an exhilaration that even today's undergraduates can find in reading Descartes; he can speak, for example, to the woman student who is in the midst of discovering for herself that she has been systematically lied to about the world and her place in it, that authorities she had trusted disagree with each other and that none of them seems to have it right, that even her own body can be untrustworthy. She may, for example, find food repulsive because even as she becomes emaciated she sees herself as hideously fat, or she may have learned from a sexual abuser to desire her own humiliation.

But, I want to argue, the Descartes we have inherited (and, more broadly, the liberal politics his epistemology partially grounds)[42] is a problematic ally for this young woman, as he is for the other women and men who have been the excluded others. Though he is not Kant, let alone Schreber (either the paranoid son or the "paranoidogenic" father),[43] the discipline of the method that lies at the heart of Descartes's constitution of himself as epistemically authoritative bears the seeds of paranoia, seeds that germinated as the revolution he helped to inaugurate moved from marginality to hegemony.

As Freud argues, the central mechanism of paranoia is projection, that process by which something that had been recognized as a part of the self is detached from it (a process called "splitting") and reattached on to something or someone other than the self. An underlying motivation for such splitting is narcissism: what is split off is incompatible with the developing ego. But it is significant to note that one obvious effect is the diminution of the self—it no longer contains something it once did. One consequence of that recognition is that it provides a motivation for thinking of that which is split off as wholly bad, perhaps even worse than it was thought to be when it was split off. It has to be clear that the self really is better off without it.

This is one way of thinking about the fate of the body in Cartesian and post-

---

[42]This is as good a place as any to note that what I find problematic in Cartesian epistemology is not peculiar to him or even to rationalism. The gender associations are, in fact, far clearer in Bacon. (See Evelyn Fox Keller, "Baconian Science: A Hermaphroditic Birth," *The Philosophical Forum* XI, 3 [Spring 1980]: 299–308; reprinted in Keller, *Reflections on Gender and Science* [New Haven: Yale University Press, 1985].) For a fuller statement of what I take to be in common in views that the usual accounts of the history of philosophy put in opposition, see my "Othello's Doubt/Desdemona's Death."

[43]The term is Schatzman's in *Soul Murder*, p. 137.

Cartesian epistemology. The self of the cogito establishes its claim to authority precisely by its separation from the body, a separation that is simultaneously liberating and totally isolating. Although Descartes goes on, under the protection of God, to reclaim his body and to place himself in intimate and friendly relation to it, the loss to the self remains. René Descartes, along with all those who would follow his method, really is a *res cogitans*, not a sensual, bodily person. One can glimpse the magnitude of the loss in Descartes's attempts to theorize his relationship to the body he calls his own, an attempt he finally abandons,[44] but the full force of it is found elsewhere, when the demand that one separate from and control one's body is joined both to Christian associations of the body with sin and to the pedagogical practices that replaced Descartes's self-conscious self-constitution.

It became impossible to empower the mind without disempowering and stigmatizing the body, or, in Foucauldian terms, anatomizing, administering, scrutinizing, and disciplining it. The body Descartes regains and bequeaths to his heirs is mechanical, not the lived body but the object of scientific practices, a body best known by being, after its death, dissected. It became the paradigmatic object in an epistemology founded on a firm and unbridgeable subject-object distinction.[45] And it became bad—because it had once been part of the self and it had had to be pushed away, split off, and repudiated. So, too, with everything else from which the authorized self needed to be distinguished and distanced. The rational mind stood over and against the mechanical world of orderly explanation, while the rest—the disorderly, the passionate, the uncontrollable—was relegated to the categories of the "primitive or exotic . . . two new interests in bourgeois society, to compensate for the estranged experience of the bourgeois self."[46]

The Cartesian God—the poisonously pedagogical parent, seen by the successfully reared child as wholly benevolent—conscripts the infinite will of the privileged son and sets it the task of "autonomously" disciplining the body, the perceptions, and the passions, with the promised reward being the revelation of guaranteed truths and the power that goes with knowledge. Evelyn Fox Keller is discussing Bacon, but she could as well be discussing Descartes—or the paranoid Schreber:

---

[44]For the attempt, see Descartes, Meditation 6, CS&M, 1, pp. 56–57; the Fourth Set of Replies (to Arnauld), CS&M, 2, p. 60; Sixth Set of Replies (to Mersenne), CS&M, 2, pp. 297–99. For further attempts and, in the face of her persistent questioning, his abandonment of the possibility of getting a rationally grounded theoretical account of the union of mind and body, see Descartes's Letters IX (a and b) and X (a and b) to Princess Elizabeth, in *Descartes: Philosophical Writings*, ed. Elizabeth Anscombe and Peter Thomas Geach (Indianapolis: Bobbs-Merrill, 1954).

[45]Barker, *The Tremulous Private Body*. See also my "From Hamlet to Maggie Verver."

[46]Donald M. Lowe, *History of Bourgeois Perception* (Chicago: The University of Chicago Press, 1982), p. 22.

> What is sought here is the proper stance for mind necessary to insure the reception of truth, and the conception of science. To receive God's truth, the mind must be pure and clean, submissive and open—it must be undefiled and female. Only then can it give birth to a masculine and virile science. That is, if the mind is pure, receptive and submissive—female—in its relation to God, it can be transformed by God into a forceful, potent and virile agent—male—in its relation to nature. Cleansed of contamination, the mind can be impregnated by God, and, in that act, virilized—made potent and capable of generating virile offspring in its union with nature.[47]

Such a self, privileged by its estrangement from its own body, from the "external" world, and from other people, will, in a culture that defines such estrangements as normal, express the paranoia of such a stance not only through oppression but, more benignly, through the problems that are taken as the most fundamental, even if not the most practically pressing: the problems of philosophy. Those problems—notably, the mind-body problem, problems of reference and truth, the problem of other minds, and scepticism about knowledge of the external world—all concern the subject's ability or inability to connect with the split off parts of itself—its physicality, its sociability. Such problems are literally and unsurprisingly unsolvable so long as the subject's very identity is constituted by those estrangements. A subject whose authority is defined by his location on one side of a gulf cannot authoritatively theorize that gulf away. Philosophers' problems are the neuroses of privilege; discipline makes the difference between such problems and the psychosis of full-blown paranoia.

IV. Beyond Madness and Method

> The new *mestiza* copes by developing a tolerance for ambiguity. . . . She has a plural personality, she operates in a pluralistic mode—nothing is thrust out, the good, the bad and the ugly, nothing rejected, nothing abandoned.[48]

> The alternative to relativism is partial, locatable, critical knowledges sustaining the possibility of webs of connections called solidarity in politics and shared conversations in epistemology.[49]

---

[47]Keller, "Baconian Science," p. 304.

[48]Gloria Anzaldúa, *Borderlands/La Frontera: The New Mestiza* (San Francisco: Spinsters/Aunt Lute, 1987), p. 79.

[49]Donna Haraway, "Situated Knowledges: The Science Question in Feminism and the Privilege of Partial Perspective," *Feminist Studies* 14, no. 3 (Fall 1988): 584.

The authorized subject thus achieves and maintains his authority by his ability to keep his body and the rest of the world radically separated from his ego, marked off from it by policed boundaries.[50] Within those boundaries, the self is supposed to be unitary and seamless, characterized by the doxastic virtue of noncontradiction and the moral virtue of integrity. The social mechanisms of privilege aid in the achievement of those virtues by facilitating splitting and projection: the unity of the privileged self is maintained by dumping out of the self—onto the object world or onto the different, the stigmatized others—everything that would disturb its pristine wholeness.

Various contemporary theorists are articulating alternative conceptions of subjectivity, conceptions that start from plurality and diversity, not just among but, crucially, within subjects.[51] From that starting point flow radically transformed relationships among subjects and between subjects and the world they would know.

One way to approach these discussions is to return to Freud. Mental health for Freud consisted in part in the acknowledgement by the ego of the impulses of the id: "Where id was, there ego shall be."[52] The German is more striking than the English: the German words for 'ego' and 'id' are 'ich' and 'es';[53] the sense is "Where *it* was, there *I* shall be." One can take this in two ways. Under the sorts of disciplinary regimes that constitute epistemic privilege, the exhortation has a colonizing ring to it. The not-I needs to be brought under the civilizing control

---

[50]Firm ego-boundaries are typically taken as a measure of mental health: one is supposed to be clear about where one's self leaves off and the rest of the world begins. An alternative view—that part of mental health, or of an adequate epistemology, consists in the acceptance of a sizable intermediate domain—has been developed by the object-relations theorist D. W. Winnicott. For a discussion of the relevance of his work to feminist theory, see Keller, *Reflections on Gender and Science*, pp. 83, 99–102; and Jane Flax, *Thinking Fragments: Psychoanalysis, Feminism, and Postmodernism in the Contemporary West* (Berkeley and Los Angeles: University of California Press, 1990), pp. 116–32.

[51]Sandra Harding and Donna Haraway are two such theorists, who also give excellent overviews of work in this area. See, especially, Haraway, "Situated Knowledges," pp. 575–99; and Harding, "Reinventing Ourselves as Other: More New Agents of History and Knowledge," in Harding, *Whose Science? Whose Knowledge? Thinking from Women's Lives* (Ithaca, N.Y.: Cornell University Press, 1991), pp. 286–95. See also three papers in which María Lugones develops a pluralistic theory of identity: "Playfulness, 'World'-Traveling, and Loving Perception," *Hypatia* 2, no. 2 (Summer 1987): 3–19; "Hispaneando y Lesbiando: On Sarah Hoagland's *Lesbian Ethics*," *Hypatia* 5, no. 3 (Fall 1990): 138–46; and "On the Logic of Pluralist Feminism," in *Feminist Ethics*, ed. Claudia Card (Wichita: Kansas University Press, 1991).

[52]Sigmund Freud, *New Introductory Lectures on Psychoanalysis*, *SE*, 22, p. 80.

[53]See Bruno Bettelheim, *Freud and Man's Soul* (New York: A. A. Knopf, 1983). *The New Introductory Lectures* were written originally in English, but the point still holds: Freud used the English of his translators.

of the ego; the aim is not to split it off but to tame it. Splitting represents the failure of colonization, the loss of will for the task of domestication. The healthy ego is unified not because it has cast out parts of itself, but because it has effectively administered even the formerly unruly outposts of its dominion. Or so goes the story one is supposed to tell. (Any splitting goes unacknowledged.)

There is another way to take Freud's exhortation. The aim might be not to colonize the "it" but to break down the distinction between "it" and "I," between object and subject. "Where it was, there I shall be," not because I am colonizing it, but because where I am is always shifting. As Nancy Chodorow puts it, in giving an object-relational alternative to the classical Freudian account, "where fragmented internal objects were, there shall harmoniously related objects be."[54] Moving becomes not the installment of oneself astride the Archimedean point, the self-made man taming the frontier of the "New World," but the sort of "world"-travel María Lugones discusses as the ground of what she calls, following Marilyn Frye, "loving perception."[55] By putting ourselves in settings where we are perceived as—and hence are able (or unable not) to be—different people from who we are at home, we learn about ourselves, each other, and the world. And part of what we learn is that the unity of the self is an illusion of privilege, as when, to use Lugones's example (from a talk she gave at the University of Minnesota), we think there is a natural, unmediated connection between intention, will, and action because if we are privileged, the world collaborates with us, making it all work, apparently seamlessly, and giving us the credit. As Frye puts it, we are trained not to notice the stagehands, all those whose labor enables the play to proceed smoothly.[56]

What is problematic about Descartes's Faustian gesture is not the idea that the world is in some sense our creation. Rather, it is on the one hand the individualism of the construction (or, what comes to the same thing, the unitary construction by all and only those who count as the same, the not-different) and on the other the need to deny any construction, to maintain the mutual independence of the self and the world. Realism ought not to require such independence on the side of the world, anymore than rationality ought to require it on the side of the knowing subject, if by realism we mean the recognition that the world may not be the way anyone (or any group, however powerful) thinks it is, and if by rationality we mean ways of learning and teaching that are reliably useful in collective endeavors.

---

[54]Nancy Chodorow, "Toward a Relational Individualism: The Mediation of Self through Psychoanalysis," in *Reconstructing Individualism: Autonomy, Individuality, and the Self in Western Thought*, ed. Thomas C. Heller, Morton Sosna, and David E. Wellbery (Stanford: Stanford University Press, 1986), pp. 197–207.

[55]Lugones, "Playfulness, 'World'-Travel, and Loving Perception"; Frye, "In and Out of Harm's Way."

[56]Frye, "To Be and Be Seen," *The Politics of Reality*, pp. 167–73.

Philosophical realism has typically stressed the independence of the world from those who would know it, a formulation that, at least since Kant, has been linked with the intractability of scepticism. But it's hard to see exactly why independence should be what is required. A world that exists in complex interdependence with those who know it (who are, of course, also part of it) is nonetheless real. Lots of real things are not independent of what we think about them, without being simply what anyone or any group takes them to be—the economy, to take just one obvious example. The interdependencies are real, as are the entities and structures shaped by them. One way we know they are real is precisely that they look different to those differently placed in relation to them. (There aren't a variety of diverse takes on my hallucinations.) The only way to take diversity of perspectives seriously is to be robustly realist, both about the world viewed and about the material locations of those doing the viewing. Archimedean, difference-denying epistemology ought to be seen as incompatible with such a robust realism. How could there possibly be one account of a world shaped in interaction with subjects so diversely constituted and with such diverse interests in constructing and knowing it?

A specifically Cartesian feature of the conception of the world as independent is the world as inanimate, and consequently not reciprocally engaged in the activities through which it comes to be known. Thus, for example, the social sciences, which take as their objects bearers of subjectivity and the entities and structures they create, have been seen as scientifically deficient precisely because of the insufficiently independent status of what they study. (The remedy for such deficiency has typically been the dehumanizing objectification of the "subjects" of the social sciences, an objectification especially damaging when those subjects have been otherwise oppressed.) But it's far from obvious that being inert should make something more knowable. Why not take 'subject' and 'object' to name not ontological categories, but reciprocal, shifting positions? Why not think of knowledge emerging paradigmatically in mutual interaction, so that what puzzles us is how to account not for the objectivity of the social sciences but for the intersubjectivity of the natural sciences?[57]

In a discussion of the problems, from an African-American perspective, with the critical legal theorists' rejection of rights, Patricia Williams suggests that rather than discarding rights, "society must *give* them away. Unlock them from reification by giving them to slaves. Give them to trees. Give them to cows. Give them to history. Give them to rivers and rocks. Give to all of society's objects and untouchables the rights of privacy, integrity, and self-assertion; give them distance and respect. Flood them with the animating spirit that rights mythology

---

[57]For a start on such an account, as well as an argument for why we should seek one, see Lorraine Code, *What Can She Know? Feminist Theory and the Construction of Knowledge* (Ithaca, N.Y.: Cornell University Press, 1991), esp. chaps. 3 and 4; and Sandra Harding, *Whose Science? Whose Knowledge?* esp. chap. 4.

fires in this country's most oppressed psyches, and wash away the shrouds of inanimate-object status."[58] One might respond similarly to the suggestion from postmodernist quarters that we discard subjectivity and agency. Rather, we should profligately give them away, invest the things of the world with subjectivity, with the ability and interest to return our gaze.[59] Realism can mean that we take ourselves as inhabiting a world in which the likes of us (whoever we may be) are not the only sources of meaning, that we see ourselves as implicated in, reciprocated by, the world.

The world as real is the world as precisely not dead or mechanistic; the world as trickster, as protean, is always slipping out from under our best attempts to pin it down.[60] The real world is not the world of our best physics but the world that defeats any physics that would be final, that would desire to be the last word, "the end of the story, the horizon of interpretation, the end of 'the puzzlement'," a desire Paul Smith calls "claustrophilic."[61] Donna Haraway imaginatively sketches an epistemology for the explicitly partial, fragmentary, un-unified knowers we are and need to be if we are to move within and learn from the complexities of the world and the complexities of how we are constructed in it. As she puts it, "[s]plitting, not being, is the privileged image for feminist epistemologies of scientific knowledge" (Haraway, "Situated Knowledges," p. 586).

A trickster reality is thus matched by a trickster subjectivity, a subjectivity that finds expression in African and Afro-American oral and written traditions. In *The Signifying Monkey,* Henry Louis Gates, Jr., builds "a theory of African-American literary criticism" (the book's subtitle) on the ground of African-American vernacular traditions.[62] Literature, the written word, was the privileged site for the attainment and display of Enlightenment rationality, the place for former slaves and the descendants of slaves to stake a claim to full membership in the human community. The signifying monkey and other traditional African trickster figures from oral traditions are for Gates a way of exploring the simultaneous appropriations and subversions of the site of writing, the attempts of African-American writers not to mimic the texts of the masters but to write themselves and their communities into history and culture by transforming the nature of writing itself, by giving voice to the written word. Gates's central trope of "Signifyin(g)" complexly spins a story about the multivocality of African-

---

[58]Patricia J. Williams, *The Alchemy of Race and Rights: Diary of a Law Professor* (Cambridge, Mass.: Harvard University Press, 1991), p. 165.

[59]See Rainer Maria Rilke's "Archaic Torso of Apollo": "there is no place / that does not see you. You must change your life." *Translations from the Poetry of Rainer Maria Rilke*, trans. M. D. Herter Norton (New York: W. W. Norton & Co., 1938).

[60]Haraway, "Situated Knowledges," p. 596.

[61]Smith, *Discerning the Subject*, p. 98.

[62]Henry Louis Gates, Jr., *The Signifying Monkey: A Theory of African-American Literary Criticism* (New York and Oxford: Oxford University Press, 1988).

American texts, the weaving of vernacular voices into literature, and the subversions, parodies, and appropriations of earlier texts. Even when the singular voice is seen as a desirable ideal, its achievement is never a simple matter, never seen as a birthright; there are always other voices playing around the edges of the text.

The unity of privileged subjectivity is mirrored in the demand that language be transparent, a demand most explicit in the now-discredited ideal languages of the logical positivists but lingering in the demands of present-day analytic philosophers for (a certain picture of) clarity, as though the point of language was to be seen through. When June Jordan writes of Black English that one of its hallmarks is "[c]larity: If the sentence is not clear it's not Black English," she might seem to be endorsing such a demand, but the clarity she extols is contextual and "person-centered": "If your idea, your sentence, assumes the presence of at least two living and active people, you will make it understandable because the motivation behind every sentence is the wish to say something real to somebody real."[63] The clarity of analytic philosophy, by contrast, is best exhibited in argumentative contexts, detached from the specificities of anyone's voice, in avoidance of ad hominem and other genetic fallacies. The clarity of Black English, Jordan explains, is grounded in the rhythms and intonations of speech, in the immediacy of the present indicative, and in an abhorrence of abstraction and the eschewal of the passive (non)voice: it is the clarity of illumination, not of the transparent medium. In contrast to the language of philosophy, which assumes its adequacy as a vessel for fully translatable meaning, Black English does not take its authority for granted. It is a language "constructed by people constantly needing to insist that we exist, that we are present."[64] It aims not at transparent representation but at subversive transformation; it is an act of intervention, used by communities of resistance and used within those communities for collective self-constitution.

There are many other theorists of trickster subjectivity. Gloria Anzaldúa, for example, in *Borderlands/La Frontera* writes in a combination of English and Spanish, refusing the demand to choose one or another "pure" language, as she moves along and across the borders that are supposed to define and separate, finding/creating herself by refusing the definitions and separations.

Teresa de Lauretis finds in some women's films a challenge to the unity of the subject. For example, Lizzie Borden's *Born in Flames* discomfits some privileged women viewers precisely in not addressing them alone, in not (re)presenting the women of color in the film *to* them, but rather addressing an audience of women

[63]June Jordan, "Nobody Mean More to Me than You / And the Future Life of Willie Jordan," in *On Call: Political Essays* (Boston: South End Press, 1985), pp. 129ff. Such accounts make evident the Eurocentrism of deconstructive sorties against such notions as presence, voice, and authorship. See, for example, Jacques Derrida, "Plato's Pharmacy," in *Dissemination*, tr. Barbara Johnson (Chicago: University of Chicago Press, 1981).

[64]Ibid.

as diverse as the women on the screen. There is no unitary viewer for the film, a move that de Lauretis takes to express the feminist understanding "that the female subject is en-gendered, constructed and defined in gender across multiple representations of class, race, language, and social relations; and that, therefore, differences among women are differences *within* women."[65]

In *The American Evasion of Philosophy*, Cornel West finds in pragmatism a challenge to the Enlightenment that can make room for a historical subject constituted otherwise than by the norms of European epistemology.[66] He sees what he calls "prophetic pragmatism" as an intellectual stance for liberationist struggles, in part because of its inheritance from earlier pragmatists, notably Dewey, of a rejection of foundationalism and individualism and an openness to the "fluidity, plurality, and diversity of experience" (West, *American Evasion*, p. 91). Knowledge and the knowing subject emerge together from continuous engagement with the world; such engagement (with our actual lives at stake) and not the abstractions of epistemology ought to be the stuff of our reflection.[67]

There is, however, an obvious problem with taking splitting and internal multiplicity as the hallmarks of liberatory subjectivity. The most striking and clear-cut cases of internal multiplicity are cases of multiple personality, a pathological condition typically caused by severe childhood abuse, that is, by the most poisonous of pedagogies.[68] Recent clinical work with people with multiple personalities suggests such multiplicity is a means of coping with the terror and pain of the child's situation.[69] Part of that coping consists in a protective amnesia of what the child can neither stop nor understand nor tell anyone about. Consequently the lines of communication between the different selves become blocked, and some of the relations between them become antagonistic as some of the selves adopt coping strategies that are at odds with those of others. Multiple personality, on such a view, is a comprehensible, perhaps even rational, response to an intolerable situation, a way of maintaining some degree of agency in the face of profoundly soul-destroying attacks on one's ability to construct a sense of self. Such construction, throughout life, but especially when one is a child, proceeds

---

[65]Teresa de Lauretis, "Rethinking Women's Cinema: Aesthetics and Feminist Theory," in *Technologies of Gender: Essays on Theory, Film, and Fiction* (Bloomington: Indiana University Press, 1987), p. 139.

[66]West, *The American Evasion of Philosophy*.

[67]George Herbert Mead has also inspired theorists of subjectivity concerned with sociality and internal diversity. See, in particular, Karen Hanson, *The Self Imagined: Philosophical Reflections on the Social Character of Psyche* (New York: Routledge and Kegan Paul, 1986); and Catherine Keller, *From a Broken Web: Separation, Sexism, and Self* (Boston: Beacon Press, 1986).

[68]Thanks to Louise Antony for stressing the importance of dealing with these issues.

[69]"Dissociative Disorder," *Diagnostic and Statistical Manual of Mental Disorders*, 3rd ed., rev. (Washington, D.C.: American Psychiatric Association, 1987), pp. 269–79.

interactively. We all are, to use Annette Baier's term, "second persons,"[70] and when those we most trust to mirror us abuse that trust, the conditions for wholeness are shattered.

In reflecting on the experiences of "multiples," Claudia Card (to whom I owe much of this discussion) suggests that we can see the main difference between them and the rest of us as lying not in their internal multiplicity but in the amnesia that both guards it and keeps it at odds. Therapy can succeed not by integrating all the personalities into one, nor by making all but one go away, but by creating the possibility for respectful conversation among them, facilitating their mutual recognition and acceptance. Analogously with oppressed communities, Card argues, multiples are internally in strife, unable to confront those who have damaged them, needing not seamless unity but effective alliance building.[71] They need from trusted others a mirror of themselves not as unitary but as united, which requires, in part, that those others be committed to the joint survival of all the selves they are and to at least some of the projects in which those selves might engage, either jointly or individually, with mutual respect.

Such an account parallels María Lugones's account of her experiences as a "multiplicitous being," a U.S. Latina lesbian who could not be unitary without killing off a crucial part of who she is, without betraying both herself and others with whom she identifies and for whom she cares.[72] Without identification with and engagement in struggle within *la cultura hispana Nuevamejicana*, the imperiled community in which she "has found her grounding," she risks becoming "culturally obsolete," but as a lesbian within that culture, she is not a lover of women—she is an "abomination." Needing to be both of the very different people she is in the *Nuevamejicana* and lesbian cultures, she works, not for unity but for connection, for the not-to-be-taken-for-granted understanding of each of her selves by the other, understanding that is cultivated by work in the "borderlands," "the understanding of liminals." Victoria Davion contends that it is such connection that can ground a conception of integrity that does justice—as she argues any usable feminist notion of integrity must—to the experiences of multiplicitous beings,[73] and it is just that connection that it would seem multiple personalities need to acquire within/among themselves.

Thus we can see the splitting characteristic of multiple personality as a response to oppression that needs resolution by the achievement not of unity but of mutual respect, an achievement that requires the loving collaboration of others. On such

---

[70]Annette Baier, "Cartesian Persons," in *Postures of the Mind: Essays on Mind and Morals* (Minneapolis: University of Minnesota Press, 1985), pp. 79–92. See also the chapter on "Second Persons," in Code, *What Can She Know?* pp. 71–109.

[71]Claudia Card, "Responsibility and Moral Luck: Resisting Oppression and Abuse," manuscript, 1989.

[72]María Lugones, "Hispaneando y Lesbiando."

[73]Victoria M. Davion, "Integrity and Radical Change," in *Feminist Ethics,* ed. Card.

a view, such splitting is the most striking example of a far more common phenomenon, seen also in experiences such as those María Lugones theorizes. I want to suggest that, without blurring the specificities of such experiences, we can recognize that the experiences even of those who identify with dominant cultures can lead in different ways to multiplicitous identities. Gloria Anzaldúa, for example, stresses the importance for *mestizas* of the acceptance of all of who they are, "the white parts, the male parts, the queer parts, the vulnerable parts."[74] But she equally calls for such self-acceptance on the part of the privileged, as the only alternative to the splitting and projection that underwrite domination: "Admit that Mexico is your double, that we are irrevocably tied to her. Gringo, accept the doppelganger in your psyche. By taking back your collective shadow the intracultural split will heal" (Anzaldúa, *Borderlands/La Frontera*, p. 86).

Erica Sherover-Marcuse suggests that all children are subject to what she calls "adultism," a form of mistreatment that targets all young people who are born into an oppressive society.[75] Such mistreatment, she argues, is "the 'training ground' for other forms of oppression," a crucial part of the socialization of some as oppressor, some as oppressed, and most of us into complex combinations of both. Central to such socialization is its normalization, the denial of its traumatic nature, the forgetting of the pain; and central to emancipation is "a labor of *affective remembrance*."[76] Alice Miller argues similarly in *For Your Own Good* that only those who have been abused become abusers, and her account focuses on the mechanisms of splitting and projection: "children who have grown up being assailed for qualities the parents hate in themselves can hardly wait to assign those qualities to someone else so they can once again regard themselves as good, 'moral,' noble, and altruistic" (Miller, *For Your Own Good*, p. 91).

The abuse of which Alice Miller writes, which ranges from the normative to the horrific, shares the requirement of amnesia, which means that the split off parts of the self, whether they be the survival-ensuring "alters" of the multiple or the stigmatized others of the privileged, are empathically inaccessible. What Sherover-Marcuse calls "an emancipatory practice of subjectivity" (Sherover-Marcuse, *Emancipation and Consciousness*, p. 140) requires memory, connection, and the learning of respect for the others outside of us. Schreber, as privileged jurist and as incarcerated madman, emblematizes the victimized child who grows up to become the dominating adult, the possessor of power—which, while real enough (as is the privilege it secures), rests on a history of abuse. As long as we hold on to the ideal of the self as a seamless unity, we will not only be marginalizing the experiences of those like María Lugones and Gloria Anzaldúa, for whom such unity could only be bought at the price of self-betrayal, but we will be fundamentally misrepresenting the experiences of even the most privileged among

[74]Anzaldúa, *Borderlands/La Frontera*, p. 88.

[75]Sherover-Marcuse, *Emancipation and Consciousness*, p. 139.

[76]Ibid., p. 140. Emphasis in the original.

us,whose apparent unity was bought at the price of the projection onto stigmatized others of the split off parts of themselves they were taught to despise.

As Quine has persuasively argued,[77] epistemology cannot come from thin air: to naturalize epistemology is to acknowledge that we need to study how actual people actually know. But one thing we ought to know about actual people is that they inhabit a world of systematic inequality, in which authority—centrally including epistemic authority—is systematically given to some and withheld from others. If our interest is in changing that world, we need to look critically at the terms of epistemic authority. Certainly there is no reason why those who have historically been dominated by the epistemology of modernity—the objects to its subjects—should accept the terms of that epistemology as the only route to empowerment.

That epistemology presents itself as universal, a universal defined by precisely that which is not different in the ways that some are defined as different: women (not men), people of color (not white people), the disabled (not the able-bodied), gays and lesbians (not heterosexuals). To echo Foucault again, none of these categories is natural or ahistorical, and they all came into existence as strategies of regimentation and containment. They all represent aspects of the multiple, shifting, unstable ways that people can be, aspects that have been split off from the psyches of the privileged, projected onto the bodies of others, and concretized as identities. The privileged, in turn, having shucked off what would threaten their sense of control, theorize their own subjectivity (which they name generically human) as unitary and transparent to consciousness, characterized by integrity and consistency. Not only is such subjectivity a myth; its logic is that of paranoia.[78]

---

[77]W. V. Quine, " Epistemology Naturalized," *Ontological Relativity and Other Essays* (New York: Columbia University Press, 1969).

[78]Louise Antony's detailed and erudite response to an earlier draft was a model of friendly, feminist criticism. It is a rare thing to have one's writing so thoroughly disagreed with and at the same time taken so seriously and with so much care. Ruth Wood was, as usual, of enormous help in clarifying the convolutions.

7

From Hamlet to Maggie Verver: The History and Politics of the Knowing Subject

I. Prologue

For Ernst von Glasersfeld and other constructivists, the subtitle of my paper is oxymoronic: the knowing subject uniquely lacks a history; it is that which constructs all histories, all knowledge. Constructivism is in the Kantian tradition of implicating the subject in the nature of what can be known—epistemology is the study not of the world-in-itself, but of the world we know because of and through our construction of it. Kant is, however, historicized in the constructivists' project. The known world and the individual and social projects of constructing it have a history, and our constructions display a discernible and modifiable method. As regards the projects of constructing the known world, constructivists, unlike Kant, can be critics and reformers.

The knowing subject, however, is taken to be the absolute given, the transcendental place from which all construction and all knowledge start. It has no history, it is not constructed, and there is nothing about it that can meaningfully be the object of critique or reform. In Wittgenstein's image from the *Tractatus*, it is the eye, that which defines, but is no part of, the visual field. Thus, what is an essential link in Kantian epistemology is broken in constructivism: for Kant, the *a priori* nature of the knowing subject correlates with the *a priori* nature of the categories that structure the knowable world. The correlation gives us the objectivity of science, as an ahistorical guarantee of intersubjective agreement.

There can be no such agreement for constructivists. The construction of the knowable world is a project, one we embark on in the first instance alone, since our knowledge of other knowers is part of what we need to construct. And as we go on, the shareability of the world we know is both a question and an ideal. As a creative project, epistemology is judged pragmatically: we need a picture of the world that works, and one we share with many others will work better than one we have alone or share with only a few. Intersubjectivity depends on the discovery

—or positing—of similarities between ourselves and others. Insofar as our encounters with and interests in the world are the same as those we attribute to others, we can be reasonably confident that our constructions of the rest of the world will match.

My aim in this paper is to suggest that the knowing subject is as historical as the known world, that, in fact, the supposedly transcendental subject is a creation of modernity and the product of particular forms of social, political, and economic organization. The transcendental subject occupies a position of privileged isolation: its clear definition, usually called integrity or autonomy, is the product of real, material boundaries. (Ego-boundaries, like any others, require fences and the power and authority to police them.) The naturalization and supposed metaphysical necessity of such a self disguise the power that maintains it, and relegate those who lack such power to "selflessness" or to being the objects of others' historical actions. A very different subject is now emerging onto the historical stage, speaking in the voices of the oppressed—notably, women and all people of the Third World.

One thing that is emerging in the sounding of these voices is that it is diversity, not similarity, that will ground the new epistemology. Selves distinguished, as the privileged self of modernity is, by their mutual independence, need similarity to constitute epistemic as well as political community. Individuality is an ironic threat to an individualistic epistemic or political order: it is the essential indistinguishability of atomic individuals that makes the liberal state possible, and, analogously, it is the discovery or positing of similarity among knowers that makes possible a workable constructivist epistemology. Difference is threatening to either enterprise, since only similarity can provide for widespread consent to the power of the state or for intersubjective agreement.

As the current state of the women's movement and of feminist theory dramatically demonstrates, similarity is not at the heart of the new epistemology. Rather, the need to find that we are all, underneath our differences, really in some fundamental way the same, has been revealed to be a lingering and hard-to-shake form of racism. As an allegedly anti-racist Pete Seeger song from my childhood had it, "You get good milk from a brown-skinned cow. / The color of your skin doesn't matter no-how." The color of all milk is white; the message is that any *other* color is irrelevant to what it is to be really human, i.e., white (and male, straight, etc.). If we start nonindividualistically with the assumption—and experience—of interconnectedness, constructing selves as we construct the world, the two projects inextricable, we will be able to learn from diversity, rather than having it pose a profound metaphysical threat—that the shared world as we know it will literally collapse around us.

This paper is part of a prolegomenon to a future metaphysics. Like Kant's prolegomenon, it problematizes the border between metaphysics and epistemology; unlike his, it explicitly recognizes that all such projects are historical and political.

II. Introduction

For reasons that I hope will become clear, I want to approach questions about the nature of the knowing subject through questions about the nature of facts, and I will turn to literature for accounts of what sorts of things facts are taken, at different times, to be—of what it is for there to *be* such things as facts.

These questions are recognizably Kantian ones: the motivating question of *The Critique of Pure Reason* concerned what the world had to be like given that scientific knowledge of it was possible. Posing that question explicitly joins metaphysics—the foundational study of what is—to epistemology—the study of what we can know. The spirit of my questions will differ from Kant's in that the answers I seek are explicitly historical, whereas Kant took his answer to be of absolute universality. That is, I want to consider the historically specific conditions for the existence of facts as we conceive of them, whereas for Kant those conditions lay in the nature of the knowing mind as such. That Kant *intended* his account to be absolutely applicable is itself of historical significance, as is his locating the conditions of facticity in the individual mind of the knower.

I will argue that this combination of individualism with universality is at the heart of the discursive formations (to use Foucault's term) that since the seventeenth century have constructed the authoritative subject and within which our supposedly pre-analytically given notion of an independent fact has its home. In premodern Europe facts existed not independently, but in acknowledged relation to the world-structuring power of the hereditary aristocracy and the Church. Thus, for example, Galileo's accusers were not being stupid or perverse in refusing to accord epistemic authority to what some unauthorized man saw looking at the sky through some unauthorized gadget. (Had the unauthorized gadget been Galileo's own eyes, the situation wouldn't have been significantly different.)

I want to suggest that it is a mark of modernity for facts to be taken both to exist independently and to be discoverable by anyone with the proper method and tools. What Kant referred to as the "scandal of philosophy," the failure to prove the knowability of the world, is a consequence of the irreconcilability of those two constraints on facts—that they be independent and that they be knowable.[1] Although Kant attempted to overcome the sceptical challenge by explicitly abandoning the demand for the transcendent independence of facts from knowers, he attempted to secure the objectivity of science by making the factual independent of anything about the knower that is empirically variable. Much of the ensuing

[1]I explore this issue in relation to constraints on the construction of gender and sexuality in "Othello's Doubt/Desdemona's Death: The Engendering of Scepticism." I argue there that patriarchally constructed female sexuality is the paradigm for that which exists independently of the knowing (desiring) subject, while being wholly open to and revealed by his penetration of its mysteries.

history of philosophy has been a debate about whether this move works, about whether, that is, empirical independence can be assured without transcendent independence. Only in the last quarter century has there been sustained philosophical discussion (following the work, for example, of Kuhn and Foucault) of the possibility that the empirical independence of the known world from the shifting conditions of our knowledge of it is in need not of proof but of exposure as an ideological chimera.

The correlative to the independently existing world of facts is the independently existing subject: the two are inextricably joined in the maintenance of the illusion of their mutual independence. Independence is the distinguishing characteristic of the modern self and the principal focus of feminist theorists' critique of its normative maleness, defined as it is by separation from everything culturally coded as female—birth, death, sexuality, bodily need, nurturance, emotion, the body. The ritual of rebirth in Descartes's *Meditations* is one from which the self emerges epistemically empowered, assured by its true father of infallibility if only it remains vigilant against the belief-inducing snares of natural impulse and the senses.

The central achievement of rebirth is the denial of the mother, or at least her relegation to the Aristotelian role of incubator and supplier of raw material. Consider the banal commonplace, supposedly presenting a deep truth we all need painfully to learn, that we are each born alone and will die alone. Rather than being a deep and painful truth, this nostrum is a deep and harmful lie—at least, about being born (about dying, it depends on the life you've made, and on luck). To accept it is to embark on the culturally mandated erasure of maternity, the first step toward becoming a self-made man.

As Marilyn Frye writes about the erasure of women (in particular, of lesbians), "there is a peculiar mode of relating belief and action . . . according to which a project of annihilation can be seen to presuppose the nonexistence of the objects being eliminated."[2] She gives the example of the North American prairie's being described by white men as a desert, which they proceeded to turn it into. Similarly, the medicalization of childbirth managed to bring it about that children born to anaesthetized mothers *were* born alone, rather than experiencing birth as a shared process of absolutely unparalleled intimacy. This positing of aloneness in the face of tangible marks of connection appears in philosophy as the so-called "problem of other minds," which starts from the assumption that experience is essentially internal and inaccessible.

Far from being an immutable given, the essential isolation of the modern subject is a cultural achievement, perilously maintained by social, political, and economic structures that are coming increasingly undone. These structures perpetuate the illusion that the subject can, through domination, bridge the gulf he has

---

[2]Marilyn Frye, *The Politics of Reality: Essays in Feminist Theory* (Trumansburg, N.Y.: The Crossing Press, 1983), p. 163.

established between himself and the world without surrendering his independence.[3] Such structures are coming undone in part through the rebellions of those who have played the roles of the objectified others by virtue of being taken to embody some aspect of humanness from which the authorized knowers have isolated themselves in order to claim full rationality and universality.

From the standpoint of a rebellious other, I would like to look at Hamlet and Maggie Verver (along with those with whom she shares *The Golden Bowl*) as representative knowers, standing respectively at the dawn and the dusk of the day of the unified subject and the necessarily correlative world of objective facts. The fictions that they move in are, I believe, to a great extent about what it is to be a subject in the world at such times. The best philosophical account I know of the world Hamlet was groping his way into is Wittgenstein's *Tractatus*. Although it was written in the trenches of World War I, a war from which that world never really recovered, it can best be seen as the apotheosis of the epistemology and metaphysics whose birth was portrayed almost three hundred years earlier in the *Meditations*. And the best mainstream philosophical account I know of the unsettling of that world is Wittgenstein's *Philosophical Investigations*, along with other of his later work that more directly places philosophical change in a broader cultural context.

III. "... that within which passes show ..."

> The world is all that is the case.
> The world is the totality of facts, not of things.
> —Wittgenstein, *Tractatus*

The *Tractatus* got its impetus from demands for the definiteness of sense. Such demands were articulated in particular by Frege but have significantly older roots, and would require of meanings that they be absolutely fixed and determinate. The *Tractatus* is the ultimate attempt to pin meanings down, to tie them to an independent realm of facts that hold firm and are knowable to one single knower, that don't require a community to constitute them. The problem of reconciling independence with knowability is "solved" by the device of an isomorphism between the structures of thought and of the world. We know the world because, although it is wholly independent of us, it is *our* world. The self for the early Wittgenstein is "of the world but not in it": his analogy was with the eye as defining the field of vision.

It has been less noticed by commentators, who tend to focus on the rigid and rigidly correlated metaphysics and epistemology in the *Tractatus*, that a large part of Wittgenstein's motivation was to protect that which he took to be uncaptured by

---

[3]I do not use 'he', 'his', etc. in their allegedly generic senses; as I argue, the normative maleness of the knowing subject is part of its essential identity, as many of us who have been generously allowed to think in drag are discovering.

the facts, an inner realm of values that occupies a space different from the logical space of all that was the case.[4] The picture that emerges is similar to the picture Kant draws of the free, rational, moral self. Existing in the noumenal realm, the self—in its truest form, the will—becomes the locus of moral worth, however at odds it may be with what actually happens in the world. Value is determined wholly independently of anything outside the confines of the autonomous ego.[5] The will alone is free and moral: the rest is billiard balls. On Kant's view, as on Wittgenstein's in the *Tractatus*, the self is protected from the world, but at the cost of any place for actual, empirically realized individuality, of any ground on which the self and the world can meet and make a difference to each other.

This problem, of inserting the self—whose independence constitutes its freedom—into the world, is the analogue in moral philosophy of the epistemological problem of establishing some relation between the world and the self—whose independence constitutes its authority. The problem is a conceptual one, for self and world so constituted, but it is also a historical one: How did these connections come originally to be figured? The problems philosophers raise—or reveal, even if they mean rather to be solving them—lie beneath the surface of practices that depend on our acting as though those problems weren't there. If we look at the times when those practices were coming into existence, we can see what are now conceptual problems arising in people's attempts to be in the world in a way the world is not yet quite ready for.

It is in this way that Francis Barker writes about Hamlet, as an emerging modern man, lost in an Elsinore that was not ready for him. Hamlet is consequently torn between a view of the situation that was constituted by the structures of the court at Elsinore, which gave a meaning to all that was happening and dictated what he was to be feeling and what he was called upon to do, and the nascent consciousness of something else, a region of interiority whose meanings were not given by the world, that was uniquely *his*, tied to the particularities of his actually lived life. As Barker describes the world of Elsinore, it is one where the distinction does not exist between private life and affairs of state. Both equally derive their meaning and their structuring authority from the will of the king: "Organized under the general form of hierarchy, sanctioned in practice by force and metaphys-

---

[4]It is less noticed in part because the realm of values Wittgenstein had meant to protect was discarded as meaningless by the logical positivists (the most immediate heirs of the *Tractatus*, a book that both at the time he wrote it and when he later repudiated it, Wittgenstein clearly intended not to have any heirs).

[5]For Kant the sensing, desiring self is outside those confines, leaving the rational self alone in its freedom. Others have attempted to bring more of the self within the confines of the truly internal and value conferring. What all the attempts have in common, from the most austerely rational to the most free-wheelingly emotive, is the abrogation of valuing to the self defined by its independence from the facts—"is" does not imply "ought"; just because things *are* a certain way says nothing at all about how they *ought* to be, etc.

ically by God the King and God the Father whose just order it reflects, the single realm describes a full place, tense with patterns of fealty, reciprocity, obligation and command. The figure of the king guarantees, as locus and source of power and as master-signifier, a network of subsidiary relations which constitute the real practice and intelligibility of the lives of subjects."[6]

In the early "I know not 'seems'" soliloquy (I. ii. 76–86) Hamlet is attempting to draw a distinction between outward appearances and inner feeling, as much to convince himself of its intelligibility as to convince his mother of its reality. He has no stable confidence in the independent existence of his inner self, let alone in its precise contents and their meanings. Consider, for example, his invidious comparison of himself to the player who "[c]ould force his soul so to his own conceit" despite its being "all for nothing" (II. ii. 515–532). The player is acting "in a fiction, in a dream of passion": he produces the outward show of emotion despite the absence of any real cause for it. Hamlet seems to be distinguishing here between the display of emotion and its inner reality, but I don't think that's quite his meaning; rather, that's how we with that distinction firmly (I'd say *too* firmly) in place are inclined to read it.

The distinction Hamlet is drawing is between two "outward" things—the expression of emotion and the occasion or proper cause for it. That the player is "in a dream of passion" points not to the inner irreality of the feeling, but to its failure to correspond to the player's actual situation. Similarly, what Hamlet imagines the player acquiring that he, Hamlet, already has is not the passion, but "the motive and the cue for passion." As Barker argues, the dissembling and secrecy that are a part of life at court are not *deep*: "This world achieves its depth not in the figure of interiority by which the concealed inside is of another quality from what is external, but by a *doubling of the surface*. . . . The deceptions of the plenum which surrounds Hamlet are always ultimately identifiable as such . . . they are never beyond the reach of its epistemology" (Barker, *The Tremulous Private Body*, pp. 28, 36, emphasis his).

Later on (III. iv. 54–88), Hamlet berates Gertrude for her marriage to Claudius by insisting that one needed only to see his father and Claudius to be aware of the differences between them. The worshipful attitude Hamlet expresses toward his father and his disgust for Claudius are both sufficiently evoked—or so he says—merely by how each of them looks. He takes it as quite beyond doubt—at least for the purposes of shaming his mother—that the outward show is an adequate reflection of the inner truth. It is unclear what exactly we are to make of his feelings about his father or about Claudius, or of his confidence in appearances, but this unclarity itself reveals something about the instability of Hamlet's situation. It was, Barker argues, quite literally the body of the king, as spectacle, that bore world-organizing power and around which the rest of the realm fell into

[6]Francis Barker, *The Tremulous Private Body: Essays on Subjection* (London: Methuen, 1984), p. 31.

place. Hamlet describes his father as having "Hyperion's curls, the front of Jove himself, / An eye like Mars, to threaten and command, / A station like the herald Mercury / New-lighted on a heaven-kissing hill— / A combination and a form indeed / Where every god did seem to set his seal, / to give the world assurance of a man" (III. iv. 56–63). The reference to his being assuredly a man is intended to contrast for Gertrude with Hamlet's characterization of her current husband, but the picture is equally importantly of a king. In reciting it, particularly at such hyperbolic length, Hamlet is attempting to reinforce the foundations of a world within which it is clear how he is to act and feel—reinforce them against the erosion caused by his own doubts about the sources and nature of meaning.

There is a similar instability around the issue of naming. Hamlet hints at the Western romantic picture of an Eden of perfect, nonarbitrary signification, which he accuses *women* of disrupting by the arbitrariness of their practices of naming: "God hath given you one face, and you make yourselves another. You jig and amble and you lisp; you nickname God's creatures. . . ." (III. i. 139–42)."[7] Margaret W. Ferguson argues that in *Hamlet*, the power of kings to impose one definitive interpretation on texts or acts is deadly, while Hamlet's subversive punning is disruptively "antic." He seizes the power of signification in his own individual hands, but can manage only to subvert it: none of the meanings he imposes in that way stick. When he does disambiguate a text or a situation to his own ends, he is acting, fatally, as a king. He uses his father's seal ring to authenticate the forged letter sending Rosencrantz and Guildenstern to what Claudius, using *his* copy of the ring, had intended to be Hamlet's own death.[8] What he does not manage is the sort of epistemology, found most explicitly in Locke, that would have all meaning reside ultimately inside the minds of individual knowers, and only derivatively in the social world of shared communication.

Barker's account of the world-structuring power of kings has an almost explicitly Kantian ring: "It establishes a constitution within which subjects are profoundly implicated not because they 'know their place' . . . but because alterity of placement is always-already encoded as unthinkable. . . . This did not prevent rebellion, but the heavy price legitimacy extracts for such an act is the burden of dismembering the frame of place and sense itself" (Barker, *The Tremulous Private Body*, p. 32). In his ensuing discussion of *Lear* Barker speaks of the "disarticulation of reality itself" that follows on the "gesture of division that . . . fissures his kingdom, his family and his reason, for on this scene the state, kinship

---

[7]Madelon Gohlke, "'I wooed thee with my sword': Shakespeare's tragic paradigms," in Carolyn Ruth Swift Lenz, Gayle Greene, and Carol Thomas Neely, eds., *The Woman's Part: Feminist Criticism of Shakespeare* (Urbana, Il.: University of Illinois Press, 1980) p. 153.

[8]Margaret W. Ferguson, "Hamlet: Letters and Spirits," in Patricia Parker and Geoffrey Hartman, eds., *Shakespeare and the Question of Theory* (New York: Methuen, 1985), p. 300.

and sense repeat and extend into each other without break" (ibid., p. 33). It is as though the Kantian role of the categories, those world-structuring prerequisites to experience, were played by the placement of the body of the king. Kant's own characterization, grounded in the individual subject of experience, thus provides an account, not, as he intended it, of any possible epistemology, but specifically of the epistemology of modernity.

Hamlet has irresolved moments of nearly being such a subject, as he begins to articulate a sense of himself as defined from the inside out. Such a sense, along with the concomitant possibility that the interior will be at odds with the external, the objective, the obdurate world of facts, can be seen as definitive of the modern self. Hamlet was on the verge of becoming such a self, though in a world that had no idea of what to make of him, he could have but little idea of what to make of himself. Although its hallmark may be its claim to self-creation, such a self is, as much as any other, a social, historical achievement. Certain structures in the world are needed to create and maintain both the modern self and its illusion of being wholly self-made.

That the modern self embodies such a contradiction is at the heart of Barker's account, and again there are Kantian resonances. He writes of the "early embarrassment for bourgeois philosophy" posed by the simultaneous positing of the self as private and as knowledgeably appropriating the world, "an I which, if it encounters the world in anything other than a quizzical and contemplative manner, must alienate itself into an environment which inevitably traduces the richness of the subject by its mute and resistant externality" (ibid., p. 36). This embarrassment is Kant's "scandal"—the inability of philosophy to secure the epistemic relation of the individual self to the world. It is not a problem Kant managed to solve, nor have succeeding philosophical generations. One "solution" to the problem is to embrace it: "a quizzical and contemplative manner" is an excellent description of Montaigne's attitude toward the world, which preceded and was largely swamped by the more vigorous attitude associated with modern science. To read Montaigne is to learn one way of more gracefully living with the contradictions of bourgeois ideology.

Another possibility, of course, is to attempt to move beyond those contradictions by moving beyond the ideology that engenders them. Although he is an unlikely (political) revolutionary, Henry James, especially in the intricacies of his later novels, gives us, I think, some sense of what it would mean to do this.

IV. Beyond "the mere muffled majesty of irresponsible authorship"

> How could human behaviour be described? Surely only by sketching the actions of a variety of humans, as they are all mixed up together. What determines our judgment, our concepts and reactions, is not what *one* man is doing *now*, an individual action, but the whole hurly-burly of human actions, the background against which we see any action.
>
> —Wittgenstein, *Zettel*

> The *pre-conceived* idea of crystalline purity can only be removed by turning our whole examination around. (One might say: the axis of reference of our examination must be rotated, but about the fixed point of our real need.)
>
> —Wittgenstein, *Philosophical Investigations*

> The novel is the expression of a Galilean perception of language, one that denies the absolutism of a single and unitary language—that is, that refuses to acknowledge its own language as the sole verbal and semantic center of the ideological world. . . . The novel begins by presuming a verbal and semantic decentering of the ideological world, a certain linguistic homelessness of literary consciousness. . . .
>
> —Bakhtin, "Discourse in the Novel," *The Dialogic Imagination*

Although the modern in philosophical terms refers primarily to the structures that put and hold in place the conception of separate realms of objectivity and subjectivity, within the arts, the modern most often designates those people, works, and movements that attempt to come to some terms with the cracks in this structure, as well as with the rebelliousness it has engendered. It is interesting to note that, if we consider the philosophical sense of modernity, then all novels are (at least) modern, and not just in terms of their dates of composition. As Bakhtin argues in the passage that is an epigraph to this section,[9] the novel as a genre resides in a world of "heteroglossia"—of multiple, interacting systems of signification, a world after the reign of world-encompassing master discourses. The novels specifically designated as modern differ from their predecessors in explicitly problematizing the relationship between the self and the world, in, for example, no longer taking as fixed the structure of time and space as framing a story. They are, that is, as Geoffrey Nowell-Smith notes about the "modern novel, since Henry James," self-consciously *discours*, rather than purportedly transparent *histoires*.[10]

One of the reasons, I think, for self-conscious modernity, for the need of novelists to mark explicitly the contingencies and specificities of their own discourse(s), is the dominance particularly in the twentieth century of the language of science, which, as Bakhtin notes, is essentially nondiscursive, claiming an absolutely authoritative transparency: "In scientific activity, one must, of course, deal with another's discourse . . . but all this remains a mere operational necessity and does not affect the subject matter itself of the science, into whose composition the speaker and his discourse do not, of course, enter. The entire methodological apparatus of the mathematical and natural sciences is directed toward mastery over *mute objects*, *brute things*, that do not reveal themselves in words, that do

---

[9]M. M. Bakhtin, *The Dialogic Imagination*, ed. Michael Holquist (Austin: University of Texas Press, 1981), pp. 366ff.

[10]Geoffrey Nowell-Smith, "A Note on Story/Discourse," in Bill Nichols, ed., *Movies and Methods*, vol. II (Berkeley, Calif.: University of California Press, 1985), p. 552.

not *comment on themselves*" (Bakhtin, *The Dialogic Imagination*, p. 35, emphasis his).

This set of attitudes is at the heart of the positivism that has functioned in many research programs as a regulative ideal not just for the natural sciences but for the social sciences and even for the study of literature. The objects of knowledge in these latter fields are neither mute nor brute, but the reduction of their self-interpretations to the status of data is an attempt to treat them as though they were.[11] Similarly, Nowell-Smith notes the ("arguable") "ambition of certain novelists, from Flaubert onwards . . . to collapse discourse into history and to naturalize events so that they seem to exist in a space defined from nowhere, [although] most often the effect has been the reverse" (Nowell-Smith, "A Note," p. 552).

It is ironic that the discursive style of the novel, its heteroglossia, is one Bakhtin refers to, quite intelligibly, as "Galilean," when one of the hallmarks of the science Galileo helped to found has become the effacement of the radical possibilities of diversity in points of view. The eye behind the telescope acquired its authority by divesting itself of all particularity. Only by adopting the view from nowhere could it lay claim to seeing the world and its facts as they really are, rather than as they (merely) appear to someone, somewhere. This disembodied, and thereby authoritative, ego has extended its hegemony throughout Western culture, turning up recently, for example, as the rational, moral agent whom Rawls in *A Theory of Justice* places behind "the veil of ignorance": the assumption is that it's what we know (about how we are particularly placed in the world) that will hurt us in our attempts to think and act as legislators.

The individualism and disembodied disinterestedness that characterize the epistemically authoritative subject in modern Western thought are as influential in literary criticism as elsewhere. In reaction to them, Henry James frequently comments in the prefaces to his novels on his particular placement as author, on the epistemic problems of narration, and on the—in his opinion, misguided—adoption by critics of an authoritative, disinterested stance toward interpretation. Such a stance characterizes many critics' attempts to evaluate—or to figure out how James is evaluating—the characters in *The Golden Bowl*, in particular to evaluate them *morally*, as individual moral agents. Such attempts have not been notably successful; the evaluations are wildly varied and tend to be quite unpersuasive to those who figure the text and its inhabitants differently: subtle differences of emphasis can lead to utterly different evaluations of someone's moral character. One reason frequently given for this difficulty is the novelist's unconditional, quasi-parental love for his creatures, and his unwillingness to judge or condemn them. But I think in this novel—as, less extremely in others of James's, especially

[11]I am indebted for this formulation to conversations with, and an unpublished manuscript by, Michael Root.

later, work—there's more going on, including James's rejection of the preroga-tives of "the mere muffled majesty of irresponsible authorship."[12]

The novel is centrally *about* the difficulty of coming to stable moral or factual judgments concerning people and situations viewed, as modern epistemology would have us do, with detachment. As Patricia McKee argues, we are faced in *The Golden Bowl* with the intentional production of judgmental vertigo both by the novelist and by characters in the novel (Adam and, especially, Maggie), alongside the attempts of other characters (notably Charlotte and the Prince) to mobilize more or less effectual resources in the attempt to maintain what they regard as stability. McKee argues that James is presenting both marriage and narrative as "the union of differences . . . absolute in its wholeness, so that it cannot be taken apart or figured out." She quotes James in the Preface to *The Awkward Age*: he refers to the artistic fusion achieved in a successful work of art as a marriage, and he addresses an imagined critic who would take the work apart better to understand it: "'You can analyze in *your* way, oh, yes—to relate, to report, to explain; but you can't disintegrate my synthesis; you can't resolve the elements of my whole into different responsible agents or find your way at all (for your own fell purpose). My mixture has only to be perfect literally to bewilder you—you are lost in the tangle of the forest.'"[13]

The Prince shares with the critics who are thus liable to bewilderment the dominant epistemology of modernity, and, since, as McKee demonstrates, Maggie is constructing their marriage with the same intent to bewilder that James brings to the construction of his novel, the Prince ends up "lost in the tangle of the forest": thoroughly married, unchanged, and uncomprehending. This Prince, like the Prince of Denmark, attempts to bring exactly the wrong resources to bear on unraveling his situation, but whereas Hamlet's resources look ahead to a world not yet realized, Amerigo's are quite well-suited to the more ordinary parts of *his* world. They are, however, woefully unsuited to the world his wife and father-in-law have woven around him. These resources—those of both princes and of the critics James is tweaking—are drawn from the epistemology shared by modern science and the market economy, an epistemology of equivalences and exchange, of separation and control, of subjects and objects that know their places.

In order for Hamlet to make sense of his incoherent gestures toward a realm of interiority set against a world of independently stable facticity, he needed the epistemology whose apotheosis was the *Tractatus*. In order for us to make whatever sense we can of the worlds that James and the Ververs wove, we can turn to Wittgenstein's later work, in which the rigid stabilities of the *Tractatus* shift, and we lose what we had taken to be our bearings. McKee's account of the

---

[12]Henry James, *The Golden Bowl* (Harmondsworth: Penguin, 1966), p. 8.

[13]Patricia McKee, *Heroic Commitment in Richardson, Eliot, and James* (Princeton: Princeton University Press, 1986), p. 270.

novel focuses on Maggie's invention of a way to think, feel, and act that will adequately express her love for the Prince and make between them a genuine, seamless marriage. I want to look at some striking similarities between this account and much of what Wittgenstein discusses in his later work concerning the relationships in which we now stand to our language and our world. Thinking of the Prince as someone still captured by the more comprehensible earlier picture of those relationships, I want to raise some questions about what can happen when the mystifications of that picture are exposed and abandoned.

Maggie's victory is not in her coming clearly to see the situation—that her husband is the lover of her father's wife—and acting decisively on that perception. Rather, it is in her managing precisely *not* to act on it, and to arrange it that no one else perceives her as acting on it. Her intentions are hidden in particular from Charlotte, even as, because of those intentions, Charlotte is being banished, on the end of a "silken cord" in Adam's hand, to the America she loathes. Maggie quite willfully constructs a version of reality in which each of the separate and separable married couples needs to pursue its own course as an internally *in*separable entity, however much pain such a course may cause to those who had ties thereby severed. (And, like a conjurer, she draws everyone's attention to herself and her father as the sufferers of severed ties, diverting attention from the tie she cannot and will not acknowledge.)

Charlotte helplessly collaborates with Maggie in this construction: deprived even of Maggie's acknowledgement of what she has learned—receiving instead an absolution that makes equally impossible both restitution and justification—Charlotte seizes on "the terms of a fair exchange: Charlotte takes Mr. Verver in return for Maggie taking the Prince. Charlotte . . . create[s] a fiction in which she can believe: the fiction of getting her own back, or the fiction of justice" (McKee, *Heroic Commitment*, p. 338).

There are, crucially, two sets of "hard facts" in the book: Charlotte and Amerigo were lovers both before and during their marriages, and the golden bowl starts out cracked and ends up shattered. As facts these are irrefutable, although before the episode with the bowl forces Maggie to devise a new strategy for dealing with the fact of the adultery, she attempts simply not to allow it to penetrate her consciousness. The shopowner's revelations to Maggie tell her something she didn't know about the extent of Amerigo and Charlotte's intimacy *before* the marriage, but they also crystallize her awareness of their more recent involvement. (The bowl is, beneath its gilding, a single crystal of transparent and colorless glass: literally blank and inarticulate, it provides shape to what can form within or around it.)

For some time previously, as Fanny says, it hadn't been "'a question of belief or proof, absent or present; it's inevitably, with her [Maggie], a question of natural perception, of insurmountable feeling. She irresistibly *knows* that there's something between them. But she hasn't "arrived" at it, as you say, at all; that's exactly what she hasn't done, what she so steadily and intensely refuses to do.

She stands off and off, so as not to arrive; she keeps out to sea and away from the rocks, and what she most wants of me is to keep at a safe distance with her —as I, for my own skin, only ask not to come nearer' " (ibid., p. 389). Only after the bowl is smashed, and thereby decisively revealed as having been always-already cracked, does Maggie acknowledge the flaw at the heart of her marriage. But she acknowledges it only to proceed to deny it any meaning.

With a boldness that merits McKee's characterization of her as heroic, Maggie takes as the figure of her desire for her marriage the bowl—not as it lies shattered nor as it was invisibly cracked—but "as it *was* to have been. . . . The bowl with all happiness in it. The bowl without the crack" (James, *The Golden Bowl,* p. 445; quoted in McKee, ibid., p. 271). The bowl cannot be made seamlessly whole; as a figure for a marriage it would seem unavoidably to represent one shattered by the revelation of a flaw that lay hidden in it from its start. But Maggie cannot and will not accept this view of the situation; to start with, it is for her *a view of the situation*, not, as we might think and Fanny does think, simply the truth. What Fanny offers Maggie, by smashing the bowl, is the option of *denying* reality, turning her back on the truth, and going on in silent sham.

But Maggie won't have it: "her faith is not separable from the reality of the golden bowl. The golden bowl is the symbol both of the reality and of Maggie's faith" (McKee, ibid., p. 326). Rather than denying reality, Maggie willfully reconstructs it; she confronts the Prince simultaneously with her knowledge and her determination that, if he chooses their marriage, she will hold it together in a way that leaves no space for any imperfection. "Maggie not only 'reconstitutes' reality but constitutes, herself, the difference between lack and fullness; she fills in the differences" (ibid., p. 327).

If the bowl had not been cracked, Charlotte would have wanted to buy it as a present for the Prince, when they found it on the trip they took together ostensibly to look for a wedding present for Maggie. Although the shopowner assures her the flaw is undiscoverable, Charlotte raises the worry that it might be revealed if the bowl is smashed—to which he replies that only intentional violence could break it. Charlotte remains undecided about the significance of the crack, but it turns out that to the Prince's magically discerning eye, it was apparent, and fatal. The Prince combines Machiavellian politics with realist epistemology: he regards it as honorable and necessary to lie and deceive on occasion, but he has a firm regard for the facts; power lies in having and using them. Charlotte's epistemology is more pragmatic; if the bowl is never smashed, if Maggie and Adam never learn of the adultery, the bowl and the marriages will to all intents and purposes be exactly as they appear to be.

The question is what those intents and purposes are. James, in the Preface to *The Awkward Age* quoted above, refers to the "fell purpose" for which critics might attempt to extract individual responsible agents from the synthesis of his novel. The melodramatic term is actually more applicable to the attempts of Charlotte and Amerigo to act as agents responsible for the happiness of their marriages and their spouses, by extracting their own agency as separable constituents of the situation. They each attempt to give and to justify a limited meaning to their marriage, one to which they can "in fact" be faithful, which rests on maintaining the innocence (ignorance) of their spouses. There are for the two of them facts in the world, real and brute, and power resides in having possession of them, in controlling others' access to them, and in being able to bring them together, keep them apart, and confer meaning on them.[14]

Maggie sees things differently. For one thing, whereas Charlotte would have been hard-pressed to afford the bowl at its discounted price, Maggie could easily have afforded it even had it been perfect. It is in part the absence of any material constraint on how Maggie values things that reveals the presence of subtler constraints of consistency and, to use McKee's terms, responsibility and commitment. She does buy the bowl because no more for her than for her father is perfection the consideration it is for the Prince, whose own value lies in his pedigree, in his being the "real thing," or for Charlotte, whose value lies in her being able to maintain a perfection of appearances. Enormous wealth and the power that goes with it have placed the Ververs above such considerations—they confer value by the mere force of their own appreciation (a baffling impasse to the Prince, who feels thwarted in his need to know just what he's worth to them). For Maggie, as for Adam, a present, in particular, "was, by a rigorous law of nature, a foredoomed aberration, and that the more it *was* so the more it showed, and the more one cherished it for showing, how friendly it had been. The infirmity of art was the candour of affection, the grossness of pedigree the refinement of sympathy; the ugliest objects, in fact, as a general thing, were the bravest, the tenderest mementos. . . ." (James, *The Golden Bowl*, p. 406). And finally, when the bowl is not only revealed as having been cracked, but is decisively shattered, Maggie conjures the power, unavailable to Charlotte, to "reconstitute" it.

The Prince and Charlotte, sharing in slightly different forms the dominant epistemic spirit of the modern world, think of the facts as hard and given, and of power as residing in having, revealing, or concealing them, in recognizing what they mean to others, and in deciding what they will mean to oneself. For Maggie —and for James—facts and those who would know and value them are much more mutually implicated, both more in flux and less arbitrary, more a matter for creative construction and less independently variable. Such an epistemology can

---

[14]McKee argues (pp. 332–40) that both the Prince and Charlotte see the situation in terms of tests, trials, proofs, knowledge, charges, justifications, and retribution, whereas for the Ververs it is a matter of faith, groundless and absolute belief, trust, inexplicable love, freedom, redemption, and commitment. Just these oppositions structure *Othello*, which becomes a tragedy when Othello accepts not the set of attitudes offered by Desdemona, but the more rational and scientific ones offered by Iago. I argue for this view of the play and its connections to Cartesian, and modern scientific, epistemology in "Othello's Doubt/Desdemona's Death."

be found in Wittgenstein's *Philosophical Investigations*. McKee's account of *The Golden Bowl*, which I have been drawing on liberally (without doing full justice to its subtlety and complexity), characterizes Maggie's and Adam's attitudes and actions in ways that are illustratative of some central themes of that book.

McKee writes, for example, about Adam's decision to marry Charlotte, that the "effect of the solution is to erase the cause for the solution" (McKee, *Heroic Commitment*, p. 283). He starts out worrying that his marriage would lead Maggie to feel he was consoling himself for losing her to *her* marriage, and comes round to thinking of his marriage to Charlotte as being as felicitous as Maggie's to the Prince's—that is, a good thing in itself rather than reparative, since no need for reparation is admitted. In his marrying as she did, he is affirming the "fusion" between them rather than healing a breach. In looking for a solution to a problem, Adam would be committed, as he quickly realizes, to a view of the situation from which there is no egress: "'Why do you demand explanations? If they are given you, you will once more be facing a terminus. They cannot get you any further than you are at present.'"[15]

Attempts to propound solutions, develop theories, and offer explanations in philosophy are, on Wittgenstein's later view, doomed. They serve only to make it more obvious that there is a problem, while they mislead us as to its nature: "The problems are solved, not by giving new information, but by arranging what we have always known" (Wittgenstein, *P.I.,* sec. 109). Wittgenstein points to "a remarkable and characteristic phenomenon in philosophical investigation: the difficulty . . . is not that of finding the solution but rather that of recognizing as the solution something that looks as if it were only a preliminary to it. 'We have already said everything.—Not anything that follows from this, no, *this* itself is the solution!'" He goes on to connect our demand for a further, deeper solution to our looking for explanations, when what we need is a description, "if we give it the right place in our considerations. If we dwell upon it, and do not try to get beyond it. The difficulty here is: to stop" (ibid., sec. 314).

On McKee's account the difficulties Maggie and Adam face and resolve are also ones of when to stop and of what will make it possible to stop: "Maggie, too, when confronted with the fact that her husband has had an affair with Charlotte, never addresses the problem, per se, at all. . . . She never asks why, how, or how could you? This refusal to talk about the problem is shocking not only in its moral but in its epistemological negligence" (McKee, *Heroic Commitment*, p. 284). Epistemological negligence is precisely the charge traditional philosophers bring against Wittgenstein: even if classical foundationalism may need to be radically revised or even scrapped, surely something must take its place, do its job of epistemic policing, arresting faulty reasoning, certifying appropriate sources of evidence, keeping knowledge in order and free from

[15]Ludwig Wittgenstein, *Philosophical Investigations*, trans., G. E. M. Anscombe (New York: Macmillan, 1953), sec. 315. Cited as *P.I.*

imposters. To say, as Wittgenstein notoriously does, "This is simply what I do" (Wittgenstein, *P.I.*, sec. 217), seems to be to abandon any standards of truth or of rationality.

Not to be negligent is to be responsible, and James and Wittgenstein are equally concerned to redefine what we take that to mean. In the tradition they are criticizing, responsibility has meant conformity to standards of thought and behavior that are given independently of that thought and behavior. (Thus, epistemic responsibility would require adherence to transcendently valid modes of reasoning fitted for ascertaining independently existing truths about the world.) Both authors suggest that if we define responsibility this way, we will end up committed to chasing a chimera and failing to attend *responsibly* to what we are actually doing. They locate our responsibility in our attention to our words and our behavior in their actual contexts, rather than in the idealized contexts of ultimately grounded explanation or ultimate moral justification (unlike, for example, Kant, who would have us judge our actions not by how they fit into the real world, but by how they would fit into the ideally moral Kingdom of Ends).

Along with exhorting us to stop chasing after explanations, both authors try to shift our attention from the supposedly more real depths (where, of course, we are sure the explanations lie) to explore the surfaces. McKee describes the use of the image of floating to characterize Maggie, referring to her sense of her actions (toward the Prince) as hovering over and detached from conviction (about his infidelity), and to Adam's sense of her passion as her being cradled buoyantly on a sea: "the image not only represents feelings, like knowledge, as something not to be gone into but insists that passion is a matter of surface rather than depth" (McKee, *Heroic Commitment*, p. 285).

In countering his interlocutor, who is held by the picture of the decisive reality of what is going on inside us when we expect or hope, Wittgenstein asks "What does it mean to say 'What is happening now has significance' or 'has deep significance'? What is a *deep* feeling? . . . What is happening now has significance—in these surroundings. The surroundings give it its importance" (Wittgenstein, *P.I.*, sec. 583). I was initially disconcerted by the conjunction in this passage of "a deep feeling" (one of profundity or perseverance) with "deep significance" (what it is that supposedly really decides the question about what state we are in). It is the same conjunction that occurs, also disconcertingly, in the passage from McKee—"feelings, like knowledge." In both passages the search for explanation, for deep understanding, is being problematized in a way that links it with the assumption that our truest feelings are the ones that lie most deeply buried: the truth has been presumed to lie beneath the surface, communicating in the causal code of signs and symptoms, decipherable to the expert and undeniably more real than the mere appearances we encounter on the surface.

Maggie faces the revelations afforded by the bowl, as Wittgenstein acknowledges the myriad of justificatory practices in which we do engage. What is being denied is the ultimate coerciveness of those revelations or those practices, a coerciveness that has been taken to lie in the supposedly special ways in which they are grounded: in Truth and Rationality. To break the hold of that coerciveness is to be free to acknowledge our role in constructing the framework in terms of which they are not just brutely there, but meaningful. We are free, that is, in McKee's paradoxical formulation, to be responsible. (The conjunction of freedom and responsibility is, of course, not a new one. But it usually turns out to be either Kantian—reducing freedom to the terms of antecedently existing moral responsibility—or Sartrean—reducing responsibility to the terms of voluntaristic, wholly unconstrained freedom.)

We need to learn not just how to find answers, but which questions to ask, and which not to. And when we do ask, we need to learn how and when to stop, how and when to "leave certain things alone . . . " (McKee, *Heroic Commitment*, p. 289). Philosophy, similarly, "leaves everything as it is," and "it cannot give it any foundation either" (Wittgenstein, *P.I.*, sec. 124). The interlocutor demands (as would Prince Hamlet, and as might Prince Amerigo, if he weren't so completely "squared"), "But, if you are *certain*, isn't it that you are shutting your eyes in face of doubt?" And Wittgenstein replies, "They are shut" (ibid., sec. 224). Amidst all the problems and attempted solutions, "the real discovery is the one that makes me capable of stopping doing philosophy when I want to.—The one that gives philosophy peace, so that it is no longer tormented by questions that bring *itself* into question" (ibid., sec. 133).

That is, philosophical problems, like the problems Adam and Maggie encounter and learn to lay to rest without "solving," are problems that call into question the nature of the enterprise (or of the self) and that consequently allow for no ground on which to stand while attempting to work them out. Epistemologies, such as those associated with modern science, that rest on the provision of successful solutions to philosophical problems—notably to the problems of scepticism—will need either to be abandoned or to be recast in ways that acknowledge the need to rest with descriptions of the practices that create and transmit knowledge, without demanding proofs that those practices are well-founded.

The need to rest with such descriptions poses a particular problem for those of us who find ourselves living in a world whose practices we find oppressive. There is on this view no mutually agreeable ground of neutrality on which to resolve the conflicts between those practices and the alternatives we envision and create. We can neither hold fast to the Enlightenment ideal of a shared rational core of selfhood that, if given voice, will lead us to agree, nor can we retreat to the acknowledgement of irreconcilable differences and effect a divorce from those whose world is different from ours.

The main reason for this latter impossibility, in the terms of *The Golden Bowl*, is that the loss is greater than we can intelligibly sustain: we cannot hold on to the confidence that, however parochial the world of values may be, the world of facts is unitary and fully shared. There is no such easy separation; that there are such things as facts, objectively ascertainable, independently existing, separate from people and what they need, want, and do, is itself a historical achievement. It depended for its accomplishment and depends for its maintenance on a specific, though to some extent variable, set of social, economic, and political institutions. And it is precisely those institutions—of capitalism and of patriarchy—that some of us are seeking to overturn.

One of the lingering temptations of foundationalism is, ironically, that it would seem to be needed to mount, and to justify, a fundamental critique of the social, political, and economic institutions that structure the production and distribution of both knowledge and power: such a critique would seem to require unshifting ground to stand on. Part of the requirement of such ground would be a universally valid epistemology, and the irony is that part of the oppressiveness of the hegemonic construction of knowledge is its claim to be providing precisely that. It is characteristic of modern scientific epistemology to claim universal validity by subsuming the purposes that might lie behind such constructions to the single one of distanced and dominating control, and to render that purpose either invisible or apparently inevitable. The purposefulness of the alternative epistemology that emerges from Wittgenstein's later work is by contrast both manifest and various.

Discussions about the political implications of Wittgenstein's writing rest on the question of whether we can acknowledge that the ground of our discourse is socially constructed and still attempt to use that discourse to mount a critique of its own ground. Or are the implications necessarily relativistic or conservative: deprived of any neutral ground to stand on, do we have to accept on its own terms any "form of life" richly enough articulated to stand on its own?[16] It is to questions like these that I think we need to turn if, as I do, we find the world that Maggie weaves, of unquestioning love, willed silences, closed-eyed faith, and seamless marriage perhaps, in McKee's term, "heroic," but definitely chilling.

Maggie's heroism comes from her envisioning and implementing a radical epistemology. But such an epistemology merely makes visible what was previously hidden—the possibility of and need for moral and political critique. By itself it does not provide that critique. Maggie's power to create reality as she would have it be comes from her (father's) wealth, and she uses it in the service of keeping the Prince as she would keep a beautiful object she had set her heart on. We may be (I am) troubled by such behavior, and by the power that makes it possible, but if we attempt to criticize her work—or that of James—by adopting the Prince's stabler, more ordered scheme of facts and values, we will end up,

[16]For a lucid discussion of this question, and an extensive bibliography on it, see Andrew Lugg, "Was Wittgenstein a conservative thinker?" in *The Southern Journal of Philosophy* 23 (1985): 465–74. Sabina Lovibond's *Realism and Imagination in Ethics* (Minneapolis: University of Minnesota Press, 1983) is an excellent extended discussion of the moral and political implications of Wittgensteinian epistemology.

as he did, "lost in the tangle of the forest." We may resist the entanglement, seeing clearly the political nature of *any* epistemology. But we need further to create the conditions for the possibility of an actual political critique that does not depend on the existence of some stable ground that is not itself subject to such critique. We need, that is, an epistemology that is radical in substance, not just in form.[17]

[17]My debt to Stanley Cavell's writing, teaching, and conversation is extensive and, I presume, evident to anyone familiar with his work. I owe a great deal, though less directly, to Michel Foucault and Jacques Derrida, in part through inheriting Barker's and McKee's indebtedness. For the relevance of Bakhtin to this essay, I am indebted to Patricia Yeager's " 'Because a fire was in my head': Eudora Welty and the dialogic imagination" (*PMLA*, October 1984). I have benefited from working in a stimulating and supportive feminist community at the University of Minnesota and in the Society for Women in Philosophy, and I have learned a great deal from recent work in feminist epistemology and philosophy of science, especially Evelyn Fox Keller's *Reflections on Gender and Science* (New Haven: Yale University Press, 1985). Thanks to the University of Minnesota for the support provided by a Bush Sabbatical Grant and by the astute and insightful editorial help of Ruth Wood, and to Michael Root for encouragement, good ideas, and tough but friendly criticism.

8

Missing Mothers / Desiring Daughters: Framing the Sight of Women

> How could she—oh how could she have become a part of the picture on the screen, while her mother was still in the audience, out there, in the dark, looking on?
>
> —Olive Higgins, *Stella Dallas*

Recent work in feminist film theory has focused on the nature of the gaze, both of the characters within a film and of the spectator addressed by the film. Questions have been raised about the relations of the gaze to subjectivity, to gender, and to sexuality, and about the relations among those three.[1] In particular, it has been argued, most notably by Laura Mulvey in her germinal essay, "Visual Pleasure and Narrative Cinema,"[2] that the cinematic gaze is gendered male and characterized by the taking of the female body as the quintessential and deeply problematic object of sight. In such accounts, the female gaze—and along with it female subjectivity—comes to seem impossible.

Yet women do, of course, see movies. Furthermore, many classic Hollywood films were made with a specifically female audience in mind, clearly not

---

This essay is a response to a number of people and events: to Stanley Cavell, who evoked my serious interest in films; to discussions with the students in a course I taught using *Pursuits of Happiness* in the University of Minnesota English and philosophy departments in the fall of 1984; and to several years of discussing related issues in a faculty reading group. My thanks to all, especially my colleagues John Mowitt, Martin Roth, and Eileen Sivert. Thanks also to Marilyn Frye for helpful discussions about the values and limits of theory, and to Michael Root for conversation, encouragement, and editing advice. I received massive and invaluable editorial help from Ruth Wood, whose strenuous attempts to produce clarity have, I hope, borne fruit. My research time was supported by a Bush Sabbatical Fellowship from the University of Minnesota.

[1]See, for example, E. Ann Kaplan, *Women and Film: Both Sides of the Camera* (New York: Methuen, 1983). See also Teresa de Lauretis, *Alice Doesn't: Feminism, Semiotics, Cinema* (Bloomington: Indiana Univ. Press, 1984); hereafter abbreviated *AD*.

[2]Laura Mulvey, "Visual Pleasure and Narrative Cinema," *Screen* 16 (Autumn 1975): 6–18; reprinted in *Movies and Methods: An Anthology*, ed. Bill Nichols, 2 vols. (Berkeley and Los Angeles: Univ. of California Press, 1985), vol. 2, pp. 303–15.

addressing that audience as though it were in masculine drag. And there are movies, in particular many of the same movies, that include women characters who see in ways that are coded as distinctively female.[3] My epigraph, from the novel on which the classic maternal melodrama *Stella Dallas* was based,[4] poignantly suggests that neither the presence of active women on the screen nor the acknowledged presence of viewing women in the audience by itself challenges the patriarchal logic of the gaze. There are, however, also specifically feminist films, made from and for an oppositional spectatorial position, and there are feminist film viewers, critics, and theorists looking at all sorts of films.[5] How shall we account for all these gazes and for the subjectivities behind them?

These issues are addressed elsewhere in feminist theory, for example, in the studies of the normative maleness of the scientist, the philosopher, the artist, and the citizen.[6] Female subjectivity, then, may often seem oxymoronic; indeed some essays appear to demonstrate conclusively the impossiblity of their having been authored.[7] There are at least three possible responses to the recognition that women do see, desire, and know despite the compelling theoretical demonstrations

---

[3]For an account of the issues raised by the centrality of women both in the narrative and in the address of a film genre, see Mary Ann Doane, *The Desire to Desire: The Woman's Film of the 1940's* (Bloomington: Indiana Univ. Press, 1987).

[4]Quoted in Kaplan, "The Case of the Missing Mother: Maternal Issues in Vidor's *Stella Dallas*," *Heresies: A Feminist Publication on Art and Politics* 16 (Fall 1983): 81–85.

[5]In addition to the works already cited, see the essays in the "Feminist Criticism" section of *Movies and Methods*; Michelle Citron et. al., "Women and Film: A Discussion of Feminist Aesthetics," *New German Critique* 13 (Winter 1978): 83–107; Judith Mayne, "Feminist Film Theory and Criticism," *Signs: Journal of Women in Culture and Society* 11 (Autumn 1985): 81–100; and Mary C. Gentile, *Film Feminisms: Theory and Practice* (Westport, Conn.: Greenwood Press, 1985).

[6]On the scientist, see Evelyn Fox Keller, *Reflections on Gender and Science* (New Haven, Conn.: Yale Univ. Press, 1985). On the philosopher, see *Discovering Reality: Feminist Perspectives on Epistemology, Metaphysics, Methodology, and Philosophy of Science*, ed. Sandra Harding and Merrill B. Hintikka (Dordrecht: Reidel, 1983); and Genevieve Lloyd, *The Man of Reason: "Male" and "Female" in Western Philosophy* (Minneapolis: Univ. of Minnesota Press, 1984). On the artist, see Linda Nochlin, "Why Have There Been No Great Women Artists?" in *Art and Sexual Politics: Women's Liberation, Women Artists, and Art History,* ed. Thomas B. Hess and Elizabeth C. Baker (New York: Collier, 1973), pp. 1–39; and Germaine Greer, *The Obstacle Race: The Fortunes of Women Painters and Their Work* (New York: Farrar, Straus, Giroux, 1979). On the citizen, see Susan Moller Okin, *Women in Western Political Thought* (Princeton, N.J.: Princeton Univ. Press, 1979).

[7]The best Anglo-American example of this phenomenon that I am aware of is Catharine A. MacKinnon, "Feminism, Marxism, Method, and the State: An Agenda for Theory," *Signs* 7 (Spring 1982): 515–44.

of the maleness of the gaze, of desire, and of epistemic authority: one is that we do it in drag, by tapping what Freud called our innate bisexuality;[8] the second is that we do it as socially constructed females, in ways masculinist regimes have uses for; and the third is that we, somehow, impossible as it may seem, do it in creative rebellion, as feminists.

The first option is *theoretically* unproblematic once one accepts that gender is socially constructed: the norms of maleness are learnable, and some girls and women, especially those of privileged race and class, have of late been allowed or even encouraged to learn some of them, such as those governing the academic and work worlds.[9] It is the latter two, more problematic but also more promising, options that interest me here. In particular, I am interested in looking at the second option for clues as to how the theoretically impossible third option—feminist subjectivity (or sexuality or desire or knowledge or agency)—can exist.

Patriarchy is like concrete: it is structured seamlessly and allows nothing through—in theory. In actuality, however, there are ailanthus trees, which can grow in any crack in the concrete and proliferate by dropping seeds into new and widened cracks, producing more ailanthus trees and less and less perfect concrete. There is nothing about ailanthus trees in concrete theory, and there is no ailanthus theory: the cracks are random from the perspective of the concrete, and the trees grow wherever they can find a foothold; there's no telling where. A theory of patriarchy is useful since its seamlessness and perfect structure provide a coherent logic that is genuinely explanatory, but such a theory does not provide the whole truth. Women's socially obedient gazes, desires, and thoughts are part of what patriarchy allows for and part of what we can theorize: they are part of the concrete. But they are also good places to look for cracks and to plant the seeds for the ailanthus trees of feminist oppositional consciousness.[10]

One possible place to start looking for oppositional consciousness is in the films Stanley Cavell discusses in *The Pursuits of Happiness*, extremely popular

---

[8]For one account of how we do this, see Mulvey, "Afterthoughts on 'Visual Pleasure and Narrative Cinema' Inspired by *Duel in the Sun* (King Vidor, 1946)," *Framework* 15–17 (1981): 12–15.

[9]Actually learning and living these norms is, of course, far from unproblematic for any woman. For accounts of the inherent tensions and instabilities, see ibid.; de Lauretis, *AD*; and Mayne, "Feminist Film Theory and Women at the Movies," in *Profession 87*, ed. Phyllis Franklin (New York: Modern Language Association of America, 1987), pp. 14–19.

[10]Similar approaches to feminist theorizing can be found in de Lauretis, *AD*, and in Harding, *The Science Question in Feminism* (Ithaca, N.Y.: Cornell Univ. Press, 1986). See also Marilyn Frye, *The Politics of Reality: Essays in Feminist Theory* (Trumansburg, N.Y.: Crossing Press, 1983); hereafter abbreviated *PR*.

films that are little discussed by feminist film theorists.[11] These comedies from the thirties and forties, particularly as Cavell discusses them, seem to offer counterexamples to the gaze-as-male theories. For example, though it has been argued that both the spectatorial gaze *at* a movie and the gazes of characters *within* a movie are normatively male—and conversely, that the female gaze is absent, stigmatized, or punished—in these films women are allowed, even encouraged, to look to (and for) their heart's content. Katharine Hepburn is told explicitly and repeatedly in *The Philadelphia Story* that to be a "real woman" she has to learn not to be a beautiful statue; she has to become a seer, not the seen. Rosalind Russell in *His Girl Friday* is a reporter, Ruth Hussey in *The Philadelphia Story*, a photographer, and Hepburn in *Adam's Rib*, a lawyer, who, although punished for making a spectacle of Spencer Tracy, transgresses—if at all—only in the nature of her orchestration of the gazes in the courtroom, not in her command of the gaze *per se*. Similarly, when Barbara Stanwyck as the Lady Eve undermines the authority of Henry Fonda's senses, we are allowed to sympathize with Fonda without concluding that epistemic authority in general is more rightfully his than hers.

On the narrative level, too, these films seem counterexemplary. They address many of the same issues raised by discussions of the gaze, particularly by those twentieth-century theories of narrative that see the gaze as gendered male by its placement in a male Oedipal frame.[12] In these theories, the Oedipus story is seen as the quintessential narrative, and exclusive focus on the male version stems from the widespread acceptance of an essentially Freudian account of the genesis of female sexuality as the learned forgoing of active desire. The female story cannot stand as its own narrative; rather, we have the story of how a girl comes to embody the desired goal and the reward of the male developmental quest. But the fates of the heroines of the *Pursuits of Happiness* films are as interesting and as connected to their own desires as are the fates of the heroes, and the paths to those fates are as complex and as much, if not more, the subject of the films: these women are hardly milestones along a male Oedipal journey.

Connecting the issues of the female gaze and of the female narrative is the issue of desire. As Cavell repeatedly stresses, a central theme of these films is the heroine's acknowledgment of her desire and of its true object—frequently the man from whom she mistakenly thought she needed to be divorced. The heroine's acknowledgment of her desire, and of herself as a subject of desire, is for Cavell what principally makes a marriage of equality achievable. It is in this achievement (or the creation of the grounds for the hope of it) that Cavell wants to locate the

[11]Stanley Cavell, *Pursuits of Happiness: The Hollywood Comedy of Remarriage* (Cambridge, Mass.: Harvard Univ. Press, 1981): hereafter abbreviated *PH*. The films Cavell discusses are *The Lady Eve, It Happened One Night*, *Bringing up Baby, The Philadelphia Story*, *His Girl Friday, Adam's Rib*, and *The Awful Truth.*

[12]See de Lauretis, *AD*, pp. 103–57.

feminism of the genre: it is the "comedy of equality" (Cavell, *PH*, p. 82). There is, therefore, an obvious explanation in Cavell's terms for the anomalous nature of these films: if their vision is explicitly feminist in embracing an ideal of equality, in approvingly foregrounding female desire, and in characterizing that desire as active and as actively gazing, then they would not be expected to fit an analysis based on films whose view of female desire and the female gaze is as passive, absent, or treacherous. If we accept Cavell's readings, these films provide genuine counterexamples to feminist claims of the normative masculinity of film (in general or in Hollywood).

My affection for these films, and the ways in which Cavell accounts for that affection, lead me to want to believe that his account, or something like it, is true; that there did briefly emerge a distinctively feminist sensibility in some popular Hollywood movies, one which unsurprisingly succumbed to the repressive redomestication of women in the postwar years. But, for a number of reasons, I can't quite believe it. Some version of the feminist critical theory of popular cinema does, in an odd way, apply to these movies: they are, to use a frequent phrase of Cavell's, the exceptions that prove the rule. Though they do have some claim to being considered feminist, their feminism is seriously qualified by the terms in which it is presented, by the ways in which female desire and the female gaze are framed.

The clue to my unease with Cavell's readings, with the films themselves, and with the feminism they embody is found in the double state of motherlessness (neither having nor being one) that is requisite for the heroines. By exploring the absence of mothers and maternity in these comedies, I want to illuminate some features of the distinctively female, though only stuntedly feminist, gaze they depict. I will argue that such a gaze is one a masculinist world has little trouble conscripting, and that its incompatibility with maternity functions to keep it within bounds. Turning then to melodrama, which, as Cavell has argued, is the cinematic home of the mother/daughter relationship,[13] I want to explore a different, but equally conscriptable, female gaze—the maternal. Finally, I want to suggest that we can open a space for the *feminist* gaze by redrawing the lines of sight.

Missing Mothers/Desiring Daughters: Take One

> . . . this turning from the mother to the father points . . . to a victory of intellectuality over sensuality—that is, an advance in civilization, since maternity is

[13]See Cavell, "Psychoanalysis and Cinema: The Melodrama of the Unknown Woman," in *Images in Our Souls: Cavell, Psychoanalysis, and Cinema,* ed. Joseph H. Smith and William Kerrigan, *Psychiatry and the Humanities,* vol. 10 (Baltimore: The Johns Hopkins Univ. Press, 1987), pp. 11–43. A revised and expanded version of this essay appears in the *The Trial(s) of Psychoanalysis*, ed. Françoise Meltzer (Chicago: Univ. of Chicago Press, 1988), pp. 227–58.

> proved by the evidence of the senses while paternity is an hypothesis, based on an inference and a promise. Taking sides in this way with a thought-process in preference to a sense perception has proved to be a momentous step.
>
> —Freud, *Moses and Monotheism*

> Lost to the daughter . . . [the mother] nevertheless rules her daughter's life with the injunctions of the culture-mother: "You must bury your mother, you must give yourself to your father."
>
> —Sandra M. Gilbert, "Life's Empty Pack"

> The question then arises of how this happens: in particular, how does a girl pass from her mother to an attachment to her father? or, in other words, how does she pass from her masculine phase to the feminine one to which she is biologically destined?
>
> —Freud, "Femininity"

Cavell explicitly acknowledges that the motherlessness of the heroines in the films he discusses poses a problem. In his most extended discussion of the missing mothers, he admits that "no account of these comedies will be satisfactory that does not explain this absence, or avoidance," since it raises "a question about the limitations of these comedies, about what it is their laughter is seeking to cover" (Cavell, *PH*, p. 57). The problem is not unique to these films: the mothers of comedic heroines are quite commonly absent—not dead or gone, but simply unremarkedly nonexistent, as they are notably in *The Lady Eve* and *It Happened One Night*. Although he recognizes the importance and the depth of this odd and troubling feature of the apparent paternal parthenogenesis of comedic heroines, Cavell goes on not to explain it, but to "offer three guesses about regions from which an explanation will have to be found" (Cavell, *PH*, p. 57)—the social, the psychological or dramatic, and the mythical. My sense is that to the extent that such explanations will be adequate, those very explanations undercut the laughter. The "limitations of these comedies" are, from a feminist perspective, fatal, if not to our pleasure in them,[14] then to our taking that pleasure seriously in the ways Cavell would urge us to do. The motherlessness of the heroines is the clue to the male framing of the desiring female gazes that provide so much of that pleasure.

In his guess about the region of the social, Cavell notes the generation to which the absent mothers would have belonged. He refers to this generation as the one that "won the right to vote without at the same time winning the issues in terms of which voting mattered enough" (Cavell, *PH*, p. 58). As a result, the following generation—that of the heroines of these films—was the first in which American women grew up with the expectation of formal political equality, one of the effects of which is to raise the hopes of substantive equality and to make the

---

[14]On the loss of pleasure attendant on feminist film criticism, see Mulvey, "Visual Pleasure and Narrative Cinema," p. 306.

traditional compromises of female selfhood no longer seem inevitable. Cavell suggests that the challenges thereby offered might appear sufficiently terrifying to account for the daughters' repression of the memory of those responsible for creating them. As an explanation, this is puzzling. The maternal erasure would seem to be in the service of the repression of the terror of those challenges, but it is integral to Cavell's account that the daughters confront the challenges: why should they repress the mothers?

More adequate explanations can be found by exploring Cavell's other two regions, the psychological or dramatic and the mythical. The two are closely connected, not surprisingly, given Cavell's reliance on Freud and Freud's on mythology.[15] Initially, however, Cavell's guess about the psychological or dramatic reasons for motherlessness is also puzzling, since it focuses not on the absence of women's mothers but on the presence of their fathers—as though one could have only one true parent. His argument is that "there is a closeness children may bear to the parent of the opposite sex which is enabling for a daughter but crippling to a son" (Cavell, *PH*, p. 57). (The "crippled sons" in a number of these films are men who are permanently attached to their mothers; they are the men the heroines mistakenly turn to in flight from their own desires.) Beyond the puzzling shift of attention from absent mothers to present fathers, there is the further puzzle about why this should be so: why should the love of a daughter for her father stand less in the way of her coming to love someone else than a son's love for his mother?

From a psychoanalytic perspective, the answer is that a girl's connection to her father is inherently more fungible—more replaceable by a substitute—than is a boy's connection to his mother.[16] The maternal connection for both males and females is the original one, the one wherein attachment is initially learned. The attachment of a girl to her father is always already a substitute; she enters into it through learning what it is to transfer love and desire from one object to another: it is the model of fungibility.

Males are supposed to learn to shift their desire from their mothers under the threat of castration attendant upon Oedipal desires. For boys the Oedipus complex "is not simply repressed, it is literally smashed to pieces by the shock of threatened castration. . . . In normal, or, it is better to say, ideal cases, the Oedipus complex exists no longer, even in the unconscious; the super-ego has become its heir."[17]

---

[15]Cavell makes his reliance on Freud explicit in "Freud and Philosophy: A Fragment," *Critical Inquiry* 13 (Winter 1987): 386–93. This "fragment" has been integrated into Cavell's longer essay, "Psychoanalysis and Cinema."

[16]I am indebted to Ronald de Sousa for the application of the concept of fungibility to emotions and their objects. See de Sousa, "Self-Deceptive Emotions," in *Explaining Emotions*, ed. Amelie Oksenberg Rorty (Berkeley and Los Angeles: Univ. of California Press, 1980), esp. pp. 292–94.

[17]Sigmund Freud, "Some Psychical Consequences of Anatomical Distinction between the Sexes," *The Standard Edition of the Complete Psychological Works of Sigmund Freud*, ed. and trans. James Strachey, 24 vols. (London: Hogarth, 1953–74), 19: 257.

In the case of a girl's attachment to her father, no such destruction is either possible or necessary: it is impossible, since in Freud's view she is already castrated, and it is unnecessary, since, being both passive and secondary, her desire for her father poses no threat to her future development. What is necessary in her case is precisely that such an attachment occur, that is, that she shift her desire away from her mother.

Freud's account of the shift in a girl's desire, which takes her recognition of "the fact of being castrated" as its primary cause, is notoriously problematic.[18] But even if one rejects completely the idea that a girl's turning away from her mother pivots on her discovery of the supposedly obvious and natural inferiority of her genitals, one still needs to explain how the socially mandated shift of love object from mother to father could occur. Presumably such a shift requires some powerfully motivating forces, however different from the ones Freud postulates. It also must leave some considerable residue of loss, a grief at the heart of socially acceptable femininity, which Freud barely glimpses. Cavell more than glimpses it, but he leaves it largely buried: unearthed it would dishearteningly reveal the costs, in the world Freud describes, of comedy, and challenge its definition of ending in happiness defined as marriage. By the rules of such a world, not only is a girl's attachment to her father not inhibiting of later attachments, but it is positively necessary in establishing her heterosexuality by breaking her attachment to her mother beyond recollection.

Cavell notes that marriage in classical romance requires the discovery of one's origins, the identity of one's parents. In contrast, the comedies of remarriage (as he refers to the films in *Pursuits of Happiness*) require that one learn and acknowledge one's sexual identity. But typically for the heroine in both sorts of narrative, the acknowledgment of parents is the acknowledgment of fathers and the mandated repression of mothers, a move that is of a piece with the acknowledgment of (hetero)sexual identity. The girl is supposed to claim heterosexuality as her genuine sexual identity, the deepest expression of self, not just as a "haven of refuge" from the ambivalences of her attachment to her mother, as Freud describes its initial attraction (Freud, "F," 22: 129). Repressing the attachment to her mother amounts to identifying her father as her true parent, forgetting the love and desire that preceded her love and desire for him. Doing that also requires learning *how* to do it, that is, learning how to dispose of desire according to demands that are external to it, through cooperating in the fiction that the desires she newly acquires are the ones that were there all along.

Through such cooperation girls are learning that there is a connection between the particular fungibility of female desire and the normative passivity of that desire. By defining female desire as responsive to male—in the first instance, paternal—desire, the culture inscribes "father-daughter incest [as] a culturally

[18]See ibid., 19: 253. See also Freud, "Femininity," *New Introductory Lectures on Psychoanalysis, Standard Edition,* 22: 126; hereafter abbreviated "F."

constructed paradigm of female desire."[19] The paradigm shapes that desire as normatively passive, as responsive to another's active desire, even if only fantasized:

> Along with the abandonment of clitoridal masturbation a certain amount of activity is renounced. Passivity now has the upper hand, and the girl's turning to her father is accomplished principally with the help of passive instinctual impulses. You can see that a wave of development like this, which clears the phallic activity out of the way, smooths the ground for femininity. If too much is not lost in the course of it through repression, this femininity may turn out to be normal.

Freud takes it that a girl's initial turning to her father is motivated by the wish of acquiring a penis from him, but, as the passage just quoted concludes, "the feminine situation is only established . . . if the wish for a penis is replaced by one for a baby" (Freud, "F," 22: 128), that is, if the desire for libidinal activity is renounced. The wish for a baby and other, ensuing, passive sexual aims require for their (fantasized) fulfillment another's (fantasized) activity. To fantasize the satisfaction of passive desires is to fantasize being the object of another's active desire. (The situation is, of course, not symmetric: one can, unfortunately, in fantasy or reality play out one's active desires on another whether the corresponding passive desire is present or not.) Thus, a father's desire—at least as represented in a daughter's mind—is a central feature of the acquisition of femininity: she learns to desire someone who (she fantasizes or believes) desires her. And, under the conditions of patriarchal control and compulsory heterosexuality,[20] her desire, if it enters into consideration at all, is meant to become fungible more or less on demand. Like Sleeping Beauty, she awakens to the man who lays claim to her.

This peculiar fungibility of female desire is very different from the fungibility of male desire. Men may be expected to shift their desires from one woman to another with ease and frequency, but they are not expected to desire automatically those who desire them. This difference is linked to the different fates of the attachment boys and girls have to their mothers. The "smashing to pieces" of the male Oedipus complex leaves the boy in possession of a large amount of power in the service of his becoming a civilized adult, largely in the form of the superego. Although he can experience this power as punitive and constraining, it is fundamentally empowering of him as an active member of society. Not so for the

[19]Sandra M. Gilbert, "Life's Empty Pack: Notes toward a Liberatory Daughteronomy," *Critical Inquiry* 11 (March 1985): 372.

[20]'Compulsory heterosexuality' is a term introduced by Adrienne Rich to refer to the complex of social, cultural, economic, political, and psychological forces that affect women's eroticism in heterosexist and male-dominant cultures. See Rich, "Compulsory Heterosexuality and Lesbian Existence," *Signs* 5 (Summer 1980): 631–60.

girl: her love for her mother is not transformed but repressed, and it succumbs to narcissistic humiliation, bitter disappointment, and a sense of betrayal. Finally, it is replaced by a love structured by her passive desires and a learned responsiveness to the desires and demands of others.

In Freud's account, not only girls' sexual identity but their gender identity is acquired with the Oedipus complex: "With their entry into the [developmentally earlier] phallic phase the differences between the sexes are completely eclipsed by their agreements. We are . . . obliged to recognize that the little girl is a little man" (Freud, "F," 22: 118). The attainment of gender identity, therefore, is portrayed as a peculiarly female problem, since girls need to turn away from the libidinal activity that is both common to all pre-Oedipal children and distinctively male.[21] In this story female gender identity gets linked both to the question of *origins*, as the gendered self comes into existence in relation to the father, and to *sexual identity*, as that relation is learned through a reorientation of desire. That is, the two forms of self-knowledge, about one's parentage and about one's sexual identity, that Cavell argues are demanded for a (true or happy) marriage, are in Freudian terms conflated in the case of women. On such an account, a woman needs to acknowledge that she came into existence as a female only in relation to the thought of her father's desire for her; that is, she needs to acknowledge him as her one true parent.

The claim of the primacy of paternity has a long history, and Freud is *descriptively* right in associating it with advances in civilization. Aristotle thought that mothers supplied only the matter that semen formed into a human being, and as Susan Bordo has argued, the seventeenth-century *homunculus* theory of reproduction is of a piece with what she calls the Cartesian masculinization of thought.[22] Although it is usually *men* that men are required to be the parents of (since they are the ones who will thereby acquire the authority that comes of being "not of woman born"), there is at least one important example of the paternal parthenogenesis of a daughter: Athena's emergence from the forehead of Zeus, who became her sole parent by, literally, swallowing her mother. The conditions of Athena's birth are essential to her role as the goddess of wisdom, as, for example, when in

[21]Nancy Chodorow discusses the "primacy of maleness" in Freud's developmental theories, along with a number of challenges to it, in "Freud: Ideology and Evidence," *The Reproduction of Mothering: Psychoanalysis and the Sociology of Gender* (Berkeley and Los Angeles: Univ. of California Press, 1978), pp. 141–58. Chodorow argues that because all children experience early undifferentiated attachment to a female caretaker, the attainment of gender identity is peculiarly a *male* problem.

[22]See Susan Bordo, "The Cartesian Masculinization of Thought," *Signs* 11 (Spring 1986): 439–56. An expanded version of this essay, "The Cartesian Masculinization of Thought and Seventeenth-Century Flight from the Feminine," appears in her book, *The Flight to Objectivity: Essays on Cartesianism and Culture* (Albany: State Univ. of New York Press, 1987), pp. 97–118.

the *Oresteia* she sides with Orestes against the matriarchal Furies, thereby helping to inaugurate patriarchal rule: she declares herself "unreservedly for male in everything / save marrying one."[23]

The requisite virginity of Athena and of other women—mortal and divine—who played her role of mediating between the worlds of maternal and paternal power (for example, the modern stereotype of the spinster school-teacher) is, I am beginning to suspect, less a matter of avoiding sex than of avoiding maternity, which, as Cavell points out in a related discussion, used to require (hetero)sexual abstinence (Cavell, *PH*, p. 59). The difficulties women encounter today when they attempt to combine motherhood and career are rooted in part in their violating a long-standing taboo against combining the symbolically loaded power of maternity with power as constituted in the extradomestic world.[24] To be allowed to exercise that second sort of power, to act like a man, has generally meant thinking of oneself as a genetic fluke—parthenogenetically fathered and sterile.

Cavell's guess from the region of myth about the absence of heroines' mothers makes reference to this tradition: "Mythically, the absence of the mother continues the idea that the creation of the woman is the business of men; even, paradoxically, when the creation is that of the so-called new woman, the woman of equality" (Cavell, *PH*, p. 57). Beyond the obvious paradox, a deeper one appears in the claim that only as fathered can a woman claim *either* public empowerment *or* feminine sexual identity. The paradox lies in the double cultural privileging of paternity—as grounding the authorities of civilization and as creating female desire. The message to a woman is clear: within the systems of male privilege neither her appropriately feminine sexual identity nor her ability to assume public power is compatible with her being her mother's daughter. (What is, of course, compatible with her having been mothered is her mothering—one reason why the heroines of these films cannot be mothers. As Nancy Chodorow argues in *The Reproduction of Mothering*, mothers are mothers' daughters.)

It appeared to Freud in his work with adult women that "insight into [the] early, pre-Oedipus, phase in girls comes . . . as a surprise, like the discovery . . . of the Minoan-Mycenean civilization behind the civilization of Greece. Everything in the sphere of this first attachment to the mother seemed . . . so difficult to grasp in analysis—so grey with age and shadowy and almost impossible to revivify—that it was as if it had succumbed to an especially inexorable repression." Freud goes on to speculate that his female patients' repression of pre-Oedipal material was reinforced during analysis with him, since the transference would have

---

[23]Aeschylus, *The Orestes Plays: The Agamemnon, The Libation Bearers, The Eumenides*, trans. Paul Roche (New York: New American Library, 1962), p. 190.

[24]For a discussion of the effects that women's bearing the sole symbolic power of infant caretakers have on a culture, see Dorothy Dinnerstein, *The Mermaid and the Minotaur: Sexual Arrangements and Human Malaise* (New York: Harper and Row, 1976).

continued “the very attachment to the father in which they had taken refuge.”[25] Women analysts, he suggests, have with more success evoked, *through* the transference, women’s attachments to their mothers. One way of thinking about this observation is that heterosexuality both depends on and reinforces the loss of a daughter’s attachment to her mother: that attachment is most likely to be rediscovered through an erotically experienced bond with another woman, or through the daughter herself becoming a mother. But in the terrain of these comedies—exclusively heterosexual and childless—the absence of even the memory of a mother is a necessary part of the identity these women embrace.

Consider the one film Cavell discusses in which the heroine does have a mother: *The Philadelphia Story*. When we first see mother and daughter together, a couple of days before Tracy’s (second) wedding and just before the arrival of Dexter and the dragooned *Spy* reporters, their relationship is extremely close. We get an intimation, however, that they live that relationship in very different ways. Tracy is affectionately bossy toward her mother (and the others she approves of) and dismissively judgmental toward her father (and the others, notably Dexter, she disapproves of). Her mother is much less severe; even when she strongly disapproves of something, she tends to hold her peace (as when she admits to Dinah that it is “stinking” of Tracy not to allow her father to come to her wedding). Mother Lord’s unconditional love, not only of Tracy, but notably of her philandering husband, can be taken, I think, as a model of how Tracy is supposed to learn to feel.

But if Tracy is meant to come to resemble her mother more closely, neither she nor the viewers of the film are meant to attend to that fate in those terms; in particular, neither she nor we are meant to pay much attention to Mother Lord. Rather, Tracy’s education, as we are shown it, is entirely in the hands of men, who lecture her on how to be a real woman. (Cavell notes that “Katharine Hepburn seems to inspire her men with the most ungovernable wishes to lecture her. Four of them take turns at it in *The Philadelphia Story*” [Cavell, *PH*, p. 56].) Tracy’s mother’s role in her daughter’s education is precisely to allow herself to be replaced, to be silent in the face of the paternal claim.

Feminist critics of the Shakespearean romances that Cavell finds echoed in these films—notably *A Midsummer Night’s Dream* in *The Philadelphia Story*—have argued that the marriages that constitute their happy endings are an assertion of patriarchal order that requires the rupture of bonds between women.[26] Since comedic heroines seem in general never to have had mothers, the mother/daughter bond is not usually among those whose rupture is enacted, but I think we can see

[25]Freud, “Female Sexuality,” *Standard Edition,* 21: 226.

[26]For a discussion of that rupture in *A Midsummer Night’s Dream*, see Shirley Nelson Garner, “*A Midsummer Night’s Dream*: ‘Jack shall have Jill/Nought shall go ill,’ ” *Women’s Studies* 9 (1981): 47–63.

its fate in *The Philadelphia Story* as emblematic of the long-buried prehistory to which Freud consigns a girl's pre-Oedipal attachment to her mother.

The scene in which Tracy's father asserts his claim to her affectionate attention contains, as Cavell notes, "words difficult to tolerate" (Cavell, *PH*, p. 137), especially as we know them to be overheard by Mrs. Lord: they are simply and unredeemably cruel. Mr. Lord makes it clear that he considers his behavior none of his daughter's business, that far from occupying the high moral ground she takes herself to be on, she's "'been speaking like a jealous woman,'" and, finally, that if he's been involved with another woman, it's *her* fault. The reason he gives for this accusation (one that I fear the film does not expect us to find outrageous) is that a man has a natural need—and, apparently, consequently a right—to be looked up to uncritically by a beautiful young woman, so if his daughter refuses to meet this need once her mother is no longer young and beautiful, she is guilty of his seeking to have it met elsewhere. It is, in Cavell's words, "essential to his aria that it occurs *in the presence of the mother*, as a kind of reclaiming of her from Tracy" (Cavell, *PH*, p. 137). But it is equally and, for the narrative, more importantly, a claiming of Tracy from her mother, an assertion of his claim to her love and attention. And Tracy goes on, oblivious to the effect of her father's words on her mother (it is not clear that she knows her to have been listening), to test what he has said against how the other men around her see her and how she wants to see herself and to be seen.

Cavell's discussion of the rupture between Tracy and her mother that follows this speech ("there is next to no further exchange between them in the film" [Cavell, *PH*, p. 138]) connects it to Freud's discussion of women's unhappy first marriages in "Female Sexuality," but the connection is an odd one. Freud suggests that a woman's difficult marriage may be replicating a difficult relationship with her mother, but the film gives us no reason to attribute any particular difficulty to Tracy's relationship with her mother. Her bossiness seems more to *manifest* itself in relation to her mother than to be a peculiar feature of that relationship or particularly grounded in it.

What the film *does* seem to be telling us, particularly in conjunction with the others in its genre and with the tradition of romantic comedy in general, is that a woman's happiness in marriage requires her abandonment both of her love for her mother and of the active aspects of her own sexuality. She needs to acknowledge her identity as a sexually desiring woman, and even to act in pursuit of those desires, but the structure of desire she needs to acknowledge is Oedipal. The right man is the one who, because of the nature of *his* desire for *her*, has a claim on her. In their unsuccessful attempts to escape the claims of the right man, the heroines of *The Awful Truth* and *His Girl Friday* turn, like Tracy Lord, to unsuitable substitutes, men who lack the power to make such a claim to a woman's desire, because they have not learned to turn their desire away from their mothers.

Thus, it seems to me that by exploring the regions of Cavell's guesses about the absence of his heroines' mothers in these films, I can adequately account for the absence, but the cost of the account is a serious compromising of the pleasure I can take in those films and of my ability to regard their endings as happy ones. Cavell is right to note that in these films "the creation of the woman is the business of men" (Cavell, *PH*, p. 57): that this creation requires for its fictional enactment the erasure of the woman's mother confirms feminist suspicions that, like Athena from Zeus's forehead, women born of men will identify with them and will at best leave a dubious legacy of female self-realization.

Missing Mothers/Desiring Daughters: Take Two

> Remind me how we loved our mother's body
> our bodies drawing the first
> thin sweetness from her nipples
>
> our faces dreaming hour on hour
> in the salt smell of her lap Remind me
> how her touch melted childgrief
>
> how she floated great and tender in our dark
> or stood guard over us
> against our willing
>
> and how we thought she loved
> the strange male body first
> that took, that took, whose taking seemed a law
>
> and how she sent us weeping
> into that law
> how we remet her in our childbirth visions
>
> erect, enthroned, above
> a spiral stair
> and crawled and panted toward her
>
> I know, I remember, but
> hold me, remind me
> of how her woman's flesh was made taboo to us.
>
> —Adrienne Rich, "Sibling Mysteries"

In the previous section mothers were missing and daughters were desired. Shifting the syntax, in this section mothers are missed, even if physically present, and daughters—problematically—desire. Along with much other feminist poetry, fiction, and theory, Adrienne Rich's poetry and prose challenge the Freudian framework, evident both in the films Cavell discusses and in his discussion of them, which constructs both female desire and female gender identity in a girl's Oedipal relation to her father. Along with feminist object-relations theorists, Rich situates gender identity pre-Oedipally; she is more explicit than they tend to be in situating the learning of specifically female desire there as well. She has criticized the heterosexism that underlies attempts to theorize female heterosexuality as the endpoint of a natural developmental path.[27] She can help us to see how *un*natural it is to turn our gaze away, as boys and men are never expected to, from the female body, which is, in a society that places early child rearing nearly exclusively in the hands of women, the source of our knowledge of love and intimacy. We may also see how unnatural it is to turn *toward* the bodies of those who are taught that our place in the world is to serve their needs and desires, and to name those needs and desires as our own.

In a discussion of *La Princesse de Clèves* Marianne Hirsch argues that Mme. de Chartres offers her daughter an alternative to the inevitable dangers of a life of heterosexual passion: "she wants to teach her daughter not only to survive but to transcend, and, to do so, she does give her a form of power, although it is a negative one. It is the power of absence, abstinence and denial, the strength to remain equal by saying 'no.' "[28] Mme. de Clèves needs to say "no" not only to the Duc de Nemours but, most important, to her own passionate desires, as they are evoked within a context of female vulnerability to male power. To succumb to her desire is not just to make herself vulnerable to abandonment and disgrace, but, more deeply, to structure her self around a willed renunciation of autonomy. Ironically, however, as Hirsch argues, the alternative her mother offers is one that denies precisely the possibility of autonomy, resting as it does on a continuing dependency on Mme. de Chartres or on her chosen successor, the Prince de Clèves. Hirsch concludes, "As feminist readers engaged in an act of re-vision, we see the strength in the Princess' uncompromised withdrawal, we see the victory of her refusal to be the female object in the exchange of love, of her insistence on attachment and continuity. Yet we cannot help but question the unbridgeable oppositions which prevent her from growing up."[29]

A number of films have played out versions of the tension between a woman's attachment to her mother and the demands of heterosexual love. Three pictures of this tension are drawn, from rather different angles, in *Now, Voyager*; *Bill of Divorcement*; and *Mildred Pierce*. The first two are melodramas, and *Mildred Pierce* is a melodrama framed by a *film noir*.[30] In his essay, "Psychoanalysis and Cinema," Cavell discusses melodrama as that genre that confronts the threats and dangers lurking in the cracks of the comedies, and he explicitly joins that discussion to the issue of women whose creation cannot be in the hands of men, whose

[27]See Rich, "Compulsory Heterosexuality and Lesbian Existence."

[28]Marianne Hirsch, "A Mother's Discourse: Incorporation and Repetition in *La Princesse de Clèves*," *Yale French Studies* 62 (1981): 85.

[29]Ibid., p. 87.

[30]See Pam Cook, "Duplicity in Mildred Pierce," in *Women in Film Noir*, ed. Kaplan, rev. ed. (London: British Film Institute, 1980), p. 71; hereafter abbreviated "D."

identity is discovered elsewhere than through heterosexual love and marriage. The mother/daughter connection is the most fundamental of those elsewheres.

As Geoffrey Nowell-Smith argues, melodrama is quintessentially familial, its family is patriarchal, and it addresses "the problems of adults, particularly women, in relation to their sexuality" and "the child's problems of growing into a sexual identity within the family, under the ægis of a symbolic law which the father incarnates." While I agree that patriarchal power structures the familial world of melodrama, Nowell-Smith's emphasis slights the presence and dramatic importance of mothers, which is one of the distinguishing marks of the genre. For example, *Mildred Pierce* is as good an example as one could find of his claim that "melodrama enacts, often with uncanny literalness, the 'family romance' described by Freud—that is to say, the imaginary scenario played out by children in relation to their paternity, the asking and answering of the question, whose child am I (or would I like to be)?"[31] But it is essential to Veda's attempt to discover herself as Monty's daughter, as it is to her subsequent attempt to become "incestuously" involved with him, that he is her mother's lover: a Mildred who is married to Monty would be someone she could, as she desperately needs to, acknowledge as her mother. (That this need is profoundly ambivalent does not, of course, make it less significant to the film.)

The story Mildred tells is a mother's story. Feminist critics have discussed the framing of her story by the detective('s) story (Cook, "D," p. 71), but equally noteworthy is Veda's attempt, internal to Mildred's story, to frame it in a way that will play out her family romance. Veda's attachment to Mildred is strong, and Bert is represented as weak and emotionally absent. (His affair with Mrs. Biedermeier seems to be justified in the eyes of the film by Mildred's "infidelity" in putting the children, particularly Veda, first.) Veda's desire to recast the facts of her own origins therefore centers on Mildred, who comes to be the target of Veda's rage when those fantasies are unfulfilled. What Veda demands from Mildred is not only the presence of money and social connection, but also the absence of those things—notably, housework and working class labor—that have no place in the sort of privileged narrative to which she wants her life to conform.

Veda has the opportunity to leave Mildred and to live a life of social and economic privilege, but she uses her marriage for extortion instead. Though Veda explicitly says she wants the money in order to leave Mildred, her actions make it hard to believe that she really means this, except as an expression of enraged disappointment—an exaggeration of the reaction Freud attributes to all daughters in the face of the discovery of the limitations of their mother's power. Instead of turning to her father at this point, Veda rebelliously "makes a spectacle" of herself, becoming not the appropriately gazed-at object of paternal and then husbandly love, but a showgirl leered at by sailors, until Mildred succumbs to Veda's fantasy

[31] Geoffrey Nowell-Smith, "Minnelli and Melodrama," *Screen* 18 (Summer 1977): 113–18; reprinted in *Movies and Methods*, 2: 193.

and marries Monty. Having had her fantasy family put in place, Veda takes to playing out the Oedipal story with the father she chose. But the available cultural scripts make the incest taboo inoperative and the misinterpretation of Veda's desire—by Veda herself and by Monty—inevitable, and fatal: at the moment of Veda's taking her desire for Monty to be a desire to take him away from Mildred, she kills him, and turns for her life back to Mildred, who cannot, this time, save her.

Mildred Pierce is in part about what becomes of motherhood when mothers lack the power to fulfill their children's dreams but are still held, by their children and by themselves, responsible for that failure. The Oedipus complex is supposed to teach both girls and boys that mothers don't have this power, that boys have it themselves and that girls are to get it from men. One of its normative results is the weakening of maternal—and, more generally, female—power. In *Mildred Pierce*, neither Veda nor Mildred has come to terms with this cultural demand, and they are both punished for their refusal. At the very end Mildred is "redeemed" by the power of the law, which, knowing the truth of her innocence and Veda's guilt, releases her, as it were, into Bert's protective custody, while Veda is left behind, believing that Mildred has betrayed her. The betrayal may be illusory, but the severing of the bond between them, as the price for Mildred's return to the social order, is not. As Pam Cook points out, the film further reminds us "of what women must give up for the sake of the patriarchal order": the closing shot of Mildred and Bert leaving the police station also frames two women on their knees, scrubbing the floor.[32]

Cook's essay places *Mildred Pierce* in the context of J. J. Bachofen's theory of "the violent overthrow of mother-right in favor of father-right" (Cook, "D," p. 69), the same transformation that Freud discusses in *Moses and Monotheism* that needs to be accomplished intrapsychically through the "successful" resolution of the Oedipal crisis. In the case of girls, the resolution of the crisis is oddly located at its inauguration, at the shift of attachment from mother to father. As hostile as Veda is to Mildred throughout the film, the root of both her rage and her rebelliousness is her refusal to make this shift, her continuing insistence on Mildred's power. Veda's desires are transgressive because they continue to have as their ultimate object the phallic mother, whose castration is demanded by the patriarchal order. Unlike Mother Lord, Mildred is unwilling to enact her own disempowerment. When the force of the law finally subdues her, it is too late for her daughters—one is dead and one is imprisoned for murder. The film closes, grimly, as a dark reflection of the remarriage comedies: Mildred walks off, reunited with her first husband, framed within a childless marriage.

In many ways *Now, Voyager* is a mirror image of *Mildred Pierce*. Bette Davis as Charlotte Vale is trapped by her mother's imperious refusal to let her go and

---

[32]See Cook, "D," p. 81, and Joyce Nelson, "*Mildred Pierce* Reconsidered," *Film Reader* 2 (1977); reprinted in *Movies and Methods*, 2: 457.

by the repressions that refusal has demanded and instilled. Unlike the Princesse de Clèves, Charlotte does not obediently accept her mother's picture of the world of heterosexual desire as lethally dangerous. Though she lives a life of renunciation of desire, it is with an undercurrent of stifled rebellion, played out —with obvious Freudian symbolism—in the hidden boxes she makes and the forbidden cigarettes she smokes. In this explicitly psychoanalytic version of the incompatibility of mother/daughter attachment and heterosexual desire, therapy is called on to undermine the attachment and liberate the desire. But, in the terms of the film, the results are ambiguous. Charlotte does acknowledge and express desire, but the terms of the acknowledgment and expression are given by the men in her life, and in the end she represses her desire for Jerry in favor of a maternal connection to his daughter.

Lea Jacobs argues that Dr. Jacquith's role is "outside desire, identified with the process of narrative itself": he makes it possible for Charlotte to have a story.[33] But the story she has is one in which her desire is expressed as her desirability, a framing that she continually resists, as Jacobs demonstrates through the close analysis of shots in which Charlotte attempts either to place herself at the site of enunciation or to resist being the visibly fetishized object of desire. Neither of these attempts is wholly successful, but her persistence undermines her recuperation into the system of desire defined by the narrative into which Dr. Jacquith's cure is supposed to insert her. Instead of taking her place as an object of heterosexual desire, she takes *his* place as an asexual substitute parent to Tina. Though we are supposed to see her as liberated from the static, prenarrative maternal realm, she chooses at the end to remove herself from the story. Her final gesture can be read as sacrificial of her happiness for Tina's, but it can equally, and subversively, be seen as a refusal of the terms on which she was offered an entry into narrative —a positioning as the object of the male gaze and a renunciation of maternity.

What is clear is that she cannot have both a consummated heterosexual relationship and an ongoing maternal one. As she tells Jerry at the close of the film, Dr. Jacquith has let her keep Tina "on probation," and Jerry's visit is a test of her will to renounce her sexual desires in favor of her maternal ones. Jacquith's initial "cure" of Charlotte was his positioning her as an object of heterosexual desire. (Like a proper father, he refrained from actively desiring her himself, but functioned as a catalyst around which her desire to be desired crystallized.) In the face of her resistance to being so positioned, he agreed to shift his definition of healthy adulthood for her, but he retained the power to keep sexuality and maternity separate—and to define them both.

The mothering Charlotte embraces at the end is a replication of what Dr. Jacquith provided for her; it hardly provides a point of connection to her own mother, who, like Tina's mother, Isobel, continues to be that from which daughters

---

[33]Lea Jacobs, "*Now, Voyager*: Some Problems of Enunciation and Sexual Difference," *Camera Obscura* 7 (Spring 1981): 94.

need to be helped to escape. Jeanne Thomas Allen, editor of the screenplay *Now, Voyager*, notes that Edmund Goulding's treatment of Olive Higgins Prouty's novel "begins the process of 'strengthening' the male figures as father-doctors in Charlotte's rebirth, while the roles of Charlotte's sister-in-law, Lisa, and friend, Deb, are minimized. The psychological midwives of the novel are replaced by doctors, who turn the midwives into nurses."[34] Thus, there is a deep instability in the film, not only between the demands of maternity and of heterosexual desire, but, internal to each of those demands, about the locus of defining authority. As Jacobs argues, "it is not that *Now, Voyager* openly subverts the conventions of romantic love but rather that in examining a woman's place within those conventions the narrative, even the film's syntax, becomes deformed. The question of how, and through whom, Charlotte Vale's desire will express itself engenders a dizzying chain of displacement and counter-displacement which will never come to rest."[35]

Another playing out of the tension between the mother/daughter relationship and heterosexual desire occurs in *Bill of Divorcement*, this time with an extremely odd twist. As the film opens, Sydney (Katharine Hepburn) and her mother, Margaret (Billie Burke), are each happily in love and about to marry. The only shadow over their happiness is the father/husband Sydney never knew and Margaret wishes to forget. Hilary (John Barrymore) has been hospitalized for what turns out to be "hereditary insanity," and his return, hopefully to his wife's love, threatens the happiness of the impending marriages. Most obviously, of course, it threatens *Margaret's* marriage. Even though she has obtained a divorce, she is as moved by the force of her ex-husband's love and need for her as she was when she married him, and her own love for another seems as without force now as her lack of love for Hilary did then. It seems to her that she has no choice but to renounce the man she loves to resume a marriage defined by another man's weakness and his intense need of her.

Hilary, however, mistook Sydney for her mother when he first unexpectedly turned up: she is, both in appearance and in manner, more like the wife he lost. She is, he says, softer, kinder, more loving than her mother has become; she is also, not altogether coherently, more like *him*. (The androgyny of both their names is further sign of their identification.) The combination forces *Sydney* to be the one whose marriage plans dissolve in the face of her father's return. She is the one, she says, who understands him and can make him happy, the one he really loves, and the one who bears the hereditary taint of insanity, hence the one who doesn't dare have children. She sends away both her lover and her mother—she literally hands her mother into the arms of a new husband—and settles down at

[34]Jeanne Thomas Allen, "Introduction: *Now, Voyager* as Women's Film: Coming of Age Hollywood Style," in *Now, Voyager*, ed. Allen, Wisconsin/Warner Bros. Screenplay Series (Madison: Univ. of Wisconsin Press, 1984), p. 20.

[35]Jacobs, "*Now, Voyager*," p. 103.

the piano with her father, willingly accepting her fate to live with and care for a man she saw for the first time the day before, but to whom she immediately feels more connected than to her mother or her fiancé.

The father/daughter bond in *Bill of Divorcement* is hardly conducive, as it is in the remarriage comedies, to the daughter's acknowledgment of sexual desire and her subsequent marital happiness. What we are explicitly told is that it is precisely *because* she is her father's daughter that Sydney has to forgo marriage: she can neither leave him nor take the risk of bearing children, and the possibility of her going mad, as he did, is too much to expect her lover to bear (as she thinks her father's madness is too much to expect her mother to bear). The film plays out too literally the fantasy of paternal parthenogenesis: Sydney seems to take her father instinctively as her true parent and to experience the bond with him as nonfungible.

The presence of her father and the knowledge of what it means to be his daughter transform Sydney's experience of her own desire. No longer is that desire compatible, as it clearly was at the start of the film, with continued intimacy with her mother or with the desire to have children. The placement of her father at the point of definition of her identity and her desire precludes both Sydney's continued closeness to her mother and the possibility of her own motherhood. We may not notice how, in the comedies, the daughter's marriage is made possible by the invisibility of her mother, but when the roles are reversed and a *daughter* retreats into the static space outside of narrative to enable her *mother's* romantic marriage, the underlying logic becomes disconcertingly clear.[36]

In the terms of this film, it is not the closeness of the mother/daughter bond that is incompatible with the daughter's heterosexual desire and happy marriage, but how that bond is experienced under the law of the father, and the connection between heterosexuality and male power, the connection Rich's poem draws so vividly. The consequences of Sydney's acknowledgment of her father highlight the peremptory violence of the claim of father-right, the violence a daughter needs to ignore in the name of "normal" heterosexual development. The violence that is done to the relationship between mothers and daughters—either its total erasure, as in most romantic comedies or the painful ruptures or sacrifices characteristic of melodrama—has its roots not simply in the daughter's need to learn to love someone else. The violence is grounded in the way in which patriarchy demands

---

[36]Ruth Wood has pointed out to me the significance of the daughter's taking on the maternal role in order to liberate her mother from it, so that the mother may enter the realm of the romantic narrative. Not only does that role need to be filled by *some*one, but it can appear positively more attractive and less confining than those associated with romance, as it did to Charlotte Vale. On a daughter's need to "rescue" her mother, see Jane Flax, "Mother-Daughter Relationships: Psychoanalysis, Politics, and Philosophy," in *The Future of Difference*, ed. Hester Eisenstein and Alice Jardine (Boston and New York: G.K. Hall and Co., 1980), p. 35.

that she learn that lesson—as a submission to male power, first in the person of her father, and as a renunciation of her belief in her mother's power and her hope for her own.

One of the messages of the maternal melodrama concerns the difficulty women encounter in denying the power and primacy of their connection to their mothers, a denial deemed essential for the development of "normal" female heterosexuality under the conditions of patriarchy. This difficulty, and the pain mothers and daughters experience through the teaching and learning of female powerlessness, are the dark underside of the laughter of the remarriage comedies. As in Shakespeare's romantic comedies, the achievement of the happy ending of marriage requires the severing of bonds between women.[37] The pleasure many women, myself included, take in such comedies, and in their bright, bold, sexually assertive heroines, is bought at the cost of not noticing what has become of their mothers and how their very brightness is figured as eager identification with a male-defined world, a world to which their fathers hold the key.

Framing the Sight of Women

> The gaze is not necessarily male (literally), but to own and activate the gaze, given our language and the structure of the unconscious, is to be in the "masculine" position.
>
> —E. Ann Kaplan, *Women and Film*

> With *Stella Dallas*, we begin to see why the Mother has so rarely occupied the center of the narrative: For how can the *spectator* be subject, at least in the sense of controlling the action?
>
> —E. Ann Kaplan, "The Case of the Missing Mother"

> To say that we wish to view the world itself is to say that we are wishing for the condition of viewing as such. That is our way of establishing our connection with the world: through viewing it, or having views of it. Our condition has become one in which our natural mode of perception is to view, feeling unseen. We do not so much look at the world as look out at it, from behind the self.
>
> Stanley Cavell, *The World Viewed*

> Women have served all these centuries as looking-glasses possessing the magic and delicious power of reflecting the figure of man at twice its natural size.
>
> —Virginia Woolf, *A Room of One's Own*

Do women as women see, or must we become "masculine" to own the gaze? Is the position of the viewer one of power or one of passivity? In "Visual Pleasure and Narrative Cinema," Mulvey argues, with respect to cinematic gazes—the

[37]See Garner, "*A Midsummer Night's Dream.*"

gaze of the characters within the film, the gaze of the camera, and the gaze of the spectators at the film—that their structures are those of masculine desire. In her analysis, the nature of this desire and the anxieties associated with it require the diversion of attention from the camera's and the spectators' gazes, through the creation and maintenance of "an illusion of Renaissance space . . . ; the camera's look [along with the look of the audience] is disavowed in order to create a convincing world in which the spectator's surrogate [the male character with whom the male viewer identifies] can perform with verisimilitude."[38]

Christian Metz makes a similar point, although problematically without attention to gender specificity,[39] in distinguishing (in Emile Benveniste's terms) between the naturalistic, gapless *story* the film presents and the *discourse* that is its telling. For Metz, narrative film gratifies a desire to be "a pure, all-seeing and invisible subject, the vanishing point of the monocular perspective which cinema has taken over from painting."[40] Such a perspective is meant to be one from which the world appears as it really is, the privileged point at which the perfect Cartesian knower situates himself.[41] Such pure subjectivity presumes a world of equally pure objectivity, a world that is both wholly independent and essentially visible. In Metz's terms, "the *seen* is all thrust back on to the pure object, the paradoxical object which derives its peculiar force from this act of confinement."[42]

Attention to the role of gender in the construction and articulation of specular desire reveals this fantasy as the self-contradictory fantasy of pornography: the essence of the woman is her desire, knowable only to the man, to be seduced/raped. The contradiction comes in the demand for this desire, as her essence, to exist independently of him—he is not responsible for it—but to be at the same time wholly exhausted by his ability to evoke and satisfy it. (This fantasy is related, of course, to the Freudian fantasy, discussed above, of the paternal parthenogenesis of feminine desire.) Such a fantasy, of an object of knowledge both wholly independent and wholly knowable, and the problems caused by the impossibility of its satisfaction are at the heart of epistemic modernity. Nature as "she" is required both to be absolutely independent of the knowing subject (as he acquires his authority by his hard-won independence from *her*) and to be fully

---

[38]Mulvey, "Visual Pleasure and Narrative Cinema," 2: 314.

[39]See de Lauretis, *AD*, pp. 24–26, 78–79, and 144–46.

[40]Christian Metz, *The Imaginary Signifier: Psychoanalysis and the Cinema,* trans. Celia Britton et al. (Bloomington: Indiana Univ. Press, 1982), p. 97.

[41]In reference to the bearer of epistemic authority in modern Western culture, the masculine pronoun is accurate and nongeneric. As in theories about the gaze, a problem for the feminist epistemologist is to account for how women have appropriated and can appropriate this authority—in particular by exploring the possibilities for going beyond claiming the individual right to "think like men" to challenging the normative maleness of authoritative ways of knowing.

[42]Metz, *The Imaginary Signifier*, p. 97.

revealed by his penetration. The irresolvable tension between these two demands gives rise to scepticism.

The conditions of vision and of visibility have figured centrally in epistemology since the Greeks.[43] Those conditions underwent a transformation, starting in the Renaissance, as the definitions of epistemic authority shifted. Such authority gradually came to be framed not in terms of an omniscient, omnipresent diety, for whom distance was irrelevant, nor in the embodied terms of an engaged practitioner, who moved among and interacted with the objects of knowledge.[44] Rather, epistemic authority was ceded to those who stood at the proper distance from the objects of knowledge and who had achieved the proper degree of independence from them—and from their own contingent "limitations" and "biases." The modern scientist, who has been our culture's epistemic hero, achieves this status by reliably accomplishing the normatively male tasks of separation and empowerment based on dissociation from everything maternal and, by extension, female.[45] The male Oedipal narrative has become the template for the processes that authorize vision and whose fantasized, effortless achievement provides (one form of) cinematic pleasure.

Cavell's account of the peculiar pleasures of movies similarly takes as definitive the wish, referred to in the epigraph to this section, to be an unviewed viewer of the world. Cavell's account of this wish seems, however, more innocent and less political. As in his discussion throughout *The Claim of Reason* of related issues concerning the troubling of our epistemic relations to each other and to the rest of the world, both our desires and the blocks to their gratification are given as *ours*—all of ours, as inhabitants of the modern, Western world, sharers of a particular culture. For Cavell, what cinema grants us is not meant to be the power

---

[43]For a discussion of the historical shifts in the epistemology of vision with particular attention to gender, see Keller and Christine R. Grontkowski, "The Mind's Eye," in *Discovering Reality,* pp. 207–24.

[44]See Samuel Y. Edgerton, Jr., *The Renaissance Rediscovery of Linear Perspective* (New York: Harper and Row, 1975), pp. 20–21.

[45]In "The Cartesian Masculinization of Thought," Bordo explicitly identifies the medieval world with the maternal and takes the attainment of epistemic modernity to consist largely in an explicit separation from a symbiotic union of the self with the (maternal) cosmos (pp. 451–56). I am dubious about that identification: the power challenged by the rise of the bourgeois epistemology was in fact nearly exclusively in the hands of men—the authorities of the Church and of a hereditary aristocracy. In a variety of complex ways, women (most notably those who were condemned as witches), and the symbolically feminine were scapegoated as the locus of archaic claims to epistemic authority and transformed into prototypes of the objects of knowledge, control, and exploitation (Mother Nature). It is, in general, a risky business for feminists to identify images of women's power in some long lost time and place as authentically female, since such images are often, as much as anything else, misogynist creations used to justify the allegedly liberating nature of male power, as in the *Oresteia*.

of the pornographer but respite from our complicity in the structuring of the world, "not a wish for power over creation . . . but a wish not to need power, not to have to bear its burdens."[46] The wish is granted by the total presentness to us of the world on the screen without our being present to it, neither implicated in it nor limited in our view of it by our particular placement in it.

The innocence of this wish is, I think, misleading. The wish to be an unseen seer may be a wish for a less troubled relation to reality, but that relation has been troubled in large measure by the cultural placement of epistemic authority precisely in the eyes of an unseen seer: movies grant us the opportunity not to notice the extent to which we are supposed to work at pushing the world away to view it truly. The world of the scientist doesn't contain the scientist, but his absence from it is neither innocent nor effortless. Thus, what Iago offers Othello is meant to be access to Desdemona's world as it is in itself, but what Othello gets is the view of a spy, of someone who by his own efforts is hidden from the world he views, seeing not Desdemona-in-herself but Desdemona-as-spied upon.[47] Kant may have tried to tell us that the world is always our world, but we haven't really learned it, and we go on trying to spy on it: no wonder we are lured by the promise of a world we don't have to hide behind a curtain to see. (We see it, in fact, when the curtain is pulled aside.)

The "we" in the last paragraph is, of course, problematic, obscuring as it does questions about whose world it is and whose view of it is authorized, or troubled by the terms of that authority. Feminist film criticism has taken as a major task the theorizing of the gender specificities of the desires, among them epistemic, that cinema gratifies, as feminist philosophy has taken as one of *its* major tasks the theorizing of the gender specificities of epistemic desires, among them visual. The analysis of the desire to know, in a culture that construes knowledge in primarily visual terms, is inseparable from the analysis of the construction of visual desire and of visual pleasure, which is in turn inseparable from the analysis of the construction of gender.

It is in this light that we need to think about the characterization of the cinematic gaze(s) as male. As Teresa de Lauretis argues, "the project of feminist cinema . . . is not so much 'to make visible the invisible,' as the saying goes, or to destroy vision altogether, as to construct another (object of) vision and the conditions of visibility for a different social subject" (de Lauretis, *AD*, pp. 67–68). This is, I

---

[46]Cavell, *The World Viewed: Reflections on the Ontology of Film*, enlarged ed. (Cambridge, Mass.: Harvard Univ. Press, 1979), p. 40.

[47]See my "Othello's Doubt/Desdemona's Death: The Engendering of Scepticism." In this essay, I discuss Othello as enacting the paranoia that underlies modern Western epistemology. My discussion is a response to Cavell's use of Othello to illuminate the origins of scepticism in the position of the modern knower (gender unspecified) in *The Claim of Reason: Wittgenstein, Skepticism, Morality, and Tragedy* (Oxford and New York: Oxford Univ. Press, 1979), pp. 481–96.

would say, a feminist project quite generally: to create the conditions for a transformed subject/object relation, in part by attending to, and redrawing, the lines of sight. The revolutions of the Renaissance and the subsequent rise of science, capitalism, and the modern state created the conditions for the existence and hegemonic power of the unitary subject, based on its separation from and domination over the object of knowledge. The revolutions of the objectified others (women and members of other oppressed and colonized groups—all those who have been scrutinized, stared at, anatomized, and ogled without being authorized to return the gaze or to see each other) will entail another transformation in what it is to know or to be known or knowable.

The lack of authority in women's looking is not, however, reason to conclude that we do not see, nor even that patriarchy does not allow or require that we see. The absence of the female gaze in some feminist theorizing is problematic, not only because such theories leave out of account significant features of the workings of masculinist power, but also because the looking that we do is a good place to seek out cracks in that power, even when we look as dutiful daughters and self-sacrificing mothers (as Tracy Lord or Stella Dallas).

In her essay, "To Be and Be Seen: The Politics of Reality," Marilyn Frye explores both the (con)scripting of female vision and the liberatory cracks it opens up.[48] Starting from her own view of the world as a lesbian, she is struck by the perception that women in general, and lesbian women in particular, are *not* seen by patriarchal eyes, whether those be the eyes of men or the eyes of women who see as men would have them see—as Virginia Woolf's enlarging mirrors.[49] Such eyes see the activities of men, against an invisible background of the enabling activities of women. In such a world, lesbian women are conceptually impossible: the positions by which women are defined are implicitly or explicitly heterosexual, and lesbians, Frye argues, are defined by their seeing of women, by the fact that women draw and hold their attention. But such attention is ontologically inadmissible; the illusion must be maintained that there is nothing there to look at: "The maintenance of phallocratic reality requires that the attention of women be focused on men and men's projects—the play; and that attention not be focused on women—the stagehands. Woman-loving, as a spontaneous and habitual orientation of attention is then, both directly and indirectly, inimical to the maintenance of that reality" (Frye, *PR*, p. 172).

Mr. Lord's demand of Tracy in *The Philadelphia Story*, that she learn to look at men in the proper way, is a demand that she reorient her attention and with it her sense of herself in the world. The attention she gives to Mike, when she goes to the library to read his book, is a sign to him and to us that she is capable of this learning, of becoming what she and we are told is a "real woman." Conversely,

---

[48]See Frye, *PR*, pp. 152–74.

[49]See Virginia Woolf, *A Room of One's Own* (New York: Harcourt, Brace and World, 1929), p. 60.

Mildred and Veda are doomed because they refuse to learn this; they can't take their eyes off each other. At the end Mildred is "saved" by having the authority of vision taken away from her: the story is no longer her melodrama, but the detective's *film noir,* and in that story she is the "redeemed" woman, marked off from Veda, who is given that genre's other female role, as "damned." As Mother Lord's and Charlotte Vale's fates illustrate, a mother may sometimes go on gazing at her daughter, provided that she remove herself from narrative space and that she consent by her silence to her daughter's incorporation into the realm of the fathers.[50]

In a study of the relationships between power and the lines of sight, Michel Foucault marks modernity in part by the directing of vision toward the subjugated, a characterization that makes the normative orientation of female vision toward men anachronistic. The modern gaze for Foucault is directed not at the powerful (who in premodern Europe had been the focal point of attention, their power figured as visual splendor) but toward the legions of the disciplined, kept in line by a diffuse, anonymous, institutionalized, and internalized system of surveillance.[51] Foucault's model of the sight lines of modernity fits the ways in which women are subject to the tyranny of the actual and internalized male gaze, including what Sandra Bartky has called, with reference to Foucault, the "discipline of femininity."[52] Female subjugation operates largely through such a disciplinary system, through our being seen and seeing ourselves as certain sorts of visual objects. But the directionality of conscripted daughterly and maternal vision does not fit this model. It runs in the wrong direction; it picks out its object as visibly distinguished and as powerful *because* visibly distinguished.

Part of the placement of such anachronistically structured female subordination in the modern world is achieved by the framing of women's vision by diffuse masculine power: neither the attentive mothers nor the adoring daughters are unseen, and they do not acquire the power that accrues to the unseen seers. Mothers, for example, are the objects of the social-scientific gaze, which judges the adequacy of their mothering from behind the two-way mirror in the psychologist's playroom. The maternal gaze is not unobserved and, although it can certainly be felt as powerful by those who are its objects, it is itself closely watched to ensure that actual empowerment flows from and not to it. Similarly, the daughter who looks up first to her father then to his surrogate is herself the specular object of his defining desire.

---

[50]See Kaplan, "The Case of the Missing Mother," pp. 82–85.

[51]See Michel Foucault, *Discipline and Punish: The Birth of the Prison,* trans. Alan Sheridan (New York: Pantheon, 1977).

[52]See Sandra Bartky, "Foucault, Femininity, and the Modernization of Patriarchal Power," in *Feminism and Foucault: Reflections on Resistance*, ed. Lee Quinby and Irene Diamond (Boston: Northeastern Univ. Press, 1988); reprinted in Bartky, *Femininity and Domination: Studies in the Phenomenology of Domination* (New York: Routledge, 1990).

The specular economy of patriarchy does not define women as exclusively either the seers or the seen. Rather, we are expected to be both, sometimes simultaneously: our subordination comes in the subtle directing of the allowable lines of sight. And it is along those lines that we can look for cracks, since they are the sites of tension. Frye's account, in "In and Out of Harm's Way: Arrogance and Love," of the tension between exploitation, which requires the activity of the exploited, and oppression, which would obliterate the possibility of that activity, is illuminating here.[53] Culturally normative male arrogance demands that women look, but, as Frye argues, the maintenance of phallocratic reality requires that we not be the authors of what we see (Frye, *PR*, pp. 165–66). We also are to be seen, but only as the beautiful objects we can make ourselves up to resemble.

Central to the resolution of the tension between these demands—between vision and blindness and between visibility and camouflage—has been the separation of women from each other: the seers must not see the seen. In particular, the happy expression of female desire, a goal of the remarriage comedies, requires the heroine never to have known—or thoroughly to forget—that it was in a woman's eyes that she was born as female and there that she first learned desire. The women in the melodramas, who in various ways possess this knowledge, are punished for it, for their inability to keep the domains of maternity and sexuality cordoned off. They need to be taught, like Charlotte Vale, that whatever power we have is had "on probation."

It is by "reading against the grain" of these injunctions that we can begin to "construct another (object of) vision and the conditions of visibility for a different social subject" (de Lauretis, *AD*, p. 68) . We need to remember that we did not come into existence—as subject, as female, or as desiring—in Oedipal relation to our fathers. When Mulvey suggests that the gaze is available to us because we have access to our pre-Oedipal masculinity, she colludes with Freud's heterosexist erasure of the mother/daughter relationship.[54] I have been arguing that, even for looking at classical Hollywood cinema, there is another gaze, which is not inscribed in the film or in the terms of its address but discoverable in the cracks along the lines of sight. Such a gaze may be untheorizable, but that may be in part because of the constraints of theory. We may need to look in the untheorizable gaps—such as those generated by the tension Frye describes between exploitation and oppression or between the impossibility and the actuality of lesbian desire—for examples of the activity of resistance, and learn from them without having or needing a theory that tells us how or whom we ought to see.

---

[53]See Frye, *PR*, pp. 52–94.

[54]See Mulvey, "Afterthoughts on 'Visual Pleasure and Narrative Cinema,'" p. 13.

III

Conversations on the Margins

9

On Competition: Some Stray Thoughts on Baseball, Sex, and Art

Imagine a zealous crusader attempting to purge baseball of the taint of competition, to make it a purely cooperative game. Where to begin? Shall we urge the pitcher and batter to cooperate on home runs, the batter and the fielders on fly balls, the runner and the base players on outs? or runs? Even if we could decide on a set of mutually agreeable goals, there wouldn't be very much fun involved in achieving them; the competition, the pitting of complementary skills against each other, is not a separable element in the game.

But there aren't just baseball teams and baseball games; there are baseball leagues, a baseball season, and the World Series. The baseball season builds toward the World Series; it aims at elimination. Team after team sinks in the ratings and bites the dust. Finally, one team wins the Series, the best team in North America (and hence, the world). Wonderful, heady stuff—but there's no one left to play with; they've all been eliminated. It's the end of the season; baseball has once again done itself in.

This sort of competition is ejaculatory; getting there may be a lot of fun, but what really matters is arriving, and once you have, it's briefly glorious and then that's it; it's all over. There's nothing to do but to go to sleep, happy and victorious—the end of the season.

It's also unfriendly. When we compete in this way, we acquire a real stake in each other's performing badly. If we're just playing baseball (I don't mean we're not taking it seriously), then we're competing toward a shared end—the most challenging, exciting game we can produce together. The competition serves the mutual end. If we're in the World Series, the mutual end of good baseball is still there, but there's another end which to some extent (not wholly, of course), *it* serves—winning the Series. And *that* can't be mutual; if I win, you lose. And my wanting to win can't help but lessen my joy in the accomplished beauty of your throws. I might feel this way in the course of a single game, might want very much to win, want that more than I want the best possible game, but it's not built into the nature of things that I do; there'll be other games, and if you play better today, I may learn from you to play better tomorrow.

This line of thought is related to the often-drawn distinction between product and process: are we aiming for some one particular thing, an object or an encapsulated end state, or are we most concerned with what's going on and how skillfully we're doing it? Two less often noted connections:

Products are detachable; they are valued, I think, in part because they can be contemplated and, often, bought and sold on their own, freed of the connection they must once have had with human labor and human bodies. We send them into the world our emissaries, cleaned up for the occasion, as though they had made themselves. Processes are embodied, undetachable from us, impure and contaminated, trapped in immanence, incapable of sauntering into the world on their own two fetishized feet.

And these notions, of disembodied, detachable transcendence and embodied immanence are tied to our cultural definitions of masculinity and femininity. Male sexuality, for example, is characterized as goal-oriented and focused on a fetishized body part that men are urged to think of as alienated, as they are urged to think of themselves as essentially separate from their bodies. As women, we learn to see—and to experience—our sexuality as diffuse, through time and our bodies, and our selves are tied to, often submerged in, that diffuseness. We are not encouraged to seek self-fulfillment in the production of enduring objects or self-definition in the transcendence of our bodies or our particular connections to others.

These differences are apparent in our perceptions of art. (Recognized) male artists have the social power to confer transcendent status on anything they please, power exercised at first on humble lives and finally on urinals, bricks, and Campbell soup cans. Women don't as a rule have this power; when women artists paint soup cans, the cans contain soup; the paintings are about nurturance, not color, line, and form. That is, they're seen this way, when they're seen as painted by a woman.

More than ever before in history some women can break away from this perception, make good the claim to the power of conferring transcendence, and of living it. We too—some of us—can create objects that will disown their sensuous connection with us, can live the lives of alienated self-definition.

Obviously, I'm less than convinced that we should *want* to do this, to stake our claim to industrial capitalism's version of the Midas touch—the ability to turn everything, including ourselves, into a commodity.

I visited the Women's Building in Los Angeles a few years ago. Kate Millet had an exhibit up—some stunningly erotic calligraphy and large papier-maché women dwarfing a shopping cart, a stove, a T.V., a telephone—beautiful pieces that could have chosen to be anywhere and chose to be there, drawing people in, benign guardians of a communal exhibit space. As I walked through the gallery

I realized I was relearning how to look at art, unlearning a particular, competitive mode.

We are taught to look at a work of art with blinders on, to encounter it in isolation. It and we need to find each other worthy of a moment of total devotion, cut off from where we each came from and where we may be going. It, of course, is not supposed to be going anywhere. Not, that is, anywhere that will change it. It can be crated and shipped from museum to museum, continent to continent, century to century, but it is expected to stay the same; it is finished. It is better than the other works it grew up with, learned from, taught, spoke with. And because it is better, only it has survived; they have been eliminated and it is left to speak with us alone. Really great works of art sometimes have whole walls or even whole rooms to themselves, the better to speak their unchanging monologues.

Something about the Women's Building kept me from treating the paintings, sculptures, and other, less well defined objects there that way. They were talking with each other, in very different voices, not always agreeing, and contributing unequally to the conversation. But the best contributor to a conversation—the most insightful, sensitive, witty, brilliant one—doesn't earn thereby the right to the others' silence. And being crated away into exalted exile would be a decidedly odd reward for that form of excellence. There was something going on in that room, something rooted in the real lives and real labor of particular real women, something I was invited briefly to join, not because I had a mind capable of aesthetic distance, but because I had a life capable of aesthetic, and political, engagement.

10

Thinking about Quality in Women's Visual Art

Think of the transformations impressionist paintings can effect in how we see the relationships between light and illuminated objects, or how cubist works can change the way we see shapes, juxtapositions, dimensionality. Think, specifically, of how photography is beginning to disabuse us of the notion of a privileged, God's-eye point of view, the central tenet of Western epistemology and aesthetics, from which the world appears the way it really is. (See Walter Benjamin, "The Work of Art in the Age of Mechanical Reproduction.") Visual art is not just art that happens to be visual (to be seen) but art that is about vision (about seeing as a distinctive form of human activity).

The premodern painter, like the scientist and the philosopher (who speak of their work in visual metaphor), laid claim to the Western point of view, or had that claim thrust upon his paintings, whatever he may have thought he was doing. And he was, of course, a "he," the painter whose point of view revealed reality as it is in itself. It has never, in what we know of our history, been women who have occupied that privileged position. We have been, both in our bodies and in our identification with nature (the landscape) the *objects* of both scientific and aesthetic vision. We are not the seers; we are the seen.

It is also true (see Marilyn Frye, "Metaphysical Misogyny: To Be and Be Seen," *Sinister Wisdom* 17) that we are not seen. We are, in Frye's metaphor, the invisible stagehands who enable the play of patriarchy to proceed. In Virginia Woolf's metaphor (in *A Room of One's Own*), we mirror men back to themselves at twice their natural size. The "real" world is the one in which men get to pretend that women (female persons) do not exist. When women see (desire) and are seen by other women, a revolution is under way. And when a woman who sees other women and sees herself as a woman paints (or sculpts or weaves or photographs or embroiders or . . .), we see her own view of her world, and an aesthetic revolution is under way. (For concrete discussions of what this revolution is like, see Lucy Lippard's essays and interviews in *From the Center*.)

Before this revolution women are both obsessively portrayed visual objects and invisible: we are, that is, camouflaged, disguised as pieces of an inanimate, dumbly maternal, hysterically chaotic, or seductively passive natural world or as artfully constructed dolls. Vision is the sense best adapted to express this dehumanization: it works at a distance and need not be reciprocal, it provides a great deal of easily categorized information, it enables the perceiver accurately to locate (pin down) the object, and it provides the gaze, a way of making the visual object aware that she *is* a visual object. Vision is political, as is visual art, whatever (else) it may be about.

Feminist visual art is about women's reclaiming of our stolen status as seers. This reclaiming is not easy: most of us who have been taught or allowed to trust the ways we see the world have learned to see it through men's eyes. ("You're different; you think/talk/write/paint/sculpt/see like a man.") We need to learn what nonimperialist ways of seeing are like: a vision of engagement and reciprocity, yielding knowledge rather than information, integrating the self and the perceived world, comfortable with being seen while seeing.

What does all of this have to do with quality? Simply this: we cannot judge the quality of something unless we know what it is for. No theory of artistic quality can exist without some account (explicit or implicit, acknowledged or hidden) of the function(s) of works of art. We need to know why we want them in our lives before we can know how to value their presence there or how to judge comparatively between them. There is no one answer to this question, no one thing art means to us, but one important answer—for visual art—is that it teaches us to see the world in surprisingly different ways and teaches us something about ourselves as seers. And if traditionally most of what we—as women—have been taught by the art we have been told was the best concerns our own objectification and powerlessness, we need to learn to judge feminist art by the extent to which it empowers us, teaches us to see the world through our own eyes.

A final note on pleasure: One might object that I make the experience of art more akin to cod liver oil than to chocolate—surely (much) art is meant to be enjoyed; one of its functions is aesthetic pleasure. I don't mean to deny this, but, rather, to raise the question of the social construction of the pleasurable. Feminist theories of sexuality have begun to explore the (politically and personally explosive) issue of female sexual desire and pleasure as shaped by a misogynist culture (see the work of Andrea Dworkin and Catharine MacKinnon), and I think we need to cast the same critical eye on aesthetic pleasure; what we enjoy looking at is not just culturally variable but deeply political.

11

Photography and the Politics of Vision

About a dozen years ago I was a New Left activist at loose ends and a graduate student in philosophy entranced by metaphysics—the nature of reality and being—and epistemology—the nature and grounds of knowledge. For me and many others, the political impetus turned inward to an examination of other "nonpolitical" parts of our lives. And what we found was, of course, politics: institutionally maintained structures of unequal power. This inward turn is part of what led to the current wave of feminist theorizing and activism. It also led to political critiques of supposedly nonpolitical academic disciplines.

I've spent the years since trying to formulate such a critique of Western metaphysics and epistemology—trying to discover alternatives to them, in practices different from the practices of science, which inform traditional metaphysics. Photography is such a practice, and I've found that I can discuss epistemology more fruitfully with the photographers I know than with epistemologists. This essay grows out of conversations I've had with a number of photographers and critics both about particular photographs and about what photography is up to. I'm writing it in the hope that the conversation will expand.

Within Western philosophy—since Descartes and until very recently—perception, particularly vision, has been thought of as passive. If you open your eyes under conditions of adequate illumination, the light reflected off objects within your field of vision will enter your eye, strike your retina, travel along your optic nerve to your visual cortex, and, assuming all that apparatus to be in sufficiently working order, produce a visual image. According to the Cartesian view, you haven't yet done anything; activity comes in when you try to decide whether the image you see of a palm tree means there's an oasis ahead or just a mirage. Perception provides the *given*, not the taken, the asked for, or the constructed: even in the case of hallucination, what we confront in perception is just there, and we just receive it.

Such a view has political foundations and implications. We think of the world we perceive as out there, independent of us, and our perception of it as either true to it or somehow distorted. Since the only thing we have to do with what we see is where we stand to see it, we think of some places as leading to distorted perception and others as affording an accurate (objective) view. The "objective position" is not conceived of as being any specific place at all; it is the nonplace one occupies when one gets to take the specifics of one's real place as irrelevant. It used to be God's place; now it is the scientist's.

The person who speaks from this privileged nonplace has no race (i.e., is white), no gender (male), no cultural identity (Western European), no class (bourgeois), no sexual identity (heterosexual), and so on. The rest of us see the world from narrow, specific, distorting perceptions: we perceive in biased, adjective-laden ways. When we write novels, make paintings, run for office, commit a crime, or do academic work, we do it as a Black person, a woman, an American Indian, a worker, or a lesbian. No matter what we do or how we do it, there's an original flaw we cannot overcome: who we are determines where we are—literally our *point* of view. That we are *there*—in some specific, nonuniversal place—means that what is given to us to see is not reality as it really is. *That* feat is reserved for those whose specificity is invisible, whose experience counts as generically human.

This critique has been developed by a number of theorists—mainly feminists building on the insights of Marxist methodology. What I have found is that the work of trying to think past this deep and pervasive piece of ideology is helped by attending to visual art and, in particular, to photography. There are photographs and photographic practices with obvious political implications. Photojournalism, for example, is often taken to present us with an objective, transparent view of reality, rather than a framed, selected, and edited one. Pornography, to which I will return briefly later, presents the viewer with a supposedly objective portrayal of women's sexuality. What I want to argue is that there are political implications to how photographs are made and looked at, no matter what their subject matter.

Visual art is not just art we attend to visually; it is also art about vision, about reflecting on how we see the world, and about coming to see it differently. Part of what we attend to in a work of art is how the artist saw some aspect of the world or of experience—perhaps not itself visual until the artist saw it. The work is a visual trace of an act of seeing. Seeing is an act whose intentionality may be attributed to it only retrospectively—in the work of art. Thus, visual art not only represents a denial of the passivity of perception, it affords us a shared access to an activity usually visible only to one person—the act of seeing itself.

There are two reasons why straight photography is particularly interesting to this way of thinking about visual art. One has to do with the democratizing potential inherent in the technology. We live in a world full of cameras, and we know that the camera that was in one place to take a certain picture could have taken a slightly different picture from slightly elsewhere. The point from which a landscape painting is depicted gets read as that privileged nonplace that shows things as they really are. The ubiquity of cameras tends to undercut a similar reading of the place from which the photograph was taken and encourages us to ask: why there? whose point of view is that?

The other reason has to do with the transparency of straight photography, the relative invisibility of surface technique. When we look at a painting (or at a manipulated photograph) our eye is drawn not just through but to the surface, to what was done to make it look the way it does. When we look at a straight photograph, we look through the considerable technique of its look to the look it represents, to the photographer's act of looking it records. This feature leads to reflection on the nature both of that act and the actor.

Both these features are culturally undermined, however, by the ways in which we are taught to see photographs. We are presented fundamentally with only two such ways, which are taken to be mutually exclusive: the informative and the aesthetic. Read as information, photographs are taken to be factual, passive, objective records of an independent reality. That is, they are read as transparent through to the object rather than to the photographer's act of seeing. The contingencies of point of view are masked. Read aesthetically, they fall under the other culturally available way of mystifying perception, the one usually applied to other visual artists: this is how things look to one singular genius, whose artist status swamps any other facts about him (or more rarely, her) and renders inquiry into them suspiciously philistine. Modern European culture, while reserving to science cognitive seriousness, has given the expression of subjectivity—otherwise rejected—to the arts, so long as the subjectivity in question emanates from "generically human" individuals, whose only specificity is that of "genius." Again, the culture subverts the potential of taking seriously the real place from which the photograph was envisioned.

Over the past ten years there have been three photographers whose work and conversation have helped most to shape my thoughts about these things. In talking with them about this article, I've come to realize how different from each other they are, and how differently their photographs help to reveal aspects of the activity of seeing. Two of the photographers are Minnesotans—Frank Gohlke and Stuart Klipper; one—Lynne Cohen—lives where I used to live, in Ottawa, Ontario.

Lynne Cohen photographs interior spaces with an 8x10 view camera. Until a few years ago she made contact prints; now the photographs are growing larger. Everything is equally, crisply in focus; we are not told where to look or what is important. Her subjects have ranged from living rooms, to reception halls, lobbies, offices, and beauty salons, to schools of various sorts—police academy, driving school, civil defense instruction classroom, hairdressing school, and so on. There are never any people in any of these rooms.

For me Cohen's photographs operate on three levels of reflexivity. The first is that of how she sees the world, something I describe as her being an intelligent

Martian, collecting a record of us to take back for Martian scientists to decode. Looking at the photographs, you know they'll get it wrong: there's no way people could move into these spaces and do what we know gets done there.

Along the opposing walls of a classroom in a beauty salon are lines of heads on shelves, most of them facing straight ahead toward empty chairs lined up in front of them, their hair either set in rollers or combed out. The faces are remarkably variable. "Remarkably" because for all the variation in skin color, nose shape, and chin line, they are utterly indistinguishable—in part as a result of their all apparently acquiring identical hairdos. The chairs are of only two types, but their legs are jauntily splayed, and they look more nearly animate than the heads. There is a door. But that creatures whose top parts resemble the things on the shelves will come through that door and sit on the chairs would never occur to the Martian scientists.

It seems not to occur to Cohen. Her photographs seem genuinely, marvelously ignorant, challenging our ready, unreflective, obvious knowledge. Try explaining to the Martians why this room looks the way it does, what goes on here, and why. What is the ground of our familiarity? After looking at a number of Cohen's photographs, I'm unsettled in the world; her alienation is contagious. There may not be anything wrong with how things look, but before that question can even be raised, we need to step back from how they look to us—enmeshed in them, knowing how to read them the way they should (why?) be read—so we can examine.

That leads to the second type of reflexivity in Cohen's photographs—our reflection on how we see them, especially if we are inclined to take her to be mocking or looking down on the human sensibilities that are responsible for the look of these places. Her gaze is steady, prolonged, cool, and constant, and the photographs do not invite us to enter into the forms of life that we know go on in those rooms. In fact, we find it hard to believe that anyone ever could inhabit those places. But when we take that look of hers to mean that *these* spaces are especially sterile or tacky, we are assuming her to feel at home with us in some place of visual warmth and good taste. And nothing in the photographs provides a ground for this.

The places she chooses to photograph are either intended to be looked at (they are decorated in some one of the many senses of that word) or places in which vision is trained (the schools can all be seen as schooling seeing). But those of us who look at art photographs tend not to look at these places nor to be trained to see in these ways. For us all this is visual Muzak; we do not know how to attend to it, nor do we find any reason why we should.

Cohen's photographs are paying close and careful attention to these places. The camera is large and cumbersome; it only records what it can gaze at steadily. In making the claim artists always make on our attention, she is saying it is worth our time to look at what we usually fail to see, and not to reserve our attention for those parts of the world deemed (by whom?) important. And if paying attention is—oddly—estranging and alienating, what does that say about us and about what is, though we may hate to admit it, our world?

The third type of reflexivity concerns the ways in which the spaces Cohen photographs are designed either to be seen or to school people in seeing—the human body as a target in the police academy, diverse heads as potentially identically coifed, a stretch of land in terms of golf strokes, or the terrain below you as affording aviation landmarks. Especially in these latter photographs, the subject matter is vision itself and the various ways of sophisticating it. The Martian who examines the photographs—to try to figure out an alien form of life —is at one end of a continuum of activity that has the people whom these spaces are designed for at the other. The activity is learning what matters and how in the visual world. Cohen's photographs add the additional questions: why? and to whom?

Cohen's photographs problematize the familiar; Stuart Klipper's frequently record his journeys to the far-flung, so-called ends of the earth—to the Arctic or Patagonia (as close as he's yet gotten to the Antarctic). He's almost in the tradition of the photographer-as-explorer, except that what he brings back is less a record of how it is out there, than a record of what it is to go out looking for it. He uses looking as a way of situating himself in the world. He is the nearly always invisible subject of his photographs trying to figure out what it is to be *there*, in that relation to shore or horizon.

He talks in ways that usually go over my analytically trained head about Heidegger and Being-in-the-World. What I understand of it is a perhaps peculiarly twentieth-century inability to be at home, to know where or what or why or how home is. How would we know it if we were? We say things like, "I find myself feeling sad." What do we mean? How and where do I find myself? Was I lost? I don't know of any other way of talking or writing about these things without sounding sophomoric (there is—hopefully—a sophomore still in each of us). But the questions are real, and Klipper's photographs pose them with a visual concreteness that makes them freshly intelligent and intelligible.

In a series of black and white photographs from the European Arctic, we find ourselves unsettlingly placed on beaches that give no clue to what lies behind us as we look out to the sea, with what may be tracks and may be the action of the tides leading to the water's edge. Other photographs unsettle our associations to terra firma: free-floating, indeterminately sized chunks of polar ice cap fill most of a picture, offering no clue to their own solidity, while in the background, clouds or mountains line the horizon alongside a definite spit of land. The trouble is, as we learn from another photograph, even the solidest land may just loom there, totally unaccommodating to our certainty that land is to land on.

We may not know, in looking at these photographs, exactly where the photographer was. But our uncertainty seems to be of a piece with his. We are, as he is, trying to find our way around, and trying to find ourselves in that activity—even (or especially) if we might not think to look for ourselves in those places. (How can I be so sure—as I am—that I could never find myself in the Arctic?)

Frank Gohlke tries to stay out of his photographs. He talks about the Wordsworthian dilemma of going out to look at the world and encountering the pesky self out there looking at itself looking at the world. When he does aerial photography, he sometimes catches a shadow of his airplane wing: he edits those shots out. (Klipper, by contrast, has a number of Arctic photographs that contain the wake of his ship.) I asked Gohlke why he did this, thinking that in-an-airplane was as specific a place as any and needed to be marked as such, given our associations of such a view with powerfully privileged authority (God, or aerial reconnaisance).

He replied, as I recall, that he hoped not to convey any such authoritative perspective, but rather to focus our attention not on him or where he was but on how things looked from there. In particular, he cared about the relations between places and people on the ground that came into view from the air—how near to each other people could be seen to be who might remain unaware of each other's presence. This attempt to find a way and a place to take photographs that carefully attend to something characterizes much of Gohlke's work, especially his records of natural devastation and natural and human recovery.

Since the eruption of Mt. St. Helens, Gohlke has been regularly returning to the mountain. His photographs are large and finely detailed; some are panoramic. He displays them with accompanying text that tells you what you are looking at and how it came to look that way—where it is with respect to the eruption, what the eruption did to it, and what has happened to it since. There are a large number of photographs: one has the impression of an attempt not to leave out any part of the mountain. The photographs are very beautiful. The blast tended to knock things over in one direction; its effects seem an oddly orderly pattern on the uneven slopes.

Owen Edwards ("In the Valley of the Shadow," American Photographer, January 1984) finds the beauty of the Mt. St. Helens photographs unsettling: what does it mean that we can respond aesthetically to the beauty in what is a scene of devastation? I take such a question very seriously, but I think it misses the point of Gohlke's photographs, which challenge a purely aesthetic way of seeing.

An important part of what these photographs do is to challenge the dichotomy between the aesthetic and the informational. Their undeniable beauty is juxtaposed to a text that tells you how to read them for information, and they have their place in a project to return repeatedly for more photographs, more text. The aesthetic and the informational are joined by the moral quality of attention, a way of looking that takes or, rather, gives time, that makes an effort to see the object of attention in a way that is true to it and not a projection of one's own desire, and that is, as well, a way of tending to, of caring for. Simone Weil and Iris Murdoch have written about this sort of attention, and Sara Ruddick finds it characteristic of what she calls maternal thinking.

In one aerial photograph we see a vast ridge curving around a lake below it; the ground is stark, rough, and furrowed. The text tells us that "these slopes" (they look too harsh for so smooth a word) "were heavily forested before the eruption." What we see shifts: this land is denuded, stripped bare; that stubble is the ghost of trees. Our awe is mixed with pity—an unsettling combination. What is it to care lovingly for something that so dwarfs us? Gohlke links our learning how to do this with our learning how not to do to the planet what a volcanic eruption did to Mt. St. Helens.

Another photograph shows, in the foreground, the rushing North Turtle River, in which sits a large rock with a small rock perched on it. The text tells us this is "an instance of erosional whimsy—unlikely to last." I'm reminded of the tree, falling unheard, but here the question is: how does it matter to the tree that its fall makes a noise? How might the earth need our attention? Or, less mystically, what would it mean for us to take the world we live in as worth our attention, our efforts at patient learning? It's only a rock sitting briefly on another rock, but in Gohlke's photograph it matters.

A practical, political consequence of my remarks on Cohen's, Klipper's, and Gohlke's photographs concerns pornography, which has the social power it does in part by relying on not being seen as I've been arguing these photographs can teach us to see. Men are taught to occupy the vantage point from which women's bodies are pornographically displayed: their experiences of alienation from this perspective are evidence of lesser manliness. The perspective itself is not to be questioned, nor is one to ask how one is being defined by one's occupancy of it. Despite the fact that the women in pornography are posed and costumed (even, as John Berger argues, when they are nude), the subjectivity behind the camera is rendered invisible. The photograph claims to reveal the essence of female sexuality, while in fact constructing it in accordance with male desire.

Lynne Cohen, Stuart Klipper, and Frank Gohlke see the world very differently, but they share a concern with responsibly attending to the world they see and to how they see it, a concern that is as moral as it is aesthetic. They help move us away from a facile and dangerous sense of passivity that masks activity we'd rather not acknowledge.

12

Art For Our Sake

Why *should* I pay for what offends me? That question haunts the discussions about content restrictions on National Endowment for the Arts funding. Many people have noted that we pay for many things, such as the violent suppression of Latin American liberation movements, that we would not choose to pay for. But the analogy is a poor one. I don't think we, or anyone else, *ought* to pay for imperialist ventures, and it seems to understate the objection ridiculously to say that some of us are offended.

Feminists have similarly argued that the language of offense used in discussions of obscenity has nothing to do with the wrongness of pornography. It doesn't matter whether anyone is offended by pornography. It is wrong for the same reason that racist hate literature or cross burnings are wrong: the speech of the privileged is deployed to effect the silence of the oppressed. I would hope that NEA review panels would refuse funding for work that functions in this way—for example, for unreflective performances of racist, sexist, or homophobic classical plays—and if I thought that such a directive might inform congressional content restrictions (given the current political scene, a preposterous suggestion), I might consider supporting them.

I do think artists have responsibilities to the rest of us, especially if we fund them. Not all art needs to be explicitly political, but all art, if taken seriously, intervenes in cultural conversations about individual and collective identities, conversations that are needed if we are to become a genuinely democratic society. And such intervention calls for responsibility. It can, for example, *require* offending those whose privileges, like vampires, can't withstand the light of day.

13

Making It All Up

1. A general characterization of the work of philosophy is the formulation of conceptions of the self and its relations to other selves and to the rest of the world. At times of major economic and political changes such conceptions become inadequate and in need of revision in terms that better reflect and facilitate altered forms of social relationship. The flourishing of modern philosophy (roughly, from Descartes to Kant) served the secularization of knowledge required by the emergence of capitalism and the modern state, the wresting of epistemic authority from the Church, and its vesting in the sorts of atomic individuals required by the marketplace.

2. These particular battles are long won and these particular intellectual tasks are long done, but no others have captured the heart of the discipline (at least not as practiced in England and the United States). This accounts, I believe, for the deep malaise that afflicts most philosophers I know at least intermittently, sometimes referred to as "loss of problems." It can seem baffling just what we are or ought to be doing and why. The feminist philosophers I know tend not to suffer from this malaise, and I want to connect this immunity to a clearly felt need within feminist politics for alternative conceptions of the self and its relations. I want to say something about this project by connecting it to some fundamentally Kantian insights that have remained underdeveloped in the individualistic metaphysics and epistemology characteristic of Anglo-American philosophy.

3. The development of the self-conceptions of liberal individualism, as respectably academic as these conceptions seem today, occurred largely outside the universities, which for a long time clung to older, scholastic notions. Similarly, it is not primarily to academic philosophers that we ought to look for emerging alternatives, but rather to radical feminist praxis and to the writings that grow out of that praxis. Adrienne Rich's poems and essays are among the best examples I know of this writing, and I want to place her work in philosophical context by

comparing it to others that reflect earlier stages of the shift toward a nonindividualist epistemology.

4. Alain Resnais's *Last Year at Marienbad* can be seen as an illustration of a straightforwardly Kantian argument against the independent intelligibility of the isolated Cartesian ego. Henry James's *The Sacred Fount* takes the argument one step further, into an examination of the ways in which specific forms of social relationship function in the construction of the self. Rich extends this line of thought to deal with the situation confronting contemporary feminists (and, although generally less intentionally, others as well) in which the mutability of these social forms becomes the object of collective self-conscious criticism and attempts at revision.

5. *Last Year at Marienbad* can be seen as a piece of experimental epistemology, as an illustration in fact of Kant's argument against Descartes on the nature of the self. My reading of the film is heavily dependent on David Bordwell's lecture on it in his course "Film: Time in Motion" at The Walker Art Center in 1981. The camera attempts to replicate the standpoint of the Cartesian ego—pure subjectivity looking out on what might or might not be a real world. What would in a narratively traditional film be establishing shots—locating characters in a shared, public space—don't work here. We are given many evocative views and grand vistas, shots of long hallways and elaborate furnishings, but they never hang together—they don't cohere into one space. Nor do the time sequences fit together; there is no one sequence of events. And, paradoxically, what we are left with seems to be pure externality: no personality, no emotion, no subjectivity. The inner, deprived of a shared, objective outer, lacks all structure, all identity, simply vanishes. The "I think" of the Cartesian cogito becomes the bare "there is thinking." Kant's point, illustrated by the film, is that the self exists only within a shared, public space and time.

6. This requirement of the existence of others is, however, purely formal: the self cannot confront the world solipsistically, agnostic about a shared reality, on pain of the loss of its own internal unity and coherence. But the demonstrated need is not for particular others in particular relation to the self, merely for a stable structure of space and time shareable by any others there might be. There may be some suggestion that, as Kant argued, it just *is* the others who, along with the self, provide the stable structure. All that could be meant by the world in *Marienbad* being real is that all the subjective shots and time references match up and provide an objective framework on which subjective perception could hang.

7. Beyond the reality of space and time, requiring the formal existence of others who in principle share it, we can ask what it is that particular others in particular relation to the self contribute to the reality of the self. On the liberal individualist view characteristic of Anglo-American epistemology, the answer is essentially nothing. Others exert, of course, causal influences of various sorts on

the development of the self and on the states it is in at any particular time, but they are not seen as providing the necessary conceptual scaffolding on which those states are hung. The self is seen as a sharply bounded black box on whose innards we can speculate on the basis of its behavior and the stimulations impinging on its surface. Such a picture is natural enough for a society that aims to justify forms of social organization based on their abilities to satisfy the independently specifiable wants and needs of the individuals who make it up. That is, the epistemology of modern philosophy characterizes the rational man (*sic*) in the marketplace.

8. The counterpart to this public world of the marketplace and the state has been the private world of the family, embodying a fundamentally different conception of the self in relation and requiring, although it has not received, an alternative epistemology. On the contrary, the family and all intimate, nonintentional association have traditionally been viewed as epistemically tainting. The project of maturity—for males—is largely one of transcending the particularistic and "biased" standpoint of the family, even of the body itself, to reach an allegedly more objective and trustworthy stance in abstraction from all such concerns. The novel is the quintessential family genre, and it is no accident that a relatively large number of novelists have been women. It is, I think, the special task of the novel to teach us the outlines of the epistemic scaffolding on which knowledge of our own and each other's inner lives is hung, a scaffolding whose existence is rendered invisible by the normatively powerful myths about the nature of the self that fit the epistemology of the marketplace and the self-made man.

9. The exploration of this scaffolding is central to many of Henry James's novels. The attempt to render it visible is hindered both by the public myths that deny it and by the fact that when it functions well, we see not *it* but the facts about us that hang upon it. Two devices he uses to throw the structure into relief are the foreigner (usually American) to the culture (usually European)—or the outsider to the family—and the revelation of deception without outright lying. Through the first device, the reader comes to share in the outsider's attempt to discover the structure in terms of which the inchoate remarks and pieces of behavior he or she observes add up for the participants to full-blown expressions of emotional life. The second device works similarly: the possibility of nonmendacious deception relies on stable expectations and associations that can be exploited to mislead without actually lying and that can be revealed when we come to wonder at how the deception was pulled off.

10. *The Sacred Fount* is barely a novel. Rather, James is playing with the devices that he usually employs to other ends than a virtuosic display of novelistic tools. The book is in many ways similar to *Marienbad*: it takes place in a remote and opulent setting in a short span of time, a year after a similar occurrence; it concerns possible romantic liaisons; and the reader is never sure just what is really going on. Unlike the film, however, the novel provides a narrator and a

well laid out spatio-temporal framework. That is, there is one observing subject who moves within a world he (and we) take as fully real, populated by indubitably real people. The narrator, however, spends the English country weekend that fills the novel attempting to figure out what is going on among and between the other characters. Or, rather, he attempts to fit their relationships and feelings into a scheme he has developed, convinced that he has insights and understanding the others lack. He is, and purposely remains, an outsider to the others' lives. This status, which he thinks makes him epistemically privileged, leaves the reader with the suspicion that he is making it all up, though we have very little idea (being even more outside things than he is) of what is really going on. That is, we are quite sure he is deceiving himself, even though we don't know what the truth is.

11. The narrator's self-deception comes about from precisely what he believes protects him—his detachment from the others and his attachment to a theory, an epistemic scaffold independent of the particular people whom he is attempting to hang on it. In particular, he sees knowledge as a one-way affair whereby an objective observer deduces how it is with the object of his observation without himself being personally implicated, vulnerable, or known. The sorts of things he wants to know, however—just who, for example, is whose lover—are not brute facts to be pinned under a microscope, but complex social constructions whose meanings are evident only to those who are in a position to read the gestures and remarks. And that reading, the seeing of significance, is not available to the external observer employing alternative explanatory frameworks. It is as though one were to employ a fluent command of English to understand conversations in French. James intends us to see the social world in this way: each of our emotional lives is experienced in a language constituted by the social interactions in which we are enmeshed.

12. We hear a lot these days of the twin deaths of the novel and the family (both spoken of as though they had existed since time immemorial in precisely the forms most beloved of modern reactionaries). One thing that *is* happening, I think, is that what we had come to think of as the stable, "natural" grounds of the forms are being called into question and, with a self-consciousness of intent, modified. We can no longer take for granted the narrative frameworks that tell us when a story—or a life—is a good one. We have—many of us—a pervasive sense of making it all up.

13. Adrienne Rich is writing from within this sense of improvisation, asking what account we can give of notions like truth and honesty, trust, deception, and betrayal once we have lost—or abandoned—a stable world against which to measure our actions and utterances. This project is, I think, the secularized version of reacting to the death of God. To say "God is dead; everything is permitted" is to assume that it was ultimately in God's name that some things were forbidden. If all along *we* (whoever that might be) were doing the forbidding and only hiding our own activity behind a facade of divine command, then God's disappearance—

or at any rate comparative unavailability—would remove not the source of the prohibitions but only the magical front we thought we needed to put on them. (We might call this the Wizard of Oz account.)

14. We have, I believe, in a similar way alienated our own activity in the construction of the social and psychological world. We have kept ourselves from seeing what James reveals and Rich describes us as finally confronted with: that the terrain of each of our lives receives its contours from the forms of social relationship in which we are engaged. The self does not stand secure in its own borders, testing the waters of the social world, deciding whether or not to take the plunge. The possibilities of self-knowledge, of self-creation, are the possibilities of what Rich (in "Women and Honor: Some Notes on Lying") calls "honorable relationships"—those "in which two people have the right to use the word 'love.'" The truth is in need of creation; lies are what we have lived, not just what we have told—and no story about correspondence to what is real will enable us to distinguish the truth from the lie. We are hanging not just the Kantian scaffolding of space and time but an elaborately articulated and deeply political framework only within which can the self encounter the world—or itself—as an object of knowledge.

15. Much of this construction has been traditional "women's work," the shaping of a world out of the materials that lie ready at hand, unchosen, obdurate, needy. Rich celebrates this work in poems such as "Natural Resources" and "Transcendental Etude": "a universe of humble things— / and without these, no memory / no faithfulness, no purpose for the future / no honor to the past." "Natural Resources," from which those lines were taken, is written in two-line stanzas, each sentence moving on through several stanzas: the patient, persistent weaving of a thought constantly interrupted, a structural metaphor for traditional women's creativity.

16. The title of "Transcendental Etude" is doubly ironic. The leaping out of space and time we are told art aims at is a lie: "The longer I live the more I mistrust / theatricality, the false glamour cast / by performance, the more I know its poverty beside / the truths we are salvaging from / the splitting-open of our lives." There is another, deeper irony: as women we are entrusted with the work of weaving the immanent world, but not only is this work devalued, it and our lives have been lived out in an enforced transcendence, a rupture from our origins in a woman's body. We learn to know ourselves in intimate connection with our mother's body, and we are meant to see ourselves as providing this connection to others. But through what Rich calls "compulsory heterosexuality" (in "Compulsory Heterosexuality and Lesbian Existence"), we learn that we must overcome (transcend) the need to receive this intimacy, and we learn to deny the eroticism of this tie to a woman's body.

17. The project of Rich's poetry is a new epistemology: a theory of knowledge that begins in trust, in contrast to the paranoid somatophobia so strikingly evident in Cartesian epistemology. "My senses have betrayed me in the past; they could

do so again: I had better not trust them at all. For all I really *know* I don't even have a body." Certainty is supposed to start when Descartes identifies himself as a pure thinking being, uncontaminated by essential connection with his own, let alone anyone else's, body, and proceeds with his proof of the existence of God, his true, trustworthy parent. (There are striking parallels between Descartes's arguments in *The Meditations* and Nancy Chodorow's account in *The Reproduction of Mothering* of the psychosexual development of males raised by women in a male-dominated society.)

18. Much has been written and said about the uncertainties of fatherhood from the father's point of view, a liability women have been sequestered to counteract. But from the *son's* standpoint this uncertainty can be seen as an asset, leaving scope for the imagination. This is one reason, I suspect, why fathers have often been considered the true parents, the mothers the mere incubators. As Dorothy Dinnerstein has argued in *The Mermaid and the Minotaur*, fathers are more remote, less intimately connected, less associated with the humiliations of dependency, more suitable parents for a self that conceives of knowledge as a disembodied encounter with a separate and independent reality. (In one case the uncertainty of paternity allowed the usually metaphoric naming of God as father to be taken literally, with striking consequences for the authority with which the son was taken to speak.)

19. To name the work Rich and others are engaged in "lesbian epistemology" is not only to give due weight to an important fact about most of the women doing this work (in addition to Rich, I am thinking here primarily of Claudia Card, Marilyn Frye, Sarah Hoagland, Audre Lorde, Toni McNaron and Jacquelyn Zita), but to say something about the sources within all women of an epistemic authority that runs counter to what Western patriarchal culture has told us is trustworthy. We need, Rich teaches us, to rediscover the sources of knowledge that spring from intimate connection and vulnerability to a world we shape within our hands, a world of need and nurturance. We need, that is, to work backward from the lure of transcendence, the temptations of autonomous authority and absolute certainty, to overcome rather than glorify the alienation from women's bodies that has been the traditional price of epistemic adulthood.

14

Coming to Know
Women's Ways of Knowing

During the quarter that I taught *Women's Ways of Knowing* my father was dying. It was fall 1987, and the class was Gender and Theories of Knowledge. We began with feminist critiques of epistemology, exploring connections between philosophical problems and the agendas of privileged masculinity: how did someone come to worry about whether there was an external world and, if there was, whether our senses reliably informed us of it, about whether we actually had bodies, or others had minds? When I had taught the course previously, we had moved on to ask what problems of knowledge confront those with other agendas —women, for example, and in planning the course for that fall, I remembered a book Anne Truax had recommended as an excellent discussion of the myriad ways in which women come to know. Mary Field Belenky, Blythe McVicker Clinchy, Nancy Rule Goldberger, and Jill Mattuck Tarule's *Women's Ways of Knowing: The Development of Self, Voice, and Mind* (New York: Basic Books, 1986), became the organizing text for the course.

Interactions of self, voice, and mind—who we are, how we speak, and how we think—are central to epistemology. In inquiring after the nature of knowledge, we need to ask how we distinguish between what we merely believe and what we genuinely know, a question partly about how we become, in our own eyes and in those of others, reliable and authoritative. We need also to ask how we express what we know, as well as how we go about finding things out, what processes or methods are fruitful and trustworthy. That is, knowing is not just one thing we happen to do, but a central node of who we are; thinking about what and how we know is a good way of thinking about who and how we are.

Belenky, Clinchy, Goldberger, and Tarule start from the cognitive stage theories of William Perry, as Carol Gilligan, in her work on women's moral voices, started from Lawrence Kohlberg's moral stage theories. Both stage theorists worked nearly exclusively with male subjects in exploring how children and young adults come to increasingly autonomous cognitive and moral stances. In both cases the feminist revisionists began as good empiricists: if the subject population from which conclusions are drawn is nonrandom, it makes sense to ask whether broadening it leads to different results. In both cases, the answer is yes: when we look at girls' and women's cognitive and moral development, the paths that emerge are distinctively different. We learn to think and to be moral in ways that are as gendered as the ways in which we learn to be sexual—a conclusion that ought to be unsurprising, given how thoroughly gendered social life is, and how thoroughly social thinking and morality are.

Such gender associations are never absolute: we are all deluged from birth with messages about gender-appropriate ways of being, but we absorb those messages in different ways. Not only do the contents of the messages vary, notably with race and class, but we vary idiosyncratically in how we take them in and in what we make of them. Gilligan's "different voice" is neither unique nor universal to women, though she does, problematically, write as though there were *one* such voice, a moral stance of caring interconnectedness alternative to the dominant one of abstract universalizing. The plural in the title is a notable strength of *Women's Ways of Knowing*, although it is not always clear whether it refers to stages or to nonhierarchical diversity. The unclarity is a problem, but it is not just the authors'.

They want to move away from a hierarchical view, emphasizing the strengths in each position and the contexts within which those strengths are appropriate, but they portray journeys toward the increasing ability to integrate one's autonomy with one's connectedness, to see oneself as an *active* participant in the *social* construction of knowledge. The unclarity is, I think, the sign of an unavoidable tension for those of us who would practice feminist (or other liberatory) pedagogy: there are directions in which we want to help our students to move, things we know or know how to do that we think it worthwhile to teach, but we need to start—and to end—by respecting the integrity of our students' lives and minds, not because we have no intention of trying to change them, but because no changes we might help to bring about that violated that integrity could be what we intended. For us, the final chapters, "Toward an Education for Women" and "Connected Teaching," are helpful contributions to a conversation we need continuously to have, with each other and our students, about how to live with that tension once we have rejected the picture of ourselves as dispensers of truths and our students as empty vessels.

That fall, for my students and me, the book helped us to place ourselves in relation to the philosophical texts we were reading and to come to articulated senses of ourselves as knowers. We interrogated the philosophers we read, and ourselves, about what one had to be like to take oneself—or for others to take one—as knowledgeable. Philosophical methods were seen as ways of identifying with and trusting certain of one's abilities and distancing oneself from others. Various of us had found such methods either empowering or shaming at different times of our lives, and we explored other methods, such as art or consciousness raising or chemical-dependency recovery, through which we had come to know and to voice what we knew.

I thought a lot that quarter about my relationship to my father, about my development of self and voice as his daughter, about how that relationship had prepared me to be a philosopher, and about how to be a loving but nondutiful daughter as I strove to find a voice and a self less shaped by the methods for achieving privileged authority (that is, a voice and a self less male-identified, but also less unreflectively white, middle class, able-bodied, and heterosexual).

In December I took my students' papers with me to New York. In the hospital room where my father was dying, I read a collection of extraordinary "epistemic autobiographies," stories of how the others in the class were negotiating journeys toward senses of themselves as knowledgeable people, and how they saw within their lives the intersections of privilege and oppression, crossroads at which they learned to trust their own voices and to listen to and learn from the voices of others. Listening to and learning from them, being a part of those conversations, helped me find the courage to embrace my father, and to let him go.

15

Changing the Subject

My colleagues, especially those who teach the introductory course, frequently lament their students' inability to write. The fault is variously placed—on the public schools, on television, on our own composition program—and various solutions are suggested, ranging from trying to have smaller recitation sections so TAs can spend more time working with students on their writing, to doing away with paper writing altogether in favor of examinations.

Recently one colleague remarked on the startling improvement in the quality of the papers he is now receiving from students in his introductory class. Using Mill's method, it is unreasonable to attribute the improvement to the public schools, to television, to the composition program, or to our talented but still overworked TAs. Rather, the one thing that has changed and that seems the obvious and, I think, correct, explanation for the improvement is the change in the nature of his paper assignments. Briefly put, he is now asking his students to communicate with him, with each other, and with the texts they are reading, and he has made it clear to them that he believes they have interesting things to say.

It seems a trivial commonplace to say that writing is a form of communication between author and reader. But many who would never go along with the trendy deconstructions of that idea seem to ignore it in their teaching, or to reduce the communication in question to the students' communicating to the teacher whether or not they can accurately and with apparent understanding reproduce what the teacher already knows. It's as though we regarded as the paradigm examples of small children's communicating with us their parroting back their best attempts at pronouncing the words we sound for them. One sign that we treated student writing, or speaking, as a mode of communication, would be our observance, and our expectation of their observance, of some of the basic norms of respectful communication: on our part, don't ask questions you know the answers to; and, on theirs, don't tell someone what you have reason to believe they already know.

Another commonplace (interestingly enough, also one for which analytic philosophers have been castigated) is that philosophy is a continuous conversation. We stage encounters between Aristotle and Descartes, and we join in. Our expectation for our students is that they, too, will participate in the conversation, but according to the usual ways of teaching, there's very little room for them to do so in an original or distinctive fashion unless they are well on the way to becoming one of us. Having something new to say, something that will be recognized as a contribution to the conversation, is hardly what we usually expect of our undergraduates. If they say something we hadn't expected, that will usually be reason to think that they hadn't quite gotten the point or understood the assignment or grasped the argument.

These assumptions on our part—that genuine contributions to the conversation that is philosophy are made by philosophers (that is, by people who think in ways similar to those who have been participants so far) and that what others say may be interesting in some way but isn't really germane—are hardly opaque to our students, who figure out that if what they are trying to do is to learn philosophy and to demonstrate that learning, they are better advised to sound as much like their teachers as they can and to say what they figure we would say rather than what they would say if they took our questions to be real ones, that is, if they took us really to care about their answers as something other than diagnoses of their abilities and achievements in coming to sound just like us.

Such considerations apply, in varying degrees, to all our students, of whatever gender, race, or cultural or economic background. And some of them will in fact respond eagerly to the terms we set: they will take on the apprenticeship, producing competently crafted work, acquiring the skills, by practicing on the arguments of others, that will allow them someday to produce original arguments of their own. There is no telling in advance who these students will be, and we need to be as ready to see the seeds of philosophical talent in a Black woman as in a white man. We need to be open to the possibility that any of our students will fall in love with the subject as it is, however traditionally it is taught, and that they will be good at it.

But they will be few. And, increasingly, the attention paid to race and gender inside and outside the university means that fewer and fewer of our students who are not white males will fail to notice or to care that nearly all of us, and nearly all the authors we teach, are. We may think they are wrong to care, that the attention is a bad and divisive thing, keeping students from claiming what could otherwise belong as much to them as to their white male fellow students. I don't think the attention is a bad thing; I think it reveals divisions that were always there though usually invisible from the side of privilege. (It's like the attention to sexual harassment, which leads many men to wax nostalgic for the harmless fun of a more comfortable, less self-conscious time. The cost of their comfort was the silence of the women who were victimized by that "harmless fun." The problem with raising awareness about race and gender is that those who had the privilege not to think about racism and sexism now have to. At least a little. Those on the other side have rarely had that luxury, and the few who have, if only in the precincts of philosophy, have had to deal with the estrangement that comes with being "the exception.")

But even if we think the attention is a bad thing, it isn't going to go away. Very few of our women students, for example, are likely to enter our classrooms as oblivious as I was in 1965 to the near absence of women from the tradition we study. Not only are they more likely than I was to notice it, more important, they are more likely to think that it matters, that it's not a dismissible consequence of the fact that before very recently women were rarely encouraged or even allowed to do philosophy. And students of color are less likely now not to notice or to care that what we name philosophy is a set of distinctively European responses to distinctively European takes on questions asked, variously, all over the world. One might well study those responses as culturally specific, but such an attempt is usually defeated by the solipsistic imperialism of high European culture, which takes the forms of its own subjectivity to be universal. And it has gotten hard not to notice how many people were never meant to count as examples of the allegedly generic man.

One way we can respond, if we take these concerns seriously, is to expand the range of voices we engage in conversation. That is, we can add to our reading lists people who speak from perspectives that are not among the privileged. We can find ways to generalize the questions to which the philosophers we have been trained to read are giving answers in ways that show those questions to have been asked and answered by others. This is not a wholly new skill for a professionally trained philosopher: on the face of it Aristotle and Descartes weren't asking the same questions, and though Descartes surely had Aristotle in mind when he framed his questions, it didn't work the other way around. It takes an imaginative leap, of the sort we are trained to make, to figure out what Aristotle might say back to Descartes, to continue the conversation.

By bringing noncanonical voices into the conversation, we can set the stage for our students' participation in it. The people we are trained to read were not talking to people like our students—in most cases not solely because people like our students weren't born yet. We need to allow our students to notice this exclusion, to get angered by it, to ask themselves whether they want to become more like the people the philosophers are addressing (who will, of course, differ, depending on the philosopher), or whether they want to change the terms of the conversation. We can encourage them to believe that they have something to say, something we do not know, something the philosopher (or those, like us, who are committed to keeping the philosopher's words alive) needs to hear. Other voices can both model this sort of engaged talking back and serve as mediators, people with whom students may well feel readier to converse, by whom they may better expect to be understood.

We need to resist the temptation to present noncanonical voices as representative, as introducing diversity by giving the Black or women's or whatever perspective. Such voices need to be diverse and to disagree among themselves. One of the sillier arguments against taking diversity as a reason for affirmative action has it that doing so presupposes that there is a distinctive perspective a member of the group in question will bring. The reality, of course, is exactly the reverse: it is when members of marginalized groups are scarce that those who are present are put in the role of representatives of their race, gender, disability, sexual identity, or whatever. One of the goals of affirmative action is to have enough members of such groups around that the diversity among them is always apparent (meaning both that there are enough people for the diversity to be represented and that they are sufficiently at home not to need to hide their diversity behind a united front).

We will, most of us, need to reach a bit to include voices from beyond the philosophical pale, and I appreciate the worry that many have about treating such work disrespectfully, out of an all-too-familiar omnivorous arrogance that picks up bits and pieces of exotica to add a little spice. It isn't enough to point out that we feel fully competent to teach, say, Plato, so how can our contemporary, the Black lesbian poet and theorist, Audre Lorde, be too great a reach: we needn't worry about arrogantly appropriating Plato. Assuaging my fears of lacking mastery is one thing; assuaging my worries about the political meaning of claiming it is quite another.

But why do I need to master the voices I invite into my classroom? I certainly need to have something to say about them, enough to introduce them to those who are unfamiliar with them, and something to say to them, some way of starting a conversation I hope the students will continue. But we worry that our treatment of a text will be superficial, that we will miss, perhaps because of cultural differences, its subtleties and depths. It would be salutary just to acknowledge this fear, to accept the likelihood that we will, in fact, miss a lot, that we are not expert guides to these texts. We can locate ourselves and the world of academic philosophy we inhabit in the broader world by drawing connections both with parts of that broader world we know very well indeed and with parts of it that are strange to us.

The connections to what we know well can involve bringing the actual, historically specific, nongeneric people we are into our classrooms, using our own experiences as touchstones for philosophical reflection. This can be hard for us to do: we, after all, are the ones who succeeded in an educational system that rewarded the disciplining of the personal, idiosyncratic voice. It is no wonder that so many academic feminist theorists reproduced the spurious universalizing for which we rightly castigated privileged men: we had learned to trust our own voices precisely to the degree that we had learned to sound like them. Having served a long and successful apprenticeship in silencing the unrulier voices in our own heads, we were not apt to be very good at hearing those coming from others'. If we are inviting into the conversation a wider range of real people, we will need to join in as real people, not as disinterested anthologizers and critics.

No one really is generic, however much privilege may encourage some to believe they are; no one has only ruly voices in her or his head.

Until we have gotten to the point where, despite long years of having been taught otherwise, students see us as real people, it will be hard for them to believe that, when they write papers for us to read, they are writing to a real person. We cannot expect that philosophy will come alive for them, will connect to the people they are, if they do not see it doing so for us, or if the enthusiasm they see us as having for our work seems so unconnected from anything they can see themselves as caring about that we might as well be another species. Especially until we are real enough to them for them to write intelligibly for our eyes it helps to have them write to and for each other, to trade papers and write responses. And taking each other seriously that way, as readers and critics, can help to break the hold of the idea that authority flows unidirectionally from text to teacher to student. We shouldn't underestimate our power in the classroom, in particular the power to say, "this is to be taken seriously; this is worth your attention; this is the real stuff."

Thus, the inclusion of other voices, authorized by their placement on the syllabus as contributors to philosophical conversation, can convey the message that what counts as philosophy is not fixed and that contributing to it does not require sounding like any of the previous participants. It may seem to us that students who bring up experiences of poverty or racism or abuse (or, for that matter, experiences of cooking or canoeing or dancing) in a discussion of Kant are changing the subject; they are no longer talking about what Kant was talking about, hence aren't contributing to the conversation we were having with Kant. But there are other senses of 'changing the subject': changing the subject matter of philosophy and changing the nature of the subject who philosophizes. In both these senses the student may well be changing the subject—if those of us charged with its preservation and canonical development have the courage and the humility to listen.

IV

The Body of Privilege

16

The Body Politic / The Impolitic Body / Bodily Politics

I am a philosopher, a woman, and a feminist. My identity as a philosopher is certified by training, diplomas, and a university appointment. My identity as a woman was not similarly earned: depending on the aspects you focus on, and how you think about them, it may be, among other things, a biological fact, or an always elusive goal, or an ineluctable liability to sexual assault. My identity as a feminist has come in large part from my attempts to make sense of those other two identities, particularly as they occur together—oxymoronically, I now think—as woman philosopher.

The main problem with being a woman philosopher is that according to our cultural norms philosophers have bodies only accidentally, and women have them essentially; women *are* our bodies. Even when the accident of corporeality is acknowledged to be universal, even necessary, and as permanent as one's identity, it still isn't essential that the philosopher have the precise body that he[1] has, and he's encouraged to regard it as a—perhaps indispensable—tool. Philosophers frequently fantasize body transfers, as they ponder the nature of personal identity. Women's bodies may be interchangeable, but not by us. Rather our bodies establish the terms under which *we*'ll be exchanged; they establish our worth, our identity.

The main problem with bodies, I have come to think, is that they are different, and the history of Western politics and epistemology[2] is the history of attempts

[1]I don't use 'he', 'his', etc. in their supposedly generic forms; the philosopher is normatively male, even if only honorifically.

[2]In referring to "politics and epistemology" I mean to be stressing that knowledge is socially created, under historically specific conditions, and that there can be no valid epistemology that is inattentive to the conditions, in particular, to the institutionalized power inequalities—the politics—under which and in response to which knowledge is created and judged.

at denying difference. I want to sketch a simplified version of that history by distinguishing between premodern and modern attempts: the premodern involve the Body Politic, and the modern involve the Impolitic Body. Feminism—as a politically responsible form of postmodernism—is epistemologically radical insofar as it abandons those projects altogether, constructing knowledge based on women's differences—from men and from each other—and on bodily experiences. Feminism is Bodily Politics.

The Body Politic

One way of dealing with the problem of diversity, of the many, is by discovering, or postulating, the one. (*Why* diversity is a problem is another question, one I haven't an answer to. What's clear is that for Western epistemology and politics it has been a problem, perhaps *the* problem.) Individual knowers and political actors may be endlessly diverse, but premodern authority resides elsewhere—in a unitary realm of Forms, in God, or in the king. An individual's claim to knowledge rests on his ability to trace its origin to the unitary source. And that source is either literally bodily—see Foucault's account of the importance of the body of the king[3]—or with a barely sublimated body: consider the anxiety about graven images and sacrificial animals for the Hebrews and the "resolution" of both those anxieties in the incarnation of Christ, the visual splendor of cathedrals, the importance of religious art and music, the veneration of relics. The sublimated body, unlike the actual one, transcends any particularity—it is not different. But the residue of bodily presence ties authority to a patriarchal memory, makes it emotionally real, and encourages the belief that we are all part of one large body, all have our proper place in its constitution.

The premodern European world was, in the root sense of the word, patriarchal. From the *pater familias* to the king as father to God the Father, the many found their place and grounded their knowledge in relation to the one who gave and sustained their lives. The most prevalent theories of reproduction denied to the mother all but a nurturant role for the male seed; even parenthood had to be singular. The ways people knew their places in the world had to do with their bodies and the histories of those bodies, and when they violated the prescriptions for those places, their bodies were punished, often spectacularly. One's place in the body politic was as natural as the places of the organs in one's body, and political disorder, as unnatural as the shifting and displacement of those organs. As Francis Barker puts it, in a discussion of *King Lear*, "Although disorder in the family, in the state and in the faculties of the soul—and, indeed, in cosmic nature—can act as metaphors for each other, their substantial interrelation is more

[3]Michel Foucault, *Discipline and Punish: The Birth of the Prison*, trans. A. Sheridan (New York: Pantheon, 1977).

profound than poetic artifice: they are all grounded at once in the same inner correspondence whose transgression risks the disarticulation of reality itself."[4]

The Impolitic Body

Against this unity of unities, the individualism of bourgeois subjectivity was genuinely liberatory. The modern self broke away from the defining bodies of the Church and of hereditary social, political, and economic power. The cost of making that break was a concurrent break with the subject's own body, a break that was characterized and experienced as fundamental to individual empowerment. As Foucault has argued most thoroughly, the modern body is disciplined, anatomized, medicalized, dissected, and surveyed by diffuse systems of power. (See also Barker, *The Tremulous Private Body*, 1984). These become internalized by a socially constituted self that is empowered by its success at objectifying and controlling its own body, that is, the body that it happens to inhabit and on which it is dependent, and for which it therefore has to assume particular responsiblity. Both our bodies and our dependence on them are embarrassments to the modern self. Even if they are regarded as indispensable, they are blamed for our failures, both epistemic and moral; they make us liable to illusions and to temptation.

Our bodies also make us different, and the authority of the bourgeois subject has resided in his sameness. So put, those claims are semantically odd: difference and sameness are relational terms—different from *what*? the same as *who*? Political logic doesn't always follow semantical, however, and sameness and difference have absolutely characterized those who do and do not fit the normative picture of the generic man—he who is authoritative because he has no characteristics that would make his point of view a partial or biased one. He is, for example, an author, not a Black or working class or homosexual or female or Third World author. The privileges of being white or middle class or heterosexual or male or European (or Euro-American) importantly include the privilege of being generic, of having one's identifying adjectives left off; they sound odd when put on.

Thus, ironically, the individualism of modern Western epistemology and politics are threatened by individuality. Without the One to forge unity from our diversity, without a stable body politic in which to find ourselves, we have to make a world from our own experiences and desires. And if those experiences and desires are diverse, we seem to have no guarantee that it will be one world that we will create. Anarchy (portrayed as the Hobbesian state of nature, a bourgeois nightmare), relativism, and scepticism are the quintessential political and epistemic anxieties of modernity (not to be confused with the real dangers, which are much more those of totalitarianism). Both science and the state require the positing of fundamental sameness among the enfranchised: difference must

---

[4]Francis Barker, *The Tremulous Private Body: Essays on Subjection* (London: Methuen, 1984), p. 33.

be merely epiphenomenal, trivialized by being relegated in political economy to the domain of consumption and in epistemology to the domain of the aesthetic. In those domains individuality is exalted, at the same time as even there it is channelled by the media and the art world, lest it get out of hand and disrupt the economy of the same.

The advances of liberalism since the seventeenth century have consisted largely in the expansion of the ranks of those who count as the same. Conversely, most of the horrors of modernity—slavery, colonialism, imperialism, the Holocaust, apartheid—have consisted largely in retrograde attempts to relegate some to the ranks of the different. Given the definition of full, exemplary humanness as sameness, the different are necessarily *less* than fully human, objects to the human subjects, and, typically, unlike the subjects, essentially embodied. The different are identified by their bodies—they are reputed not only to look different but to smell different and to have different capacities and tolerances—and it is obsessively their bodies that are mythologized, feared, loathed, exploited, tortured, or destroyed. Until relatively recently the struggles against these horrors have consisted in claims by the different to fundamental sameness—for example, Shylock's "do I not bleed?" The slogan of Black nationalism in the United States, "Black is beautiful," symbolizes the emergence of an alternative mode of struggle, one that challenges sameness as the basis of modern political and epistemic enfranchisement. That challenge is the reason why Third World nationalism has at least the potential to be both radical and progressive, unlike the earlier European and American versions, which, grounded in the epistemology of sameness, were ineradicably imperialist.

Bourgeois white women (usually, following the rules about who gets "adjectivized," referred to simply as 'women') have had a unique position in the modern scheme of things—different but supposedly not lesser. The pedestal is a place neither for a person nor for a devalued object: it is meant for an object that is cherished and cared for. Such women's alleged special virtues were meant to mark them as different, but as equal to or even—morally and aesthetically—superior to men. The arguments around women's suffrage in the United States in the late nineteenth and early twentieth centuries attest to the hold of this conception of womanhood on the imagination of even the proponents of suffrage, many of whom argued for it precisely because of the allegedly unique contribution of women's finer moral sensibilities. (The opponents of suffrage tended to believe rather that the corrupting atmosphere of politics would irreparably damage those fine, but delicate, sensibilities, rendering them unfit for the essential tasks of nurturing children and humanizing men.)

Sojourner Truth, a Black woman born a slave, responded to a litany about the sanctity of womanhood delivered by an opponent of women's suffrage, with a counter-litany of the differences of her life from the privileged, protected, pampered life "women" were said to lead. Her refrain was "Ain't I a woman?" The questions she was raising—who and what are women, who does the defining, how are women different from men and amongst ourselves, and what differences should those differences make—have defined the struggles of feminism for the last century. And, in conjunction with the analogous questions raised by the anti-imperialist struggles of the Third World, they point toward a revolution in political epistemology as radical as the one that marked the move into modernity. Also analogously with those struggles, feminism has to confront the definition of women in bodily terms against the backdrop of a culture that privileges the self defined as only accidently embodied. The disciplines that control the impolitic body confer power and authority on those who master them: sublimation is the Freudian term for this process as applied to one's own(ed) body. Those who *are* their bodies are disciplined, mastered by others: they are those who lack the moral power of sublimation. Lacking authority, they do not make culture.

Bodily Politics

Postmodernism is, most profoundly, a revolt against the social, political, and economic structures that have held in place the unified subject and the correlative world of objective facts. Too often, however, the revolt is staged against the ideas of that subject and of that world, or against the supposed illusion that those structures are still in place. There is frequently no recognition of the need for concrete political struggle to effect the material changes that would actually make the unified subject an anachronism, rather than just exposing it as historically conditioned. Postmodern epistemologies that are political only negatively—only in their exposure of the emperor's new clothes, the revelation of the historicity of modernity—cannot provide a politically usable epistemology. The major strength of modern epistemology is that it is politically usable: it grounds both science and the liberal state. And it needs to be challenged by an epistemology that grounds and is grounded in an alternative set of political practices, that is, that bears a positive relation to some particular set of such practices. Subversive playfulness is not enough, nor is a noncritical pluralism.

Humberto Maturana's epistemology is, I think, such a noncritical pluralism.[5] To argue, as Maturana does, for the existence of a plurality of cognitive domains and for the absence of hierarchical relationships between them, is, I agree, to undercut one of the pillars nodern epistemology. Such an argument is a political move, and an important one, since that epistemology legitimates a wide range of strategies of domination. However, a noncritical pluralism like Maturana's sees as reactionary the attempt, or even the desire, to choose in more than a situational way between competing epistemologies. Figuring out how to explicate and guide such choices is, I want to urge, the task of any politically

[5]Humberto R. Maturana, "Elemente einer Ontologie des Beobachtens," in *Materialität der Kommunikation*, ed. Hans Ulrich Gumbrecht and K. Ludwig Pfeiffer (Frankfurt: Suhrkamp, 1988).

responsible postmodern epistemology. (If 'politically responsible' and 'postmodern' sound contradictory, that's part of the problem.)

Another way of posing this problem is as the problem of when and how to say *we*. The epistemology of sameness had an easy answer: insofar as I have thought myself out of my own particularity, including out of my body (a move that Kant, for example, equates with the attainment of autonomy), I can say *we*, confident that only those who cannot or have not so abstracted themselves will disagree. A claim to objectivity is a claim to speak for all whose voices count; it is a license not to listen. (I may, of course, need to listen in order to *achieve* objectivity; others may be helpful in pointing out my biases and may provide me with information I lack. But ultimately one voice will do, the one that speaks the truth.)

Women have become justifiably suspicious of this *we*: men have spoken for us (or for all mankind, which may or may not have included us), and we have known or discovered that what they have said is not what we would have said, had anybody asked or listened. The initial exhilaration of the wave of American feminism that started in the '60s lay largely in the discovery and evocation of a new *we*, the different voice that women spoke, the different world that we inhabited. It subsequently came as quite a shock to have it pointed out to us—mainly middle class white women by mainly women of color—that we had been spuriously generalizing from our own experience, commiting precisely the epistemological and political sin we had been attacking in masculinist thought. The case against saying *we* seems overwhelming: politically as a piece of imperialist presumption, and epistemologically as a fiction that equates autonomy with universality.

The epistemological and political need to say *we* remains, however. Neither a theory nor a politics of irreducible singularity seems very promising. The very political activism that led to the problem—the need to build a theory that would further the fight against the various forms of oppression of *all* women—requires its nonsceptical solution. It is not surprising that feminists are charged—in particular by French poststructuralists—with remaining in thrall to the bourgeois conception of the subject, as well as to such concomitant liberal ideals as rights and autonomy. It is not even surprising that sometimes (though not as often as it is made) such a charge is justified. Those who have always been denied the status of *the same* are less likely to be attracted by the rebellious thrill of spurning its privileges, and it is extraordinarily difficult to do without the fundamentals of one epistemology in the absence of a developed alternative—not, that is, unless one has the privilege of being able to afford a cheerful nihilism (and only men get to play at being naughty boys).

One of the standard ways in which the quest for the same has engaged philosophy is essentialism—the idea that the properties of objects are distinguishable into the essential and the merely accidental, and that it is the former that make something the sort of thing that it is, those properties that it has in common with all others of its kind. It has come to seem, even to those who would mean to repudiate essentialism, that one cannot meaningfully theorize about—or politically organize—a group of people one cannot *define*: how, we are asked, can there be a movement for women's liberation if we cannot define what is meant by 'woman', if we cannot tell who is and who is not one? With respect to women (and at least many other oppressed groups) the situation is complicated by the centrality of the body to the oppressor's definition. That is, something which in modernity is relegated to an accidental feature of being human, and is the repository of all the accidental, individuating features of particular people, becomes, with respect to oppressed groups, the locus of generic definition rather than of individuality.

If the problem with the bodies of middle class white men is that they get in the way of those men's claims to objectivity by making them liable to bias and partiality, the problem with the bodies of the rest of us is that they define us as interchangeable with others in our group, exchangeable as workers or as sex objects. For the privileged the body expresses the anarchic play of individual differences, which threaten one's authority unless one has the power to channel and control them. For the oppressed the body expresses the stereotyped difference that defines—in the oppressor's terms—group membership; the possibilities of individuality seem to lie in a retreat from the body. Since, paradoxically, the privileges that attend membership in the fellowship of the same lie that way too, the incentives are strong for the oppressed also to regard their bodies as merely accidental.

There are two sorts of problems with succumbing to those incentives. The hope for individuality if one can escape being defined by one's body is illusory, since, given currently available escape routes, the likeliest escape is into the realm of privilege, where the body is tamed in the name of sameness. And the politics of such escapes is necessarily elitist: one escapes precisely by breaking the perceptions of one's ties to others in one's oppressed group; one becomes the exceptional one. What is needed is rather a conception of individuality that is compatible with a historically specific *we* of political identity and alliance. Such a *we* must be collectively articulated and situationally flexible: it must be *usable*.

The question of constructing such a *we* is of more than academic interest: for example, transsexual men claim really to be women, trapped in a male body that they frequently choose to have surgically altered to correspond better with their sense of their own gender identity. Are they women? Who is to decide? What does the question mean? Why does it matter? Particularly for groups who have been defined by their oppressors, the need for *self*-definition can seem particularly acute. There are, for example, deep controversies among Jews and lesbians about how membership in those groups is to be internally defined, and what relation there should be between the internal definition and the definitions that target some people for anti-Semitic or homophobic violence. Such collective self-definitions need to be grounded not in some timeless essentialism, but in sensitivity to the actual political circumstances, to the needs for alliance building and empowerment. That is, the conceptual work that has typically been done by a politics of oppression masquerading as a metaphysics of bodily essences needs to be done by an explicit politics grounded in the complex interrelationships between individuality and group identity, both of them culturally encoded, and hence lived, as bodily.

Just as group definitions have been a part of the politics of oppression, the definitions of the normative self have been part of the politics of dominance and privilege. At least since Descartes, the Western normative self has been not only disembodied, but, as I have argued, consequently stripped of individuality. It has also, in a political economy based on private property, been obsessively concerned with boundaries, with where it leaves off and the not-self begins. The reconstitution of community among atomized selves has been a central task of philosophy and political theory: sociality, along with the body, has become metaphysically inessential to modern man. If we take both the body and sociality rather to be essential, we need a rethinking of the nature of the self: Descartes's *res cogitans* will no longer do. The defensiveness of the well-bounded self, sure of its borders (since nothing else distinguishes it from all the other atoms), needs to give way to an image of the self in community and uniquely valuable, that is, as an essentially embedded *locus of idiosyncracy*, a place from which one acts and interacts, in that style which is distinctively—*differently*—one's own, oneself. Boundaries—like group membership—become not definitive but situational and flexible.

Such a conception of the self—as a locus of idiosyncracy—is, I think, a starting point for an epistemology that avoids the apolitical nihilism that so frequently seems to follow the postmodern undermining of the foundations of modernity. By putting flesh back on our bones, it would allow us to be responsible while acknowledging that there is nothing beyond ourselves to be responsible to.

17

Your Ground Is My Body: The Politics of Anti-Foundationalism

A number of central philosophical problems involve the possibility or impossibility of bridging a gap: between mind and body, the knowing subject and the external world, perceptions and objects, the self and others, words and their referents, language and reality. In each case one of the sides is taken to be epistemically unproblematic (or at least less problematic), while the other side is taken to be in need of shoring up, of being provided with a foundation more secure than it has on its own, a foundation to be provided by showing how it is connected to the first, less problematic side. For a number of reasons foundationalist projects of deriving statements about the dubious side from conjunctions of statements about the secure side have fallen out of fashion. While analytic epistemology used to be largely concerned with projects that were in one way or another phenomenalist, and continental European philosophy used to be largely concerned with projects that were in one way or another phenomenological, both sorts of projects have been for the most part abandoned as unworkable and misguided. I want to explore what I think are the underlying motivations for such projects and say something about why they have become unworkable and about what might replace them.

Many of the gap-spanning problems have analogues in Greek philosophy, but as we know them they are peculiarly modern,[1] and their dissolution is one of the many signs of postmodernity, that notoriously vague but irresistibly descriptive category. Like most of the problems of philosophical modernity, these find their clearest expression in Descartes. Empiricists and rationalists and, later, analysts and phenomenologists have differed on exactly how to put the problem and on how to go about trying to solve it, but there is a general form of the problem that

---

[1]Wallace Matson, "Why Isn't the Mind-Body Problem Ancient?" in P. Feyerabend and G. Maxwell, eds., *Mind, Matter and Method: Essays in Philosophy and Science in Honor of Herbert Feigl* (Minneapolis: University of Minnesota Press, 1966).

we can find in Descartes that has motivated nearly all European philosophy since his time.

Descartes was faced with a dilemma. The epistemic framework he inherited and in which he was taught was coming undone. That framework traced epistemic warrant up to divine origins and ran justification down through culturally authorized channels. The challenge to it meant that authority and power—religious, political, and economic—were no longer stably invested in hierarchies that existed independently of the individuals who happened to people them. But with increasing democratization came the threats of religious schism, political anarchy, economic chaos, and scepticism.[2] If everyone could think for himself,[3] what guarantee was there that what different people came up with would be sufficiently congruent to sustain social order, a working economy, or anything that could count as shared knowledge about the world? Descartes's project, which has been the dominant project of modern philosophy, was to provide grounds for assurance that such congruence was possible and to develop a method for ensuring that it would be realized.

The threat of scepticism or anarchy arises from the recognition of diversity among those whose voices count, and the classically modern response to those threats has been to deny deep significance to that diversity, to render it merely superficial, and to locate authority not in individuals as they happen to be in their full particularity, but in those parts or aspects of individuals that are supposed to transcend the differences among them. Methods are developed to aid individuals in achieving this transcendence, in abstracting their true (rational, moral) self from the irrelevant idiosyncrasies in which it is enmeshed. The apparatus of Kant's categorical imperative is one such method,[4] as is Rawls's updated version, the original position.[5] More elaborately, much of the scientific method, that diverse and shifting set of practices and reflections on practices, functions largely to make irrelevant to the justification of hypotheses and theories the particularities of the researchers. The original of all such methods is, of course, Descartes's.[6]

The point of Descartes's method is to authorize individuals epistemically without thereby dissolving knowledge into a cacophony of diverse opinion. In

---

[2]Richard Popkin, *The History of Scepticism from Erasmus to Descartes* (New York: Assen, Van Gorcum, 1964).

[3]My use of the masculine pronoun is deliberate. As I will argue below, the newly authorized subject was normatively male, that is, conforming in relevant respects to the norms of masculinity, even if, in other respects the actual person was female.

[4]Immanuel Kant, *Foundations of the Metaphysics of Morals*, trans. Lewis White Beck (Indianapolis: Bobbs-Merrill, 1959).

[5]John Rawls, *A Theory of Justice* (Cambridge, Mass: Harvard University Press, 1971).

[6]René Descartes, *Discourse on the Method of Rightly Conducting the Reason*, in Elizabeth Sanderson Haldane and G. R. T. Ross, eds., *The Philosophical Works of Descartes*, vol. I (Cambridge: Cambridge University Press, 1931), pp. 79–130; and Descartes, *Meditations on First Philosophy*, in Haldane and Ross, vol. I, pp. 131–200.

order to do this, he has to locate the sources of diversity and to provide a means of isolating the trustworthy, because nonidiosyncratic, parts of the subject from those sources. They are essentially two: the subject's own body and other people. The body accounts for sensory illusions, as well as for misperceptions due to disease or disorder, and confusions due to the emotions. Other people provide untrustworthy testimony and pass along the results of their less than careful reasoning. The trustworthy self is the isolated self of the cogito. What that self knows it knows with unshakable certainty; unfortunately, it doesn't know very much, and it seems barred from finding out anything more.

The challenge for Descartes, as for those who followed him, was to extend the range of what the individual could know without decreasing the certainty with which he knew it. Since the certainty available to the self of the cogito came precisely from its isolation from any potentially contaminating influences, which meant the isolation from anything beyond its own disembodied mind, the task seems impossible in principle. Descartes thought he had solved the problem by calling on God to underwrite his forays beyond the confines of his own mind, to guarantee that, if he was totally vigilant about how he used them, his senses could be trusted to provide reliable information about the world. Other people could never be guaranteed in this way, a problem that led Descartes to reject all but the most menial direct assistance with his research, urging those who wanted to aid his scientific work either to do it by and for themselves or to send him money (Descartes, *Discourse,* pp. 126–27).

Descartes's solution has worked for nearly none of his successors,[7] who were left with the problem of how to acquire knowledge without incurring liability to error. What liability to error has meant, operationally, has been the possibility of intractable disagreement: however truth has been theoretically defined, it has in practice been whatever could, with reasonable certainty, be taken to be agreeable to all those whose opinions mattered. Thus, Descartes, in principle a staunch realist, admitted, when pushed, that even if angels were to see things differently (and, presumably, in some sense more truly), what we meant by truth was what could never be discovered by us to be false.[8] What's needed is control: we need to be certain that none of the possible contaminating influences will get in the way of our ability to know the world, an ability whose existence has not typically been taken to be in need of positive verification. Rather, what has been needed is reassurance that it can be exercised in a way that keeps it free from corruption. Not: how can we know the world at all?, but: how can we make sure we don't get deceived?

One way this fundamentally paranoid epistemology has played itself out has

---

[7]Naomi Scheman, "Othello's Doubt/Desdemona's Death: The Engendering of Scepticism."

[8]René Descartes, "Reply to Second Objections," in Haldane and Ross, vol. II (Cambridge, Cambridge University Press, 1931), p. 41.

been by projecting onto people other than the authorized knowers the error-producing liabilities and corrupting influences. The most basic of these, which underlies all the others, is embodiment itself, not a feature of the human condition from which anyone can seriously believe himself exempt. What can, apparently, be seriously believed is that the demands and influences of one's own body can be experienced by, and will thereby contaminate, others. Thus, modern epistemic authority has attached to those who did minimal physical labor, who neither bore nor reared their own children, grew or cooked or cleaned up after their own food, built or maintained their own homes, produced or cleaned their own clothing, nor nursed the illnesses or eased the deaths of those close to them. Symbolism as well has been borne by the less privileged: women embody sexuality—as do men of (some) races other than white—and racial difference is figured as contaminating darkness, in contrast to the light of reason.

The epistemic project of the privileged (or of those who would seek to be allowed to join their ranks) has been: first, to distance themselves sufficiently from the contaminating influences of the body so that what they believe will come to have the status of knowledge (because it will either be replicated by those who similarly abstract themselves from anything that could lead them to think differently or will be challenged by those who can be dismissed because they've failed to purify themselves); and, second, to enter into a relationship with the world they've pushed away that's sufficiently rich to allow them to say something about it. It's not easy, and it's no surprise that the abyss of scepticism has opened up at the feet of many who've tried to maintain just the right balance of approach and avoidance.

Foundationalist projects have been attempts to keep the subject's feet firmly planted on the safe side of the abyss and to bring parts of the world into his purview by deploying argumentative lassos that corral the elusive (because feared) stuff on the other side. Strategies have been various. Phenomenalism, for example, works by exploiting the aesthetic attitude, in which the subject's mind is entered by emissaries from the other side, toward which he adopts an attitude of distance, which allows for contemplation without inducing belief: the subject remains uncommitted to, hence unsullied by, what he aesthetically contemplates. Then, cool reason steps in and ascertains whether any sufficiently certain inferences can be drawn from those emissaries about the external world and recommends just the right degree of commitment to any beliefs about it.

One striking feature of this procedure and of others that have the same aim of acquiring grounded knowledge without getting one's feet dirty, is that all the apparent labor is purely mental. One of the features of the separation of the context of discovery from the context of justification is precisely to sweep behind the curtain all the physical labor that went into the framing and testing of the hypothesis in question. As Dorothy and her friends are frantically exhorted by the Wizard of Oz, as he faces unmasking, "Don't look at the little man behind the curtain. I am Oz the Great and Powerful. What I don't tell you is not important to know." If we're not supposed to look at the professor from Kansas, still less are we supposed to look at the Munchkins (or whoever) who keep up the wizard's chambers.

What we are not supposed to notice is that it is actual physical labor and actual embodiment that connect the knowing subject with what he knows, that hold body and soul together. It is supposed, from within the context of justification, that it is irrelevant to what is assembled there how it came to be and to be there. Kekule is said to have dreamt of a snake biting its tail and to have awakened with the idea of the benzene ring; it doesn't matter if it was something he ate.

A recent controversy in biomedical ethics illustrates the problem starkly.[9] Robert Pozos, a University of Minnesota-Duluth researcher into the effects on humans of hypothermia, has been faced with the decision about whether or not to use the results of experiments on the effects of immersion in cold water performed during World War II by Nazi scientists on concentration camp inmates. The scientists were well-trained and their motivation for obtaining accurate results was presumably high: the research was designed to be of use to the German Navy. They seemed to have followed proper scientific methods, assuming, as much of the discussion has assumed, that ethical questions are separable from scientific ones. Most of the dispute surrounding the ethics of using these data has taken it for granted that what will or will not be used are facts. When doubts are raised about the factual status of the data, they concern such things as whether or not the physical condition of the research subjects was comparable to that of members of the German Navy, that is, about alleged deviations from standard scientific norms.

Most of the discussion is thus similar to discussions about whether or not a politically progressive organization ought to accept funds from a source whose politics or morality are repugnant. The status of the money as money is not at issue in such cases; rather, debate concerns the legitimating effect on the donors, the disrespect shown toward those whose victimization led to the profits that are the source of the offered funds, and the complicity in that victimization, even if it is entirely in the past, that would follow from benefiting from it. The money itself is entirely fungible: that is, after all, the point of money. Questions about its origin may be of political and moral importance, but they don't, for example, make a million dollars worth only eight hundred thousand. We can isolate the question of how much money is there from questions about how it came to be there. Scientific method is designed, I have been arguing, to do the same for facts and theories. If we can ascertain that the Nazi scientists did follow proper scientific

---

[9]My discussion here is adapted from my comment, "Discussion of Harding's 'The Method Question'," in the American Philosophical Association's *Newsletter on Feminism and Philosophy* 89, no. 3 (1989).

methods, then we can be assured that their data are factual and their theories sound, even if we decide that the circumstances of their experiments are so evil that we ought to refrain from benefiting from their results.

The view of science and of scientific method in which facts are fungible emerges from the fundamental interest of modern industrial and, to an even greater extent, postindustrial, capitalism in the production of facts as commodities — exchangeable objects whose value lies in their relations to each other and in their exchangeability, rather than in their relationships to the conditions of their production or to their ability to satisfy preexisting human needs. That is, facts-as-commodities are, in Marx's term, fetishized.[10] Rather than being appraised within the complex human circumstances of their production and of the needs they might meet, they are abstracted from those circumstances and appraised according to standards of value developed primarily to emphasize their independence from everything but each other and those standards: hence, the separation of the context of discovery from the context of justification and the notion that to be concerned with the former is to commit the "genetic fallacy."

If we were not to fetishize facts, we would need to recognize that their existence and meaning are inseparable from the social, embodied lives of those who framed them. Fetishization allows us to think that facts are connected causally to each other, referentially to the world they are about, and inferentially to our knowledge of other facts, and that these connections jointly exhaust our properly epistemological interest in them. Fetishization allows the facts we call data to be deployed rather like the children in upper class Victorian families: brought out and put on display to testify to the father's worthiness, they must first be cleaned up and tamed by anonymous people behind the scenes who, acting on the directives of the father, are responsible for their care and for making them presentable, which means making sure that nothing about them is evident beyond those virtues that fit with the place they hold in their father's view of the world. In particular, they should show no traces of the influence of their anonymous caretakers, whose activity should appear to be a transparent enactment of the will of the father, rather than an expression of their own values, desires, or attachments to the children.[11]

What I think is most deeply at issue in the Nazi data case is precisely the assumption that scientific method can and should assure the fungibility of facts.

---

[10]Karl Marx, *Capital: A Critique of Political Economy*, trans., Samuel Moore and Edward Aveling (New York: The Modern Library, 1906).

[11]There is an excellent discussion of child rearing done as the alienated fulfillment of another's will in Barbara K. Rothman, *Recreating Motherhood: Ideology and Technology in a Patriarchal Society* (New York: Norton, 1989). She is critical of the extension of such practices from the Victorian family to the current relationship of middle and upper class employed mothers to those they hire to care for their children.

If, as feminist epistemologists and philosophers of science are arguing,[12] the historically specific placement of researchers is always relevant at every level of their research, then the acceptance of the results of the research of others is always a matter of acknowledging a commonality of interests, and always a matter of extending trust in the integrity of the other. You may be able to take the money and run, but you cannot take the data and run.

As Dr. Arnold S. Relman, editor of the *New England Journal of Medicine*, asked, "Given the source of the information and the way in which it was obtained, how can anyone believe it? How can anyone want to believe it?" (*New York Times*, 12 May 1988). Believing it, on the grounds that it was scientifically, hence, reliably, obtained, requires the use of descriptions such as the ones I used above, referring to "experiments," "researchers," and "research subjects," rather than to torture, torturers, and torture victims.[13] Believing for those reasons requires admitting the people whose word we are taking for it into a community of trust. Methodolatry leads to the assumption that we can narrowly cordon off the region of that trust, and limit our vulnerability to betrayal.[14] (Such vulnerability is laid bare in the scientific community's reactions to cases of scientific fraud, which make it evident that there is no way to eliminate altogether the need to trust the integrity of others, while Descartes's solution of not relying on it is no longer even imaginable.)

It may seem that present-day scientists share enough interests with the Nazi researchers to make it a good bet that their results count as data, perhaps even reliable data, about cooling bodies. Their interest in minimizing the effects of hypothermia is presumably not relevantly different from ours. (Similar considerations were presumably invoked to justify the use by the United States after the war not only of the results of German rocketry, but of the services of German rocket scientists. We shared with the Nazis an interest in getting things into the air and having them land where we wanted them to.) But admitting the results of torture into the category of scientific experimentation indicates both a deeper, troubling common interest—in science as distanced, controlling, and objectifying

[12]Sandra Harding, *The Science Question in Feminism* (Ithaca, N.Y.: Cornell University Press, 1986); Ruth Bleier, *Feminist Approaches to Science* (New York: Pergamon Press, 1986).

[13]We might believe it on other grounds, as I am inclined to think we should. We believe, on the basis of records kept by the Nazis, many things about, for example, the effects of Zyclon B, the gas used in gas chambers, on human beings, but we don't call those who ran the death chambers experimenters or their victims research subjects. Such distinctions are not "merely semantic": the epistemic warrant conferred by calling something a scientific experiment is undetachable from moral notions such as trust. It matters not only what we believe but why we believe it.

[14]The term 'methodolatry' is Mary Daly's. See Sandra Harding, "The Method Question," *Hypatia* 2, no. 3 (1987): 19–36.

—and, serving that interest, a faith on our part that scientific method, narrowly defined, can render irrelevant any other divergence in interests or in moral perspective. (Ironically, the Nazis didn't share this faith in fungible fact. They were notoriously prone to committing the "genetic fallacy" in what they admitted and excluded from epistemic respectability, for example, in their systematic rejection of what they called "Jewish science.")

Feminist epistemologists and philosophers of science, along with others who have been the objects of knowledge-as-control, are attempting to understand and to pose alternatives to the epistemology of modernity. As it has been central to this epistemology to guard its products from contamination by connection to the particularities of its producers, it must be central to the work of its critics and to those who would create genuine alternatives to re-member those connections, to overcome the alienation of knowers from the known. It is becoming respectable in the philosophical mainstream to view science as a social practice; we need to take the logical next step of seeing its products—data, facts, theories—as social products, shaped and thought of in the ways our society has for shaping and thinking of products. One of those ways involves fetishization, the decontextualizing of something and its recontextualizing in a setting that revalues it according to a logic alien to and alienated from the circumstances of its production and from its ability to meet human needs.

Scientific method has typically functioned to abstract from explicitly moral and political questions—to whom should we extend trust and with whom do we share interests—and to focus instead on the denatured question of determining adherence to itself as a purifying device, allowing the scientific community to transcend the limitations of political or historical parochialism. What we have learned is that scientific method has introduced a parochialism of its own, a systematic set of biases, through its very definition of objectivity in terms of separation from the body and closely associated functions of the mind (notably, the emotions) and from the particularities of connections to others. Such methodological and epistemological considerations have implications not only for scientific methods, but for the shaping of scientific hypotheses.

For example, the hegemony of individualism in the political and economic spheres partly explains the hegemony of atomism as the aim of explanation in physics: scientists were supposed to find the ultimate tiny hard things that, secure within their own boundaries, entered into, rather than being constituted by, the flux of interrelationship. Explanations are explanatory not in the abstract, but for particular people at particular times and places, taking themselves already to understand some things and in some particular ways. Ever since Plato the dominant position in Western philosophy and science has been that substances precede relations, that the fundamental givens, at the end of analysis, are atomistic, a position that reflects not how the world is but what those framing the explanations took as explanatory: at what point could an explanation satisfyingly stop?

What atomism, individualism, and the fetishization of facts have in common is the attempt to pin down identity, the demand that we be able to say with clarity and finality what something is, rather than having to deal with the full complexity and particularity of it and with all the relationships in which it is implicated. Both the knowing subject and the world he claims to know are defined by their mutual independence.[15] Scepticism would be unavoidable, as Kant argued, if that independence were real.[16] But it isn't. It comes to appear so by the invisibility, to the authorized eye, of the labor that holds things together, that bridges the gaps between body and mind, nature and culture, and, in so doing, creates and sustains the knowable identities of people and things, identities of full particularity and essential interconnection.[17]

The alienation of labor under capitalism functions in part to obscure the role of physical labor in production, to make it appear that commodities enter the world independent of the people who made them. Children, too, are fetishized in this way: maternal labor needs to be finally invisible, allowing the self-made man to stride onto the world stage. Similarly, facts and theories about facts are required not to bear the marks of those who framed them, to be independent of the labor that brought them to the light. The obscuring of such labor is aided by various myths of paternal parthenogenesis: commodities, children, and theories obviously come from *some*where, and they need to be provided with a fictive lineage that underwrites their self-contained identities, to replace the literal one that makes visible their dependence. Thus, the normative shift in male psychosexual development from the mother to the father as the true parent is mirrored by the "history of ideas" way of connecting texts with other texts, theories with other theories, in a series of intellectual begats.

A number of apparently unrelated twentieth-century developments are challenging these immaculate conceptions. Foundationalist projects have largely crumbled; European poststructuralism reflects this disintegration, as do Quinean holism[18] and Kuhnian historicism.[19] It no longer seems possible for reason to bridge the gaps, although explanations for the impossibility are varied, as are thoughts about what else, if anything, there is for philosophy to do. We need, I

---

[15]Naomi Scheman, "From Hamlet to Maggie Verver: The History and Politics of the Knowing Subject."

[16]Immanuel Kant, *Critique of Pure Reason*, trans. Norman Kemp Smith (New York: St. Martin's Press, 1965), B274–79.

[17]Eva Feder Kittay and Diana T. Meyers, eds., *Women and Moral Theory* (Totowa, N.J.: Rowman & Littlefield, 1987); Susan Moller Okin, *Women in Western Political Thought* (Princeton, N.J.: Princeton University Press, 1979); Adrienne Rich, *The Dream of a Common Language: Poems 1974–77* (New York: Norton, 1978); and Sara Ruddick, "Maternal Thinking," *Feminist Studies* 6, no. 2 (Summer 1980):342–67.

[18]W. V. Quine, "Epistemology Naturalized," in *Ontological Relativity and Other Essays* (New York: Columbia University Press, 1969).

[19]Thomas Kuhn, *The Structure of Scientific Revolutions* (Chicago: University of Chicago Press, 1970).

think, both a better diagnosis of what has happened, as well as a better sense of where we might go from here.

One place to start is by taking seriously the positions of those whose labor has, materially, bridged those gaps, by enculturating parts of the natural world, producing artifacts, and bearing and rearing children—making sense out of the stuff of life. It has been quite literally on the bodies and the bodily labor of such people that the foundations of modern thought have rested, while, precisely because they did and were defined by this labor, women, the working class, and people of color have been denied the authority to make knowledge out of their experiences and perspectives. What they thought about the world was relegated at best to mere opinion, precisely because they were incapable of distancing themselves from the bodily realm. They were not taken to know how to bridge the gaps because, from their perspectives, there were no gaps to bridge. Since they did not constitute themselves by creating a gap between themselves and the world, they were discounted as reliable knowers of that world: they were too close to it to be trusted.

Perhaps the most significant thing, in this regard, that has happened in the twentieth-century is that increasing numbers of women, members of the working class, and people of color have listened to the universalistic language of modernity and believed or claimed that it applied to them, and they have been increasingly able to make those claims stick, in part because liberal epistemology hasn't a leg to stand on. Everywhere you look it says people are created equal, and, though no one who originally said that meant it, there's nothing in the theory to keep those words from meaning what they say. Except that the only way successfully to stake a claim to be among the authorized knowers is to enact the strategies of distantiation, and that is much easier for some than for others. It is one thing, and hard enough, for a middle class white man to conform to the norms of middle class white masculinity; it is much harder, though by no means impossible, for someone who is only one or two or none of those. Insofar as some of us have done just that, the ground underneath all our feet, the ground that the newly enfranchised among us used to help to constitute, gets predictably unsteady. In noting the increasing instabilities of subjectivity, the prophets of postmodernity are merely functioning as effective seismographs.

Where do we go from here? One question is who "we" are. Those who have always benefited from the solely theoretical democratization of knowledge have typically responded with violence to the mere suspicion that their control over the gaps and over what lay on the far side of them was being challenged. Nature, women, and people of the Third World have all suffered from what were always presented as preemptive strikes. Now that the challenges are real, not the paranoid fantasies of those who required total control to feel safe, such violence will seem even more justified to those who see their privileges being undermined.

For those who are claiming authority, the situation is complicated. Liberalism seems to promise enfranchisement, and no matter how problematic the terms of that promise may be, it may be hard to break with those who are allies, even if only on their own terms. But increasingly women and people of color are rejecting the terms of the liberal promise and demanding enfranchisement neither in drag nor in white-face. One reason for the rejection is the recognition that to accept it is to stand on the bodies of others, as well as to reject one's own identity.

I do not believe that we can give up altogether on epistemology, if by that we mean the attempt to characterize knowledge, meaning by *that* sets of beliefs we can all share and that are collectively usable. But we will need to give substantive answers to who we all are and what we want to use knowledge for. Epistemology thus becomes part of the politics of coalition building. Communities both constitute and are constituted by the knowledge they construct and share and by the methods for constructing and sharing it. Such communities will be of very different sizes and degrees of homogeneity, depending on what sort of knowledge is at stake: are we describing the structure of the helium atom or of the economy? In either case what matters is who wants to know and why, and with whom do they need to know it, that is with whom do they need to work in a way that utilizes such knowledge?

Features of the ecology and the potential for nuclear destruction mean that for an increasing range of questions the relevant community is all of humankind, since, if objectivity no longer requires us to bracket the interests we have in the acquisition of knowledge, we are free to recognize those interests that we do, in fact, universally share. Even so, such urgently required universalizability cannot be achieved by methodolatrous fiat, but only by the political struggle to recognize the need for such a community of interests and to make it materially real. Interests in not starving millions of people or decimating the rain forests or polluting the water supply have to take precedence over competing interests in profits and the economic benefits of imperialism in order for knowledge about such things to become common property. To the extent that such fundamental interests are not shared, those we know with will be those with whom we are allied in struggle.

We cannot know now just how different knowledge so constructed will look. What we now take ourselves to know, on the authority of the powerful, is like a small square of a larger painting. There is no telling ahead of time what contributions will be made by those who see beyond that frame. Not only will we learn about parts of the canvas thought to be empty, but what we learn will change how we see what we thought we knew, as we learn how to see it as an expression of privilege by seeing how it fits into the broader picture. Arguably, the characteristic tenor of European modernity was set largely by discoveries that led to various responses to threatened decenterings: of the earth in the cosmos, of humans in creation, of Europe in the world. From that perspective, postmodernity is the end of the road for all the defensive strategies of modernity that have worked to maintain the illusion that privileged subjectivity is at the center of the world.

Foundationalist projects dreamed of knowledge that was absolutely universal, but that universality was obtained by writing out of the universe of knowing subjects those whose labor made possible any knowledge at all. Reason was supposed to be able to construct foundations that would obscure the real foundations of bodies and physical labor on which all theories and all knowledge rest. When those who do such labor theorize, the ground of their theoretical labor will not be an imperious fiction, but the actual earth we live on. We need to come to a picture of that earth from the vastly varying perspectives of its inhabitants that will be, in its own, richer, more complex, and less romantic way, as comprehensive as the space photographs of this lovely and vulnerable planet.[20]

[20]An earlier version of this paper was presented to the Philosophy Club at Cornell University, and the discussion was extremely helpful. I want to acknowledge especially Richard Boyd's extensive comments and the criticisms and suggestions of Susan Sauvé.

18

Who Wants To Know?: The Epistemological Value of Values

The question "who wants to know?" is a gangster movie staple: it signifies the value of knowledge, the ways in which having or withholding it are forms of power, and the dangers of its falling into the wrong hands. The question to which it is a response is often straightforward enough ("What is your name?" or "Where is Lefty?"), as is the true answer, no matter how unlikely it is that the questioner will ever receive it. The answer, the knowledge in question, is taken to be a quite definite thing, a fact or a set of facts. One either has it or one doesn't. Viewed this way, "knowledge is power" means that facts are useful things. You can do things with them, especially if you have some that other people don't.

The essays in this section,[1] in a number of related ways, problematize all these assumptions. They lead us to see that "Who wants to know?" may challenge more than someone's right to obtain possession of a preexisting commodity. In the cases that concern the authors of these essays, if we don't know who wants to know—and why—we won't know how to understand, let alone to answer, the question posed, whether that question concerns the technical feasibility of forms of reproductive technology, cross-cultural commonalities of gender, or the interpretation and evaluation of Afro-American literature and criticism.

More deeply still, reflection on these essays reveals that the values that constitute communities of knowers and motivate the pursuit of knowledge shape that knowledge, which is consequently never value free. The request for "just the facts, ma'am," meaning the bare truth unadorned by interpretation, is ultimately

[1]See Ruth G. Doell, "Whose Research Is This? Values and Biology"; Micaela di Leonardo, "Contingencies of Value in Feminist Anthropology"; and Joyce A. Joyce, "Black Woman Scholar, Critic, and Teacher: The Inextricable Relationship among Race, Sex, and Class," all in *(En)Gendering Knowledge: Feminists in Academe*, ed. Joan E. Hartman and Ellen Messer-Davidow (Knoxville: The University of Tennessee Press, 1991). The present essay appeared in this volume as a response to these three.

incoherent. Without interpretation and value-laden human social activity, there are no facts. On this view, "knowledge is power" means that knowledge is socially constructed in accordance with norms of authoritativeness and thus both embodies and furthers the values and interests of the powerful; or, alternatively, knowledge is constructed as subversive challenges to those norms, values, interests, and power. On such a view, truth is not straightforward, value-neutral conformity with the world, and the notion that it *is* is an ideological fiction that renders invisible the workings of the dominant norms of authoritativeness.

Think of the question "How long is the eastern coastline of the United States?" To get an idea of the problems in answering it, take a piece of curly-leafed lettuce and tear a strip about an inch from the curly edge. Hold the strip taut along a ruler and note the length. Then tear that strip again, this time one-half inch from the edge, and measure it again: depending on how curly the lettuce is, the difference in length will be anywhere from significant to astounding. Obviously, if you keep on tearing, the length will keep on getting longer: how long the edge is depends on how close to the edge you're measuring. It won't work to say that the true answer is the one that measures right at the edge: you *might* be able to do it for the lettuce leaf (try it sometime), but it doesn't even make sense for the coastline. Which of the irregularities of the coastline count? Depending on which we conform to and which we skim over, we'll come up with radically different answers. It's not a matter of more or less accurate figures; answers will differ by orders of magnitude. We get stable answers by having an idea of why we want to know. Do we want to drive the distance? On interstates or back roads? If we want to sail, will we be hugging the shoreline, or will we be at sea? Or do we plan to fly? Until we know who wants to know, and why, the question about the length of the coastline is unanswerable.

Even so apparently simple and objective a question as length depends on the purposes for which we are measuring, and those purposes reflect the values of those who are asking the question, even if such values are only a preference for coastal sailing over plying the open sea. Even if we grant the realist's contention that the true answer is the one that conforms to the world, we need to have some idea of how closely we are to conform, which of the irregularities of whatever we are examining are of significance, and which are to be smoothed out in our representation.

If truth is to conform to the world, however closely, it would seem that we need, in our pursuit of it, varying degrees of pliancy and flexibility. According to the *Oxford English Dictionary*, a "lesbian rule" is "a mason's rule made of lead, which could be bent to fit the curves of a molding" (the reference is to Aristotle's *Nicomachean Ethics* V.x.7). Such flexible rules would seem to be called for if knowing the world requires conforming to its curves. But the figurative meaning of "lesbian rule" is, presumably, less favorable: it means "a pliant principle of judgment." Principles in the world of orthodox epistemology cannot be pliant, ought not to bend to fit the circumstances. Their rigidity is what restores the knower's virility, which was challenged by the requirement that his knowledge pliantly conform to a world independent of his will. The pursuit, at least, can be in his control; he can and should go straight. As necessary as it would seem to be that knowledge conform to the world, on the level of methodology, of rules, we are taught to be suspicious of those that bend, to reject the pliant for the upstanding. Knowledge, of course, does not remain unaffected by the rules governing its pursuit. If nature, with its slippery curves, cannot be captured, we can wait until it dies, or kill it; rigor will set in and the straight rule will work.

There is another sense in which the rule determines the measurement of the world. Thinking of the literal lesbian rule, the flexible mason's tool for measuring moldings, we can see that length will depend in part on exactly how flexible the rule is. Moldings, like lettuce leaves and coastlines, will be of very different lengths depending on how closely the rule measuring them hugs their perimeters. (Were we to go down to the molecular level, the molding around my study, for example, would be measured in miles.) The choice of the rule will be dictated by interests and values. Contemporary philosophers of science will, for the most part, acknowledge the sort of relevance of purpose represented by the coastline example. They will acknowledge, that is, that values and interests influence what questions people care to ask—or to fund, hire, or tenure others for asking. But they will also maintain that once the question is specified precisely enough (once we know how we want to travel down the coast), it will have one answer, and all competent researchers will arrive at it.

To ensure this interchangeability of authorized knowers, the rules they use should not be differently flexible in different hands: once the rule is formulated, it should be pliant neither to the values and interests of those who are using it nor to the filigreed complexities of the world they are studying. Values, interests, and other ways in which people differ from each other can and must be segregated so as not to contaminate the process of finding the one true answer. Authorized knowers cannot have, as individuals or groups, distinctive epistemic styles, or their results will not be replicable and will not count as knowledge. Authority consists in being trusted to use the straight rules that guarantee uniformity. The rules determine one's epistemic orientation, and, in this domain, as in the sexual one, straightness, not deviance, is normative.

As Evelyn Fox Keller has argued in *Reflections on Gender and Science*,[2] the epistemology of modern science developed around interrelated conceptions of knowing subjects and their methods, both of them fully constituted prior to the act of knowing and untransformed by it. The object of knowledge, by contrast, is inert; it does not tell us how it wants to be known (it does not shape the

[2]Evelyn Fox Keller, *Reflections on Gender and Science* (New Haven, Conn.: Yale University Press, 1985).

rule), nor does it know us in return. In her accounts of the geneticist Barbara McClintock,[3] Keller explores the workings of a different epistemic orientation, one in which knowledge emerges dialogically from the evolving relationship between the knower and the known, a relationship that changes them both, one whose terms are not laid down in advance.

When we turn from the acquisition of knowledge to its transmission, we need to consider other perspectives and other ways of posing the question of who wants to know. In addition to the knower and the known, there are those with interests in learning what the knowers know, as well as those who will be affected, whether they like it or not, by what comes to taken as knowledge. From the perspective of traditional epistemology, they don't make a difference, any more than it makes a difference to what my name *really* is or to where Lefty *really* is whether it's the boss or the cops that want to know. Knowledge—so the story goes—consists in facts, and facts are facts, no matter who has them or wants them or why. People who are rich or powerful are more likely to get their questions answered (especially questions that directly concern the acquisition and maintenance of wealth and power), but their money and their power, if the rules are working properly, are supposed to have no influence on what those answers are. Our culture's separation of production from consumption is apparent here: consumer demand sets the whole apparatus in motion, but consumers are external to the processes of production and passive with respect to them. Still less do those who are "passive consumers," affected by knowledge created in the interests of others, have any say, any more than do those who live downstream from a toxic chemical plant.

It needn't be like that. Imagine breaking down the distinction between the producers and the consumers of knowledge: we all come to learn what we all need to know. Clearly such an ideal is unworkable in those terms as soon as we need to know more than the barest basics about ourselves and the world. It is impossible that we could all come to learn for ourselves what we would have to know for our cars to run, our bread to be baked, our illnesses to be cured, our roofs to keep the rain out, our currency to be stable, and our airplanes to fly. But when we face analogous problems of scale in the political realm—when we recognize that the town meeting won't work for polities larger than towns—we abandon direct democracy, not for autocracy, but for representative democracy. (That is, we do so in theory; the reality of our political process is quite different.) Why, in the realm of epistemology, do we make the opposite choice? We don't (in theory, anyway) divide the political realm into the governors and the governed, those who produce government and those who consume it: why do we do that in the epistemic realm?

Ideally, at least, in a representative democracy those who govern do so in the name of the others, who are the final authorities. Their values and interests are meant to inform the processes of government at every level: elected officials are

[3]Evelyn Fox Keller, *A Feeling for the Organism: The Life and Work of Barbara McClintock* (New York: Freeman, 1983).

their surrogates, even if in the name of doing that job well, they have to become more expert about features of the political world than any of their constituents. Epistemologically, by contrast, experts are accountable to each other and to no one else (professionalism and academic freedom are meant to insure this). Certainly (again, in theory), academic experts of various sorts are supposed to be discovering truths because it will be good for all of us to have those truths: in that sense, they, like elected officials, are supposed to be doing what they do on our behalf. But, unlike the constituencies of elected officials, we are not supposed (even in theory) to have anything at all to say about whether academic experts are doing their job well. When a purported discovery is presented, the jury of peers called upon to judge it is drawn very narrowly from among those whose disciplinary mastery authorizes their opinions. The rest of us are presumed incompetent even to have an opinion, let alone to have one that carries any weight.

It is hard to imagine how it might be different. Certainly, once academic experts are inside a research program, taking for granted what questions to ask, what research methods to use, what background knowledge to draw upon, which experts to consult, and which educational methods to rely on for the training and certifying of new researchers (within, that is, a paradigm, in Kuhn's sense),[4] most questions *will* have determinate and uncontroversial answers. Producing such agreement is precisely one of the functions of paradigms: within them, experts can make progress, as those working in the field build on each other's previous successes. But such progress leaves as an open question whether the paradigm provides effective strategies for acquiring what everyone should take to be truths about the world, or whether it just ensures that its initiates—the experts—will share a common set of delusions. That is, what reasons do *we*, the nonexperts, have for believing what the experts believe, beyond the fact that they are socially authorized to produce what is supposed to count as knowledge? Why should we be any more respectful of that authority than our founding political documents tell us to be of *political* authority in which we have no ultimate say?

Scientific realists (those who argue that science does, by and large, lead to truths about the world)[5] will often refer at this point to the successes of scientific methods (the flight of airplanes, the moon landing, the eradication of or cures for diseases, the stability of bridges, the explosion of bombs) as providing grounds for believing that such methods produce not delusions, but truth, since they are effective in predicting and controlling nature within certain temporal and spatial bounds. The evidence for such effectiveness is, even from our lay perspective, quite good: that is, science does what it was designed to do. But what we

[4]Thomas Kuhn, *The Structure of Scientific Revolutions*, 2nd ed. (Chicago: University of Chicago Press, 1970).

[5]See Jarrett Leplin, ed., *Scientific Realism* (Berkeley: University of California Press, 1984), esp. Richard N. Boyd's essay in that volume, "The Current Status of Scientific Realism," pp. 41–82.

are increasingly discovering is that science as we know it is not very good at understanding the interconnectedness of diverse phenomena beyond those spatial and temporal bounds. As we are learning, mostly to our terror, phenomena interconnect far beyond the bounds of our investigations—that is, beyond the bounds of our prediction and control—and something that was done there and then is coming back to haunt us here and now. Even (especially?) scientists are unprepared for these discoveries, in part because drawing spatial and temporal bounds, defining a problem, and specifying the parameters of investigation are integral to scientific method. But if, for example, the eradication of the smallpox bacillus counts as reason to believe that scientific method is reliably truth producing, why don't the long-term, unforeseen complexities of atmospheric changes count as reason to believe that it might not be?

Scientific knowledge also categorizes. It is general, not specific. It is knowledge of the type and not the individual. To know scientifically, we look for similarities, particularly those that bring diverse phenomena under the same law. Their obedience to that law is what they have in common, and it is the most important thing about them: it is how we understand them. The diversity—say, between the tides, the orbits of planets, and the behavior of dropped objects—is demonstrated to be merely apparent. They all exemplify the law of gravity, and it is their falling under the same law—the way in which they are tokens of the same type of phenomenon—that, scientifically, allows us to understand them, in abstraction from the specificities of water, heavenly body, and homely object.

These two features of scientific knowledge, the attempt to delimit interconnectedness and the reduction of diversity to underlying similarity, are repudiated in current feminist theorizing. Feminists working in a wide range of fields[6] have argued that women tend to see the world and themselves in it in terms of a web of interconnectedness, rather than as isolated atoms or as links in linear causal chains—and that to do so is an ability worth cultivating, not just a product of women's oppression (though it is, problematically, that as well).[7] Many have focused on the related idea of responsibility as a relationship to people and events that is not defined by the scope of one's power and control.[8] Work in feminist

[6]Caroline Whitbeck, "A Different Reality: Feminist Ontology," in *Beyond Domination: New Perspectives on Women and Philosophy*, ed. Carol Gould (Totowa, N.J.: Rowman and Allanheld, 1984), pp. 64–88; and Carol Gilligan, "In a Different Voice: Women's Conceptions of Self and Morality," *Harvard Educational Review* 47, no. 4 (November 1977): 481–517.

[7]For a discussion of the problems of valorizing features of women's characters under patriarchy, see Joan C. Tronto, "Beyond Gender Difference to a Theory of Care," *Signs* 12, no. 4 (Summer 1987): 644–63.

[8]On an ethic of responsibility, see the essays in Eva Feder Kittay and Diana T. Meyers, eds., *Women and Moral Theory* (Totowa, N.J.: Rowman & Littlefield, 1987). Issues of responsibility are central to Sarah Lucia Hoagland's *Lesbian Ethics: Toward New Value* (Palo Alto, Calif.: Institute of Lesbian Studies, 1988). Claudia Card is working on a comprehensive study of the nature of responsibility and its place in feminist moral theory.

ethics has also stressed the need to attend to the particularities of persons and of situations, rather than, as traditional moral theorists would have us do, identifying "morally relevant features" in order to treat all like situations alike.[9] And attention to diversity (most centrally in the work of women who saw their lives and perspectives ignored or misrepresented in the work of women of privilege) has shifted the attention of many feminist theorists away from the attempt to describe and explain what all women have in common.[10]

The two ideas—of interconnectedness and particularity—are related. If we are attempting to make sense of the world, whether through science, literature, or common sense, we need to find patterns, ways things hang together. One way to do that is both to narrow sharply and define the scope of our inquiries and to look for similarities that allow a reduction in the number of laws that govern phenomena. (The search for a Unified Field Theory is the ultimate goal of this line of thought: it would epitomize the ideal of elegance by subsuming all physical phenomena under one overarching set of laws.) If we resist doing this, by insisting both on the importance of following the web out beyond the limits of our own agency and on the irreducible particularity of individuals and the value of differences, we will need a new epistemology, one which takes as central not similarities, but connections. It is no accident that the new politics forged by feminists and others in liberation movements has led to the same conclusion: not what we have in common, but how our lives and choices affect each other, is what ties us together and makes coalitions possible. We need, epistemologically as well as politically, the ground for trust, and we need to acknowledge that such ground needs to be literal, lived, and struggled for, not the imagined result of the application of abstracting rules.

Attention to interconnectedness can also make possible an epistemology that doesn't start by positing a separation between the knower and the known, and then enforcing that separation in the name of maintaining objectivity. Such an epistemology would also acknowledge the irreducible particularity not only of the objects of knowledge, but of knowers, as well as the ways in which both are shaped by the forces around them, including, for knowers, the forces of race, class, gender, and other systems of domination and privilege. Knowledge would always be seen as especially problematical when it was constructed only by those

[9]On the ways in which particularity enters into moral thinking, see Kittay and Meyers, eds., *Women and Moral Theory*; Lawrence A. Blum, *Friendship, Altruism, and Morality* (London: Routledge & Kegan Paul, 1980); and Sara Ruddick, "Maternal Thinking," *Feminist Studies* 6, no. 2 (Summer 1980): 342–67.

[10]On the need to attend to the diversity in women's experiences and perspectives, see bell hooks, *Feminist Theory: From Margin to Center* (Boston: South End Press, 1984); María C. Lugones and Elizabeth V. Spelman, "Have We Got a Theory for You! Feminist Theory, Cultural Imperialism, and the Demand for 'The Woman's Voice,'" *Women's Studies International Forum* 6, no. 6 (1983): 573–81; and Elizabeth V. Spelman, *Inessential Woman: Problems of Exclusion in Feminist Thought* (Boston: Beacon Press, 1988).

in positions of privilege that afforded them only distorted views of the world. When experts were trusted to discover for us things too obscure to be generally evident, we would always want to know as much as we could about how they went about finding them out, and part of our trust would be grounded in our knowing that the values that structured their investigations were ones we shared. The experts, that is, would be our representatives in the laboratory or the archives or the field, as the members of Congress are supposed to be our representatives in Washington.

Ruth G. Doell's recommendations for the composition of an oversight commission on germ-line therapy and human embryo research (more than half nonscientists, equal numbers of women and men) reflect these concerns and could, if implemented, have more than a braking effect. It isn't just that some research is potentially too dangerous or too ethically questionable to be undertaken. The politics around AIDS research is a clear example of how attitudes of privilege (heterosexism and homophobia in the early days, now also racism, classism, and sexism) can prevent or stall research that is urgently needed. What Doell's essay, "Whose Research Is This?: Values and Biology," points toward is precisely a representative democratic model of science, where the orientation of research is set dialogically by all those who have an interest in it, rather than monologically by those who are encouraged to think they own it.

Oversight groups are also potentially sites for the forging of coalitions, as people from diverse social positions discover common interests and confront the issues that divide them. Knowledge is supposed, abstractly, to belong to everyone, but such abstract universality masks the exclusivity of privilege. We would go further in reaching universality by working to make knowledge concretely shared among individuals and groups that seem initially to see the world in very different ways but who have a real interest in finding an account of things complex enough to do them all justice. Thus, for example, groups overseeing reproductive research would need to include people with interests in overcoming infertility, as well as those with interests in the possible use of fetal tissue to counter the effects of Parkinson's disease, as well as those with interests in not defining the female body primarily in terms of an ability to produce babies *or* fetal tissue.

Not all research ought to be guided by specific practical agendas. What many scientists report as a spirit of play—curiosity given free rein—is undoubtedly valuable, and not only because we cannot predict in advance which hunches will pay off. But what is usually taken to follow from that observation—that scientists should be left alone to follow their muse—is false to actual scientific practice (which is always deeply influenced by what others than scientists find it important to look at), while it obscures attempts to examine just why the spirit of play, of supposedly unconstrained curiosity, leads in some directions and not in others, or how differently socialized and rewarded scientists might hear a different muse, beckoning them in different directions.

An interest in unconstrained pure science, to the extent that there is such a thing, is not the only interest we have, and it needs to be balanced with others, ranging from the immediate and practical (a cure for AIDS) to the concretely political (genuine, noncoerced reproductive choice for all women) to the foundationally political (the effective empowerment of people who now correctly perceive themselves as impotent with respect to the creation and use of the knowledge that structures their lives). Professionalism and academic freedom, at their best protectors of heterodoxy, have become guardians of unexamined privilege, in part because of the enormous amounts of money involved in research (especially in the sciences), but equally because of the ways in which academics of all sorts are selected and socialized. A large part of graduate education, for example, consists in learning which people, groups, ideas, and approaches are to be scorned.

Democratization, rather than stifling creativity, could open up a world that is becoming progressively more closed, not only to outside, nonscientific influence (except, of course, for the military, government, and corporate funding of whatever issues are currently important to them), but to potentially revolutionary work within science. As Kuhn has argued,[11] major scientific breakthroughs often come from people marginal to the field, people whose view of things is not shaped by the paradigm their theory challenges. If only recognized experts are allowed to have any say, such breakthroughs will be harder to effect. Similarly, research agendas are unreflectively shaped by the interests of those with economic and political power, with little or no influence from those without the clout to make their interests heard. Democratization would serve both to make evident the influence of nonscientists and to diversify that influence. Without such democratization, what we have is an ideology of unfettered research conducted by independent scientists and a reality of skewed research controlled by those with economic and political power. That essentially the same groups of people effectively control the nominally democratic processes of government serves to point out the need for democracy to be substantively guaranteed, not just formally decreed.[12]

Micaela di Leonardo, in "Contingencies of Value in Feminist Anthropology," argues for a radically dialogical epistemic democracy in the cross-cultural anthropological situation, especially when, as is nearly always the case, the ethnographic subjects are, in a variety of ways, less powerful than their ethnographers. If the meanings of facts, and even the facts themselves, are the products of culturally embedded interpretive practices, then Western feminist anthropologists need not only to understand the complexity of those practices in the societies they study but also reflectively to examine their own and the relationships of power between them. Di Leonardo cautions us against a too-facile perception of similarity and

[11]Thomas Kuhn, *The Structure of Scientific Revolutions*, pp. 132f.

[12]I keep waiting for a Soviet or Chinese or Eastern European reformist to respond to the questioning of American reporters about what they think of democracy in the United States with a paraphrase of Gandhi on Western civilization: "It would be a wonderful idea."

urges that we bridge cross-cultural gaps, not by aiming to discern commonality beneath the differences but by attending closely to the interconnections between the lives of others and our own. Not only do we need to attend, for example, to the ways in which our standard of living as affluent Americans depends on the exploited labor of Third World women (and men), but we need to learn about the webs that constitute the meaningfulness both of their lives and of our own.

Both Doell's and di Leonardo's essays make clear that, whatever knowledge may ostensibly be about (the efficacy of a technique for *in vitro* fertilization or an ethnographic account of a community), it is always in part about the relationships between the knowers and what they know. The acquisition of that knowledge always further shapes those relationships and others as well, including relationships between the original knowers and those who, actively or passively, consume that knowledge, and between those consumers and what has now come to be known, which may be a part of their own lives. The values that inform those relationships are always implicated in the acquisition of knowledge, in ways that typically are neither democratic nor equitable.

Doell and di Leonardo help us see how knowledge could be constructed differently, informed dialogically by the values and perspectives of all those who are implicated in it. Part of the difference of such knowledge would be its explicit inclusion of reflectiveness about those relationships, about how they were constituted and about how they have been changed—for example, how the experience of pregnancy and parenthood is changed by reproductive technology,[13] or how relationships between communities are changed when members of one do an ethnographic study of the other. We need, as di Leonardo stresses, to come to these understandings in the context of forming alliances. Questions of who wants to know, and why, need to be answered not in terms of pursuing pure research for its own sake, but in terms of developing a common vocabulary for social and political action.

The need to develop such a vocabulary is at the heart of a debate now going on in feminist inquiry. One central question concerns the usefulness of attempting to find and to articulate commonalities among all women: is it necessary to do so in order to have a theory and a politics that will be genuinely about and for (all) women? Or is the very attempt necessarily either falsely essentializing or spuriously universalizing, trapping women in a limiting and unchangeable definition, or applying to all women features of the lives of some, usually those with the privilege to have their accounts recognized by those even more privileged than they? Are there really two jointly exhaustive and mutually exclusive categories—men and women—with cross-culturally applicable necessary and sufficient conditions? Or is the dichotomizing of gender, perhaps even of sex, itself a

[13]For a discussion of such changes and a challenge to the ideology that knowledge is always a good thing, see Barbara Katz Rothman, *The Tentative Pregnancy: Prenatal Diagnosis and the Future of Motherhood* (New York: Viking Penguin, 1986).

cultural artifact? If so, to what extent do we need to use it (at least to describe the cultures in which it applies), and to what extent do we, in using it, reify it?

To avoid gender essentialism, some feminists assert that it is a social rather than an essential taxonomy, while arguing that without some unified account of gender, without some universal claims about what it is and how it operates as a social taxonomy, we will lose the political point of doing this work; our theories will fail to be usable.[14] Certainly, much of the deconstructive challenge to a unified theory of gender is, explicitly or implicitly, anti-political (although it needn't be: Teresa de Lauretis, for example, is explicit about the importance of the political usefulness of theory).[15] But worries about universally applicable definitions of gender need not come from deconstructionists.

Such a worry can, for example, be raised about the assertion that gender, as a taxonomy, is defined by the power of men over women, yielding an oppression distinctive of women as a class. One problem with this assertion is that, stated universally, it isn't true. We need to ask: power of *which* men over *which* women? As Elizabeth V. Spelman has argued in *Inessential Woman*,[16] we need to be very careful about statements about "women" and "men" and the relationships between them, given the ways in which gender is constructed always in relation to race and class. Spelman points out, for example, that, in the United States during slavery and its aftermath, gender has not been about the power of *Black* men over *white* women: they have had no such power. Spelman's book makes clear that universal statements about "women" have been challenged most tellingly not by deconstructionists (whom she never mentions) but by women of color and others who found themselves misrepresented—or failed to find themselves at all—in the histories and theories of white middle class academic feminists. That is, the

---

[14]For feminist accounts of gender as a culturally variable social taxonomy, in conjunction with attempts to provide cross-cultural generalizations to ground a global feminist politics, see the essays in Michelle Zimbalist Rosaldo and Louise Lamphere, eds., *Women, Culture, and Society* (Stanford: Stanford University Press, 1974). Denise Riley addresses the question of what happens to feminist politics when we fully acknowledge the social-constructedness of the category "woman" in *Am I That Name? Feminism and the Category of "Women" in History* (Minneapolis: University of Minnesota Press, 1988). See also Sandra Harding, "The Instability of the Analytical Categories of Feminist Theory," *Signs* 11, no. 4 (Summer 1986): 645–64; and the references in n.26.

[15]See de Lauretis's introductory essay in Teresa de Lauretis, ed., *Feminist Studies/ Critical Studies* (Bloomington: Indiana University Press, 1986). De Lauretis, *Alice Doesn't: Feminism, Semiotics, Cinema* (Bloomington: Indiana University Press, 1984), p. 95, approvingly quotes Julia Kristeva: "Believing oneself 'a woman' is almost as absurd and obscurantist as believing oneself 'a man'. I say almost because there are still things to be got for women: freedom of abortion and contraception, childcare facilities, recognition of work, etc. Therefore, 'we are women' should still be kept as a slogan, for demands and publicity."

[16]Spelman, *Inessential Woman*, chap. 5.

critique is a deeply political one, aimed not at depoliticizing gender theory but at making that theory responsive to the demands of a more inclusive politics.

Gender *is* about power, but so are race, class, and other institutionalized systems of inequality, and the ways in which they interact render suspect any simple statement of who, with respect to any one of them, has power over whom. Gender and race in the United States, for example, have been in part about the power of white men—over white women, who are infantilized; over Black men, who are terrorized, in alleged response to what Angela Davis has named, "The Myth of the Black Rapist";[17] and over Black women, whose rape and exploitation are supposed to reflect, not their abusers' bestial nature, but their own. To speak simply of men's power over women reinforces the racist assumption that Black men, because they are men, do have some sort of power over white women, even in circumstances where a Black boy can be lynched for daring to whistle at a white woman.

What is true is that dominant models of masculinity in the United States normatively include power over women, so that men who in any real sense lack this power often experience that lack as emasculating. They may also respond to their emasculation with violence against women, but when that violence (if the woman is white) evokes not the trivializing indifference of society to rapes committed by privileged men, but cries for the death penalty, it can hardly be considered an expression of *power*, however horrible it may be for the woman who suffers it. We need to be clear about these matters, not out of a desire for theoretical sophistication but out of the need to overcome the white solipsism that has blocked alliances between white women and women of color.

Such alliances—and theories of gender that facilitate them—needn't be grounded in similarities, whether an unchanging essence of womanhood or the features of socially constructed genders. Rather, they can be grounded in our interconnectedness, in how our very different ways of being constructed as women have implicated each other, how we have been used against each other, threatened by each other, and learned to see each other as an enemy, a rival, or a dreaded alter ego. To look for commonalities necessarily simplifies all our lives; when we look instead at webs of interconnection, we can do justice to the complexities of those lives.

Certainly any culture that constructs gender dichotomously will make categorical *normative* claims about all and only women in that culture (that's just what it means to construct gender dichotomously). But in any real woman's experience, those claims will be mediated by other features of her life, including whether or not those like her are meant to be fully included in the normative construction of womanhood. The normative claim about women in contemporary American culture, for example, that domesticity is the central arena for self-definition, is

---

[17]Angela Davis, *Women, Race, and Class* (New York: Random House, 1981), chap. 11.

experienced differently by the upper class, nonemployed, suburban wife and mother; by the undocumented immigrant woman who tends that woman's children, hoping to earn enough to bring her own children from Mexico; by the single mother who works outside the home; and by the career woman who has resisted family pressures to marry and have children. For some of these women, the normative claim is simply false (though they are not unaffected by its normativity); for others it is true, but in very different ways. As a statement of something they are meant to have in common, it is unilluminating. As a way of organizing how their lives interact, it can be helpful.

Classification can be illuminating, but we need to attend to our own agency in constructing any classificatory scheme, whether it be of elementary particles or of people, and not mistake it for how the world itself divides up. The warnings of the deconstructionists about dichotomization are apt here: Western thought has been so structured around binary oppositions that we fall into them "naturally" and find them satisfyingly explanatory, when what we are doing is finding in them not an illumination of the subject matter but a reflection of our own need to divide the world in two. Such dichotomies serve to blur the complexities that the real world has a nasty habit of multiplying. Thus, much recent feminist theory has attempted to repudiate unified models of gender oppression, emphasizing instead the irreducible—albeit socially constructed—differences among people, along lines of gender, race, class, sexual identity, etc., and arguing for a politics of equality not based on the denial of diversity.

We block the development of such a politics by posing questions about gender fairness that assume that the only alternatives are equality-as-sameness (which holds everyone to the identical set of standards, usually framed around the experiences and needs of privileged men), or gender essentialism (which tailors standards to the supposedly fundamentally different experiences and needs of women). We need to know what "fundamentally different" can mean, if we reject essentialism; certainly all people are fundamentally different from each other, and those differences are partly a matter of their membership in various groups that are constructed and maintained hierarchically. But how can we speak of *two* fundamentally different *kinds* of human beings without either essentializing gender or glossing over the roles of race, class, sexual identity, and so on in people's lives?

In our society gender *is* constructed as a binary opposition. Not all cultures have two, but ours does so with a vengeance, surgically or hormonally "correcting" those whose bodies fail to put them securely in one box or the other. But we need to be careful not to reify gender, even as a pair of *social* categories, not to give it more reality than it has. One way to see this point is to think about race. Race, on the face of it, is not a matter of binary opposition, but of complex amalgams of genetic and cultural differences. Whatever else we can say about race, we can safely say that there are more than two of them; race is not dichotomous. Or so one would think, were it not for the workings of racism, which precisely dichotomizes the world's peoples into white and nonwhite (or people of color, or Third World people; it is hard to find a respectful term for a category the existence of which is an artifact of racism). Nonwhite people, after all, have no more in common with each other than any one group of them has with white people, except within the grammar of racism, in which what matters above all else is whether one is white or problematically other.

One point of calling race or gender a "discourse" is to argue that these categories have a logic, a grammar—that is, a structure that works in some ways like the structures of a language—and that we can learn something about how they work by looking at language and people's use of language—how race and gender are talked about, how they are used as metaphors to explain other things. To note what I have noted about the logic of racism (not just the social-constructedness, but the instability and illogicality of the categories) ought not to undermine the possibility of an anti-racist politics.[18] Joan Scott, for example, argues well for the value of discourse-based theorizing, within a context that is explicitly and always political.[19] But the problems many feminists and others find with academic poststructuralism are nonetheless real, and painfully evident in Joyce A. Joyce's essay, "Black Woman Scholar, Critic, and Teacher: The Inextricable Relationship among Race, Sex, and Class." These problems bring us back to the fundamental questions about who wants to know and why. Research questions and methods do not exist in a vacuum; they are developed and used by people situated in various ways in various institutions, with various loyalties, values, responsibilities, privileges, and identifications.

Joyce is clear about her responsibilities as a Black woman critic and English professor. Central among them are bringing out the potential of works of literature to empower those who can challenge the oppressions of race and gender. It is to such people, groups, and movements that Joyce holds herself accountable and to whom she is loyal. Academic professionalism, by contrast, has won for those it authorizes and protects the right to be subject only to the opinions and the demands of those who are similarly authorized (one's "peers"—most of whom, of course, are privileged by race, class, gender, and so on). A professional's loyalty is supposed to be given, concretely, to those "peers" and to the academic institutions they inhabit and, abstractly, to the subject matter, the discipline itself, and the supposedly disinterested pursuit of knowledge. Joyce's loyalties are, from this

[18]Whether or not a discourse-based analysis *does* undermine anti-racist politics is part of what is at stake in the disputes discussed in Joyce A. Joyce's essay. For examples of such analyses, by people who for the most part at least *intend* their work to be politically usable, see *"Race," Writing, and Difference*, a special issue of *Critical Inquiry* 12, no. 1 (Autumn 1985); and *The Nature and Context of Minority Discourse,* two special issues of *Cultural Critique* nos. 6 and 7 (Spring and Fall 1987).

[19]Joan Scott, *Gender and the Politics of History* (New York: Columbia University Press, 1988).

perspective, subversive. It is clear to her that the academy could accept her fully only if she appeared both in white-face and in drag: the "protection" that academic freedom offers from the opinions and demands of those outside the charmed circle fails to protect the integrity of those whose identities, let alone words, challenge its authorizing practices.

It is precisely those outsiders who rightly claim Joyce's loyalty, as they ought to claim the loyalty of all of us who write and teach as feminists or as Afro-Americanists, even as we work in colleges and universities, publish in academic journals, and train and accredit others as we were trained and accredited. It is no mean feat. Especially for those who are in some way privileged (notably, by being white or male), the academy is seducing: it more and more frequently acts as though it can accept us for who it thinks we really are, rewarding our loyalty to it and punishing us if our loyalties are perceived to lie elsewhere. Crucially, many of the tools we use for whatever we do were forged in the academy by others whose loyalty to it was far less ambivalent. What are we, any of us subversives, doing?

In an essay critical of what she calls the "race for theory," Barbara Christian concludes that her major objection to the hegemony of theory over literature "really hinges on the question, 'for whom are we doing what we are doing when we do literary criticism?'" Her answer is that she writes what and how she does in order, literally, to save her own life. Literature for her is a confirmation that her perceptions are not hallucinations and that "sensuality is intelligence, that sensual language is language that makes sense." She writes as a response to the writers she reads (notably Toni Morrison) and to their other readers, out of the knowledge that the academy has an interest in their voices' being lost (since they speak from points of view the academy presumes not to exist, and certainly not to carry authority), and that "writing disappears unless there is a response to it."[20]

As someone who does read Toni Morrison, I am among those to whom Barbara Christian writes, although, as a white woman, my relationship both to Morrison's novels and to Christian's criticism is necessarily different from that of a Black woman or another woman of color (as either's will, of course, be different from the other's). If Morrison's and Christian's writing—and my own—are to save my life, the ways and means need to be different. I need, for example, to discover that some of what I have been taking for clear-eyed perception *is* a hallucination of sorts. One role of privilege in my life (beyond that of race, there are those of class and sexual identity) has been to make me feel thoroughly at home in the world of academic philosophy and to make it difficult for me to see through the eyes in my own mortal, embodied, female head, rather than through the lenses of disembodied reason. One way I can come, literally, to my senses is by listening to the voices of those who have come, through however different a journey, to

---

[20]Barbara Christian, "The Race for Theory," *Cultural Critique* 6 (Spring 1987): 51–63; quotation, p. 61.

theirs. More particularly, the writings of women of color can help replace the hallucinated version of the world privilege provides with the complexity of reality, whose hallmark is that it looks different depending on where you're seeing it from.

The academy thrives on theories and rewards those who produce them, but a major problem with theories is that they flatten that complexity. However much diversity went into their construction, they are ultimately monologic. In order to construct one, you may need to listen to a lot of people, but then you retire to a quiet place and put it all together, in one maximally anonymous voice. Christian's preference for the verb ("theorizing") reflects in part the concern that the conversation not stop, that one voice not presume to speak for all the others. In the multivocality of theorizing, we are both discovering the complexity of reality and, simultaneously, constructing ourselves and each other as creatures and creators of that reality and as speakers and listeners in the conversation about it.

I've written something here about my sense of myself in these conversations, in part because I want to discuss a particular unease I feel reading the essays in *New Literary History* that form part of the background to Joyce's discussion.[21] The exchange there began with an essay of Joyce's sharply critical of the use of deconstruction and other currently fashionable literary theories to discuss Afro-American literature. Her essay was followed in the same issue by responses from a number of the theorists she criticized, notably Henry Louis Gates and Houston Baker, whose replies to Joyce I find painfully cruel. It is hard to focus on what they are saying about their own practices as "critics of Afro-American literature" (significantly, a designation Gates prefers because it is "less ethnocentric" than "the Black Critic").[22] It is hard not to get stuck in the pain, hard not to wonder what they are really arguing about (if arguing is an appropriate term for what they are doing). And, for a white reader, it's hard not to feel embarrassed, as though I were eavesdropping on a painful, intimate family scene. I feel awkward and confused in part because it's not that I have stumbled in where, as a white person, I wasn't wanted or expected; these essays appear, after all, in *New Literary History*.

Beyond the pain in these particular essays is a question that currently haunts theoretical and academic work that would claim solidarity with liberatory movements. Some of the theoretical tools that seem most powerfully subversive in our hands have met with acclaim from the very disciplines and institutions we aim

---

[21]*New Literary History* 18, no. 2 (Winter 1987). The essays under discussion are: Joyce Ann Joyce, "Reconstructing Black American Literary Criticism" (pp. 335–45); and "Who the Cap Fit: Unconsciousness and Unconscionableness in the Criticism of Houston A. Baker, Jr., and Henry Louis Gates, Jr." (pp. 371–81); Henry Louis Gates, Jr., "What's Love Got to Do with It: Critical Theory, Integrity, and the Black Idiom" (pp. 345–63); and Houston A. Baker, Jr., "In Dubious Battle" (pp. 363–69).

[22]Gates, "What's Love Got to Do with It?" p. 349.

to subvert. And those who most skillfully wield those tools have been rewarded in ways that it is hard not see as attempts at co-optation. However committed such individuals are to resisting what amounts to a bribe, divisiveness inheres in the singling out of a few for acclaim by a system that still disdains and disparages—if it notices at all—the work of the many others that sustain the conversation that gives sense and importance to the voices being isolated from it. Individuals can, of course, use their positions and influence for collective empowerment, and we need to honor those who use their power in this way, but that doesn't change the uneasy fact that institutions of privilege decide who is to have such power and what achievements are to be rewarded.

Thus, it is hard not at least to suspect that those Joyce is critical of are academically rewarded less for the work they have done preserving and presenting the writings of African-American women and men than for the theoretical discourses they have mastered and helped to shape. My suspicion here comes from my own experience as a feminist theorist, noting that the deployment of sophisticated maneuvers against the tradition, however radical in content, is more acceptable than is opening up the conversation to academically untrained voices. It can seem sometimes that almost anything one says is acceptable so long as only the initiated can understand it—something that ought not to surprise us, since the exclusionary effect of incomprehensibility serves in fact to protect the structures of privilege we take ourselves to be so brilliantly skewering.

We need as individual theorists to grapple with these issues, but we need also to recognize that we come to them differently because of how we are placed in the world. So, for example, as the academy and much of the rest of American society stands today, it is easier for me to act in perceived solidarity with Baker and Gates than with Joyce, much as I would like to think I would choose otherwise. As argued by bell hooks,[23] the liberation of Black women challenges the structures of domination in a fundamental way; it is inconceivable on any merely reformist agenda. Black men and white women in the academy, by contrast, share the experience of divided identities, mixtures of privilege and oppression. (Maleness may be problematically a privilege for inner-city Black men living in poverty; it is clearly a privilege for Black male academics.) Racism and sexism function as, among other things, back-ups for each other. Those who are oppressed by one can—and often do—take refuge in the other. That is, they do if they can: if they are white or male. It is on this most uncomfortable of grounds, linked to Black men by our guilty participation in conflicting privileges, that I find myself, as a reader of the *New Literary History* essays and of Joyce's essay.

It is not where I want to be. Joyce is right to see the issues as those of responsibility (as she says in "Black Woman Scholar, Critic, and Teacher"), as well as of identity, "perspective, commitment, involvement, and love-bonding"[24]

[23]Hooks, *Feminist Theory*.

[24]Joyce, "Who the Cap Fit," p. 381.

(as she says in her reply to Baker and Gates). The Black teacher/critic needs, she argues, to "merge the roles of critic and political activist."[25] Analogous arguments have been made about the role of the feminist teacher/critic (or teacher/theorist), and feminist journals and anthologies these days are full of debates about the relationship of feminism as a political movement to academic theory, especially to poststructuralism and deconstruction.[26] If those debates are marked by less intimate rancor than this one, it is in large measure because the participants, being for the most part white academic women, are divided only by theoretical affiliations and are joined by the ambivalence of their positions in the academy.[27]

Baker argues that the theories that he and others use and develop "bring their work into harmony not with a *mainstream*, nor with an academic *majority* (both of which remain wedded to an old literary history), but with an avant-garde in contemporary world literary study."[28] Within this avant-garde, the nature of the literary canon is being profoundly challenged, as is the nature of literature itself, in order to provide a comparativist, non-Eurocentric theoretical framework for studying the literatures of the world. This is an aim I find hard to fault, as I find it hard to disagree with deconstructive moves against European and Euro-American theoretical hegemonies, whether in literature or elsewhere. (Most of my own work, in fact, consists in performing such moves against the philosophical tradition.) But Baker's words, and the attitudes in his and Gates's essays, make me very uneasy.

---

[25]Ibid., p. 377.

[26]See, for example, Jane Flax, "Postmodernism and Gender Relations in Feminist Theory," *Signs* 12, no. 4 (Summer 1987): 621–43, along with Daryl McGowan Tress's "Commentary," *Signs* 14, no. 1 (Autumn 1988): 196–200, and Flax's "Reply" in the same issue, pp. 201–3; Linda Alcoff, "Cultural Feminism versus Post-structuralism: The Identity Crisis in Feminist Theory," *Signs* 13, no. 3 (Spring 1988): 405–36; Nancy Fraser and Linda Nicholson, "Social Criticism without Philosophy: An Encounter between Feminism and Postmodernism," *Theory, Culture, and Society* 5, nos. 2–3 (June 1988): 373–94; Donna Haraway, "Situated Knowledges: The Science Question in Feminism and the Privilege of Partial Perspective," *Feminist Studies* 14, no. 3 (Fall 1988): 575–600; Susan Bordo, "Feminist Scepticism and the 'Maleness' of Philosophy," and Naomi Scheman, "Further Thoughts on a 'Theoretics of Heterogeneity'" (abstract), both in *Journal of Philosophy* 85, no. 11 (November 1988): 619–29, 630–31; and Frances E. Mascia-Lees, Patricia Sharpe, and Colleen Ballerino Cohen, "The Postmodernist Turn in Anthropology: Cautions from a Feminist Perspective," *Signs* 15, no. 1 (Autumn 1989): 7–33.

[27]There *are* deep and painful divisions around "the theory question" among feminist academics, though not usually in print, and these do, I think, have a lot to do with differences in how (many) older and younger women have experienced the academy and themselves as women or as feminists in it—that is, with at least perceived differences of privilege. See Annette Kolodny, "Dancing between Left and Right: Feminism and the Academic Minefield in the 1980s," *Feminist Studies* 14, no. 3 (Fall 1988): 453–66.

[28]Baker, "In Dubious Battle," p. 366.

It's the avant-garde that has me worried. The current situation is reminiscent of that of the avant-garde in the arts in the early part of this century. What started out as a profoundly political challenge to the repressive structures of the art world, as they were embedded in and abetted other structures of domination, became the accepted, prestigious, expensive art of the Establishment. Duchamp's urinal was, in the end, far less potent than the gallery wall on which it was hung. At the heart of the canonization—and taming—of the avant-garde was the undermining of its democratic impulses: when humble objects became art, it was because those the powerful recognized as artists elevated them. Only Andy Warhol could make a Campbell's soup can into art: in the hands of a woman painter it would have remained full of soup, a dismissible emblem of women's preoccupation with the domestic.

Things are now at a similarly critical point. The underlying impetus for postmodernity is the struggle of peoples of color and of women against the terms on which white men might be persuaded to offer equality to a token few of us—namely, our ability successfully to impersonate them. That struggle takes the form of a fundamental challenge to the norms of selfhood that white men have formulated for themselves, using tropes of darkness and effeminacy against which to define themselves. Deconstruction can be a powerful tool to expose the logic of domination, as it lurks in the egalitarian rhetoric of the Enlightenment; it has a place in a revolutionary's toolbox.

But deconstruction is as undiscriminating a tool as were the shock tactics of the artistic avant-garde. Its appeal is that it *can* dismantle the master's house.[29] But it dismantles *our* houses just as effectively, and, unlike the master, we are unlikely to have multiple residences. So the master faces us scornfully, after we've collaborated in the playful tearing down of our houses, and we are left homeless, as he moves on to his ten-room *pied-à-terre* overlooking Central Park or his Tuscany villa or his Vail condominium. Privilege, as Elizabeth Spelman demonstrates in *Inessential Woman*, has many hiding places, and one of them is nihilism: if the world can't be adequately known from where I stand, it can't be known at all.[30] Such nihilism will appeal primarily to those who know deep down that, however many houses are torn down, they will not be on the streets.

We do need to tear down the master's house, along with the badly built ugly houses many of the rest of us have been told were the best that could be done by way of affordable housing. But we need, with equal urgency, to build new, sturdy, beautiful houses, and for that task the master's tools are worse than useless. That's where the writing—of Toni Morrison and others—that saves Barbara Christian's life and inspires Joyce A. Joyce's passion as a teacher/critic comes in, and that's where questions of loyalty, responsibility, identity, commitment, involvement,

[29]Audre Lorde, "The Master's Tools Will Never Dismantle the Master's House," in Lorde, *Sister Outsider* (Trumansburg, N.Y.: Crossing Press, 1984), pp. 110–13.

[30]Spelman, *Inessential Woman*, pp. 183 ff.

and love-bonding have their greatest force. Some of us—in particular, white women and Black men—are co-optable by the masters, who are showing an increasing willingness to indulge us in our house wrecking. It's a heady and empowering activity, but we need to listen to the Black women and others who warn us about what we are to likely to end up having done.

We need, those of us who aspire to be feminist academics, to take seriously the contradictions in that aspiration. Both feminists and academics are concerned with coming to know aspects of the world and with sharing that knowledge with others. But each of these roles (not to mention all the others we play, as the actual people we are) carries with it values that shape what counts as knowledge and how it is reliably obtained. We have, to use Sandra Harding's term from her essay "Who Knows? Identities and Feminist Epistemology," "perverse identities,"[31] and we need to learn to live them responsibly—responsible, that is, to the values we affirm and to the communities with which we identify, as well as those with which we wish to ally. As academics we need to question the loyalty expected of us to the structuring norms of disciplinarity and exclusive "peer" accountability. We need to think concretely about the colleges and universities where we work, about all the people who constitute them and whose lives are affected by them. Our loyalty should be that of the loyal opposition, committed to challenge and transformation.

Those with perverse identities (perhaps everyone, but certainly every feminist and other radical academic) can have no easy answers to what counts as acting responsibly; we have no straight paths to follow. The perversity we have chosen means that we cannot walk directly from where we are to where we need to be, since we have chosen to walk on the grounds of institutions that have laid out their paths according to plans we do not fully share, to lead to places we do not choose to go. If we have reasons for staying (and we need to be clear about what they are), then we need to get good at taking detours. To change the metaphor, we need, in Emily Dickinson's words, to "tell all the truth but tell it slant."[32]

The slant will come in part from our using tools that were developed by others who do not share our interests, tools that were designed to construct knowledge by and for those who benefit from structures of domination and privilege. But the maintenance of domination is not the whole story about the social construction of knowledge, even at the privileged sites for that construction; if it were, universities would be no place for any of us. Just as the egalitarian language of the founding documents of the United States has been usable in generations of liberatory struggles, despite those documents' having been drafted by and for

---

[31]Sandra Harding, "Who Knows? Identities and Feminist Epistemology," in *(En)Gendering Knowledge: Feminists in Academe*, ed. Joan E. Hartman and Ellen Messer-Davidow (Knoxville: The University of Tennessee Press, 1991).

[32]Emily Dickinson, *Complete Poems*, ed. Thomas H. Johnson (Boston: Little, Brown, 1960), poem no. 1129, pp. 506–7.

propertied male slave-owning Europeans, so can the epistemology of liberalism provide points of entry for radical critique, despite having primarily served to empower straight white middle and upper class males and those who can impersonate them. Conceptual tools are not neutral, but neither are they untransformable in the hands of those who were never meant to touch them.

Sheer numbers are of great importance: it is far easier to "pass"—that is, to agree to the tacit bargain to bracket your nonprivileged identity as the price of being taken seriously—when there's no one else like you around. It becomes a lot harder to pretend that *everyone*'s a middle class straight white man if most of the people in the room aren't. When people are empowered to speak in their own voices, out of their own bodies, lives, and communities, not as impersonators of the privileged, the tools of thought are transformed. Truth becomes a goal of ever-broader coalitions, the hallmark of knowledge shareable by more and different particular others, for more and different particular ends. Who those others and those ends are become explicitly political questions, revealed behind the liberal façade of supposedly anonymous, value-neutral universality.

Thus, it is especially important to write and teach in ways that include in the conversation those whose liberation we say we champion. Hegemonic theorists have often said that they had the best interests of the disadvantaged at heart and that they knew better than those unfortunate others what those best interests were. Feminist and other radical academic theorists risk perpetuating that arrogance. Bringing about revolutionary change is conceptually, as well as practically, difficult; it is not meant to be easy to see through the obfuscations of privilege and to reveal the deep structure of domination. Academically sophisticated conceptual tools can be of use in this labor. But such sophistication itself is an expression of privilege, and like all privileges, needs to be acknowledged as such and used responsibly. Romantic downward mobility is no more an adequate response to the privilege of academic training than it is to the privilege of class. (Only those whose family backgrounds have allowed them to take decades of formal education for granted are likely to toss it away frivolously.) The harder, more honest course consists in acknowledging privilege, its limitations *and* its advantages, and putting those advantages to use, in alliance with others who do not share them. The success of such a course depends in part on our reliability as allies, which in turn depends in part on whether we use the sophisticated languages we have learned as shareable tools or as marks of exclusivity. We need to ask ourselves, as we embark on a piece of research, who wants or needs to know what we are trying to find out—and why. And we need to be open to the ways in which the answers to that question subtly shape the work we do.[33]

---

[33] As this paper went through successive drafts, Joan Hartman and Ellen Messer-Davidow were of enormous help in clarifying both the issues (which became in the process more complex) and my expression of them (which I hope became simpler).

V

(In)Conclusion

19

Who Is That Masked Woman?: Reflections on Power, Privilege, and Home-ophobia

> Be patient to all that is unsolved
> in your heart
> And try to love the questions themselves
> Do not seek the answers
> that cannot be given you
> Because you wouldn't be able to live them
> And the point is to live everything
> Live the questions now
> Perhaps you will gradually without noticing it
> live along some distant day into the answers
>
> —Rainer Maria Rilke

In the summer of 1987 I gave a talk to a symposium of mostly European mostly literary theorists in Dubrovnik. I had been invited by one of the conveners, Hans Ulrich Gumbrecht (then at the University of Siegen in the Federal Republic of Germany), whom I had met at a literary theory conference at Indiana University and who had become excited by the challenge of feminist theory as an accepted and institutionalized part of the academy, a development much further along in the United States than in Europe. My talk was entitled "The Body Politic/The Impolitic Body/Bodily Politics," and it had to do with the different representations of the body in premodern, modern, and postmodern European and Euro-American thought, and with how those representations were inflected by race and gender. Afterward I wrote it up, and it was translated into German by the other convener, Ludwig Pfeiffer, also at Siegen, and published in a collection of papers from the symposium.[1] I have never read the translation all the way through, something it would be quite hard for me to do.

The paper was written for strangers. It is meant to stand alone, presupposing no ongoing conversation. I wrote it knowing it was to be translated into German, and it reads to me as though it had started in German and been translated into English (except for the title, which in German is clumsy and awkward). While writing it I felt as though I had broken into a cathedral and was pounding out Buxtehude on the organ (or so I said: I can't play the organ, and I couldn't

[1]"Der Körper des Gemeinwesens/Der unpolitische Körper/Körperpolitik," translated by K. Ludwig Pfeiffer, in *Materialität der Kommunikation*, ed. Hans Ulrich Gumbrecht and K. Ludwig Pfeiffer (Frankfurt: Suhrkamp, 1988).

recognize a piece of music as Buxtehude's). I felt freed of the expectations of my more domestic audiences: for (analytical) philosophical rigor and concision and for (American) feminist grounding in experience and connection to practice.

I subsequently read the paper (in English) to several different audiences made up mostly of strangers and of nonphilosophers. Then, with some anxiety, in the fall of 1988, I read the paper at a meeting of Midwest SWIP (the Society for Women in Philosophy) in Northfield, Minnesota.

Bringing the paper home, although frightening, was something I needed to do. Most of what I write begins life as a talk at some distant place, in response to invitations to address audiences made up entirely or nearly entirely of strangers. I enjoy traveling, and I especially like being places where I'm responsible for nothing except my end of lots of conversations, and where I'm the center of attention for a fixed period of time, fussed over, and then left alone in a comfortable, anonymous hotel room. Writing happens later, when I'm pleasurably alone with my Macintosh. But, as much as I like it (or, precisely because I like it), I have become increasingly suspicious of the effect on my work of such a combination of solitude and life among strangers.

Most of my life, however, is spent neither alone nor with strangers. Most of the time I am teaching and interacting with friends and colleagues. From 1986 to 1989 I was chairing the women's studies department, and I have been the Vice President of the board of directors of a feminist theater company, At the Foot of the Mountain, since 1980. For the past several years we have been struggling to transform the theater from an essentially white women's theater to a genuinely multicultural arena, while in Women's Studies we've been involved in analogous efforts involving hiring, the curriculum, alliances with ethnic studies departments, and, in 1987, working in an academic/community, multicultural coalition to host the National Women's Studies Association annual meeting. What was troubling me was the contrast between what I thought I believed—in theorizing not only from but in these interactions with students, friends, and colleagues and my work in the community—and what I actually did, which was to theorize alone or as a stranger.

When I read the "Body" paper at SWIP, I asked for help in bringing what I did back home, in exploring how it fit with what others closer to me were doing. In a long conversation afterward María Lugones, a philosopher at Carleton College and a friend, challenged me in ways I hadn't quite anticipated. She pointed out that, although ostensibly concerned with the conditions for constructing a politically usable and nonimperialist first person plural in which to theorize, I had in the paper kept the role of theorist to my solitary self. I appealed to the "experiences" of people of color to provide the raw material for a more adequate theory, which it would remain the prerogative of people like me to create and authorize.

The other side of that arrogance was my elision of the specificities of my own actual life. Although the paper began on what seemed to be an autobiographical note, placing myself in what I argued was the oxymoronic position of a woman philosopher, I said nothing of how I came to be in that position, how I came to do theory, why it mattered to me, to whom I felt myself to be connected, and so on. Just as only those like me were really theorists, apparently only those unlike me had experiences worth noting: theorists learn from experiences (whoever's they are); they are not shaped by them.

There is little point in saying that, of course, I don't want or mean to do any of these things, that I am, in fact, committed to deploring them in my own and others' work. The point is that I do, usually, write from an insufficiently examined place, in an insufficiently examined voice, and, most important, in insufficiently examined relation to several audiences and communities. I write most easily and fluently from the academy, as a theorist, and for strangers. I want to try to examine some of what I have thereby obscured or elided, some of the voices other than my own, as well as some of my own voices, that I have silenced or (mis)interpreted. I am assuming that my experiences are not wholly idiosyncratic (although I know them not to be shared even by many who are demographically similar to me: white, Jewish, female, middle class, academically successful and rewarded, heterosexual), and I hope that the exploration will reveal things others will find useful, whether they are prone to theorizing as I do or have found themselves angry at others who do, or both.

I start with the recognition that I am in many ways more comfortable among strangers or acquaintances or relatively distant colleagues than among those to whom I am more closely related. I find it comforting to be expected to perform, to jump through some set of hoops, to earn approval. It is obviously relevant to my comfort that those around me with the power to grant or withhold approval have mostly set me tasks I could perform, and they have not withheld the approval I earned. Among the tasks I am best at are those associated with theorizing: seeing connections among apparently disparate things, explaining those connections imaginatively and clearly, and speculating on what holds them all together. I learned to theorize as a student of philosophy and, before that, as my father's daughter, both of which I was very good at and for which I earned a great deal of approval. What it is to theorize as a feminist and as my mother's daughter is both less clear to me and more frightening, and something more important than approval is at stake. Thus, my "home-ophobia": pun, of course, fully intended.

The preceding four paragraphs are a slight revision of a proposal I sent to the organizers of a conference on "Feminisms and Cultural Imperialism: Politics of Difference" at Cornell in the spring of 1989. Although the people at the conference were predominantly strangers, there was a difference that unsettled my usual ease: most of those on the program and many of the audience were people of color, and things infinitely more important than being clever or even profound were at stake. And I had decided to talk as the very specific person I am, in particular, as a Jew.

As I went on to say in the proposal, an important piece of the puzzle has to do with power and privilege and the ways I have learned, as a daughter and as a theorist, both to identify with the privileged and to fight them, usually in the name of some oppressed others. (I came of age on the edges of the civil rights movement and later the anti-war movement.) I have rarely had to fight for myself, and I need to examine the consequences of my fighting for others from a position of ease with their oppressors. And I need to examine my fear of and uneasiness with those whose causes (as I understand them) I champion. One obvious piece of the fear is that of losing my voice.

If the position that I have doesn't distinctively well equip me with the tools and talents for theorizing—that is, if I recognize that others (for example, women of color) can speak for themselves, and theorize for themselves—then my own theorizing seems privileged neither in the way of the old Archimedean point from which reality appears as it really is, nor in the way of the vantage point of the oppressed. For many feminist theorists the recognition of the nonexistence of any Archimedean point was compensated for by the (originally Marxist) idea that the standpoint of the oppressed was one of epistemic privilege, and that, as women, we occupied such a standpoint. But, as we reluctantly learned, there is no such standpoint that all women share, and, for many of us, myself included, the place where we stand is shaped more deeply by privilege than by oppression, and consequently seems to partake of the epistemic liabilities we so clearly point out in the case of men.[2]

While trying to find the time and the courage to figure out how and why to theorize neither as the Grand Canonical Synthesizer nor as a representative of the oppressed, but as the particular person I am and with the particular others I am variously connected to, I continued to travel. In the spring and summer of 1989, before and after the Cornell conference, I went to a meeting of the Revisioning Philosophy Program on gender and philosophy at Esalen, then back to Dubrovnik, and then to the program's conference on Philosophy and the Human Future at Cambridge. The Dubrovnik talk, "Your Ground Is My Body: The Politics of Anti-Foundationalism," like its predecessor, was translated into German by Ludwig Pfeiffer. My talk at Cambridge was entitled "If Your Ground Were Not My Body, What Might Our Ground Be?" It's never been written, and the present essay can be taken as its translation, not into a language I can barely read, but into my native tongue, what in Yiddish is called the "mame-loshn," the mother tongue. (I do not really know Yiddish. To the consternation of my elderly relatives, what I

---

[2]For a critical account of feminist standpoint epistemologies, see Sandra Harding, *The Science Question in Feminism* (Ithaca: Cornell University Press, 1986); and for a critique of the effects of unexamined privilege on feminist theorizing, including the assumption that privileged women can articulate universal female experience, see Elizabeth V. Spelman, *Inessential Woman: Problems of Exclusion in Feminist Thought* (Boston: Beacon Press, 1988).

understand of it comes mainly from what I understand of German. But Yiddish feels natural to me: it sounds like home.)

There has been a recent rich conversation about the meanings of home to feminists of different races and ethnicities. In 1983 Barbara Smith edited *Home Girls: A Black Feminist Anthology,*[3] with an introduction in which she discusses her choice of the title, the resonance of "home" for Black women: "Home has always meant a lot to people who are ostracized as racial outsiders in the public sphere. It is above all a place to be ourselves" (Smith, *Home Girls*, p. li) Bernice Johnson Reagon in her essay in that volume, "Coalition Politics: Turning the Century," stresses the importance of not confusing the comfort of home with the frequently uncomfortable work of coalition building. Too often, she argues, white feminists have taken the women's movement to be their home, and wondered why more women of color didn't want to join them in it, not noticing that, like all homes, it bore the marks of its proprietary occupants. White feminists have not left behind as much of our original homes as we have often wanted to think we have, nor have most women of color been eager to follow suit. Even if the new feminist homes were not so recognizably white, the detachment from family and community that can feel like a liberating gesture for a woman of privilege is likely to be both a loss and a betrayal for a woman of color.

For Barbara Smith home is not necessarily comfortable: being oneself there may at times be a struggle. But even if it is not always the place of refuge and sustenance Reagon writes of, home as an arena of struggle is markedly different from a coalition. The difference is one of history and its connection to identity. The decision not to sever one's ties with home is a decision—or a recognition—that who one is is not detachable from that place or those people. One of the arguments women of color have made to white women is that we need to acknowledge those ties, the ways in which homes we may think we have left have shaped us, and we need to take responsibility for where we have come from.

In thinking about how to do that in my own life, I turned to Minnie Bruce Pratt's autobiographical narrative, "Identity: Skin Blood Heart,"[4] and an essay on it called "Feminist Politics: What's Home Got to Do with It?" by Biddy Martin and Chandra Talpade Mohanty[5] (both of whom were at the Cornell conference). Martin and Mohanty trace Pratt's journey from a Southern girlhood, marriage, and motherhood to an explicitly anti-racist lesbian feminism, noting how her

[3]Barbara Smith, ed., *Home Girls: A Black Feminist Anthology* (New York: Kitchen Table Women of Color Press, 1983).

[4]Ellie Bulkin, Minnie Bruce Pratt, and Barbara Smith, *Yours in Struggle: Three Feminist Perspectives on Anti-Semitism and Racism* (Brooklyn, N.Y.: Long Haul Press, 1984).

[5]Biddy Martin and Chandra Talpade Mohanty, "Feminist Politics: What's Home Got to Do with It?" in Teresa de Lauretis, ed., *Feminist Studies/Critical Studies* (Bloomington: Indiana University Press, 1986).

narrative of the journey problematizes her relation to the various homes she has had and made. Far from abandoning who she had been, by "leaving home" (becoming the feminist version of that American icon, the self-made man) according to Martin and Mohanty, "Pratt . . . succeeds in carefully taking apart the bases of her own privilege by resituating herself again and again in the social, by constantly referring to the materiality of the situation in which she finds herself" (Martin and Mohanty, "Feminist Politics," p. 194).

In thinking about the issues of home and privilege, I began as a white woman, but the specificities of Pratt's narrative made it clear to me that among the many differences between her life and mine, a particularly salient one for exploring the meanings of home was my Jewishness. I was born in 1946 of parents born in New York. Although the Holocaust barely preceded my birth, I was brought up in a suburban world that was carefully constructed to feel safe: at Passover seders Hitler merged in my mind with the Pharaoh as a vanquished oppressor who had been forced finally to "let my people go." But, despite the safety, it's become clear to me that home for me is not the stable place from which one sets out into the world, secure that, whatever else changes, it will still be there. Home is where, if you can't flee from it fast enough, they will kill you or take you away. Home is where pogroms happen; like most American Jews, I have only the vaguest idea of where my grandparents were born, and there are surely no relatives still to be found there.

Jewish "cosmopolitanism" needs, of course, to be seen in this light: our survival as a people has depended on our individual and communal ability to survive in diaspora, finding ways of making a living and making a life in a strange land, on the margins. (The stubborn brutality of Israel's response to the Palestinian people and to the Intifada is, I think, an indication of the extent to which the moral integrity of Jewish identity was tied to the conditions of diaspora and marginality and has not been sufficiently reconfigured to fit the conditions of being at home and the different sorts of responsibility that come with that.) In my own life, although I never feared being chased from the home I grew up in, it never occurred to me to remain there, certainly not in the Long Island suburb that felt like a nursery, a place designed to be grown out of, and which I barely remember, though I lived there from when I was two until I started college.

For the past fifteen years I have lived in places that are foreign to me, first in Canada, then in the Midwest. I like Minneapolis and have no desire to leave, but I cannot imagine thinking of it as home, as where I am from, no matter how long I live here. Part of what I like about it is precisely that it is not and never will be home. Before I could feel comfortable, though, I had to drive between here and the East Coast. Until I'd done that (a couple of years after I moved here), I had attacks of a sort of agoraphobia: there was far too much continent all around. I needed to know where the nearest ocean was, not because I like oceans (which I do), but because I needed to know where to flee to. Just in case.

There is, of course, more than a little romantic posturing in all this. But I do see in my own life and in my sense of myself in the world the influence of the position of privileged marginality of many contemporary American Jews (a position that a significant number of German Jews enjoyed before the ascendancy of Nazism and that made it difficult for them to acknowledge the murderousness of their countrymen's intentions toward them). In feminist theory marginality has most often been contrasted with privilege; the position on the margin is precisely the position not shaped and limited by the myopias of privilege. But much Jewish experience, including my own, questions this association. Not all positions on the margin are the same. The place of usury in premodern Europe is an example: being forbidden to Christians, it was taken up by Jews, who came to play a vital and necessarily well-remunerated role in economic life, while being, precisely because they played this role, even more marginalized to core conceptions of privileged European identity.

Philosophers are, I think, in an interestingly analogous position. As I have argued elsewhere,[6] philosophical problems, notably the core epistemological problems of scepticism, can be seen as the residue of the construction of privileged subjectivity. Insofar as authority rests in one's ability to lay claim to a self essentially detached from bodily needs and desires, from emotions, from defining connections to other people, and from manual labor, one will find it problematic whether and how one can ever really know, for example, if one actually has a body, whether there is any world out there at all, whether other people have minds like one's own. The detachments that constitute authority stigmatize everything culturally assigned to women, to the working class, and to members of races other than white. Thus, racism, classism, and gynophobic misogyny are at the heart of the subjectivity whose construction gives rise to the problems of philosophy.

The serious work of actually exercising that authority—in science, politics, or business—is hardly compatible with worrying about such notoriously intractable questions, so they are shunted off onto philosophers, hopelessly impractical, abstracted eggheads, who serve as cultural scapegoats for the neuroses of privilege. Such a position is certainly marginal (necessarily so, since the questions that trouble philosophers can't be taken seriously), but it is not lacking in privilege.

It is a position I took to with an ease that now, as a feminist, I find troubling. The problems of philosophy seemed wholly natural to me. I said when I discovered philosophy, my first year in college, that I felt immediately at home with it, as though I was hearing my native tongue spoken for the first time. But it wasn't, of course, my mother tongue, and its naturalness to me is a reflection of the extent to which I was then my father's daughter. I was at Barnard, a women's college, and my teachers were women, which certainly made it much easier to feel that I could be a philosopher, but being a woman was not taken to mark any important difference, certainly not in one's relation to philosophical problems and methods.

---

[6]In addition to "Your Ground Is My Body," see "The Unavoidability of Gender," and "Though This Be Method, Yet There Is Madness in It: Paranoia and Liberal Epistemology."

In a logic class at Columbia, much was made of my being a woman; at Barnard it seemed irrelevant.

I don't now think it is irrelevant, since I no longer believe (and am trying to stop acting as though I do believe) that theorists are essentially disembodied and ahistorical. My choice to inhabit problems that arise from the construction of privilege signified my willingness to disaffiliate with other women, that is, not to identify with those who rejected or were never offered the privilege of being treated like (privileged) men. It was a choice to identify with my father and with others who offered me approval if I learned my lessons well. It was, for reasons I do not yet fully understand, a less frightening choice than that of identifying with my mother.

It is too easy to say (though it is true) that my choice is understandable, that is, looks wholly rational, given the greater power associated with the world of men. What that explanation leaves out is the fear, which was—and is—not just the fear of (relative) powerlessness. It was—and is—the fear of home, the fear of women: home-ophobia. It is connected to my attitudes about the seasons, in particular, to the transition between winter and spring. April, for me, is the cruelest month[7] (except in Minnesota, where we still have blizzards then; here it's May). The "mixing [of] memory and desire," the re-emergence of what has been safely frozen, is frightening. In the winter, boundaries are well-marked; things and people know their places. Spring brings thaw, the blurring of the boundary between inside and outside, a generally promiscuous mingling. I can tough out the winter: it makes demands on me. There are rules to follow, clear things to succeed at; it calls for hardness and rigor. Spring is another matter. It doesn't make demands at all, but it has hopes and expectations. It won't punish those who aren't up to its promises, as winter will punish those who aren't up to its threats, but it will be disappointed, saddened by those who can't or won't rise to its occasion. You can't tough out spring.

Heterosexuality is, for me, like winter. There is a lot I straightforwardly like about both, moments of intensest pleasure, and certainly desire. But there is also little I fear. I know what the challenges are, and I enjoy them, and if worse comes to worst, I know how to survive. With respect both to winter and to heterosexuality, my fearlessness is, of course, born of privilege: there are many for whom one or the other can be literally deadly, and in both cases there is no guarantee that my privilege will continue, or that it will be enough. But I feel safe.

As I don't in the spring, or with women. Where, objectively, I am, and know myself to be, safer, I feel frightened, because none of the tricks I have learned will do me any good. They're unnecessary, but without them I feel defenseless, and it does no good to say there's nothing for me to defend myself from.

---

[7]T. S. Eliot, "The Waste Land," in *Collected Poems 1909–1962* (New York: Harcourt, Brace and World, 1970), p. 53.

That's just the problem. I don't need the mask, but I'm seized with anxiety that underneath it, there's no face. Politically, personally, and as a theorist I am most comfortable when I feel least at home, when being myself is the last thing I have to worry about.

I remember a talk I gave soon after coming to Minnesota. In the front rows sat my new, senior colleagues, the people who would in a few years decide whether or not I got to keep my job. In the back were students and faculty from Women's Studies, my friends, people with no power over my future in the university. I spoke with ease, even bravado, certainly no fear, as long as I focused on the front rows. When my eyes went toward the back, my pulse raced and my throat grew dry. They—my friends, the people who I knew really cared about me—could, I was sure, see through the cleverness, would want more from me than that. With no power to make or enforce demands, they needed and expected me to speak honestly, to say things that mattered. It's a lot easier to be clever.

Among the things that matter: in the midst of increasing tension between Blacks and Jews some people are trying to make connections between the two groups and to heal the rifts. As part of this attempt, there are Black and Jewish Women in Dialogue groups, and I belong to one in the Twin Cities. One of the things we have tried is to reach some common understanding of the alliances between Blacks and Jews during the forties, fifties, and sixties, alliances that Jews typically remember far more fondly than Blacks do. For many Blacks, the memory is mixed: the support given to the civil rights movement by Jews is acknowledged and appreciated, but it didn't feel like an alliance between equals. Jews were too often in the role of the masked woman (or man)—the benefactor riding into and out of town, doing good from behind a mask and atop a horse.

Jewish cosmopolitanism translated into marginality, not as on the edges but as at the interstices, strategically located socially, economically, residentially, between more privileged whites and Blacks. While recognizing the moral courage of chosen solidarity with those more oppressed, we need to acknowledge that many Jews, even among those truly committed to the civil rights agenda, compromised that solidarity by turning toward the greater safety of privilege. (Rumor has it that some have even become Republicans.) The movement of many Jews from major cities to the suburbs was in the name of safety, a resonant term for post-Holocaust parents. But, as Lata Mani pointed out to me when I discussed these issues at the Cornell conference, the "danger" Jews were fleeing was not Nazis, but the changing face of the inner city, too often summed up by the movement into Jewish neighborhoods of Blacks, the very people with whom they were supposedly allied.

Privilege is a very tricky thing. It allows one to do things that are genuinely valuable (like living in neighborhoods where children can go out to play without risking their lives and where the schools are well-equipped and not overcrowded): only those who have always had it are in a position to think it's worthless. But it is systematically distorting of our perspective and of our values: it demands our loyalty to the unjust structures that grant it.[8] An understandable response to discovering that we have it at the expense of others, on whose backs it rests, is to try to use it on their behalf, to take advantage, for them, of our ability to move with relative ease among the oppressors. As a strategy, that may have its place, but as a way of life, it doesn't work. No one out there knows us well enough to keep us honest.

Bernice Reagon urges us not to think we are at home when we are in coalition; equally important, as she also notes, we have to be at home somewhere, not only for our own mental health, but precisely, as Barbara Smith puts it, "to be ourselves," which for some of us may be the hardest thing of all to be.

---

[8]See Adrienne Rich, "Disloyal to Civilization: Feminism, Racism, Gynephobia," in *On Lies, Secrets, and Silence* (New York: W. W. Norton & Co., 1979).

20

Undoing Philosophy as a Feminist

During the academic year 1966–67, I was passionately engaged: in Wittgenstein's *Tractatus*, with Students for a Democratic Society, and to the man I married that June. The fledgling philosopher, the student activist, and the fiancée had nothing directly to say to each other. When they communicated, they spoke in migraine, and, although I could hardly ignore the medium, I managed to miss the message, if there was one. Mostly, I think, they were just fighting to maintain their mutual independence. They really didn't—yet—have much to say to each other, nor did they share an intelligible language.

It was feminism that provided both the content of the subsequent conversations and the language in which to have them. Unlike the women in the New Left in Sara Evans's *Personal Politics*,[1] I didn't learn about sexism in SDS. My not having a leadership position had, I thought (if I thought about it at all), to do not with my gender but with my major: I wasn't good at or interested in politically useful things like sociology or history or economics or political science. Even within philosophy, my passion was for epistemology and metaphysics, which I described as like pure mathematics, having nothing to do with politics or with anything else remotely practical. What it did have to do with was harder to say, but whatever it was, doing it felt as natural and as inevitable as breathing.

My earliest encounters with philosophy, in Virginia Held's introductory class my freshman year at Barnard, felt to me like hearing my native tongue spoken for the first time. In the following two years, as I took and retook every class Mary Mothersill and Sue Larson taught, I continued to feel myself fully a part of this two and half millennia long conversation. Not even graduate school tarnished my sense of full enfranchisement, even though up to that point the Harvard philosophy department had hired only one woman and had tenured none. Those

[1]Sara M. Evans, *Personal Politics: The Roots of Women's Liberation in the Civil Rights Movement and the New Left* (New York: Knopf, 1979).

facts seemed scandalous and anachronistic, the product of a sexism that infected the world in which philosophy was done but which, it seemed to me, if I thought about it at all, had nothing to do with the subject itself.

I continued to think this way about philosophy, at least about the parts of it that most engaged me, even as it pained me to do so, even as I envied my friends among the Radical Philosophers whose interests in moral, political, and social philosophy gave their intellectual and political lives an integrity mine lacked. My desire for seamless coherence in these parts of my life seemed ineluctably blocked by the obdurate bent of my intellectual passions, just as my later envy of my lesbian friends for the analogous coherence of their feminist politics with their desire seemed blocked by the obduracy of my (hetero)sexuality.

I was wrong about nearly everything.

I was wrong, in the first instance, about myself. My passions, intellectual and otherwise, were far less obdurate than I had believed. And discovering that meant acknowledging the stake I had had in believing otherwise, and in romanticizing the positions of those whose passions put them outside the arenas of mainstream approval and acceptance. And I was wrong in the ways I thought about and valued seamlessness, coherence, and integrity.

What I took to be my native language, the characteristic musings and sceptical probings of philosophers, was not my mother tongue. Its familiarity to me had its roots in long years of apprenticing as my father's daughter, in learning how different I was from my mother and from other girls and women. As a "red diaper baby" I also grew up alienated from the world of my classmates and teachers: I recall my fury at Kennedy during the Cuban missile crisis and the ease with which I accepted, even took pride in, my estrangement from the very different mood of nearly everyone around me. Finding philosophy was like realizing the fantasy of having been left as a foundling on one's purported parents' doorstep by real parents who were unimaginably grander. Philosophy was another world, the one I really belonged to, in which I could find my way around, in which I would be intelligible.

My earliest philosophical passion was for Wittgenstein; he has stayed with me through a dissertation and on into a seminar I am now teaching on Wittgenstein and feminism. Only now am I coming to see (helped, painfully, by reading Ray Monk's biography)[2] how central to the connection I feel to Wittgenstein is his deep estrangement: willfully from the culture in which he lived, painfully from the people around him, and notoriously from philosophy itself. His misogyny is complexly implicated in that estrangement and is not something I want to—or could—overlook, while finding something worthwhile in what he says, something detachable from his life. Misogyny as culturally encoded self-hatred provides a

[2]Ray Monk, *Ludwig Wittgenstein: The Duty of Genius* (New York: The Free Press, 1990).

clue to the complex workings of identity and identification as these are played out in his work.

Patricia Hill Collins has theorized the perspective of the "outsider within"[3] as one of clarity and creativity, grounded in the critical achievement of self-knowledge, including knowledge of where one stands in relation to the structures of privilege and domination that constitute one's marginality. Such knowledge can start from felt experiences of alienation and estrangement, but its achievement requires, even as it grounds, a politics, an account, however provisional, of one's identity as a member of an oppressed or marginalized group and the conscious, chosen identification with that group, an identification that provides ground to stand on different from the ground that defines one as outsider.

However complex Wittgenstein's multiple identities, at least two were, in the worlds in which he lived, not only marginal but life-threateningly stigmatized: he was a homosexual, and he was a Jew. The question of his homosexuality is hotly debated,[4] but what seems clear is that he experienced intense homoerotic desire, which, whether he acted upon it or not, produced equally intense feelings of self-loathing. He was Jewish not by belief or upbringing but by the racist definitions of his murderously anti-Semitic times, and Jewishness, too, occasioned self-loathing. He was, Monk persuasively demonstrates, profoundly influenced by Otto Weininger's *Sex and Character*, which gave him the idea that only genius could redeem him from the capital sins of Jewishness and sexual desire, both of which were associated, not only by Weininger, with effeminacy. That is, in neither case was the stigma anything he had *done*; it was who he *was*, and his obsession with honesty, integrity, and self-knowledge only compounded his inability to stand on the ground that seemed to him both to constitute his identity and to be incompatible with his self-respect.

My own entry into philosophy was considerably less anguished: I thought I belonged there, and I felt like an insider. Only later, as the feminism that made so much sense everywhere else in my life led me to question the apparent political neutrality of epistemology and metaphysics, did I come to a sense of myself as an outsider within philosophy. I think now that my early attraction to Wittgenstein was an encoded perception of the alienation I could not yet feel. I was drawn precisely to his recognition that there was something *wrong* with the questions philosophers asked and with the answers they sought, as well as to his apparently superficial puzzlement. "Back to the rough ground," he urged (*Philosophical*

[3]Patricia Hill Collins, "Learning from the Outsider Within: The Sociological Significance of Black Feminist Thought," in Mary Margaret Fonow and Judith A. Cook, eds., *Beyond Methodology: Feminist Scholarship as Lived Research* (Bloomington: Indiana University Press, 1991); reprinted from *Social Problems* 33, no. 8 (1986): 14–32.

[4]See Monk, passim and esp., "Appendix: Bartley's Wittgenstein and Coded Remarks," pp. 582–86; and W. W. Bartley III, *Wittgenstein*, 2nd. ed. (LaSalle, Ill.: Open Court, 1985).

Investigations, sec. 107), away from the seductive depths, but there never was any ground on which Wittgenstein could actually stand, though he tried to find it on the remote coast of Norway, in the trenches of World War I, and among school children in the mountains. Feminism for me has meant, as much as anything, a willed attentiveness to the actual ground beneath my feet, the placement of my body in the world, and the structures of privilege that have supported me and the philosophy I have done so naturally.

I have argued elsewhere[5] that philosophical problems are the neuroses of privilege, the unassuageable worries that arise from the simultaneous needs both to keep one's body, the world, and other people at a distance and to hold them close enough to be securely known. Philosophers take on these worries as though they were intellectual puzzles, while the more powerful go about the business of life oblivious to the gaping and unsuturable incisions that would threaten to undermine everything they think they know. Wittgenstein in his early work took on the labor of suturing the self and the world: his need to know himself to be a "genius" was, he thought, met by the crystalline structure of the *Tractatus*. World and self were held unshakably together, laced by language, which perfectly mirrored them both. Having done that, having placed himself securely in the world in the only way he could, putting metaphysics in the place of human community, logically deducing what he could not otherwise believe—that the world was his world, that he belonged in it—Wittgenstein left philosophy. There was nothing left to do.

His later work shatters the crystal, shows it to be a hall of mirrors, in which what we take for metaphysics are the reflections of our own activity, the long accretions of human community and practices, our natural history and forms of life. But how are we to take this? What are we to do once we have broken free from the grip of a picture that says that this is how things *have* to be, once we see that our practices constitute the patterns of meaningfulness that allow for the talk of intention, emotions, understanding, grief, pain, and joy? What, especially, are we to do if those practices and consequently those patterns are in deep ways abhorrent to us? Wittgenstein never quite says, although scattered through his posthumously published writing we find, as we should not be surprised to find, ample evidence that he found much about his world abhorrent and, although he was clear that it was not to be the task of philosophy to go about reforming it, it did need reforming. ("The sickness of a time is cured by an alteration in the mode of life of human beings, and it was possible for the sickness of philosophical problems to get cured only through a changed mode of thought and of life, not through a medicine invented by an individual.")[6]

---

[5]"The Unavoidability of Gender."

[6]Ludwig Wittgenstein, *Remarks on the Foundations of Mathematics*, ed. G. H. von Wright, R. Rhees, and G. E. M. Anscombe (Cambridge, Mass.: The MIT Press, 1967), p. 57.

As a feminist, I start from the idea that much about the world needs reforming, and dissolving philosophical problems is the least of the reason why. But those problems can be read as symptoms of what is wrong: we can learn from Wittgenstein not to take them at face value, not to take on the task of solving them, as though we could reason away the estrangements that structure subjectivity. What we cannot learn from Wittgenstein is how to change our "mode of thought and of life" or even what it is about our lives that needs changing and why. Nor can we learn from him how to distinguish the disease that comes from the assumption of privilege from that which comes from marginality and which can provide the creatively critical ground Collins speaks of.

We feel ourselves at a distance from the world, disconnected from our bodies, from other material things, and from other people. We need not to prove that the distance is an illusion but to ask why we experience it, and the answers will vary. We may, as part of the assumption of privilege, have learned to hold the world away from ourselves, to constitute ourselves by a willed estrangement from it. Or we may find ourselves at a distance from the representations of ourselves that others take as real, and we may need to move away or to learn that we aren't in fact where they or we took us to be. To be a woman and a philosopher is to encounter oneself in the world in confusingly contradictory positions: the quintessential knower and the archetypal known, the generic self and the paradigmatic other, the introspected mind and the spectated body, the exemplar of reason and the embodiment of passion, the moral agent and the primordial source of temptation.

We cannot hope to find ourselves, integrally whole, awaiting discovery and rescue. We are what we and the others around us make us up to be.[7] We can work at distancing ourselves from the social definitions of women, claiming the privileges of generic humanness, positioning ourselves as unequivocal insiders, denying the dissonance of a definition we reject. We may succeed. If we do, we will speak with voices as univocal and single-minded as those of the men we emulate; we too will have integrity and autonomy. And we will, like them, have philosophical problems. We will feel the need to prove—or at least to provide good reasons for believing—that the bodies we are no longer defined by are real and in some sense ours, that the other people we no longer depend on to tell us who we are are not mere automata, that the world from which we have declared our independence truly exists.

If we resist these projects and these problems, we remain—or constitute ourselves as being—outsiders within philosophy. We learn not to silence the voices in us that remind us of our mothers, of the girls we avoided, or of ourselves as children. We can resist the lessons that would teach us to see internal diversity as pathological, to value integrity and single-mindedness, to admire the person

---

[7]I owe this concept of our making each other up to María Lugones; see her "Playfulness, 'World'-Traveling, and Loving Perception," *Hypatia*, 2, no. 2 (1987): 3–19.

who always seems the same, to strive for seamless coherence in our lives. Multiple subjectivities have been most associated with the survival strategies of victims of childhood abuse and as such are hardly models of health.[8] However, the pathology may not be in plurality *per se* but in the mutual hostility among the diverse voices, the silencings and failures of recognition and acknowledgment.[9] At the end of her essay Collins suggests that the stance of the outsider within has something to teach even the privileged, those who, if anyone is, are the real insiders. Insider status, whether to sociology, or to philosophy, or to any other disciplinary structure, comes at the price of the elision of one's personal history, one's idiosyncrasies, and, especially, any efforts one may have made to silence any dissident, dissonant voices in one's own head. Misogyny, homophobia, racism, and all the other ways we learn to stigmatize the other have their internal counterparts, as we learn to rout from our own psyches the voices that sound too shrill or too soft, that speak of forbidden desires or shameful fears, that laugh or cry at inappropriate moments, that mark us as "different."

To philosophize as a feminist has meant for me the ongoing effort to undiscipline my mind, to learn the sounds of voices other than the one that seemed so natural to me in Virginia Held's class, to let go the need for imposed coherence, to enter into conversation with no idea of where it's going to go, to upset and unsettle, to distrust the clear and the distinct. To speak not nonsense, but sense. As Barbara Christian writes, "sensuality is intelligence . . . sensual language is language that makes sense."[10]

---

[8]Louise Antony has challenged me to distinguish a liberatory nonunitary subjectivity from the splitting that characterizes the survivors of abuse. See my "Though This Be Method, There is Madness in It."

[9]I am deeply indebted here to conversations with Claudia Card and to her unpublished manuscript, "Responsibility and Moral Luck: Resisting Oppression and Abuse." Card is exploring the connections between the experiences of people with multiple personality disorder and those of oppressed communities. It is her hypothesis that in both cases health lies not in speaking a single voice but in building the conditions for respectful conversation and in finding ways of living together.

[10]Barbara Christian, "The Race for Theory," *Cultural Critique*, no. 6 (Spring 1987), p. 61.

21

Confessions of an Analytic Philosopher Semi-Manqué

Feminist philosophers have often been accused of analytic philosophy bashing. For example, H. E. Baber, in a letter to the editor of the *Feminism and Philosophy Newsletter*, expresses her "discomfort with the direction that some of the most vocal feminists in the profession have taken, most particularly with the denigration of the assumptions, methods, preoccupations and customs of analytic philosophers."[1] I want to respond to Baber and to those who share her discomfort both as someone who is almost certainly among those who discomfit her (if I fail to be among them, I suspect that's only because I haven't been sufficiently vocal within her hearing), and as someone who in complex ways identifies herself as an analytic philosopher.

My identity as an analytic philosopher seems in many ways analogous to my identity as a New Yorker. With respect both to New York and to analytic philosophy, I came of age in and around the "center," and it was that center that gave the suburbs their meaning and toward which I gravitated. My "assumptions, methods, preoccupations and customs" were shaped by those centers and by my position with respect to them, including my desire to be as close to the center as I could be. I no longer have that desire, although I'm still tugged by something stronger than nostalgia: I care in a special way for those who are still there and for the fates of those places. In both cases those centers are where I take myself to be from, and those origins are revealed in my characteristic inflections and intonations, though more noticeably to those from elsewhere. Those who still live there are more likely to pick up the influences of the intervening years, although, conversely, I do often sound more like a native when speaking with others who are; I pick up the rhythms. For the past couple of decades I have been moving elsewhere, and for the foreseeable future I expect to be a feminist philosopher living and working in Minneapolis. But I don't think of either feminist philosophy

[1]H. E. Baber, letter, in *Feminism and Philosophy Newsletter* 89, no. 1 (Fall 1989): 90ff.

or Minneapolis as where I am from (it is in part their chosenness that appeals to me), and I do think it is important for people, for me, to acknowledge where we are from, where and who we were before we found/placed ourselves where we are now.

So when I'm critical of analytic philosophy, it's in part because for me that's what I mean by philosophy unmodified, a usage whose imperiousness is at least somewhat mitigated by the fact that what I learned as analytic philosophy was decidedly eclectic. And becoming a feminist philosopher during the early days of the "pluralist" challenge to the APA leadership, it never seemed to me that the pluralists were any more open than were those identified as analytic philosophers to the sorts of plurality that I cared about, including attentiveness to issues of class, race, and sexual identity, along with those of gender. I didn't and don't see any reason to believe that switching allegiances from one bunch of fathers and sons to another is likely to further any feminist agenda I care about, and the bunch I spring from have at least the virtues of an easy cosmopolitanism and a taste for irreverence.

All that acknowledged, it remains true that in some sense I have left analytic philosophy and that I have no intention of returning. The reasons why have a lot to do with issues of postmodernism. It's notoriously difficult to state just what postmodernism is. Architecture may be as clear an arena as there is for detecting the postmodern, but it's far from obvious how to transfer to philosophy the look of buildings with arches, pediments, and teal trim. Much of the difficulty stems from differing conceptions of the modern. In different fields it refers to work of very different time periods. The distinctively modern novel, let alone the skyscraper, hardly dates back to the canonical dawn of modern philosophy—Descartes's stove-stoked meditations in November of 1619. Postmodernism in philosophy is largely shaped by the rejection of the legacies of those meditations —the "assumptions, methods, preoccupations and customs" that all European and Euro-American philosophers have, however fractiously, inherited. Thought of in this way, most current analytic philosophy is postmodern, for example, in its rejection of foundationalism and in the growing permeability of its boundaries. The cosmopolitan eclecticism of analytic philosophy has made the postmodern tendencies of recent mainstream work less evident, so it can look as though those who are most self-reflectively critical about developments in the field are leaving it for some other school of philosophy with more clearly named identities and loyalties.

As analytic historians of philosophy have come increasingly to stress over the past twenty years, philosophy doesn't have an autonomous, text-based history. The self whose relations to the world and to the others in it generate the problems of philosophy is a historical being; those relations and consequently those problems are historically shaped. It is, paradoxically, one of the distinctive marks of modernity that that self is taken, explicitly though problematically, to be generic: we are to ask, for example, about *the* relation of *the* mind to *the* body. Were the historicization of the history of philosophy to include the present and the recent past, the problematic status of such a subject would, I think, become clear, and with it the problematic status of the "assumptions, methods, [and] preoccupations" that structure philosophical investigation. In this sense, current analytic philosophy is, by what ought to be its own lights, neither sufficiently nor sufficiently self-reflectively postmodern.

Postmodernity is best seen not as a philosophical position or methodology. When it is seen in that way, I agree with the criticisms that Susan Bordo has brought against it—briefly, that it undermines attention to the specificities of, and hence precludes our political responsibility for, the historically conditioned subject positions we in fact occupy.[2] Postmodernity is, rather, the condition of the world we inhabit, and, consequently, the condition shaping the self whose problems philosophy undertakes to (dis)solve. My main quarrel with analytic philosophy is that, while it acknowledges some of how this subject is differently placed in the world than were his (or her? Maybe.) forebears, in particular, in taking knowledge to be more a matter of social *bricolage* than of individual, rationally guaranteed, linear construction, it still takes that subject to be the individual of modernity—definitively bounded and generically endowed. That is, contemporary analytic philosophy for the most part still embraces individualism and shuns individuality.[3] However differently contemporary philosophers may address the mind/body problem, for example, there is still taken to be such a problem. However gussied up with the latest in cognitive science, philosophy of mind (or of psychology) still asks questions about the connections between the generic mind and the generic body, questions that lose their sense when we take seriously that minds and bodies are variously constructed for those differently placed, and that the generic self is a modernist fiction whose identity as normative rests on political, social, and economic structures that are (many of us hope) coming undone.

The undoing of those structures is a matter of both global and local politics. The relevant revolutions—of, for example, anti-imperialism, postcolonial nationalisms, gay and lesbian liberation, ecological awareness, economic democracy,

---

[2]Susan Bordo, "The View from Nowhere and the Dream of Everywhere: Heterogeneity, Adequation and Feminist Theory," *APA Newsletter on Feminism and Philosophy* 88, no. 2 (March 1989): 19–25. See also her "Feminism, Postmodernism, and Gender Scepticism," in Linda J.Nicholson, ed., *Feminism/Postmodernism* (New York: Routledge, 1990).

[3]One interesting exception that proves the rule is the recent spate of work that argues against individualism in the philosophy of psychology, in particular, in discussions of the attribution of propositional attitudes. Notions like narrow content are then formulated to allow one to hold onto an apparantly undeniable core of individualism in the content of the mental in the face of arguments about the social nature of meaning. See, for example, the articles in C. Anthony Anderson and Joseph Owens, eds., *Propositional Attitudes: The Role of Content in Logic, Language, and Mind* (Stanford: CSLI Press, 1990).

as well as feminism—are as profoundly radical as those that birthed the modern subject. There is little reason to believe that conceptions of subjectivity, epistemic authority, morality, integrity, selfhood, and so on, that, for all the timelessness of their accompanying rhetoric, were crafted to serve the needs of the emerging bourgeoisie will equally well serve the needs or reflect the perspectives of present and future revolutionary subjects.

It is in this sense that I take the project of a seriously feminist philosophy to be postmodern, while recognizing that revolutions aren't made overnight, and that part of the work of achieving one will involve using currently hegemonic methods and ideals to press the boundaries, reveal and deepen the cracks. Thus, for example, it can be important to press within existing structures for universal political and economic enfranchisement, not only for the immediate tangible benefit of some but in order to reveal the structural impediments to its full achievement, impediments that are likely to remain otherwise invisible. Similarly, the rhetorically generic nature of the modern philosophical self can be revealed as an exclusionary fiction when more variously diverse people claim that self as their own. We are more likely to see ourselves as passing as honorary men or whites or heterosexuals or members of the middle or ruling or leisure classes when we are surrounded by others who, like us, are "different."

Postmodernism, however, doesn't usually mean this sort of thing. Most often it refers to various currents in contemporary academic, intellectual, and cultural life, tributaries of a highly theorized and, for all its naughty appropriation of pop cultural icons, utterly elitist river. I would like to think that it is my politics as much as my analytic training that makes me impatient with writing that seems designed to defeat my attempts at comprehension. There is a difference between being challenged and stretched to work hard at understanding something difficult, and being sneered at, being made to feel that the likes of me were never meant to understand. But, despite my frequent impatience and anger, I have found myself emboldened and invigorated by postmodern academic writing, by the rushing of its streams past the fields I work in.

For example: my analytic education taught me to abstract arguments from their textual settings, to discard as irrelevant the language in which they came clothed, to "restate them in my own words," to see clarity as a matter of transparency through to the world or at least to an argument about the world. It is largely through developments in the world of literary theory—various tributaries of the academic postmodern river—that I have come see those "assumptions, methods, . . . and customs" as highly problematic. Whatever one makes of the textualization of the world, attention to the textuality of *texts* is surely salutary; they are not just the neutral conveyors of arguments. Analytic philosophy needs to move further away from the positivists' dreams of a purely denotative language, to a fuller recognition of the irreducible role of metaphor in all explanation and argument, and, with that recognition, attention to the exclusionary and marginalizing nature of language that implicitly positions the generic subject as male, able-bodied, heterosexual, white, and middle class.

But such concerns are not well served by most academic postmodern writing, which seems to confirm the suspicion that one can get away with, even be rewarded for, saying the most radical and subversive things just so long as one says them in a way guaranteed to be unintelligible to nearly everyone but a few similarly elitely educated people. If attention to language teaches us anything, it ought to teach us to notice the ways in which our words and our syntax can string themselves out like so much barbed wire and broken bottles set out to bloody anyone who, lacking an invitation, tries to scale the walls. Nor does such writing, in its clotted complexity, well serve what it might well whet—an appetite for the sound, texture, and imaginative vividness of language. At least with bad analytic philosophical writing, of which there is a great deal, I'm not being asked to attend especially closely to the fabric of the prose, but rather to see through it to the body of argument it clothes.

In the twenty-five years that I have been doing it, analytic philosophy has become increasingly "naturalized." Epistemology and philosophy of mind attend to empirical research on the workings of the human mind, ethics and moral philosophy attend to the actual circumstances of moral deliberation, aesthetics attends to the institutionalization of the production and experiencing of art, philosophy of science attends to the history and current practices of science. Naturalizing the subject (in both senses) of philosophy is an inherently postmodern move, but in the current state of the center of the field that move is stymied by the failure to take the logical next step, as feminist philosophers and others who philosophize from explicitly liberatory perspectives have done: that is to problematize, not just to theorize, the actual historical nature of that subject. The true postmoderns are those who in their personal and political practice are forging new nongeneric subjectivities and with them new philosophical problems. Analytic philosophy will either recognize and embrace this shift, in part through fidelity to its own commitment to specificity, or it will risk becoming the scholasticism of the twenty-first century.

Index

Alice (example of discovering anger), 24–25, 29
Alice (in Wonderland), 11, 12, 14
Allen, Jeanne Thomas, 144
Amerigo, Prince (in *The Golden Bowl*), 117–124
Antony, Louise, xvii
Anzaldúa, Gloria, 96, 101, 104
Archimedean point, 85, 99, 158, 161, 232
Aristotle, 20, 109, 135, 206
Asante, Molefi Kete, 83n14
Athena, 135–136, 139
Auden, W. H., 64n36, 65–66
Austin, J. L., 12n3, 31n12

Baber, H. E., 245
Bachofen, J. J., 142
Bacon, Francis, 64, 65, 67, 74, 94n42, 95
Baier, Annette, 103
Baker, Houston, 220–222
Bakhtin, M. M., 115–116
Barker, Francis, 73, 91n37, 95n45, 111–114, 186–187
Bartky, Sandra, 151
Belenky, Mary Field, Blythe McVicker Clinchy, Nancy Rule Goldberger, and Jill Mattuck Tarule (authors: *Women's Ways of Knowing*), 174
Benjamin, Walter, 158
Benveniste, Emile, 147
Berger, John, 166
Bertram (in *All's Well that Ends Well*), 59, 61
Bettelheim, Bruno, 97n52
Blum, Lawrence A., 211n9
Borden, Lizzie, 101–102
Bordo, Susan, xiii–xiv, 7–8, 135, 148n45, 247
Bordwell, David, 169
Boyd, Richard, 209n5
Burge, Tyler, 37n5

Card, Claudia, 103, 173, 210n8, 244
Carroll, Lewis, 11, 14
Cavell, Stanley, xvi, 57, 63n28, 128–130, 131–139, 146, 148–149, 149n47
Chambers, E. K., 59
Chodorow, Nancy, 45–51, 52, 98, 135n21, 136, 173
Christ, 48, 186
Christian, Barbara, 88n28, 219, 223, 244
Clark, Lorenne, 44n14
Clément, Catherine, 75
Clèves, la Princesse de (in *La Princesse de Clèves*), 140, 143
Code, Lorraine, 99n57
Cohen, Lynne, 162–164, 166
Collins, Patricia Hill, 241, 243–244
Cook, Pam, 141–142

Daly, Mary, 199n14
Davidson, Donald, 36n3, 37n4, 41n9
Davion, Victoria, 103
Davis, Angela, 216
De Lauretis, Teresa, 101–102, 128n9, 128n10, 149–150, 152, 215
De Sousa, Ronald, 27n6, 132n16
Derrida, Jacques, 101n63

Descartes, René, 3, 6, 23, 36, 58, 62, 64, 65, 66–71, 71n62, 73, 76, 78, 83–86, 89–90, 91, 93–95, 98–99, 109, 160, 168–169, 173, 192, 193–195, 199
Desdemona, xvi, 63–64, 66–70, 69n53, 72–73, 149
Dewey, John, 102
Di Leonardo, Micaela, 205n1, 213–214
Dickinson, Emily, 224
Dinnerstein, Dorothy, 45–46, 50–51, 52, 136n24, 173
Doane, Mary Ann, 127n3
Doell, Ruth G., 205n1, 212–213, 214
Dworkin, Andrea, 159
Dworkin, Ronald, 42

Edwards, Owen, 165
Edgerton, Samuel Y. Jr., 148n44
Eliot, T. S., 236n7
Evans, Sara, 239
evil genius (in Descartes's *Meditations*), 66, 84

Ferguson, Margaret W., 113
Fetterley, Judith, xvi
Flax, Jane, 7–8
Foucault, Michel, 91–92, 95, 105, 108, 109, 151, 186, 187
Frege, Gottlieb, 110
Freire, Paulo, 92n38
Freud, Sigmund, 8, 8n14, 15, 23, 26n5, 30–32, 45–48, 50, 52, 66n46, 67, 79–81, 80n11, 80n12, 89, 94, 97–98, 128–129, 130–138, 139, 142, 147, 152
Frye, Marilyn, 71n62, 88n27, 98, 109, 128n10, 150, 152, 158, 173

Galileo, 108, 116
Garner, Shirley Nelson, 60n17, 63n28, 66n44, 137
Gates, Henry Louis Jr., 100, 220–222
Geertz, Clifford, 22, 90
Gibson, Mary, 43n11
Gilbert, Sandra M., 131, 133–134
Gilligan, Carol, 174–175, 210n6
Glaserfeld, Ernst von, 106
God, 3, 67, 81–83, 85–86, 95–96, 112, 165, 171, 173, 186, 195
Goethe, 89
Gohlke, Frank, 162, 165–166
Gohlke, Madelon. See Sprengnether, Madelon.
Grand Canonical Synthesizer, xiii, 232
Grimshaw, Jean, 2
Grontkowski, Christine, 70–72, 84n20, 148n43
Gumbrecht, Hans Ulrich, 229

Hamlet, 110, 111–114, 117, 123
Hampshire, Stuart, 27n7
Hanson, Karen, 102n67
Haraway, Donna, 96, 97n51, 100
Harding, Sandra, 88, 97n51, 99n57, 128n10, 215n14, 224, 232n2
Hartmann, Heidi, 49n18
Hawkes, Terence, 64, 65, 66n43
Heidegger, Martin, 164
Heilman, Robert B., 71–72
Helena (in *All's Well that Ends Well*), 60–61
Hepburn, Katherine, 63n29, 129, 137, 144
Higgins, Olive Prouty, 126
Hirsch, Marianne, 140
Hoagland, Sarah, 173, 210n8
Hobbes, Thomas, 50
hooks, bell, xiii, 211n10, 221
Hume, David, 3

Iago, 58, 64–66, 72–73, 120n14, 149
Irigary, Luce, 57n3

Jacobs, Lea, 143
Jaggar, Alison M., 7n13
James, Henry, 114, 115–117, 119–120, 122, 169–172
Johnson, Jill, 36
Jordan, June, 101
Joyce, Joyce A., 205n1, 218–223

Kahn, Coppelia, 61
Kant, Immanuel, 65n41, 93–94, 93n41, 99, 106–107, 108, 111, 113–114, 122–123, 168–169, 172, 194, 201
Kaplan, E. Ann, 146
Keller, Evelyn Fox, 7–8, 67n48, 70–72, 84n20, 94n42, 95–96, 148n43, 207–208
King Lear, 57
Kirsch, Arthur, 59, 60n18, 61
Klipper, Stuart, 162, 164–165, 166
Kohlberg, Lawrence, 174
Kolodny, Annette, 222n27
Kripke, Saul, 4
Kristeva, Julia, 215n15
Kuhn, Thomas, 109, 201, 213

Lacan, Jacques, 71n62
Laing, R. D., 29
Lather, Patti, xin1
Levin, Michael E., 6n10
Lewis, David K., 36n3, 37n4
Lippard, Lucy, 158
Locke, John, 75, 113
Lowe, Donald M., 95n46
Lord, Tracy (in *The Philadelphia Story*), 137–138, 150–151
Lorde, Audre, 173, 180, 223n29
Lovibond, Sabina, 124n16
Lugg, Andrew, 124n16
Lugones, María, xii, 75, 97n51, 98, 103–104, 211n10, 230, 243n7

MacKinnon, Catharine A., 127n7, 159
Mahler, Margaret, 71n62
malicious demon. See evil genius.
Mani, Lata, 237
Martin, Biddy, 233–234
Marx, Karl, 44n14, 52, 198
Mason, H. E., 5n7
Masson, Jeffrey Moussaieff, 80n10
Matson, Wallace, 193n1
Maturana, Humberto, 189
Mayne, Judith, 128n9
McClintock, Barbara, 208
McKee, Patricia, 117–124
McNaron, Toni, 64n35, 173
Mead, George Herbert, 102n67
Metz, Christian, 147
Mill, John Stuart, 6–7, 75
Miller, Alice, 79, 80, 92–93, 92n39, 104
Millet, Kate, 156
Mitchell, Juliet, 50
Mohanty, Chandra Talpade, 233–234
Monk, Ray, 240–241
Montaigne, Michel de, 58–59, 62, 65, 66, 74, 85, 114
Morrison, Toni, 219, 223
Moulton, Janice, 76n2
Mulvey, Laura, 126, 128n8, 131n14, 146–147, 152
Murdoch, Iris, 165
Murray, Timothy, 69n53

Neely, Carol Thomas, 58n5, 60n17, 63n28, 68n52, 69n53
Nowell-Smith, Geoffrey, 115, 116, 141
Nowottny, Winifred M. T., 64n37, 72

Oedipus, 47–48, 129, 132, 134–136, 142, 148, 152
Okin, Susan Moller, 50n19
Othello, xvi, 57, 58, 62–73, 120n14, 149
Oz, Wizard of, xii–xiv, 172, 196–197

Perry, Ruth, 83n15
Perry, William, 174
Pierce, Mildred (in *Mildred Pierce*), 141–142, 151
Pierce, Veda (in *Mildred Pierce*), 141–142, 151
Pierre (Saul Kripke's example), 4–5, 7
Plato, 70, 72, 200
Popkin, Richard, 58, 62, 66, 194n2
Pozos, Robert, 197
Pratt, Minnie Bruce, 233–234
Price, Vincent, 23n2
Putnam, Hilary, 17n7, 37n4, 41n9

Quine, W. V., 39, 40n7, 78, 105, 201

Rawls, John, 43, 116, 194
Reagon, Bernice Johnson, 233, 238
Relman, Arnold S., 199
Resnais, Alain, 169
Reyes, Angelita, 91n35
Rich, Adrienne, 60n15, 134, 139–140, 145, 168–169, 171–173, 238
Riley, Denise, 215n14
Rilke, Rainer Maria, 229
Root, Michael, 116n11
Rothman, Barbara K., 198n11, 214n13
Ruddick, Sara, 165, 211n9

Sartre, Jean-Paul, 44, 71n60, 79, 123
Schatzman, Morton, 80, 92
Schreber, Daniel Gottlieb Moritz (father of Daniel Paul Schreber), 80, 92–94
Schreber, Daniel Paul, 78–83, 89, 91–92, 94–95, 104
Scidentop, Larry, 43
Scott, Joan, 218
Seeger, Pete, 107
Shakespeare, William, 57–58, 59, 61n23, 62, 65, 74, 137, 146
Sherover-Marcuse, Erica, 104
Sleeping Beauty, 82, 134
Smith, Barbara, 233, 238
Smith, Paul, 90, 100
Snyder, Susan, 63, 63n30, 68

Spelman, Elizabeth V., 2n4, 28n8, 211n10, 215, 223, 232n2
Sprengnether, Madelon, 61n23, 63n29, 72, 113
Stant, Charlotte (in *The Golden Bowl*), 117–121
Stroud, Barry, 90n33
Sulzer, J., 93

Taylor, Charles, 44
Taylor, Harriet, 6–7
Thomas, Gary, 82n13
Thoreau, Henry David, 51n22
Tronto, Joan C., 210n7
Truth, Sojourner, 188–189

Vale, Charlotte (in *Now, Voyager*), 142–144, 145n36, 151, 152
Verver, Maggie (in *The Golden Bowl*), 110, 117–124

Wallace, John, 5n7
Walrus (in *Alice in Wonderland*), 11, 12, 14–17
Warhol, Andy, 223
Weber, Sam, 79–80
Weil, Simone, 165
Weininger, Otto, 241
West, Cornel, 102
Whitbeck, Caroline, 71n62, 210n6
White, Morton, 75–76, 83, 85, 88
Wilde, Oscar, 23n2
Williams, Patricia, 99–100
Winnicott, D. W., 71n62, 97n50
Witt, Charlotte, xvii
Wittgenstein, Ludwig, 4–5, 8, 8n15, 13n4, 18, 40, 78, 88n28, 105, 110–111, 114–115, 117–118, 121–124, 239–243
Wolff, Robert Paul, 44n14
Wollstonecraft, Mary, 6–7
Wood, Ruth, 145n36
Woolf, Virginia, 22n1, 146, 150, 158
World Series, 155

Zita, Jacquelyn, 7–8, 173